D1382707

Governing with the Charter

Law and Society Series
W. Wesley Pue, General Editor

The Law and Society Series explores law as a socially embedded phenomenon. It is premised on the understanding that the conventional division
of law from society creates false dichotomies in thinking, scholarship,
educational practice, and social life. Books in the series treat law and
society as mutually constitutive and seek to bridge scholarship emerging
from interdisciplinary engagement of law with disciplines such as politics,
social theory, history, political economy, and gender studies.

Of interest and also in the series:

Gerald Baier, *Courts and Federalism: Judicial Doctrine in the United States,*
Australia, and Canada (forthcoming)

W.A. Bogart, *Good Government? Good Citizens? Courts, Politics, and Markets*
in a Changing Canada (2005)

Christopher P. Manfredi, *Feminist Activism in the Supreme Court:*
Legal Mobilization and the Women's Legal Education and Action Fund (2004)

Roy B. Flemming, *Tournament of Appeals: Granting Judicial Review*
in Canada (2004)

A complete list of the books in this series is available at www.ubcpress.ca.

LAW AND
SOCIETY

James B. Kelly

Governing with the Charter: Legislative and Judicial Activism and Framers' Intent

UBCPress · Vancouver · Toronto

© UBC Press 2005

All rights reserved. No part of this publication may be reproduced, stored in a retrieval system, or transmitted, in any form or by any means, without prior written permission of the publisher, or, in Canada, in the case of photocopying or other reprographic copying, a licence from Access Copyright (Canadian Copyright Licensing Agency), www.accesscopyright.ca.

15 14 13 12 11 10 09 08 07 06 05   5 4 3 2 1

Printed in Canada on acid-free paper

Library and Archives Canada Cataloguing in Publication

Kelly, James B. (James Bernard), 1968-
  Governing with the Charter : legislative and judicial activism and framers' intent / James B. Kelly.

(Law & society series, ISSN 1496-4953)
Includes bibliographical references and index.
ISBN-13: 978-0-7748-1211-5 (bound); 978-0-7748-1212-2 (pbk.)
ISBN-10: 0-7748-1211-7 (bound); 0-7748-1212-5 (pbk.)

  1. Canada. Canadian Charter of Rights and Freedoms. 2. Political questions and judicial power – Canada. 3. Judicial power – Canada. 4. Legislative power – Canada. 5. Canada. Supreme Court. I. Title. II. Series: Law and society series (Vancouver, B.C.)

KE4381.5.K44 2005   342.71'042   C2005-905081-0
KF4483.C519K44 2005

Canadä

UBC Press gratefully acknowledges the financial support for our publishing program of the Government of Canada through the Book Publishing Industry Development Program (BPIDP), and of the Canada Council for the Arts, and the British Columbia Arts Council.

This book has been published with the help of a grant from the Canadian Federation for the Humanities and Social Sciences, through the Aid to Scholarly Publications Programme, using funds provided by the Social Sciences and Humanities Research Council of Canada.

UBC Press
The University of British Columbia
2029 West Mall
Vancouver, BC V6T 1Z2
604-822-5959 / Fax: 604-822-6083
www.ubcpress.ca

This book is dedicated to my parents,
   James and Elizabeth Kelly,
and to my wife, Michèle Friel

Contents

Acknowledgments

Governing with the Charter is the result of a Standard Research Grant from the Social Sciences and Humanities Research Council of Canada. I am very grateful to this organization for providing me with financial support at the beginning of my academic career. This book has been published with the help of a grant from the Canadian Federation for the Humanities and Social Sciences, through the Aid to Scholarly Publications Programme, using funds provided by the Social Sciences and Humanities Research Council of Canada. It was completed with the help of several research assistants at Concordia University and Brock University, including Tamara Levy, Christopher Dueck, Daniel Lafferty, and Bohdana Diduch.

In the course of researching and writing this book, I incurred a number of personal debts that I want to acknowledge. Randy Schmidt was an outstanding editor and was the first to approach me to write a book on the *Canadian Charter of Rights and Freedoms*. I want to thank him very much for his patience, as he knows the circumstances under which this book was written. Several scholars read parts of this book and provided important feedback, particularly Richard Schultz and Christopher Manfredi. Richard Schultz suggested that I focus on the Charter's effect on parliament as an institution after interviewing senators and members of the House of Commons in late 2002. This conversation changed the direction of the book and improved it significantly. Though Manfredi disagrees with my assessment of the Charter and judicial power, he was very supportive and provided critical guidance. I want to thank him for his good humour when listening to my latest critique of conservative judicial critics. I discussed this book with F.L. Morton during a meeting at the London School of Economics in January 2004 and benefited from his suggestions. Cor Vandermeer, a retired detective and staff sergeant from the Niagara Regional Police, read Chapter 4 and provided useful comments. Patrick James read the manuscript in its entirety and provided critical suggestions for its improvement. Janet Hiebert read parts of the manuscript in an early form, and I benefited from her suggestions for improvement and wish to thank her. Finally, I would like to thank the anonymous reviewers of this book who provided critical and instructive comments that significantly improved this work.

In addition, I interviewed a number of senators, members of parliament, and public servants, and it was during these sessions that the theme "Governing with the Charter" entered my thinking. I'd like to thank senators Serge Joyal, Raynell Andreychuk, and Gérald Beaudoin for their time. After interviewing the senators and reviewing the important Charter scrutiny performed by the Standing Senate Committee on Legal and Constitutional Affairs, the criticism of an unelected Senate seems trite. Also, I had the privilege to interview Irwin Cotler before his appointment to cabinet as minister of justice, as well as the following members of the Standing Committee on Justice and Human Rights during the second session of the 37th Parliament: John Maloney, John McKay, and Chuck Cadman. Former prime minister Pierre Elliott Trudeau granted me an interview in 1997, and I incorporated the research findings in this book. Finally, I conducted 100 interviews with public servants in every province and the federal government, including former Department of Justice deputy ministers Roger Tassé and John Tait and Justice Barry Strayer of the Federal Court.

My research on the Charter of Rights and its effect on Canadian constitutionalism and governance began at McGill University, where my dissertation was supervised by Richard J. Schultz, Christopher P. Manfredi, and Hudson Meadwell and was defended in April 1999. Few truly know the burden of supervising an Irishman (or hide the scars so well). Most of the writing of this book occurred when I moved back to Montreal in June 2003 to join the Faculty of Political Science at Concordia University after spending three years at Brock University. The writing was finalized in Wellington, New Zealand, in May 2004 during a research trip on the *New Zealand Bill of Rights Act 1990*. The conclusion to this book is based on the research findings from New Zealand, and I would like to thank former attorney general Margaret Wilson and former prime minister Sir Geoffrey Palmer for granting interviews. Further, I interviewed the following members of the Justice and Electoral Select Committee: Tim Barnett, Russell Fairbrother, and Judith Collins. As always, I conducted interviews at the Ministry of Justice, Crown Law Office, Parliamentary Counsel Office, and the Human Rights Commission, as well as with members of the Faculty of Law, Victoria University of Wellington.

I want to thank my wife, Michèle, who is probably the most grateful that this book is finally completed. Michèle compiled the bibliography and case list, and I want to thank her for all her love and support during the writing. I'm very lucky to have found her.

This book is important to me because it is the one I told my dad I would write shortly before he died from cancer in June 2002. I began the writing about a week before he was diagnosed in May 2002, and during the times I drove my dad to his treatments and sat with him, he asked me about my research and I sketched out the chapters for him. I didn't realize this would be the last time I was alone with my dad, and I cherish these memories. The talks would end too soon, and I had to write this book without him. I miss you, Dad, and wish you were still working in your garden with Mom.

Permission Note
I am grateful for permission to incorporate material from the following publications:

James B. Kelly, "Governing with the Charter of Rights and Freedoms," *Supreme Court Law Review*, 2nd ser., 21 (2003): 299-337.

James B. Kelly, "The Supreme Court of Canada and the Complexity of Judicial Activism," in Patrick James, Donald E. Abelson, and Michael Lusztig, eds., *The Myth of the Sacred: The Charter, the Courts and the Politics of the Canadian Constitution*, 97-122 (Montreal and Kingston: McGill-Queen's University Press, 2002).

James B. Kelly, "Reconciling Rights and Federalism during Review of the Charter of Rights and Freedoms: The Supreme Court of Canada and the Centralization Thesis, 1982-1999," *Canadian Journal of Political Science* 34 (2001): 321-55.

James B. Kelly and Michael Murphy, "Confronting Judicial Supremacy: A Defence of Judicial Activism and the Supreme Court of Canada's Legal Rights Jurisprudence," *Canadian Journal of Law and Society* 16 (2001): 3-27.

James B. Kelly, "Bureaucratic Activism and the *Charter of Rights and Freedoms:* The Department of Justice and Its Entry into the Centre of Government," *Canadian Public Administration* 42 (1999): 476-511.

Christopher P. Manfredi and James B. Kelly, "Dialogue, Deference and Restraint: Judicial Independence and Trial Procedures," *Saskatchewan Law Review* 64 (2001): 323-46.

Acronyms

AHRC	Alberta Human Rights Commission
BCMAG	British Columbia Ministry of the Attorney General
CACP	Canadian Association of Chiefs of Police
CACSW	Canadian Advisory Council on the Status of Women
CBA	Canadian Bar Association
CCLA	Canadian Civil Liberties Association
CCMC	Continuing Committee of Ministers on the Constitution
CHRC	Canadian Human Rights Commission
CJC	Canadian Jewish Congress
CLS	Critical Legal Studies
DOF	Department of Finance (Federal)
DOJ	Department of Justice (Federal)
FLA	*Family Law Act* (Ontario)
FMC	First ministers' conference
HRLS	Human Rights Law Section (Department of Justice)
IRPA	*Individual's Rights Protection Act* (Alberta)
LMSS	Legal mobilization support structure
LRA	*Labour Relations Act* (Ontario)
LRC	*Labour Relations Code* (British Columbia)
LSU	Legal service unit
MP	Member of parliament
NCR	Not criminally responsible
NDP	New Democratic Party
NACSW	National Action Committee on the Status of Women
NZBORA	*New Zealand Bill of Rights Act*
OMAG	Ontario Ministry of the Attorney General
PCO	Privy Council Office
PMO	Prime Minister's Office
QHRC	Quebec Human Rights Commission
RFL	Request for legislation (British Columbia)

SGC	Senior general counsel
SHRC	Saskatchewan Human Rights Commission
SJC	Special Joint Committee on the Constitution of Canada
TBS	Treasury Board Secretariat
YOA	*Young Offenders Act*

Governing with the Charter

Introduction

Since the introduction of the *Canadian Charter of Rights and Freedoms,* the question of judicial power and its relationship to parliamentary democracy has been a central issue. This book contends that critical assessments of judicial activism have unfairly portrayed the Supreme Court and its increased power as a direct challenge to the cabinet and its legislative agenda. However, while the Supreme Court is a political actor, the cabinet's and the bureaucracy's responses to the Charter are also political decisions.[1] Although the principal institutional outcome of the Charter's introduction has been a further weakening of parliament, this has not been the result of the Supreme Court's political choices involving the Charter, but of the cabinet's decision to govern with the Charter from the centre. Like the central agency reforms of the Trudeau era, which were designed to offset bureaucratic power, the political response to the Charter has been an attempt to offset judicial power through similar reforms to the machinery of government. As a result, the cabinet's response to both bureaucratic and judicial power has had the same outcome: a strengthening of the cabinet and a weakening of parliament as an institution.

Governing with the Charter advances a cabinet-centred approach to the question of judicial power and parliamentary democracy, arguing that the principal reaction to the Charter has been in the political arena, as the cabinet has institutionalized Charter scrutiny under the control of the Department of Justice (DOJ). In effect, this book challenges the judicial-centred paradigm that has dominated the Charter debate among legal and political analysts.[2] Because the Charter's impact has primarily affected the ability of the cabinet to advance its legislative agenda and has required institutional changes in the bureaucratic arena to conform to the new policy environment, I introduce the concept of "rights activism" to broaden the debate beyond the narrow confines of the judicial arena. My analysis of the Charter of Rights is based on the argument that multiple forms of activism, and not simply its judicial manifestation, structure the document's relationship to Canadian democracy.[3] Instead of simply focusing on judicial activism and power, this study suggests that three forms of activism have emerged in response to the Charter. Perhaps more importantly, it argues that these distinctive but interrelated forms of activism function as checks and balances preventing the emergence of judicial supremacy.

It is the complexity of rights activism and its three manifestations – democratic activism, judicial activism, and legislative activism – that has ensured the proper functioning of constitutional supremacy in Canada. Democratic activism refers to the intentions of the Charter's framers to ensure greater textual and institutional protection for rights generated by both the Supreme Court and the cabinet, supported by the DOJ. It serves as the foundation of the Charter project and has guided both judicial and political responses to the entrenchment of rights. The term "judicial activism" is much maligned in the Canadian debate on judicial review, and this is an unfortunate development. The most balanced definition has been provided by Peter Russell, who considers it simply to be "judicial vigour in enforcing constitutional limitations on the other branches of government on constitutional grounds."[4] Conservative critics have used the term to suggest the unconstrained growth of judicial power derived from the court's discretionary interpretation of rights. In this book, judicial activism is viewed as essential to the emergence of constitutional supremacy and, thus, is not considered an independent creation of the courts, but a legitimate response to the intentions of politically accountable actors who drafted the Charter and ensured its final entrenchment in 1982.[5] As none of the distinct manifestations of rights activism functions independently of each other, but is constrained by countervailing forces within the judicial, legislative, and bureaucratic spheres, the effect of judicial activism on Canadian democracy is far more nuanced than either the supporters or critics of the Supreme Court of Canada suggest.

In fact, it will be suggested that judicial activism has generally had a positive effect on Canadian democracy, as it has led to important institutional changes within the legislative process, which are designed to limit the unconstrained growth of judicial power. This study refers to these changes as "legislative activism." There are two distinct elements of legislative activism – parliamentary and bureaucratic – that capture the complementary roles performed within a rights-structured policy environment. Of the two, parliamentary activism is the less institutionally advanced form of legislative activism in Canada, which is a reflection of the general weakness of parliament as an institution and as a policy actor.[6] It also suggests that a cabinet-centred response to the Charter has contributed to the decline of parliament. While the Senate and the House of Commons have standing committees that periodically review legislation for its relationship to protected rights, the executive-dominated nature of parliamentary democracy in Canada undermines the effectiveness of parliamentary scrutiny of legislation at this time. Indeed, the weakness of parliamentary scrutiny of legislation in regard to rights considerations in Canada is apparent when the Australian, New Zealand, and British examples are evaluated. Despite the absence of either an entrenched or statutory statement on rights and freedoms, the Australian senate and the states of Victoria and Queensland have institutionally advanced parliamentary scrutiny committees that ensure legislation is consistent with basic rights and freedoms.[7] With the incorporation of the *European Convention on Human Rights* into domestic law, the British parliament has instituted a Joint Committee on Human Rights that reviews legislation for its relationship to the *Human Rights Act 1998*.[8] In New Zealand, under section 7 of the statutory *Bill of Rights Act*, the attorney general is required to engage in pre-legislative rights scrutiny of bills and to inform parliament of any proposed bill that is inconsistent with the *New Zealand Bill of Rights Act*.[9] Ironically, these countries possess weak courts that cannot invalidate legislation but strong legislatures that ensure bills presented by the cabinet conform to domestic rights guarantees.

In Canada, however, the limited effectiveness of parliamentary scrutiny committees is of little practical significance because of the advanced development of pre-legislative review of bills for their rights consistency, which I have referred to as bureaucratic activism. This form of legislative activism refers largely to the Charter review process within the bureaucratic arena, which has been under the direction of the DOJ at both the federal and provincial levels. This government-wide process sees the DOJ, in partnership with line departments, thoroughly assess the risk of judicial nullification of proposed statutes and restructure policy proposals to limit the potential for judicial nullification on Charter grounds.[10] In this sense, it is an activist exercise that has been directed to countering the potential for judicial supremacy by engaging in a similar Charter review before legislation becomes law.[11] Further, while not every statute is subjected to judicial review on Charter grounds, every potential statute is subjected to bureaucratic review on such grounds. This is a significant difference that prevents the emergence of judicial supremacy and allows the prime minister and cabinet, supported by the machinery of government, to offset judicial power and generally achieve their legislative agenda.

The implications of legislative activism, however, are not all positive, as this process is driven by its bureaucratic component and supports the cabinet, and parliamentary scrutiny of legislation from a rights perspective is quite underdeveloped in Canada. Indeed, the present "parliamentary" approach to ensuring that Charter values are advanced in the legislative process is decidedly cabinet-centred, as it has empowered the DOJ as the lead government agency responsible for an internal Charter review during the development of policy. The attempt to govern in a rights culture has seen the federal DOJ, along with the Ministry of the Attorney General in Ontario and British Columbia and the Quebec Ministry of Justice, emerge as central agencies, as the minister of justice is responsible for certifying to cabinet that legislation introduced by line departments is constitutional or, at the very least, a reasonable limitation on a Charter right. Central agencies do not empower parliament as a policy actor but ensure that the machinery of government is directed to advance the policy agenda established by the cabinet. At present, the debate has focused on the question of judicial supremacy and has suggested that this is the likely institutional outcome of the Charter's introduction, though much disagreement exists on this point. I will suggest that executive supremacy, not judicial supremacy, has been the primary outcome of the Charter's introduction, as bureaucratic-driven legislative activism has further marginalized parliament and the provincial legislatures as policy actors. This development has transpired in all jurisdictions and is particularly acute at the provincial level, where unicameral legislative assemblies are generally dominated by the governing party, and inadequate checks exist on the cabinet.

Despite the institutionalization of Charter scrutiny in the legislative process, the invalidation of statutes will continue to occur. This is not evidence of judicial supremacy or the failings of legislative activism but of the continued importance of political actors in a parliamentary democracy. Constitutional advice provided by the DOJ is just that – advice that the cabinet has the discretion to accept or not. There may be times when the cabinet disagrees with the constitutional assessment of the DOJ or feels that a policy that infringes a right is a reasonable limitation and therefore constitutional, despite Justice's analysis to the contrary. Further, a proposed policy that raises constitutional concern at the DOJ may be a central commitment made by a government during an election campaign and necessary to satisfy a critical constituency. The Charter has not removed politics from the legislative process or reduced the decision-making ability of the cabinet or the prime minister. It has simply meant that these decisions can be reviewed outside the parliamentary arena and challenged as unconstitutional. Judicial activism, therefore, may be the clearest illustration that the cabinet remains the political centre in Canada.

Undoubtedly, there was a tendency toward intense judicial activism during the first years of Charter review, but since this initial activist phase, the court has settled into what Peter Russell has described as a moderately activist approach to rights and freedoms.[12] Some commentators have suggested that the waning of judicial activism, measured by declining success rates of rights claims and a reduction in the number of statutes invalidated as inconsistent with the Charter, is the result of growing judicial acceptance of parliamentary limitations on rights and freedoms.[13] This is only a partial explanation, and it should not be viewed as proof that the level of rights activism has declined. Rights activism has not waned, but has simply been distributed more efficiently across judicial and legislative activism. Focusing solely on judicial activism and adopting a judicial-centric analysis of the Charter obscure the transformative potential of rights activism for cabinet and the machinery of government that supports the political executive.

A Cabinet-Centred Analysis

Like Janet Hiebert, I view the introduction of the Charter as ushering in a new relationship between courts and political actors.[14] However, I do not advance a parliament-centred but a cabinet-centred approach because the principal political response to the Charter has occurred at the cabinet level and has been the result of prime ministerial leadership. While the prime minister is more than "first amongst" equals in the cabinet, the political response to the Charter has not been directed by bureaucratic actors who directly support the prime minister, such as the Privy Council Office or the Prime Minister's Office, but by bureaucratic actors who directly support the cabinet, as the traditional role of the minister and Department of Justice has been to serve as the cabinet's legal advisor. The increased importance of Charter vetting, and the requirement that all memoranda to cabinet be scrutinized by the DOJ for Charter compliance, have seen the centre of government expand. While the increased importance of the cabinet's legal advisor and the corresponding significance of the DOJ have allowed the cabinet to govern with the Charter, it has occurred outside the parliamentary arena and within the machinery of government that directly supports the cabinet and its legislative agenda.

A recent innovation in Canada has been the inclusion of preambles within legislation that serve to outline the cabinet's interpretation of rights and freedoms.[15] Legislative preambles have been used in situations where the cabinet has introduced legislative responses to overcome judicial invalidations of statutes as a violation of the Charter. The significance of a preamble is that it allows the cabinet to challenge the judiciary's interpretation of a right, to justify the act as a responsible attempt to advance the Charter, and to assert the constitutionality of a statute. Further still, the decision by the DOJ to appeal a lower-court decision that invalidates an act indicates a willingness by the cabinet to challenge judicial interpretation of the Charter and judicial determination of what constitutes a reasonable limitation on a right or freedom.[16] Within the parliamentary arena, neither the Standing Committee on Justice and Human Rights nor the Standing Senate Committee on Legal and Constitutional Affairs has a formal mandate to engage in legislative scrutiny of bills for their compatibility with the Charter, but select parliamentarians have begun to perform this task, albeit in an ad hoc manner.[17] This rights scrutiny by the DOJ in support of the cabinet's legislative agenda is significant, therefore, because it challenges the orthodox interpretation of the Charter as being primarily judge-centred and judicially determined.

A central claim in this book is that the present debate over judicial activism in Canada has established a false dichotomy, in which judicial activism is said to undermine democracy and judicial deference serves to advance it.[18] My claim is that the court's particular approach to judicial review advances a certain form of democracy, not democracy itself, with judicial activism necessary to ensure that the intention of the framers for a more vigorous level of rights protections is achieved.[19] Indeed, it is argued in this book that the components of rights activism function as a system of checks and balances that prevent judicial supremacy from being the primary institutional outcome of the Charter. In this regard, I agree with F.L. Morton and Rainer Knopff that "to view the courts as part of an institutional system of checks and balances, one need not deny the *political* dimension of their work. Checks and balances, after all, are designed to pit different *political* perspectives, grounded in different institutional structures, against each other in the hope of securing more moderate, consensus-based policy outcomes."[20] However, they conclude that judicial finality on the meaning of rights has been the primary outcome of the Charter because of the limited effectiveness of these checks on judicial power within the Canadian constitutional system.[21]

The position advanced in this book is much more optimistic because it rejects judicial-centred analyses that downplay the importance of alternative forms of activism that serve to constrain judicial supremacy. Instead, more attention should be devoted to the cabinet and bureaucratic reforms designed to confront and contain judicial power associated with the Charter. There are a number of formal checks on judicial power in Canada that ensure the protection of rights and the determination of their meaning remain a shared responsibility between cabinet and the Supreme Court. The most obvious limitation on judicial power is section 33 of the Charter, the notwithstanding clause, which allows parliament and the provincial legislatures to override judicial nullification of statutes in limited areas of the Charter for a renewable five-year period. Christopher Manfredi views the notwithstanding clause as "a legitimate instrument within liberal democratic theory for preventing the slide from constitutional to judicial supremacy" and tends to emphasize the use of formal checks on judicial power.[22] While a revitalized section 33 would directly confront judicial supremacy, it is unnecessary because of several informal checks available to the cabinet.

The most important constraint on judicial power is the emergence of a rights culture within the bureaucratic arena that represents a significant change from the situation that followed passage of the *Canadian Bill of Rights*, when the DOJ functioned simply as the government's legal advisor and saw its mandate as protecting the Canadian government from successful rights claims.[23] This resistance to rights-based litigation fundamentally changed with the Charter, as the DOJ broadened its mandate to actively promote the protection of rights within the design of legislation as a way to protect the cabinet's lead role in public policy. Former deputy minister of justice John Tait saw the introduction of the Charter as an opportunity for the cabinet to remain the centre of public policy and disputed the claim that the Charter had transferred decision-making authority to the courts. He wrote that "working together on the Charter is part of the necessary cultural change toward horizontality in government that goes well beyond court requirements or the law itself. Working with the Charter increases the government's ability to maintain the lead on policy issues, establish the right balance between courts and governments, and to reflect, reaffirm and interpret Canadian values."[24] Indeed, many of the internal political and bureaucratic responses to the Charter have been overshadowed by the more public judicial approach to rights, but this should not be taken as evidence that the cabinet has ceded guardianship of rights to the Supreme Court.

The failure to recognize the importance of the cabinet's response to the Charter within the bureaucratic arena has led many to conclude that judicial power has weakened parliamentary institutions. The Charter has not weakened parliament: the cabinet's response to the Charter and the empowering of bureaucratic institutions at the expense of parliamentary scrutiny have nonetheless produced this result. Janet Hiebert has remarked that "most observers assume that the principal effect of a bill of rights is on courts because it gives the judiciary a more authoritative role to evaluate legislation in terms of its consistency with protected rights. But what should not be overlooked is the potential of a bill of rights to encourage more responsible and principled parliamentary decisions."[25] The improvement of the legislative process and the emergence of more principled decisions by the cabinet have occurred, but principled parliamentary decisions have not, because of the cabinet-centred nature of parliamentary institutions in Canada. The full attainment of the Charter's promise of greater protection for rights requires both legislative and judicial activism, as neither actor can fully protect civil liberties without effective checks on either the power of the cabinet or the power of the Supreme Court.[26]

Toward the Charter

The activist responses to the Charter are essential to the emergence of constitutional supremacy, but this study does not view the distinct components as necessarily equal, because there is a clear order of importance that ensures the Charter project is fundamentally democratic. Both judicial and bureaucratic activism are responses to democratic activism and the desire by Trudeau and the major drafters of the Charter to provide greater textual and institutional protections for rights and freedoms. The paramount status of democratic activism is clearly evident in its relationship with bureaucratic activism, as the cabinet has ensured that the machinery of government has responded to the rights culture introduced by the Charter. In an interview I conducted with Pierre Elliott Trudeau, the former prime minister outlined his desire that the Charter act as an internal check on both parliamentary and bureaucratic actors, as well as to facilitate principled policy decisions by the cabinet: "I had not articulated the Charter as part of my broader project of restructuring the political executive's relationship with the administrative state, but I had conceptualized the Charter in such a way. My prime ministership was concerned, among other things, with democratizing the policy process within government, and this was the intention of my attempts at central agency reform. The Charter was therefore an extension of this larger project, and consistent with my philosophy of checks and balances, because it requires the administrative state to develop policies consistent with the values of a democratic society."[27]

Democratic activism is associated with a new framers' intent to distinguish the activist intentions of the Charter from its predecessor, the *Canadian Bill of Rights,* and to suggest that comparisons involving the court's approach to the Bill of Rights and the Charter are highly problematic. The deferential approach advanced under the *Canadian Bill of Rights* was textually required because the judiciary was restricted to protecting rights that "existed and shall continue to exist" at the time of the statute's enactment by parliament in 1960.[28] What reinforced the restrained and deferential approach to rights and freedoms within section 1 of the Bill of Rights was the strict adherence to the principle of parliamentary supremacy found within the document's preamble, which stated the judiciary would interpret "a Bill of Rights which shall reflect the respect of Parliament for its constitutional authority and which shall ensure the protection of these rights and freedoms in Canada."[29] In effect, judicial review was constrained through the constitutional principle of parliamentary supremacy and a frozen rights approach to the Bill of Rights, as the document only applied to the Parliament of Canada.

The same constraints on judicial review are not present within either the text of the Charter, the post-1982 constitutional principles that structure judicial review, or the activist intentions of the document's framers. What justifies an activist approach to the Charter by the Supreme Court is the substitution of the preamble to the Bill of Rights with section 52 of the *Constitution Act, 1982,* which states that "the Constitution of Canada is the supreme law of Canada, and any law that is inconsistent with the provisions of the Constitution is, to the extent of the inconsistency, of no force or effect."[30] As well, this new activist approach is further legitimized by the wording of section 24(1), which requires a court of competent jurisdiction to implement remedies that it considers "appropriate and just in the circumstances."[31] The textual variations between the Bill of Rights and the Charter are not insignificant, and, more importantly, much of the court's activism involves the three most important textual differences between the two documents: the reasonable limitations clause (section 1), section 24(2) – the exclusion-of-evidence rule – and, finally, equality rights protected by section 15(1) of the Charter. In accepting that textual variations exist in the very areas in which the Supreme Court has been activist, and, incidentally, areas in which the text is least precise, the contention that this has facilitated judicial supremacy is, in my opinion, very debatable.[32]

Judicial activism does not threaten democracy, because it is consistent with the intention of the Charter's framers. The Charter can be viewed as an explicit rejection of the Bill of Rights and the approach to civil liberties that the judiciary adopted during its interpretation of this statutory document.[33] The suggestion that the Supreme Court has departed from the specific meaning of the text and, thus, supplanted constitutional supremacy with judicial supremacy is open to dispute, given that the framers largely engaged in speculation as to how the courts would approach specific sections of the Charter. Perhaps more importantly, the framers of the Charter possessed a more positive view of the institutional role performed by the judiciary and viewed the courts as complementary and not competitive actors in a constitutional democracy. As this book will argue, the perception of a Supreme Court as a political actor is quite different in a parliamentary democracy based on a fusion of power than it is in a system based on a separation of power, as in the American context. In a parliamentary democracy, the judiciary has generally been viewed as a complementary actor, and Dicey contended that judicial legislation is secondary legislation because these decisions can be reversed through acts of parliament.[34] Though this insight has been lost in the Canadian debate and its preoccupation with American theories concerning the finality of judicial decisions, the Canadian Charter is not a paler and northern version of the American Bill of Rights. In moving toward the Charter, therefore, we must move away from the American debate and return to Diceyan principles of constitutionalism that recognize the central role of political actors in the policy process. This remains true despite the introduction of the Charter, as judicial legislation, for the most part, remains secondary legislation because cabinet retains the discretion to decide how to respond to judicial findings of unconstitutionality.

Parliamentary Democracy and the Protection of Rights
A more difficult issue for critics of judicial activism to reconcile is the fact that the framers of the Charter did not view judicial activism as usurping the democratic will, but saw it as essential for a properly functioning

constitutional system. For instance, Trudeau considered judicial activism necessary to ensure greater protection for language rights and "long realized that he would need to enlist the courts as allies to implement bilingualism at the provincial level."[35] This positive view of the judiciary is clearly illustrated in the 1968 policy paper *A Canadian Charter of Human Rights,* in which an explicit limitations clause was absent, and it was left to the courts to define the scope of rights and freedoms and, perhaps more importantly, the appropriate limitations on entrenched rights and freedoms.[36] Janet Hiebert has argued that "Trudeau indicated a faith in the judiciary's ability to develop the appropriate limits on rights when the exercise of the right conflicts with an important social value."[37] It would be a mistake to overemphasize Trudeau's role, as the Charter was the result of significant political and social struggles that began in 1929, as Christopher MacLennan noted.[38] However, Trudeau's perception of the judiciary as a complementary actor reveals an important difference between Canadian and American constitutionalism, which has been overlooked in the academic debate on judicial power.

A central issue not addressed by conservative critics in their adoption of American theories of constitutional review is whether a compound republic with a clear separation of powers and an emphasis on limited government is a good model for a parliamentary democracy with a fusion of power.[39] In truth, too much of the works of James Madison and Alexander Hamilton has been used in the Canadian debate, and there has not been enough reflection on the work of A.V. Dicey, who did not view the judiciary as a threat to democratic governance within the parliamentary tradition.[40] Dicey recognized the tension between judicial review and parliamentary supremacy, but he saw it as essentially reconcilable: "This judicial legislation might appear, at first sight, inconsistent with the supremacy of Parliament. But this is not so. English judges do not claim or exercise any power to repeal a Statute, whilst Acts of Parliament may override and constantly do override the law of judges. Judicial legislation is, in short, subordinate legislation, carried on with the assent and subject to the supervision of Parliament."[41] The suspicion of power is a notable feature of American constitutionalism, but is not a characteristic of Canadian constitutionalism and Westminster democracies.

Why then should the Canadian debate over judicial review be conducted in the same manner as its American counterpart, where the judiciary is viewed with suspicion, and the primary role of the constitution is to limit the concentration of power? The Canadian debate needs to emphasize the constitutional principles that structure a parliamentary democracy and move out from the shadows of the American debate.[42] While Canada has moved beyond parliamentary supremacy, the critics have focused on judicial activism and have concluded that it represents the final word when the Supreme

Court invalidates legislation. Canadian judges are more powerful than English judges, but "judicial legislation" should still be viewed as subordinate legislation because of the important role performed by cabinet and bureaucratic actors during the legislative process and their ability to respond when legislation or the common law is invalidated as inconsistent with the Charter.

In criticizing the Supreme Court, conservative critics have relied on the distinction between interpretivist and non-interpretivist judicial review. In interpretivism, judicial review is legitimate because the courts simply apply the explicit meaning of the constitution, as determined by the framers. Non-interpretivist judicial review is considered problematic by conservative critics because it requires the courts to be activist and to create the meaning of constitutional provisions. Thus, non-elected actors depart from the intended meaning of political actors. This is the paradox of judicial power: if the constitution is a set of rules to constrain power, by creating the constitution's meaning, the courts are not bound by constitutional rules, and judicial power is unchecked.[43] Interpretivism, therefore, is considered more consistent with constitutional supremacy, whereas critics associate non-interpretivism with judicial supremacy. In their estimation, because the Supreme Court has departed from interpretivism, it has weakened constitutional supremacy in Canada.

There is a fundamental limitation with the distinction between interpretivist and non-interpretivist review and their use to evaluate the Supreme Court of Canada and its approach to the *Canadian Charter of Rights and Freedoms:* these are judicial theories developed in relation to American political culture and are not relevant distinctions in a parliamentary democracy established to promote peace, order, and good government.[44] Specifically, judicial theories developed for a limited constitution where the state is viewed as the principal threat to individual liberty are problematic in a society where the state has been an important and activist actor designed to advance individual liberty and collective freedom through the use of public power. Janet Hiebert has argued that "the liberal-constitutional emphasis on the limited state to regulate political power has its roots in eighteenth- and nineteenth-century assumptions that have little resonance for a modern welfare state."[45] Unlike the American founders, the framers of the Charter did not intend the courts to be the bulwark of a limited constitution through narrow interpretivist review but to prevent the limited constitution through an activist approach to the Charter. This activist duty was not placed simply on the judiciary, but on all actors required to govern with the Charter after 1982.

In a comparative assessment of United States, Canada, Britain, and India, Charles Epp contends that the success of a rights revolution depends on the ability of a legal mobilization support structure (LMSS) to place civil liberties cases before a Supreme Court for resolution. The turning point in the American rights revolution, according to Epp, was not the ascendancy of the "liberal" Warren court in the 1960s, but the emergence of an LMSS and rights advocacy organizations staffed by legal activists committed to cause litigation. In the United States, Epp contends, the rights revolution was delayed until the 1960s because the LMSS was underdeveloped and the ability to move civil liberties cases through the court system to the United States Supreme Court for final review was prevented by societal barriers that limited access to justice and legal education for minority communities. Thus, by the 1960s, the very communities that created rights advocacy organizations in the early part of the twentieth century had the legal personnel committed to civil liberties issues and their resolution by the Supreme Court through "progressive cause lawyering."[46]

In his assessment of Canada, Epp contends that this country has been "a great experiment in constitutional engineering," largely because he believes that Canada has mirrored the American approach with the creation of an LMSS, though one that relies primarily on public and not private funding.[47] While Epp does offer a compelling alternative to the judicial-centred paradigm, there is a serious limitation in his analysis that is directly the result of the pluralist assumptions that inform his model. In particular, Epp does not consider the positive role that the political and bureaucratic arenas can have in the advancement of the rights revolution, largely because his model is dependent on pluralist assumptions that the political arena is generally a reflection of inter-group competition, and the outcome of this competition is public policy involving civil liberties issues. Further, this model overlooks the domestic manifestation of rights revolutions and seeks to measure success by the replication of the American approach in different countries. The emphasis on the LMSS is a valid approach in political systems where sovereignty resides in the people and also in systems that emphasize limited government, such as the United States. However, this model is not directly transferable to parliamentary systems or those with an activist state, such as Britain, Canada, and India.

The limitation of this approach is most evident in the case of Britain, which, contrary to Epp's view, has had a successful rights revolution within the parliamentary and bureaucratic arenas despite the underdevelopment of the British LMSS. For instance, the domestic demand for greater attention to human rights led to the Labour Party's campaigning on an explicit platform of constitutional reform that saw the incorporation of the *European Convention on Human Rights* into domestic law as the *Human Rights Act* in 1998, but with application delayed until 2000.[48] During this two-year delay, the British parliament established the Joint Committee on Human Rights with an explicit mandate to scrutinize legislation for its conformity to the *Human Rights Act*. As well, the Lord Chancellor's Department was reorganized to include the Human Rights Unit, which assumed responsibility for creating an internal scrutiny process during the development of legislation within the bureaucratic arena.[49] Epp has interpreted this as a modest rights revolution because his model emphasizes societal activism to the neglect of legislative activism directed at ensuring that principled policy decisions are reached before either the judiciary or rights advocacy organizations attempt to become policy actors through litigation.

Canada is a great experiment, but not in the way envisioned by Epp. The Commonwealth approach to bills of rights, which prioritizes the attempt to develop legislation that conforms to rights commitments and does not rely heavily on judicial review to achieve principled policy, is distinct from the American approach, which is decidedly judicial-centred.[50] To invoke this model of constitutionalism, as it relates to bills of rights, we must be aware of the limitations of theories of judicial review developed in a political system inconsistent with the principles of parliamentary democracy.

Courts and Legislatures

Between 1982 and 2003, 52 percent of Charter decisions by the Supreme Court involved the conduct of police officers. Perhaps more importantly, the nullification rates of statutes have been drastically declining in recent years.[51] The significance of these trends is that they offset the democratic critique of the Supreme Court because they show that the instances in which the judiciary directly challenges the policy choices of the cabinet at the federal or provincial level represent a minority of the court's Charter jurisprudence. When the discretionary conduct of the police clearly violates legal rights, the Charter allows for the exclusion of evidence under section 24(2). Canadian democracy is not threatened when judicial activism requires the agents of law enforcement to respect the rule of law, and this suggests that a paradox exists within constitutional democracies that provide for judicial review. Specifically, judicial activism does not necessarily lead to judicial supremacy, but it can have a positive effect on the democratic quality of a country when it challenges the conduct of police officers, as it ensures that the discretionary conduct of the police is accountable to the values of Canadian society entrenched in the Charter.

The balancing mechanisms within the Charter are significant, but they do not function in isolation from the parliamentary arena. Rather, they serve to reinforce the shared responsibility for rights in Canada. Peter Hogg and Allison Bushell developed the Charter dialogue metaphor to describe the interaction between legislatures and the courts when statutes are nullified and the ability of legislatures to introduce legislative sequels to overcome the invalidation of laws. They state that, "in most cases, relatively minor amendments were all that was required in order to respect the *Charter*, without compromising the objective of the original legislation."[52] Along with Christopher Manfredi, I have challenged the conceptualization of the dialogue metaphor, suggesting that not all legislative sequels qualify as Charter dialogue and that a positive legislative response is necessary to facilitate genuine dialogue between courts and legislatures.[53] With these caveats aside, the ability of the cabinet, at both levels of government, to respond to the courts tempers the force of judicial activism. Perhaps more importantly, statutes that violate the Charter and are determined to constitute an unreasonable limitation on protected rights and freedoms generally demonstrate an inherent flaw that necessitates their invalidation. Specifically, many of the statutes nullified by the Supreme Court demonstrate a lack of legislative precision in their drafting, and thus the flawed statutes do not simply exceed what constitutes a reasonable limitation, but either constitute a total limitation[54] – as in the case of *Ford v. Quebec* and *Rocket v. Royal College of Dental Surgeons of Ontario* – or suffer from overbreadth in the type of activity regulated – such as in *R. v. Heywood* and *Osborne v. Canada*.[55]

Instead of viewing nullification as the crudest example of judicial power, an alternative approach is presented in this book. In essence, legislative precision has emerged as a principle of Charter review because the new policy environment requires legislation to be drafted in a manner that demonstrates greater respect for rights. Taken together, Charter dialogue and the call for greater precision in the drafting of statutes provide the cabinet and the bureaucracy with the ability to effectively respond to the new policy environment and to achieve substantive elements of the cabinet's agendas. While judicial discretion is an important variable during Charter review, it is rarely used by the Supreme Court to limit the policy options of cabinet at either the federal or provincial level. The increasing frequency with which cabinet introduces amendments to ensure the constitutionality of nullified statutes and attempts to develop legislation that is more consistent with the Charter highlights the complementary relationship between the Supreme Court and the cabinet in an age of rights. It also highlights the emergence of coordinate constitutionalism in Canada, as the cabinet and the Supreme Court have shared responsibility for the Charter and its interpretation.[56] Brian Slattery refers to the coordinate model that "sets up a complex scheme of constitutional duties and review powers that are distributed among governments, legislatures, and the courts."[57] The significance of this model is that it requires all actors to govern with the Charter and views the responsibilities of courts and legislatures as reciprocal and complementary.

Legislative Activism and the Cabinet

The principle of legislative precision as an emerging criterion of judicial review has been put in practice within the bureaucratic arena that supports the cabinet in achieving its legislative agenda. However, the Charter debate has generally ignored legislative activism and has focused on important but marginal actors within the policy process, such as interest groups and their litigation strategies.[58] If the Charter's impact on the constitutional order is as broad and encompassing as Alan Cairns and others have suggested it is, then the evaluation of that impact must extend beyond the peripheral realm of interest group politics and into the centre of the policy process, which remains under the direction of the cabinet. The relative obscurity of legislative activism is understandable because of the generally closed nature of the policy process and the principle of cabinet solidarity that limits an appreciation of the influential role performed by the minister of justice and the attorney general of Canada.[59] However, the importance of the minister of justice in ensuring that cabinet properly addresses Charter issues cannot be denied. As former Ontario attorney general Ian Scott has suggested, "an independent attorney general should bring to policy-making in government a particular concern for principle, for constitutionalism and for rights."[60] Indeed, Scott has documented the ability of the attorney general to effectively pressure cabinet to seek amendment of legislation the attorney general considers to be unconstitutional, such as the prohibition in the *Ontario Human Rights Code* that prevented complaints based on sex discrimination in sports, and the prohibition in the *Vital Statistics Act* that prevented a child's taking the maiden name of the mother. According to Scott, "in both of these cases the Cabinet accepted the advice of the attorney general that the sections were unconstitutional, and told us to prepare the appropriate amendments and to concede the issue."[61]

Legislative activism under the leadership of the minister of justice or provincial attorney generals at cabinet, however, is typically the last stage of rights activism before legislation becomes law and could be significantly bolstered by the development of a more thorough parliamentary scrutiny of legislation for rights consistency in Canada.[62] Ideally, an elected Senate with a Charter scrutiny committee could check executive supremacy in Canada and would be particularly important in creating a legislative record of the alternative approaches considered in the design of legislation. It would also act as a useful resource for the DOJ in defending statutes as either consistent with the Charter or a reasonable limitation in a free and democratic society. More practically, a joint committee of the Senate and the House of Commons with the same mandate could be achieved through non-constitutional means, but would require prime ministerial leadership and commitment to address the democratic deficit through a reform of cabinet-centred parliaments that dominate the policy process in Canada.

Legislative scrutiny involving the Charter does exist in Canada at the present time, but it is hidden within the bureaucratic apparatus that supports the cabinet and its attempt to govern with the Charter from the centre. The establishment of effective parliamentary scrutiny committees would complement the Charter screening process that exists under the direction of the DOJ and would act as the public face of this important exercise. Bureaucratic activism is distinct from judicial activism because it is directed to ensure that policy decisions remain centred in the cabinet. Judicial activism, therefore, may indeed facilitate democratic control of the policy process in the long run because of the behavioural and institutional changes it causes within the administrative apparatus that supports the cabinet and its legislative agenda. Thus the initial "flight from politics" that Peter Russell identified in the court's early activist approach to the Charter has come to have its wings clipped by bureaucratic activism.[63] The dilemma, however, is to produce a political response to the Charter that empowers parliamentary institutions and not simply the cabinet.

Beyond instigating the important review functions performed by the DOJ, the introduction of the Charter has facilitated the emergence of this department as a central agency. Donald Savoie has suggested that the centre of government remains the same despite the introduction of the Charter, but the importance of bureaucratic activism and the leadership role of the DOJ in a rights-based policy environment challenge this conclusion.[64] The central agency reforms introduced by Trudeau were designed to increase the cabinet's control over the bureaucracy and to control the direction of public policy. In particular, Trudeau created bureaucratic centres of power to offset the dominance of operating departments in the policy process. A similar problem faces the cabinet with the Charter: how best to ensure that policy decisions reflect the priorities of cabinet and prevent judicial nullification of policy as inconsistent with the Charter. Those who dispute that the DOJ is now a central agency have not considered whether the traditional central agencies can offset the judiciary's challenge to the cabinet's legislative agenda. The Charter's introduction has expanded the central agency rationale beyond simply a consideration of bureaucratic power and the threat this poses to the cabinet to one that must also confront the potential of judicial power. The emergence of legislative activism and its relationship to democratic activism suggest that judicial power can be reconciled with political power and democratic control.

Organization of This Book

This study seeks to address the tendency in the Charter debate to focus on the negative implications of judicial review for constitutional supremacy and federalism in Canada. Instead, it questions whether judicial activism in all its manifestations, and the different relationships between the judiciary and state actors that Charter review creates, necessarily threaten constitutional balance in Canada. Judicial review is simply one variable that determines whether a constitutional order that combines parliamentary democracy, federalism, and rights can facilitate institutional balance. Indeed, the question of democratic activism takes centre stage in this study, as it suggests that judicial activism is not an independent creation of the judiciary but is consistent with both the intentions of the Charter's framers and broader societal trends in Canada after the Second World War that sought to constitutionalize rights and freedoms.

The first chapter considers the theoretical questions underpinning the Charter and democracy debate in Canada. It challenges the dominance of the judicial-centred paradigm for understanding the Charter because that paradigm does not consider the attempt by cabinet, supported by the bureaucracy, to govern with the Charter through a reformed policy process. Instead, this chapter suggests that a cabinet-centred approach is preferable because of the Charter's origin as a political project and because of the continued leadership of the prime minister and cabinet in developing legislation that advances rights and freedoms. Chapter 2 considers the constitutional politics in the period immediately preceding the Charter's introduction and the competing agendas of the Trudeau government and the provincial premiers, who attempted to preserve the principle of parliamentary supremacy. The activist intentions of the Trudeau government triumphed, and the role of the Special Joint Committee on the Constitution of Canada is considered in this chapter. As the protections in the draft Charter were strengthened during the proceedings of the Special Joint Committee, the argument that judicial activism is a violation of the framers' intent lacks a textual and historical basis. This idea is advanced further in Chapter 3, where the issue of framers' intent is considered and the conservative critique of judicial activism is challenged. A new framers' intent surrounded the Charter's introduction, and it is decidedly activist.

Chapters 4 and 5 focus on the Supreme Court, its approach to Charter review, and the emergence of coordinate constitutionalism. Chapter 4 considers the largest category of Charter review: the conduct of public officials and the effect of legal rights on the administration of justice. Unlike previous assessments, which conclude that the provision of legal rights has resulted in a due process revolution by emphasizing the legal rights of the accused at the expense of victims' rights, I contend that this was never the intention of the Charter's framers, who sought to reform the crime control model and its sole emphasis on protecting victims from crime with elements of due process. My conclusion is that the Charter's introduction has stirred but not shaken crime control in Canada, and the court's approach to legal rights and the exclusion-of-evidence rule in section 24(2) has balanced the objectives of crime control with the rights of the accused. Perhaps more importantly, this is generally consistent with the legislative intent surrounding these Charter provisions, making the due process thesis questionable. The relationship between the Supreme Court, the cabinet, and its provincial counterparts when statutes are the focus of judicial review is considered in Chapter 5. This chapter expands on the theme of coordinate constitutionalism and provides an analysis of statutes invalidated as inconsistent with the Charter. I contend that much of the evidence used to demonstrate the growth of judicial power involves legislation that was enacted before the Charter's introduction. Indeed, very few statutes enacted in the 1990s have been invalidated as inconsistent with the Charter, which is the result of institutional reforms to the legislative process by federal and provincial governments. As legislative actors are committed to governing with the Charter, and judicial activism is mainly confined to pre-1982 statutes or those enacted immediately after the document's entrenchment, the judicial power thesis comes to rest on a precarious empirical foundation.

The importance of coordinate constitutionalism demonstrates the "guardian of the constitution" role, which the court invokes to defend its approach to the Charter, exists in two dimensions. In the purely legal sense, the Supreme Court is the guardian of the constitution, but the actual functioning of the constitution demonstrates that this is a responsibility shared between the cabinet and the Supreme Court. In Chapter 6 it is suggested that the purview of the guardian role is broader than simply rights and encompasses both federalism and constitutional supremacy. This chapter argues that both the Supreme Court and provincial cabinets have protected the federal character of Canada and that the suggested incompatibility between rights and federalism is incorrect. The advancement of provincial autonomy and federal diversity is the result of the Supreme Court's sensitivity to this principle in its Charter jurisprudence, but is also due to the flexibility to policy variation that section 1 of the Charter has come to provide. The protection of federalism, however, is not simply a judicial responsibility, and this chapter argues that the introduction of pre-legislative Charter vetting in all provincial governments has guarded this essential characteristic of the Canadian constitutional order. Thus, the protection of federalism and the responsibility shared between the Supreme Court and provincial cabinets clearly highlights the significance of coordinate constitutionalism in Canada and the continued relevance of Dicey for Canadian constitutionalism.

Chapter 7 is an analysis of legislative activism in Canada and the further marginalization of parliament as a policy actor since the Charter's introduction. While the cabinet governs with the Charter and the claims of judicial power are overstated, the democratic deficit thesis does have merit in regard to the relationship between the cabinet and parliament since the Charter's introduction. The imbalance within legislative activism is significant and supports the suggestion that executive supremacy has not been challenged by judicial review and the Charter's introduction. This book concludes with a consideration of the intra-institutional conclusion on executive supremacy and advocates parliamentary scrutiny as a necessary but underused dimension of legislative activism and the attempt to govern with the Charter.

Part 1
Democratic Activism and Constitutional Politics

1
Democracy and Judicial Review

The relationship between democracy and judicial review has been a central issue in Canada since the passage of the *Canadian Charter of Rights and Freedoms* in 1982. While the Canadian public has concluded that the Charter has been a positive addition, no such consensus exists within the legal and academic communities that debate the impact of Charter review by the Supreme Court.[1] This highly polarized debate has produced enthusiastic supporters of the Charter and the activist jurisprudence of the Supreme Court, who view the court as the lead actor responsible for the evolution of Canada from a legislative to a constitutional state.[2] The supporters of judicial activism have been equally matched by Charter critics, who see a more pronounced institutional revolution in which the constitutional state has been overwhelmed and replaced by the judicial state.[3] Though the supporters and critics disagree as to the outcome of constitutional interpretation of rights by the Supreme Court, their analyses occur within the same judicial-centred paradigm that emphasizes the judiciary as the agent responsible for fundamental political and social changes. For instance, their analyses focus on the legitimacy of judicial review and the appropriate role of the courts in a constitutional democracy. While these are important considerations that have generally dominated the Charter debate, the discussion has been cast in terms too narrow to fully capture the complexity of the Charter and the multiplicity of forces that have contributed to its evolution.

Supporters of judicial activism defend the Supreme Court on too narrow a foundation and deny the political role of the court in interpreting the Charter. While they defend the Supreme Court and its jurisprudence as essential to the emergence of constitutional supremacy, their theory of checks and balances largely pertains to legislative actors, and no such check is considered appropriate, or even necessary, for judicial actors, save within the context of judicially determined Charter dialogue.[4] For the defenders of judicial activism, such as Lorraine Weinrib, the legislative state is seen as unprincipled at times and as the institutional actor that poses the greatest

threat to rights and freedoms.[5] Because this position downplays the important role performed by the cabinet in protecting rights, as well as in sharing
responsibility for determining the Charter's meaning, this defence of judicial activism cannot be sustained within the paradigm of constitutional
supremacy. The reliance on judicial hegemony serves to heighten the tension between democracy and judicial review, as the supporters view this
reconciliation as simply the cabinet's compliance with judicial decisions.

Though Charter critics on both the left and the right have made a solid
contribution that has identified the potential democratic deficit associated
with Charter review,[6] this critique has failed to break free of the judicial-
centred approach. Specifically, in this view the relationship between the
Charter and democracy is largely determined by judicial responses to the
document, while societal and political responses to rights activism outside
the judicial arena are not part of the analysis or, when they are considered,
are overwhelmed by judicial power.[7] While it is not particularly surprising
that left-wing critics have sustained a judicial-centred analysis of the Charter, as this critical position is drawn primarily from Canada's law schools,
the same cannot be said about the analytical approach of conservative judicial critics, such as F.L. Morton, Rainer Knopff, and Christopher Manfredi.
This critical school is drawn from the discipline of political science and has
correctly identified the growth of judicial power and the emergence of the
Supreme Court as a political actor since the Charter's introduction.

Quite rightly, this critical school rejects the claims of judicial hegemony
over the determination of rights and has questioned the democratic potential of unconstrained judicial power. Despite the importance of this perspective, these scholars have generally focused on the rise of the judiciary
as a political actor and downplayed developments within political institutions, such as the cabinet, that prevent the emergence of judicial supremacy.
An important exception to this is their support of the Charter's notwithstanding clause as a political response to unacceptable judicial interpretations of this document.[8] In this sense, both left- and right-wing critics share
common ground with the supporters of judicial activism, as all three positions minimize the importance of legislative activism and ignore the institutional reform of the machinery of government that directly challenges
judicial hegemony over the Charter. As a result, this court-centred analysis
leads conservative critics to conclude that judicial supremacy has been the
primary outcome of the Charter, largely because they focus on the institutional apparatus that supports the judiciary,[9] as well as on the methods of
judicial review believed to advance judicial power.[10] In effect, right-wing
critics have correctly identified the rise of judicial power but have overstated its effect on Canadian democracy by ignoring the institutions of Canadian democracy that confront and contain judicial power.

In this chapter, the legitimacy debate that has dominated legal and academic analyses of the Charter is examined. This debate is divided between the supporters of judicial activism, who are referred to as the judicial democrats because they view both the protection and determination of rights largely as the domain of the courts,[11] and the judicial critics, who question whether the courts, as unrepresentative and unaccountable institutions, can actually advance democracy beyond its concern for the rule of law. My refusal to accept the positions advanced by the judicial democrats and the critics is directly related to their decision to focus on important yet secondary actors in the development of public policy: the judiciary and the social movements that seek policy victories in the courts. The judiciary does not possess the institutional capacity to emerge as the type of policy actor suggested by right-wing critics, and it lacks the ability to implement its decisions, as it requires the cabinet and parliament to accept judicial invalidation. The neglect of the cabinet and its response to the Charter is not a reasonable limitation in a debate that seeks to understand the relationship between rights, democracy, and judicial review in Canada.

Critical Positions Reconsidered

The limitations of the contemporary debate are reminiscent of the one involving the Judicial Committee of the Privy Council (JCPC), particularly Alan Cairns's insight that too much importance was attributed to judicial decisions: "Courts are not self-starting institutions. They are called into play by groups and individuals seeking objectives which can be furthered by judicial support. A comprehensive explanation of judicial decisions, therefore, must include the actors who employed the courts for their own purposes."[12] The contemporary debate has the same fervour and the same limitations that Cairns identified in his study of the JCPC.[13] For instance, the judicial democrats have correctly identified the importance of judicial activism, but the hierarchical relationship between the Supreme Court and cabinet that is implicit within their analysis is incompatible with constitutional supremacy. This creates a questionable dichotomy in which the courts are considered principled, and the defenders of rights and cabinets and parliaments are viewed as the principal threat to constitutional protections. Without a careful consideration of legislative activism, and with an inability to accept that alternative interpretations of rights by cabinet and parliament are as legitimate as those of the court, the judicial democrats provide only a partial defence of judicial activism and its relationship to constitutional supremacy.

While judicial critics have challenged the assumptions of the court-centred paradigm and question the democratic elements of judicial activism, they overstate the case that Canadian democracy has suffered as a result of the

Charter's introduction and the court's interpretation of this document. It is my contention that their participation in the legitimacy debate is directly influenced by ideological positions that do not reflect Canada's moderate, centrist, political culture.[14] Indeed, the left-wing critique is more an attack on liberal democracy than it is an analysis of Charter review by the Supreme Court.[15] Advocates of this critical position lament that Charter review has reinforced liberal democracy and its inherent limitations, which can only be overcome, they argue, with a systemic shift to social democracy that advances substantive equality.[16] While left-wing critics do appreciate the important advances made in the areas of substantive equality for gays and lesbians, they consider these advances partial because of the limitations of legal liberalism.

Even though this study agrees with the right-wing critique of the court-centred model of Charter analysis, my position neither mistrusts the judiciary nor feels pessimistic about the cabinet's ability to effectively respond to judicial activism. The emergence of legislative activism is designed to ensure that the cabinet advances the constitutional guarantees entrenched in the Charter *before* the judiciary reviews legislation for its constitutionality. In those instances when the Supreme Court invalidates legislation, the cabinet may still respond to "judicial legislation" with positive legislative sequels that amend legislation to clarify the attempt to protect rights in nullified legislation. Therefore, judicial decisions can remain as secondary legislation because of the ability of the cabinet to prevent judicial invalidation during the development of legislation. A cabinet-centred analysis of the Charter does not reject the important role played by the judiciary in protecting rights, but it refuses to accept the dominant role assigned by the supporters and critics of judicial activism. In truth, conservative critics have explored the limitations of the Charter solely within a court-centred paradigm. What is needed, therefore, is an institutional approach to the Charter that looks simultaneously at judicial, political, and bureaucratic responses to rights in a context that reflects the unique elements of Canadian constitutionalism.

Judicial Democracy and the Charter

The belief that the judicialization of politics is necessary to create the proper institutional environment for rights is reflected in the writings of Torbjörn Vallinder, who discussed two related phenomena associated with the global expansion of judicial power: judicialization from without and judicialization from within.[17] The first dimension of judicial power exists in political systems where judicial review is an established practice and the courts can require democratic actors to honour constitutional protections. The second dimension, judicialization from within, occurs when judicial values and processes become internalized within the decision-making structures of the legislative arena. The importance of Vallinder's approach is that it clearly reveals the assumptions advanced by the judicial-centred analysis of the Charter and the Supreme Court. For instance, a deeply held belief of judicial democrats is that rights are best protected when the courts are activist. According to Weinrib, the Supreme Court has been essential in moving Canada away from the minimalist view of democracy as simply adherence to majoritarianism, and toward a more mature democracy that demonstrates its respect for the rule of law by entrenching constitutional supremacy and, further, protecting the fundamental rights of citizens through judicial review of government action.[18]

This critical position reveals a fundamental assumption that rights are only fully protected in the constitutional state under judicial supervision. This assumption is clearly revealed in Weinrib's discussion of the institutional roles under the Charter performed by courts and legislatures: "Courts of law, independent from the political arena and expert at articulating and elaborating principle on a case by case basis, are to deliberate upon questions of rights and limits constrained to supreme law values; legislatures shoulder the political responsibility for denial of rights under conditions that intensify the democratic function."[19] The difficulty with this characterization is that it does not acknowledge that both the Supreme Court and cabinet deny and limit rights during the legislative and judicial dimensions of Charter review.[20] Indeed, the Charter requires the Supreme Court to choose among competing rights claims, most evidently in legal rights cases that pit the due process claims of the accused against the rights of the victim.[21] It is not clear how this process is any different from the legislative process when the cabinet, supported by the Department of Justice, attempts to balance competing rights claims as it designs legislation that becomes the future basis of Charter decisions by the court.

This defence of judicial activism, therefore, comes to rest on the claim that the Supreme Court is more principled and the more capable institution to act as the guardian of the constitution. In defending the principled nature of judicial review, Weinrib has correctly identified the past injustices of parliamentary democracy and its treatment of religious minorities. But this approach discounts that the effect of the Charter has been to facilitate the emergence of principled policy decisions by the cabinet, as both political and bureaucratic review attempt to hold legislation to the highest standard before the courts replicate this process. The emergence of a principled policy process within the bureaucratic arena in support of the cabinet suggests that judicial activism is necessary for the effective protection of rights but not essential. The view that the Supreme Court is simply a principled actor would be a more convincing defence of judicial activism if section 1 of the Charter, the reasonable limits clause, was not a critical aspect of Charter review. While the Supreme Court is required to make principled decisions about rights when statutes are challenged, this is simply the first stage of judicial review. This principled review quickly proceeds to the second stage, which sees the court make policy decisions about the reasonableness of legislative schemes that limit rights. In effect, there is very little difference between this process and the principled decisions of cabinet, unless one accepts the claim that the Supreme Court is more principled and does not deny rights during judicial review.

The supporters of judicial activism appear unwilling to accept that the cabinet's approach is as valid as judicial attempts to protect rights. Indeed, this reluctance is reflected in their view that judicial restraint is counter-productive to both the protection of rights and the democratic character of Canadian governance.[22] The difficulty with this view of deference is cap-tured in Guy Davidov's statement that "since deference means a relaxation of standards and an easing of the constraints on the state, it undercuts con-stitutional rights."[23] This is a zero-sum approach to constitutional protec-tions because it re-creates the faulty assumption that the cabinet encroaches on rights and the Supreme Court protects rights. The limitation of this po-sition is clearly its failure to recognize that contending principled approaches to Charter review exist and, further, that judicial deference is not simply the result of a lessening of constitutional standards by the Supreme Court, but may be the result of principled attempts by the cabinet to fulfill its commitment to protect Charter rights.[24] Indeed, the emergence of legisla-tive activism lessens the importance of judicial activism, as principled ap-proaches to the Charter occur at a lower stage of the policy process.[25] Thus, judicial deference is not simply evidence of the decline of rights protections or a relaxing of standards by the courts, but verification of attempts by the cabinet and bureaucratic actors to design principled legislation that pro-tects rights or, at the very least, limits rights in a reasonable and principled manner.[26]

Charter Dialogue and Judicial Accents

The dialogue metaphor represents a promising attempt to defend judicial activism by the Supreme Court. The originators of this approach, Peter Hogg and Allison Bushell, developed this metaphor in a 1997 article in *Osgoode Hall Law Journal,* and it has quickly become the dominant paradigm for understanding the complex institutional relationship between courts and legislatures that results from Charter review.[27] The dialogue theorists chal-lenge the myth of judicial supremacy and contend that judicial invalida-tion of a statute begins a dialogue between courts and legislatures that "causes a public debate in which *Charter* values play a more prominent role than they would if there had been no judicial decision."[28] For the dialogue theo-rists, judicial invalidation is not problematic because it allows a legislative response in which "the legislative body is in a position to devise a response that is properly respectful of the *Charter* values that have been identified by the Court, but which accomplishes the social or economic objectives that the judicial decision has impeded."[29] Further, Charter dialogue is suggested to occur if it results in a democratic decision that responds to a judicial invalidation by reversing, avoiding, or modifying a constitutionally suspect statute. In the 1997 study, Hogg and Bushell analyzed sixty-five cases in which the courts invalidated statutes and suggested that Charter dialogue occurred in two-thirds of the cases (forty-four) because the responsible legislative body introduced legislative sequels to the judicial invalidations. Perhaps more importantly, Hogg and Bushell contended that in "most cases, relatively minor amendments were all that was required in order to respect the *Charter*, without compromising the objective of the original legislation."[30]

Another supporter of the Charter dialogue theory is Kent Roach, who views the "Charter not so much as a revolution, but as a continuation and enrichment of the ability of courts and legislatures to engage in a dialogue under the common law."[31] Like Hogg and Bushell, Roach contends that judicial activism advances Charter dialogue because the Supreme Court never prevents the competent legislature from introducing a legislative response to reverse a court decision. Instead, Roach contends that judicial activism is not problematic because the Canadian combination of strong courts and strong legislatures prevents judicial supremacy under the Charter.[32] This democratic nature of this dialogue, according to Roach, is the result of legislatures' retaining the ability to decide how to respond to judicial invalidation of legislation as an unreasonable limitation on a Charter right. Perhaps more importantly, Roach believes that the responsibility for judicial policy making remains in the parliamentary arena because "when the Court has the last word, it is because the legislature and the people have let it have the last word."[33]

The dialogue theory as advanced by Roach does attempt to respect the distinct institutional roles performed by the Supreme Court and cabinet, as Roach provides a more advanced approach to legislative responses than Hogg and Bushell. For instance, Hogg and Bushell view any legislative response as evidence of Charter dialogue, irrespective of the judicial remedy employed by the court and whether this remedy allows an independent response by the cabinet.[34] However, the remedy employed by the Supreme Court does structure the cabinet's response and raises the question whether all legislative responses advance Charter dialogue. The attempt by Roach to view Charter review as a democracy-enhancing exercise, as opposed to one of judicial empowerment, is reflected in his analysis of judicial remedies during the second decade of Charter review. Roach believes that the complexity of judicial remedies during the past decade, in which the Supreme

Court is employing more suspended decisions when it considers legislation to be a violation of the Charter, provides the cabinet with greater discretion in deciding how to respond to judicial invalidation of legislation.[35]

Accepting that Charter dialogue is initiated by the courts is accurate if one accepts that the protection of rights is fundamentally a judicial responsibility. In effect, the dialogue theorists have been clear that judicial activism is necessary to initiate the institutional dialogue between the Supreme Court and the cabinet, and then to ensure that Charter values attain a prominence in legislative sequels that would be absent without an activist court.[36] What Hogg and Bushell fail to recognize is that they are analyzing a particular form of Charter dialogue, as the cabinet and bureaucratic actors engage in Charter dialogue during the design and implementation stages of a policy exercise.[37] Neither is Charter dialogue initiated by the courts, but it is the result of political attempts to protect rights when legislation is being developed. The main criticism of Charter dialogue, as developed by Hogg and Bushell, is that it occurs within a judicial-centred paradigm that ignores the development of rights dialogue by the cabinet, advanced by the Department of Justice (DOJ). In truth, Charter dialogue is initiated not by judicial actors but by cabinet and bureaucratic actors who attempt to reach principled policy decisions that accommodate the Charter during the legislative process.

This is a cabinet-centred form of Charter dialogue that is initiated within the bureaucratic arena by the DOJ when it advises client departments on the implications of legislative approaches and their consistency with the Charter.[38] This Charter dialogue continues throughout the machinery of government and transpires in the absence of judicially initiated Charter dialogue.[39] Further, this dialogue on rights interacts with its parliamentary form when the responsible standing committees of both the House of Commons and the Senate engage in parliamentary scrutiny of legislation to determine whether the bureaucratic arena has adequately advanced Charter values during the initial design of legislation. Indeed, these standing committees regularly call DOJ officials as witnesses and thus facilitate a parliamentary dialogue over the Charter of Rights between legislative and bureaucratic actors responsible for the development of legislation in the age of rights.[40] Contrary to what Hogg and Bushell and the dialogue theorists claim, charter values take a prominent place in cabinet discussions well before judicially structured Charter dialogue influences the Canadian discourse on rights and freedoms.

The supporters of judicial activism demonstrate skepticism about political power and the effectiveness of parliamentary institutions. This skepticism, however, comes at the expense of an appreciation that the Supreme Court is a political actor when it decides Charter issues and is thus subject to the same institutional limitations as the cabinet or parliament. While the judicial democrats are correct about the fallibility of cabinet and parliament, their belief in the infallibility of judicial actors prevents them from recognizing the necessity of legislative activism for the effective protection of rights and the development of the Charter as an institution of Canadian governance. Because they view the success of Canadian democracy as resting on the activism of judges that produces a democratic dialogue on the meaning of Charter values between the cabinet and the Supreme Court, their position does not capture the complexity of Charter dialogue that takes place outside the judicial arena.

Critical Positions on Liberal Democracy

The left-wing perspective has been unquestionably important in exposing the limitations of the legalization of politics and the litigation difficulties faced by certain individuals and groups when Charter issues are raised before the Supreme Court. Indeed, I am in full agreement with left-wing critics that the Charter was intended to be an activist document, but I do not share their overall disappointment with the Supreme Court's use of the Charter. There have been important advances made as a result of judicial activism, such as the extension of equality rights protections to gays and lesbians in *Egan v. Canada,* and the nullification of statutes that devalue and demean same-sex relationships, such as in *M. v. H.,* where the definition of "spouse" in Ontario's *Family Law Act* was found to be in violation of the Charter.[41] Further, the court's activism has ensured the protection of vulnerable groups in society, such as women and children in sexual assault cases in decisions like *R. v. Mills* and *Darrach,* and the hearing impaired in *Eldridge v. B.C.,* in which the court ruled that equal access to medical treatment requires the provision of sign-language interpreters in hospital emergency rooms.[42] Finally, and most surprisingly, is the recent favourable approach by the court to issues of organized labour and trade unionism.

The Critical Legal Studies (CLS) position is the predominant branch in the left-wing perspective and includes such commentators as Michael Mandel, Joel Bakan, Judy Fudge, and Allan Hutchinson. They suggest that there are inherent limitations in Charter review that act as impediments to social equality and democratic participation.[43] In particular, those who hold this critical position conclude that Charter review simply reinforces the limitations of liberalism because the Charter is fundamentally a liberal document that advances a negative conception of freedom.[44] Perhaps more importantly, the progressive nature of the Charter is limited by the conservative character of the judiciary, which fails to address the power imbalances in Canadian society through an activist approach to the Charter. In essence, the CLS position claims the Charter has not facilitated a more representative democracy by empowering marginalized groups in Canadian society, but instead has seen the emergence of "legalized politics," which further reduces the progressive nature of the Canadian state because of the conservative nature of legal liberalism.[45]

Advocates of the CLS position argue that the deficiencies of liberalism are so entrenched in the Charter that judicial interpretation is counterproductive to their goal of societal reform and substantive equality. In fact, Allan Hutchinson and Andrew Petter admonish their fellow left-wing Charter critics, such as David Beatty, to stop waiting for the Charter to transform Canada into a just and progressive society, as defined by the CLS position. Instead, they challenge their counterparts to turn their reformist zeal toward replacing "liberal individualism and engendering a more open ended form of social democracy."[46] In fact, those who hold the CLS position argue that the legalization of politics creates a policy environment where the corporate sphere is provided with the means to undermine the welfare state and organized labour. They claim that, "far from loosening the grip of the economic elite on the public policy-making agenda, judges tighten the establishment's hold on its substance and style. The law's empire is built upon the frustrated dreams of a democratic imagination."[47] Andrew Petter has echoed Hutchinson's sentiment by suggesting that the Charter is "a 19th century document let loose on a 20th century welfare state. The rights in the Charter are founded on the belief that the main enemies of freedom are not disparities in wealth nor concentrations of private power, but the state."[48]

Judy Fudge sees the liberal distinction between the private and public sphere, and the focus on negative liberties and individualism, as serious constraints on the reformist potential of the Charter: "Together, they constitute a block on the development by the judiciary of the social and collective rights necessary for redistributive policies."[49] In truth, the left-wing position is more a critique of the broader failings of liberal democracy than it is a critique of the Supreme Court and its interpretation of the Charter. Critical legal theorists do not deny that the Supreme Court has been activist, but they simply reject the direction of this activism, which has been to further legitimize liberalism and the public/private distinction that is considered the root of inequality in Canadian society. Michael Mandel is particularly critical of the democratic thesis surrounding the Charter, claiming that the Charter does not substitute a new form of democracy for the one that it replaces.[50] Mandel's solution to the legalization of politics under the Charter is unapologetic as he concludes that "legalized politics cannot simply be abolished. It must be made to wither away."[51] Thus, the Charter is undemocratic for Mandel and other left-wing critics because it has not advanced their desired form of democracy. Interestingly, if judicial activism had facilitated the emergence of social democracy, it is clear that the left-wing critique of the unrepresentative and unaccountable nature of judicial review would lessen, and the democratic virtues of judicial review would be celebrated by those who take this critical position.

Aside from a series of early Charter decisions in which the court concluded that secondary picketing was not protected under freedom of expression[52] – particularly *Retail, Wholesale and Department Store Union v. Dolphin Delivery,* where the court reconfirmed that striking was not protected under freedom of association – there are few concrete examples to demonstrate the negative impact of the Charter on organized labour. Indeed, the recent jurisprudence by the Supreme Court has undermined much of the left-wing's position that the court has an anti-labour bias and that the Charter will be used by corporations to reduce the legal protections available to organized labour. For instance, in *Dunmore v. Ontario,* the Supreme Court ruled that the exclusion of agricultural workers from the *Labour Relations Act* violated freedom of association,[53] and in *UFCW, Local 1518 v. Kmart Canada Ltd.,* the Supreme Court decided that prohibitions on the distribution of leaflets at secondary picketing sites did not constitute a reasonable limitation on freedom of expression. In this case, the Supreme Court found that the definition of picketing in the *Labour Relations Code* was too broad to be constitutional because it restricted far too many legitimate practices of organized labour.[54] This victory for organized labour was extended in *RWDSU, Local 558 v. Pepsi-Cola Canada Beverages (West) Ltd.* when the Supreme Court ruled that primary and secondary picketing engaged freedom of expression, thus increasing the level of constitutional protection available to organized labour under the Charter and effectively reversing an important element of the *Labour Trilogy.*[55]

The latest labour trilogy has removed many of the features of the original labour trilogy, which supported the left-wing critique and its assessment of the Charter and its impact on organized labour and collective action. The positions presented by left-wing critics reveal a disdain for liberal democracy that is presented as a critique of the Charter. If liberal democracy is as discredited as the CLS position suggests, then it is unrealistic to assume that it could be sustained simply through judicial decisions and, thus, must be supported by societal and political institutions that provide liberal democracy with the legitimacy that is required for it to endure. Though there are important insights provided by the left-wing perspective, the limitations of a judicial-centred analysis within an ideological position that is out of step with Canadian political culture casts doubt on the accuracy of its analysis of the Charter.

Conservative Judicial Critics

American theories of judicial review rest prominently in the conservative judicial critics' assessment of the *Canadian Charter of Rights and Freedoms,* particularly the distinction between interpretivism, where the judiciary is simply a legal actor that interprets the constitution consistent with the clear meaning of the text, and non-interpretivism, where the judiciary acts as a political actor that potentially changes the constitution's meaning by exceeding and at times defying the original intention of the text.[56] Judicial critics, such as Morton, Knopff, and Manfredi, reject the idea that the introduction of the Charter has strengthened Canadian democracy and suggest that the emergence of an activist, non-interpretivist Charter jurisprudence has weakened both representative democracy and constitutional supremacy.

To account for the undemocratic nature of Charter politics, conservative judicial critics turn their attention away from the Charter as a document and toward the constellation of actors who take their cue from this document.[57] In particular, Morton, Knopff, and Manfredi are critical of the Supreme Court's activist approach to the Charter, which they suggest encourages interest groups to engage in the politics of rights and to abandon the parliamentary arena for judicial politics.[58]

Manfredi contends that the "legal seduction of politics" has fundamentally altered citizens' perception of the policy process because judicial activism encourages the use of litigation strategies by interest groups and thus undermines the parliamentary arena as the centre of public policy. Morton and Knopff are concerned that the court has extended the "living tree" doctrine of federalism to its Charter jurisprudence, a development considered serious by conservative judicial critics because the expansion of rights limits the policy capacity of the parliamentary arena and allows the judiciary to substitute legislative policy preferences for judicial preferences.[59] This further erodes the Charter's compatibility with liberal democracy because it reduces the importance of majoritarian politics in Canada. According to Morton, "rather than accommodating legislative problem solving, judges are encouraged to find better solutions. The constitutional judge is encouraged to read new meaning into the constitutional text in order to correct legislative errors. Courts are given the authority to dictate to the legislature what it may not do or even must do. The political roles are reversed. The constitutional judge decides policy, and the legislator implements judicial choice."[60] The right wing is very critical of this development because it is said to transform the judiciary into a policy actor that rivals parliament and the provincial legislatures and, at times, dominates parliamentary actors in policy areas where the judiciary lacks legitimacy and institutional capacity.[61]

Manfredi suggests that the Charter complicates the proper functioning of constitutional supremacy because the court's activist jurisprudence undermines public debate in representative and accountable forums, where policy solutions are suggested to be the result of deliberation and compromise. In an earlier work, Manfredi noted that the court's approach to the Charter raised an important normative issue, as "the spectre of unelected, virtually life-tenured officials reviewing the decisions of elected legislators poses a special dilemma for democratic theory, especially one that recognizes the doctrine of parliamentary supremacy."[62] Instead of becoming the "citizens' constitution," according to right-wing critics, the Charter has become the constitution of special interests that advance a liberal, reformist agenda through the judicial arena. Charter politics, therefore, has displaced democratic politics because it takes its cue from what Morton has referred to as the "new imperial judiciary."[63]

Evaluating the Conservative Critique

After reading the scholarship of conservative judicial critics, one is left with the impression that the Supreme Court approaches the Charter in a highly activist manner that has undermined Canadian democracy; that it has used the Charter in such a way that the cabinet has ceased to be the dominant policy actor; and that as a result of judicial invalidation of provincial statutes, Canadian federalism has been seriously weakened. This position suffers from a number of empirical and normative limitations, however, which challenge its general conclusion that judicial supremacy has been the primary institutional outcome of the Charter's entrenchment. The most significant limitation is the weakness of the majoritarian critique against judicial review, which has dominated the right-wing position. For instance, conservative critics focus primarily on judicial invalidation of statutes and suggest a particular relationship between institutional actors under the Charter that weakens both representative government and constitutional supremacy. The analysis presented implies that a confrontational relationship exists between courts and legislatures, as judicial invalidation of statutes represents the primary focus of Charter review by the Supreme Court.

This, however, is not an accurate characterization of the Supreme Court's Charter jurisprudence, as statutes represent a minority of the court's Charter cases.[64] Between 1982 and 2003, the focus of Charter review has been on the conduct of public officials such as the police; 52 percent of Charter cases have involved such challenges.[65] As a result, the conservative critique of judicial review as anti-majoritarian is based on a minority of Charter reviews, as much of the judicial review sees the Supreme Court challenge the discretionary conduct of the police and not the policy choices of the cabinet. Further, the rate of activism between 1982 and 2003 has been 33 percent, as rights claimants have not been overly successful in challenging the constitutionality of government acts or the conduct of police officers. These empirical limitations lead to a further unsustainable normative claim that the impact of judicial activism is the same whether it involves the policy choices of the cabinet or actions of the police. Indeed, the right-wing analysis fails to consider whether judicial activism against the police can advance the rule of law and constitutional supremacy, as this critical position simply concludes that judicial activism has detrimental implications for democratic governance.

The absence of critical analysis of judicial activism undermines the persuasiveness of this position. As I argue, starting in Chapter 4, the effect of judicial activism is complex and is directly influenced by the actor at the centre of a Charter challenge, and, more importantly, judicial activism against the police has advanced Canadian democracy by creating an important check on the discretionary power of an unelected actor. Neglecting to make important distinctions between state actors, I would contend, is a direct result of ideological considerations that structure critics' analysis of the Charter and the Supreme Court. For instance, the right-wing position is critical of judicial activism involving the police because it directly conflicts with the right wing's preferred model of criminal procedure, the crime control model, in which the rationale of the legal system is to have the police prove "factual guilt" and not the judicial system prove "legal guilt."[66] While judicial activism that checks the discretionary conduct of the police may complicate the crime control model, it cannot be suggested that the emergence of an effective check against the police under the Charter weakens Canadian democracy or supports the anti-majoritarian critique presented by conservative judicial analysts.

In a number of important Charter cases, the court has not favoured the attempt by rights claimants to increase social policy spending by governments. In *Egan,* the appellants James Egan and John Norris challenged the definition of spouse in the *Old Age Security Act* as an infringement of equality rights protected under the Charter.[67] The appellants were a homosexual couple, and Norris applied for spousal allowances under section 19(1) of the act upon turning sixty years of age. In a highly divided judgment (five to four), in which four judges found that the *Old Age Security Act* did not violate section 15(1) and four judges found that the act violated section 15(1) and did not constitute a reasonable limitation, the constitutionality of the *Old Age Security Act* was determined by Justice Sopinka, who decided that the section 15(1) infringement was a reasonable limitation. The court ruled the definition of spouse to be constitutional and, therefore, did not compel the federal government to increase the level of spending on pensions or to rewrite the definition of spouse in the act.[68] Further, in *Adler v. Ontario* the court rejected the assertion that lack of public funding for Jewish schools violated section 15(1) and freedom of religion, and thus maintained provincial policy autonomy in an important area of responsibility.[69]

Even in section 15(1) cases where the court has found an equality rights violation, it has tempered the force of its activism by rendering decisions that do not place any fiscal obligations on the state. For instance, in *Vriend v. Alberta,* the court concluded that the exclusion of sexual orientation as a characteristic protected against discrimination by the *Individual's Rights Protection Act (IRPA)* violated section 15(1) of the Charter and read sexual orientation into the *IRPA.*[70] While this is an example of an activist decision and of the court functioning as a policy actor – two elements of the court's Charter jurisprudence that the right wing is particularly critical of – the decision is less problematic than conservative judicial critics conclude it to be for Canadian democracy. Specifically, this decision simply extends a negative freedom to homosexuals and lesbians and does not place a substantive obligation on the state to address discrimination through public expenditure. Perhaps most importantly, it is a form of activism that advances a conception of rights and equality that conservative judicial critics favour, that being formal equality and negative freedoms. Conservative judicial critics' opposition to decisions like *Vriend, Egan,* and *M. v. H.,* like their critique of judicial activism involving the police, is generally influenced more by ideological considerations than the claimed inconsistency of these decisions with their preferred theory of judicial review.

The characterization of the Supreme Court's Charter jurisprudence as activist is only partially correct and obscures a fuller appreciation of the impact of Charter review on Canadian democracy.[71] In truth, the court's Charter jurisprudence defies being labelled as either activist or restrained, just as the individual judges cannot be labelled as liberal or conservative, because there is no general approach to the Charter by the Supreme Court. Indeed, the court has approached the Charter as a complex document that has seen both activism and deference emerge in its jurisprudence. What is even more important, the method of judicial review employed generally corresponds to the type of state actor at the centre of a Charter challenge. The court has been activist in its relationship with police officers, but more restrained when Charter review creates a direct relationship between the Supreme Court and the cabinet. Thus, judicial activism has occurred in those areas where the Supreme Court arguably has the institutional capacity to be an effective policy actor, such as criminal law and procedure, but the court has been equally restrained in policy areas where its institutional capacity is limited, such as social policy and areas of public expenditure.[72]

This textured approach to the Charter was not an original feature of the court's Charter jurisprudence, but as the Charter has evolved as a document and the court has reflected on the implications of rights jurisprudence, a more mature approach to the Charter has emerged.[73] The growing deference on the part of the court to the policy choices of the cabinet and its provincial counterparts, however, is not evidence that the Supreme Court is less committed to rights than it was during the height of judicial activism. The decline of judicial activism involving statutes is directly related to the emergence of more principled policy decisions by the cabinet, which limits judicial invalidation through legislative activism.

Conservative critics overplay the policy-making capacity of the Supreme Court under the Charter and have added too much weight to the ability of judicial decisions to determine public policy. According to Morton and

Knopff, "the Supreme Court now functions more like a *de facto* third chamber of the legislature than a court. The nine Supreme Court justices are now positioned to have more influence on how Canada is governed than are all of the parliamentarians who sit outside of cabinet."[74] This assumes that judicial decisions represent the final and most important stage in a policy exercise and, further, that the courts can ensure the implementation of their judgments. In a certain sense this is a contradictory approach, as these critics dispute the Supreme Court's ability to design policy, but then suggest a high institutional capacity during the implementation stage. Conceptually, it is difficult to understand how the Supreme Court can overcome these limitations during the design stage and then ensure the implementation of judicial decisions by the cabinet. This analytical difficulty is rooted in the suggestions that the Supreme Court is a policy actor possessing the same institutional ability as the cabinet to implement its policy decisions and that the court can dominate the cabinet and the bureaucratic arena to achieve its agenda.[75]

These claims are suspect because the Supreme Court does not control the legislative form that policy responses to judicial decisions take, and, perhaps more importantly, the court has no role in choosing the instruments used to implement these legislative responses.[76] I would contend that conservative critics in Canada have fallen prey to the belief that judicial decisions, on their own, can bring about fundamental social change – what Gerald Rosenberg referred to as the "hollow hope" of judicial activism.[77] In effect, these critics focus solely on the discretionary choices available to the Supreme Court when it is deciding on the remedies for constitutional violations, but they downplay that this policy-making power is limited, as the court is generally reliant on the cabinet's complying with its judgments. Because the Supreme Court must rely heavily on the cabinet and the bureaucratic apparatus that supports it during legislative responses to invalidated statutes, judicial legislation must be viewed as subordinate legislation due to the pre-eminent role of the cabinet in the policy process, regardless of judicial invalidation of statutes.

Legislative Responses to Judicial Power

What has been overlooked in the debate surrounding the global expansion of judicial power is the fact that parliamentary systems have addressed this phenomenon in distinctively different ways than the American presidential system or those that are based on popular sovereignty. The limitations of the present Canadian debate reflect this general weakness, as neither the supporters nor critics of judicial activism have considered the institutional responses to the Charter by the cabinet and bureaucratic actors. Both supporters and critics consider the implications for democracy to be dependent on the approach by the judiciary, but they discount the role of political institutions in advancing democratic governance in the era of rights. The lack of attention to the parliamentary arena has been addressed in the work of Janet Hiebert, who attempts to demonstrate the ability of parliament to advance an interpretation of the Charter that is an alternative to that of the Supreme Court.[78] However, Hiebert distances her relational approach to constitutional interpretation from the dialogue theorists because she contends that the dialogue theory allows a judicial-centred approach to constitutional interpretation to dominate. Hiebert is concerned that Charter dialogue simply allows the court's approach to the Charter to structure the legislative remedy that parliament introduces in response to a judicial invalidation and thus perpetuates the assumption that the guardianship of rights is solely a judicial responsibility.[79]

The importance of focusing on parliamentary actors is evident because of the growing significance of legislative activism and the emergence of a rights culture within government.[80] Many of the claims made by participants in the judicial activism debate have been based on an incomplete assessment of the Charter's impact on the primary institution responsible for public policy in Canada. Indeed, the claim that judicial activism is essential in order for Charter values to attain prominence in the legislative process assumes that the cabinet, bureaucracy, and parliament ignore the Charter during the development of legislation and that the judiciary must fill this Charter void in the policy process. Instead of viewing judicial activism as either essential to democracy or a process that results in a loss of decision-making authority for the cabinet, it must be conceived as part of a mutually reinforcing activist approach to rights that originates with the cabinet and the bureaucratic arena that supports its legislative agenda. The Charter debate has largely discounted the ability of legislative activism to ensure that the cabinet, supported by the machinery of government in the bureaucratic realm, remains the centre of public policy. Further, the debate has overlooked the cabinet's engagement in significant institutional and cultural reform to advance the values of the Charter that both supersedes and marginalizes judicial activism as the primary force behind the presence of Charter values in public policy.

Judicial invalidation is more a reflection of the institutional failure of legislative activism to fully ensure that Charter values are addressed in the design of legislation than it is an indication of the danger of judicial supremacy. In truth, judicial invalidation indicates the danger of cabinet dominance and the dysfunctional parliamentary policy process this facilitates.[81] While this study contends that legislative activism can function as a check on judicial activism and allow the cabinet to remain the centre of public policy, it acknowledges that the full benefit of legislative activism has been limited by the underdevelopment of parliamentary scrutiny of legislation from a rights perspective. Indeed, of the two distinct components of legislative activism, parliamentary activism is underdeveloped in comparison to bureaucratic activism because of an executive-dominated parliamentary process. Further, the advanced development of bureaucratic activism allows the cabinet to dominate the legislative process during Charter review, as the bureaucratic apparatus is at the disposal of the cabinet in the legislative process, and not of parliament and its standing committees.

This is where my analysis departs from that of Hiebert, who focuses on the role of parliament in determining the meaning of Charter values in legislation, but does not address the question of the role of an executive-dominated parliament in sharing responsibility for the Charter and the determination of its meaning. This issue will be the focus of Chapter 7 as part of an analysis of legislative activism and its limitations within an executive-dominated system. The Canadian parliament does not have an effective role to play in interpreting the Charter and is not as efficient as it could be in comparison to functional parliamentary systems, such as those in Britain, Australia, and New Zealand. Parliamentary activism in Canada, at the present time, effectively means that the minister of justice or the provincial attorney general certifies, first to the cabinet and then to parliament, that legislation conforms to the Charter. In many regards, the approach to rights activism has not changed since the time of the *Canadian Bill of Rights* and the requirement under section 3 that the minister of justice examine all bills for their relationship to the Bill of Rights and report any inconsistencies to the House of Commons.[82] The presence of a cabinet-dominated manifestation of parliamentary activism is evident in the writings of John Edwards, who, reflecting on the importance of the attorney general in requiring that legislation conform to the Charter, said that "an imaginative and politically sensitive Attorney General can be counted upon to show a marked awareness of the alternative options at his disposal in meeting confrontations clothed in the language of the Charter."[83]

Legislative activism is generally equated with the review process conducted by the minister of justice and government lawyers directly answerable to this political actor, as Huscroft suggests that "many governments have procedures requiring *Charter implications* to be formally identified and referred to the Attorney-General for review before a matter can proceed to Cabinet."[84] In effect, a paler version of parliamentary activism presently exists because of the shadow cast by a cabinet-dominated process. An alternative interpretation of judicial activism would be to suggest that a cabinet-centred parliament gets the policy outcomes it deserves when legislation is invalidated because parliamentary actors outside the executive are constrained in their ability to thoroughly assess the Charter implications of legislation. This is a sentiment expressed by members of the Standing Senate Committee on Legal and Constitutional Affairs for the 37th Parliament, including senators Joyal, Andreychuk, and Beaudoin,[85] as well as by members of the Standing Committee on Justice and Human Rights, including Chuck Cadman of the Canadian Alliance and Irwin Cotler of the Liberal Party of Canada.[86] Parliament wants a role in ensuring that the legislative process reaches principled decision on Charter values, but the cabinet has dominated this process to date.

The imbalance within legislative activism in favour of the cabinet is evident when bureaucratic activism is considered. While important institutional reforms have been implemented to ensure that legislation is subjected to an extensive Charter scrutiny, and this process has prevented a loss of policy autonomy, it has clearly strengthened cabinet in the parliamentary arena. Indeed, the development of a rights culture within government has not challenged executive control but has strengthened it, because bureaucratic activism can ensure that the policy choices of the cabinet survive Charter scrutiny by the courts. Perhaps more importantly, bureaucratic review occurs outside the parliamentary arena, and the Charter certification of legislation by the minister of justice to cabinet is based on the scrutiny performed by the DOJ. This formalized Charter review has no equivalent review within the parliamentary arena, as neither the House of Commons nor the Senate has established a standing committee with formal responsibility for Charter scrutiny of legislation. Peter Russell called for the establishment of such a committee in 1969, saying that it "would provide Canadian citizens with a more reliable and accessible device for examining the libertarian aspects of public policy than would the opportunity to appeal to a judicial system, which not only might fail to take the libertarian's concerns seriously, but will charge him thousands of dollars and make him wait several years to find this out."[87] This committee, however, has not been established in parliament or any provincial legislative assembly.

When parliamentary scrutiny has occurred, as it periodically does in the Standing Committee of Justice and Human Rights as well as the Standing Senate Committee on Legal and Constitutional Affairs, it has been at the behest of select parliamentarians who raise Charter issues. Interviews that I have conducted with members of the Standing Committee on Justice and Human Rights and the Standing Senate Committee on Legal and Constitutional Affairs attest to the weakness of parliamentary scrutiny of legislation, as parliament is informed by the minister of justice that legislation is certified for its constitutionality, but no documentation is provided that verifies this claim.[88] Indeed, parliamentarians can rely on few resources with which to challenge the certification of legislation by the minister of justice, so appearances before parliamentary committees are merely a required formality for the minister and members of the DOJ in an executive-dominated legislative process.

Parliamentary reform in the last forty years has generally resulted in strengthening the cabinet vis-à-vis ordinary parliamentarians, and the central agency reforms implemented by Pierre Trudeau and Brian Mulroney were designed to achieve this end.[89] The development of a rights culture within government has been consistent with central agency reform because bureaucratic activism has strengthened the capacity of the centre. Indeed, the strengthening of the centre via the DOJ has occurred in all governments, including those of the territories.[90] At the federal level, Mary Dawson analyzed the initial response to the Charter and concluded that the changing role of the DOJ in the policy process resulted in the emergence of Justice as a central agency, equal in status to the Department of Finance and the Privy Council Office (PCO).[91] The process of bureaucratic activism is discussed in Chapter 7, where it is concluded that the institutional changes in the policy process under the direction of the DOJ have elevated this department to the status of a central agency or, more correctly, an executive support agency.

Although the ascendancy of legislative activism is driven by its bureaucratic form, there is a relationship between this process and the decline of judicial invalidation of legislation as inconsistent with Charter protections. Former Chief Justice Brian Dickson was clear on the importance of legislative activism as an effective check on judicial power: "The fact of the matter is that the scope of judicial power under the Charter is very much dependent on the extent to which government takes the Charter seriously. The more government works constructively in ensuring Charter values are taken into account in drafting and implementing legislation, the less the courts will end up second guessing the legislature's decisions."[92] My contention is that the decline of judicial activism is not an indication that the commitment to rights has decreased in Canada, but that the cabinet has increased its commitment to principled policy decisions through a reformed policy process that attempts to reconcile policy objectives with Charter values. Further, the emergence of a Charter review within the legislative arena has been under the direction of the DOJ and has elevated this department to the status of a central agency. DOJ's new status as a central agency has been disputed by Donald Savoie, who contends that the centre of government remains the traditional executive support agencies and, further, that the concentration of power at the centre has changed in favour of the prime minister and the PCO.[93] However, the changes in the policy process since the Charter's introduction challenge Savoie's conclusion because of the important Charter review function performed by the DOJ.

The institutional and procedural changes that transformed the Department of Justice into a central agency are the subject of Chapter 7, but an initial case will be made that bureaucratic activism has seen the DOJ move into the centre of government. The DOJ has a unique institutional structure; there is a central office, but there are also legal service units (LSUs) that reside in line departments. Crown lawyers seconded to line departments remain the responsibility of the DOJ but are involved in the development of policy with client departments. Since the introduction of the Charter and the development of a rights culture within government, the cabinet has used LSUs to perform a substantive review of legislation for its Charter implications.[94] This Charter scrutiny at the departmental level does not simply involve the LSU, but also involves the Department of Justice, as the LSU relies on the Human Rights Law Section (HRLS) within the DOJ to ensure that Charter values receive adequate attention in the design of legislation. Further, once the line department in consultation with its LSU drafts a memorandum to cabinet, the DOJ provides advice to the PCO regarding the attempts taken to ensure that the proposed policy is constitutional or, at a minimum, a reasonable limitation on a Charter right.

Once the cabinet approves the policy and it is passed into law by the Parliament of Canada, the DOJ has the final responsibility for drafting the act into law. The importance of the DOJ in the post-Charter period has been undervalued, and it has not been recognized as a new type of central agency because it lacks the organizational structure of a traditional central agency. The traditional central agency, such as the Privy Council Office, is staffed with policy generalists who must review the proposals of policy experts in line departments, and thus the relationship is one of policy generalist versus policy expert, with experts in line departments clearly in the dominant position. This relationship is reversed in Justice's interaction with line departments because of the importance of a Charter review conducted by the DOJ for client departments. Charter experts confront Charter generalists within line departments, and policy experts, therefore, must change policy proposals to conform to the Charter. This relationship has transformed the DOJ into a powerful central agency, possibly the most powerful within the federal government, save the Department of Finance.

Legislative activism directly challenges the dialogue theorists' position that Charter values only attain prominence once the courts invalidate legislation as a violation of the Charter. Though an executive-dominated version of legislative activism exists in Canada, it has succeeded in ensuring that a vertical transfer of decision-making authority to the judiciary has not been the primary outcome of the Charter's entrenchment. This activist approach to rights has seen the emergence of principled legislative decisions that indicate the presence of an important dialogue on rights at the cabinet level, which is implemented at the bureaucratic level by the DOJ. The invalidation of legislation by the judiciary should not be viewed as evidence of a paradigm shift to judicial supremacy but of the internal constraints placed on Charter dialogue by the cabinet within the parliamentary arena. Unfortunately, the imbalance of legislative activism only intensifies at the provincial level, where the cabinet is a larger entity in relation to the size of the legislative assembly, and parliamentary scrutiny is virtually non-existent due to the underdevelopment of the legislative committee system.

Conclusion

The introduction of the Charter has resulted in an intense debate surrounding the implications of judicial review for Canadian democracy. My objective in this chapter has not been to dispute the importance of judicial activism, but simply to suggest that the evolution of Canadian democracy is the result of more than the judiciary's approach to rights and freedoms. Indeed, the Charter's introduction has resulted in multiple forms of activism, which have ensured that Canada has evolved to a system based on constitutional supremacy, and that public policy makers reach principled decisions consistent with the Charter. In advancing this objective, I have attempted to outline the important theoretical gains made by scholars who interpret the Charter through a judicial-centred approach, while at the same time suggesting that this approach can only present an incomplete assessment of the relationship between judicial review and democracy. The maturing of Canadian democracy has not been monopolized by any actor, but has been the institutional outcome of Supreme Court, cabinet, and DOJ attempts to govern in a rights culture. In several respects, the supporters of judicial activism overestimate the influence of judicial decisions and the importance of the Supreme Court. In truth, judicial activism is not the barometer of rights protections in Canada that its supporters claim.

While conservative judicial critics have identified the limitations in the analysis presented by the supporters of judicial activism, I am concerned that they are too willing to concede the overpowering force of judicial review and the ability of judicial actors to determine the constitutional status of a political entity. For instance, these critics focus on the most explicit – and least used – political check on judicial decisions, as the use of the notwithstanding clause figures prominently in their analysis. In this chapter, I have suggested that important political checks on judicial power exist within the policy process, as the attempt to govern in a rights culture has seen the creation of important Charter review functions within the bureaucratic arena in support of the cabinet's agenda. Conservative judicial critics' focus on the Charter's notwithstanding clause, and their criticism of the Supreme Court, occur without a critical evaluation of the decision-making processes that result in the public policies eventually subjected to judicial review. Without an evaluation of the decision-making processes that support the cabinet in achieving its agenda, the conservative judicial critique is thus open to dispute.

The use of a cabinet-centred paradigm suggests that constitutionality of statutes is principally the responsibility of the cabinet and the DOJ. In advancing this notion, my position is complementary to that of Brian Slattery, who focused on the interplay between constitutional duties and constitutional rights in his "coordinative model" of the Charter.[95] Slattery suggested that the protection of rights was a responsibility shared between courts and legislatures and that multiple guardians of the constitution would be needed for rights to attain their full potential as constitutional standards in Canada. In the remainder of this book, the importance of coordinate constitutionalism and the response to the Charter by democratic, judicial, and legislative actors is considered. Unlike previous scholarly works that have started their analysis of the Charter at the Supreme Court and have focused on Charter decisions, my analysis begins with the period of constitutional politics that preceded the Charter's entrenchment in 1982. Before analyzing the legitimacy of the Supreme Court's approach to the Charter, it is important to establish the intentions of its framers and the mandate to govern with the Charter placed simultaneously on the cabinet and the Supreme Court after 1982. As the Charter began as a political project of the Trudeau government and not a judicial project of the Supreme Court, the next two chapters consider the important political choices – and battles – that preceded the first Charter decision by the Supreme Court in 1984.

2
Constitutional Politics and the Charter

The entrenchment of the Charter was a watershed event, as it marked the formal shift from parliamentary to constitutional supremacy. Though constitutional supremacy was an informal principle since Confederation, Canadian political culture was clearly structured by the principle that legislatures were supreme within their spheres of jurisdiction.[1] The political culture implications of this principle were evident in the Supreme Court's approach to the 1960 *Canadian Bill of Rights*, as the court continued to demonstrate deference to the policy choices of parliamentary actors.[2] The *Canadian Bill of Rights* articulated the principle of parliamentary supremacy, as the preamble was clearly in the tradition of British constitutionalism.[3] Thus, parliament placed an obligation on itself to pass acts that honoured this commitment to rights, and the judiciary, within this tradition, deferred to parliament's attempt to comply. This resulted in only one statute being partially invalidated as inconsistent with the Bill of Rights between 1960 and 1982.[4]

The formal transition to constitutional supremacy occurred in 1982, with the inclusion of section 52(1) of the constitution.[5] Peter Russell has referred to this event as part of the constitutional odyssey that resulted from an intense period of mega-constitutional politics, which saw the entrenchment of the Charter, the patriation of the constitution, the inclusion of a domestic amending formula, and minor changes to the division of powers.[6] In this chapter, the framework of constitutional politics will be used to understand the political events that preceded entrenchment. A limitation in the present debate is the tendency to begin the analysis of the Charter, and the Supreme Court's subsequent interpretation, at the period of entrenchment.[7] However, the Charter went through several drafts and important substantive revisions as a result of constitutional politics, both within the institutions of executive federalism and the declaration of unilateral patriation between July 1980 and December 1981. Indeed, the strategy of unilateral patriation temporarily changed the process of constitutional politics, as the Special Joint Committee on the Constitution of Canada (SJC) provided the public with the rare opportunity to participate in constitutional change.[8] Though the Charter had been part of Pierre Trudeau's political agenda since his entry into federal politics in 1965,[9] this is the critical time frame that determined the structure of the document that was entrenched in 1982.

In this chapter, the evolution of the Charter and the period of constitutional politics that surrounded the creation of the present document will be analyzed. The chapter will show the competing agendas and the eventual triumph of the activist intentions of the Trudeau government over the reservations of the provincial premiers.[10] Indeed, this is a central development in the subsequent legitimacy of Charter review, as some Charter critics have contended that the Supreme Court has departed from framers' intent in its interpretation of this document. In contrast, it will be argued here that there is an activist framers' intent surrounding the Charter, and the textual evolution of the document from the compromise discussion draft tabled 4 July 1980 to the final document passed by the Senate on 8 December 1981 demonstrates this.[11] The influence of the premiers was to weaken the Charter by securing language that required a high degree of deference to the policy choices of elected assemblies, as well as to the conduct of public officials such as the police. However, the strategy of unilateral patriation fundamentally altered the rules by which constitutional politics were played in Canada.[12] While the premiers did secure important amendments such as the notwithstanding clause, the final Charter lacked the deferential language that characterized the document produced by elite accommodation among the first ministers.

There were three critical periods of constitutional politics between the return of the Trudeau Liberals to power in 1980 and the entrenchment of the Charter in 1982 that will be considered. The first period is associated with the pledge by Trudeau to renew federalism in the event of a defeat of sovereignty-association in the 1980 Quebec referendum.[13] Though Trudeau's position vis-à-vis Lévesque was strengthened after the "Non" forces triumphed, this did not alter his position within the institutions of executive federalism. During this period of constitutional politics, the draft resolution presented to parliament reflected the premiers' intention that, if a Charter was entrenched, the principle of parliamentary supremacy as it related to provincial autonomy would emerge relatively unscathed. While the principle of parliamentary supremacy was compromised by a written constitution and judicial review, the Canadian variant of this principle accepted that each government would be supreme within its sphere of jurisdiction as delineated in the *British North America Act, 1867 (BNA Act)*. The second period represents a break from the traditional approach to constitutional politics that had taken place within the framework of executive federalism. The strategy of unilateral patriation challenged both federalism and the principle of unanimity that had existed in all previous constitutional amendments involving the division of powers. Once these two important constraints were ignored, the Trudeau government transformed the process of constitutional politics by allowing public input through the SJC, which was established to consider the draft Charter.[14] This is a critical period as, for the most part, the interest groups that appeared rejected the draft Charter as an uninspiring document that did not adequately protect rights from legislative encroachment. The new constitutional politics of citizen participation rejected the intention of the premiers to preserve significant aspects of parliamentary supremacy, and this had a direct impact on the textual evolution of the Charter.[15]

The final phase of constitutional politics saw the Trudeau Liberals return to the institutions of executive federalism because the Supreme Court determined that substantial provincial consent was required before parliament could exercise its legal duty to request changes to the constitution by the British parliament. Trudeau returned to the bargaining table, however, with a fundamentally different Charter that had been greatly strengthened as a result of the SJC. While substantial provincial consent was secured, the premier of Quebec refused to be a signatory. Though the Supreme Court did not fully endorse this new approach to constitutional politics, its decision revealed a fundamental weakness in the amending process that existed until 1982: while the process was informally federal and based on unanimity, it was legally a unitary amending process, as only parliament could request changes to the *BNA Act*. While the Charter project began and ended as an exercise in executive federalism, the substantive content of the Charter was determined outside the constraints of this process. The Trudeau vision of an activist constitution with an entrenched Charter ultimately prevailed over the deferential intentions of the first ministers as a result.

Constitutional Politics and Executive Federalism: July to September 1980

Though the absence of a domestic amending formula did complicate the process of constitutional politics, executive federalism had been the process used to secure changes to the *BNA Act*. This amending process was based on unanimity, as all the constitutional changes requested by the federal cabinet and agreed to by the British parliament had first received unanimous consent from the provincial premiers.[16] The federalist victory in the 1980 Quebec referendum saw the Trudeau government return to the issue of patriating the constitution, with primary emphasis placed on the entrenchment of a Charter.[17] While this was generally reflective of his commitment to "renewed federalism," it was the ordering of constitutional objectives and prioritizing the Charter that resulted in serious opposition from the provincial premiers. While the first ministers largely agreed on the need to patriate the constitution with a domestic amending formula, there was little enthusiasm for an entrenched Charter. Further, the federal government was lukewarm to the premiers' view that the division of powers needed realignment in their favour. As a result, neither constitutional agenda satisfied the principle of unanimity, as even the sequence of constitutional reform caused serious disagreement. For instance, the Trudeau government favoured entrenching the Charter and a domestic amending formula and then returning to the division of powers in a future round of constitutional reform. This was the complete opposite of the approach desired by the premiers, who wanted changes to the division of powers before returning to the entrenchment of the Charter in a future round of mega-constitutional politics.

Before the Trudeau government decided to proceed unilaterally on 2 October 1980, the provincial premiers considered three draft Charters presented by the Delegation of the Government of Canada and responded with a joint proposal on 28 August 1980. The evolution of the Charter, therefore, bore the implications of executive federalism and the principle of unanimity that structured the negotiations between the first ministers. Though the Trudeau government was widely condemned for this strategic move, it was a procedural change in regard to patriation and did not at first affect the substance of the draft Charter. Indeed, the proposed resolution presented to parliament on 6 October 1980 generally incorporated the concerns of the provincial premiers and had been significantly changed as a result of federal-provincial negotiations that occurred between July and September 1980. It was not until the draft Charter moved beyond the institutions of executive federalism to the SJC that the substance of the document changed. At this stage in constitutional politics, the premiers had generally succeeded in protecting provincial jurisdiction from judicial review under an entrenched Charter.

In this section of the chapter, the evolution of the draft Charter until the proposed resolution of 6 October 1980, which marked the beginning of the period of unilateral patriation, will be examined. What emerges is the importance of federal-provincial negotiations in the evolution of the draft Charter and the influence of the premiers in the substantive content of rights protections. Indeed, the proposed resolution may have been presented to the SJC on 6 October 1980, after the declaration of unilateral patriation by Trudeau, but this resolution represents the height of the premiers' influence on the Charter's substantive content.[18] The subsequent proceedings of the SJC challenged the premiers' defence of parliamentary supremacy and succeeded in strengthening the level of rights protections provided, as well as increasing the role of the Supreme Court. While the premiers were successful in securing concessions from the Trudeau government during the first ministers' conference (FMC) in November 1981, which was held as a result of the Supreme Court's decision in *Attorney General Manitoba et al. v. Attorney General Canada et al (Patriation Reference),*[19] they were unable to regain the degree of influence that was evident in the proposed resolution presented to Parliament on 6 October 1980.

Though all draft Charters were influenced by federal-provincial negotiations and have a tremendous amount of overlap, there were significant changes designed to satisfy the premiers and the requirement of unanimous consent. For instance, in his opening remarks to the Continuing Committee of Ministers on the Constitution (CCMC), which met 8-11 July 1980 to consider the draft Charter of 4 July, Justice Minister Jean Chrétien indicated that the federal government was willing to change the wording of draft provisions to ensure provincial agreement. In particular, the federal government acknowledged that the provinces were resistant to legal rights, but it was adamant that these protections should be entrenched in the Charter: "The federal government appreciates the difficulties involved in applying some of these rights throughout the legal system and you will find us reasonably flexible when we come to discuss the precise language to be used."[20] Perhaps more importantly, the Trudeau government indicated in its background notes the importance of entrenching non-discrimination rights despite the opposition of the premiers and the open-ended nature of this provision: "Because it has been very difficult to reach an agreement on a complete enumeration of these grounds, the federal 'discussion draft' includes a general clause rather than a list."[21] This is significant, as the Supreme Court's subsequent activism in equality rights provisions after 1982 has been widely condemned by conservative judicial critics as a violation of framers' intent.[22] However, the initial approach to non-discrimination did not narrow the discretionary authority of the courts, but invited it through a general clause that did not specify the protected grounds of protection.

Before turning to the decision to proceed unilaterally, I want to address the notion that the process of unilateral patriation gave the Trudeau government a free hand to change the Charter at the expense of provincial autonomy. The draft Charter that most catered to the premiers and their interests was the document introduced immediately after the decision to proceed unilaterally, suggesting that the substance of the Charter, at this point, was the product of elite accommodation between the first ministers. Though the draft Charter changed greatly once it was subjected to public scrutiny in the SJC, this was an unexpected outcome and largely attributed to parliamentarians, the novel involvement of interest groups in the process, and the use of televised proceedings.[23] Roger Tassé has discussed the importance of the public in strengthening the Charter, stating that, "while the constitutional project started as an attempt to patriate the constitution, patriation did not generate enthusiasm and the Charter became the centre of the public's interests ... The reason this constitutional exercise succeeded was that the people became interested and saw something in the Charter for the public."[24] The text that was eventually entrenched, therefore, was not the result of constitutional brinkmanship by the Trudeau Liberals, but of public consultation and criticism of the draft Charter created to appease provincial opposition in the institutions of executive federalism.

Draft Charters Presented to the Premiers

The draft Charter that was the focus of the 8-11 July 1980 meeting of the CCMC was tabled by the Delegation of the Government of Canada on 4 July 1980 and was notable in a number of respects. This draft Charter did not contain a general limitations clause, but provided a series of internal limitations attached to each specific right, with the exception of language rights.[25] Indeed, the internal limitations were more specific than the general limitations clause that would appear in subsequent draft Charters, as the limitations on fundamental freedoms could be made in the "interests of national security, public safety, order, health or morals or the rights and freedoms of others."[26] The limitations on legal rights clearly reflected the Trudeau government's experience during the 1970 October Crisis, as most legal rights could be suspended in times of emergency under section 6(3) "to the extent strictly required by the circumstances of the emergency."[27] Though the provinces were opposed to entrenching the Charter, they were strenuously opposed to the 4 July 1980 approach to limitations on rights, which was viewed as favouring the federal government by making it easier to justify federal limitations on rights. For instance, declarations of emergency situations could not be made by provincial governments, nor were the provinces responsible for issues of national security. As a result, there were fewer justifiable grounds for limiting rights available to the provinces, which created the impression that the Charter would be a more serious constraint on provincial governments, as most of the limitations, such as national security, were only available to the federal government.[28]

Fundamental freedoms and democratic rights are present in this draft Charter and are very similar to those in the final text entrenched in 1982. The one difference is that freedom of peaceful assembly and association is listed as one right under section 2(c). This would endure until 12 January 1981, when freedom of association was listed as a separate category under section 2(d). The legal rights in this draft specified that an individual could only be deprived of life, liberty, and security of the person according to "due process of law," similar to the wording in the *Canadian Bill of Rights*.

This would eventually be changed in the 3 September draft to "the principles of fundamental justice" to appease the provinces, which felt that the phrase "due process" would be interpreted as "substantive due process," as it had been by the United States Supreme Court.[29] The premiers preferred an approach to legal rights that placed limited constraints on state power.

Section 7 outlined non-discrimination rights, which would be changed to equality rights in the 12 January 1981 proposed resolution before the Special Joint Committee. In the 4 July draft, the non-discrimination clause was open-ended and stated "everyone has the right to equality before the law and equal protection of the law without distinction or restriction."[30] While the protection against discrimination invited judicial discretion because it did not specify the characteristics to be protected, section 7 of the 4 July draft included a very broad limitation clause that allowed these rights to be limited by a "distinction or restriction provided by law that is fair and reasonable having regard to the object of the law."[31] This broad limitation clause also allowed for reverse discrimination by protecting programs that targeted disadvantaged groups or persons from invalidation as inconsistent with non-discrimination law. Thus, the qualification on non-discrimination rights in section 7(2) protected provincial autonomy by allowing an important area of provincial jurisdiction, social policy, to deviate from non-discrimination rights.

This aspect of the draft Charter continued in the section 8 protections for mobility rights, which were designed to secure the free movement of Canadians and permanent residents, as section 8 was not an absolute right but was subject to existing provincial or territorial laws that did not discriminate on the basis of current or previous residency. Mobility rights were further weakened by a limitation clause that permitted "such limitations prescribed by law as are reasonably justified in a free and democratic society in the interests of national security, public safety, order, health or morals."[32] In addition, property rights were included in section 9, but these rights were limited within the right itself, as individuals and associations could not be deprived of property "except in accordance with law and for reasonable compensation."[33] Property rights were further limited by section 9(2), as "nothing in this section precludes the enactment of or renders invalid laws controlling or restricting the use of property in the public interest or securing against property the payment of taxes or duties or levies or penalties."[34] Finally, if governments were unable to limit property rights via sections 9(1) and (2), there was the general limitations clause in section 9(3) attached to all but language rights in the 4 July 1980 draft Charter.

The strongest protections provided were for language rights, as the Trudeau government sought to constitutionalize the equal status of English and French in the proceedings of Parliament and the legislatures of Ontario, New Brunswick, Manitoba, and Quebec. The use of English or French in the court proceedings of these jurisdictions was also protected, as was the right to communicate in either official language, with both the federal and the provincial governments listed in section 13. While a majority of provinces were excluded from the language rights guarantees, the draft Charter did make provision for these provinces to provide these services "to the greatest extent practicable accordingly as the legislature of the province prescribes."[35] While the Trudeau government intended to entrench the *Official Languages Act* in sections 12 to 15 of the proposed Charter, a tremendous amount of flexibility existed, which allowed a majority of the provinces to decide what level of services to provide.

Edward McWhinney has suggested that the absence of controversy in the area of language rights was generally the result of the Trudeau government's attempt to respect provincial responsibilities.[36] This is most apparent in regard to minority language education rights in the July draft Charter, as it was left to the legislature of each province to decide whether the size of minority language populations in parts of the province warranted the public provision of educational instruction and facilities.[37] Thus, a right to minority language education existed, but it was left to the discretion of provincial governments whether to provide this service. In contrast, the final Charter changed the remedy for minority language education rights violations, as courts – and not legislatures – would determine whether numbers warranted the provision of educational services for official language minorities and would also determine the extent of those services.

The difficulty facing the Trudeau government was that the draft Charter did not receive ministerial attention during the 4 July 1980 meeting of the CCMC. Upon returning to power, the Trudeau government indicated that it would proceed on the assumption that the Charter would be entrenched, whereas the premiers virtually ignored the Charter and focused on the division of powers. Jean Chrétien responded to the opposition to an entrenched Charter by outlining the advantages of entrenchment and suggesting that "entrenchment is therefore not a redistribution of powers between governments, rather it is a redistribution from governments to the people."[38] In addressing the concern regarding the empowerment of judges, Chrétien demonstrated a belief that judges would interpret the Charter as part of a broader network of actors responsible for governing in a rights culture: "Courts do not exist in a vacuum. Judges and the lawyers who appear before them reflect many of the same ideals and attitudes found among elected legislatures and other citizens."[39]

The draft Charter attempted to incorporate the principles of both parliamentary and constitutional supremacy by entrenching rights but allowing governments a tremendous amount of discretion through generous limitations on most rights. The federal draft was clearly intended to appease the provincial premiers by providing a series of safeguards that would shield

provincial jurisdiction from the full force of constitutional rights.[40] However, this draft Charter clearly favoured the principle of parliamentary supremacy and was more a symbolic attempt at protecting rights in a
constitutional document. While a remedy clause was provided in section
19, which allowed a court to determine a just and appropriate remedy when
a right was infringed, the limitations available to governments effectively
weakened the ability of individuals to establish a rights violation. The provinces' opposition to an entrenched Charter caused the federal government
to introduce a compromise document intended to appease the provinces in
exchange for federal concessions on the provincial constitutional agenda
and its emphasis on the division of powers. Constitutional rights, therefore, were sacrificed to the dynamics of federal-provincial negotiations and
the need to achieve unanimity among the first ministers.

The Second Draft Charter
A second draft was presented to the CCMC by federal officials on 22 August
1980, but, like the 4 July draft, it was not the focus of the meeting that took
place in Ottawa from 26 to 29 August 1980. This would be the last meeting
of the CCMC before the FMC scheduled for 8-12 September 1980. The latest
draft Charter was very similar to the 4 July version but did contain a number of important differences designed to generate support among the provincial premiers. Roger Tassé chaired a meeting of the Sub-Committee of
Officials on a Charter of Rights and released a report that discussed provincial concerns with the 4 July draft. Opposition was rooted in the premiers'
defence of parliamentary supremacy and their desire to prevent a loss of
authority for state actors that an entrenched document would ensure: this
outcome was to be prevented by securing a limited document with sufficient deference to parliamentary actors and their agents, such as the police.
This report directly influenced the 22 August draft that was presented to the
CCMC at the 26-29 August meeting in Ottawa, as the provincial officials
wanted legal rights limited to criminal and penal matters, and less restrictive standards applied during police investigations and interrogations.[41] A
large majority of the provincial officials wanted property rights excluded,
and seven provinces opposed including non-discrimination rights.[42] Further, provincial officials wanted mobility rights narrowed to simply allow
citizens to enter, remain in, and leave Canada, and they had serious reservations regarding the application of language rights at the provincial level.
The issue of judicial remedies for constitutional violations also concerned
the provincial officials despite the provision in the minority language education rights section (section 16) that allowed legislatures to decide when
numbers warranted the provision of educational services for official language minorities. As section 19 of the 4 July 1980 draft provided the courts
with the responsibility to find remedies "appropriate and just in the cir-

cumstances," provincial officials were concerned that section 16 violations could still be subject to judicial remedy.[43]

The negotiations surrounding the draft Charter represent a classic example of executive federalism, as the concerns raised by the premiers were addressed, to a large extent, in the 22 August draft Charter. The most notable change was the creation of a new section 1 that served as a general limitations clause for the Charter instead of having a series of limitation clauses attached to each specific right. In the 22 August draft, the rights in the Charter were "subject only to such reasonable limits as are generally accepted in a free and democratic society."[44] The textual change was significant in a number of respects, as it addressed the concern among provincial officials that the specified grounds favoured the federal government and made it more difficult for the provinces to justify a limitation. Further, the use of the term "generally accepted" implied a high degree of deference by the courts to the policy choices of parliamentary actors and clearly suggested that the attempt to reconcile parliamentary supremacy with judicially enforceable rights would favour the reasonableness of policy decisions by political actors.[45]

A further concession to the provincial premiers was the decision to omit property rights from the 22 August draft, as the premiers opposed the transformation of their jurisdictional responsibility for property and civil rights into a Charter right, subject to judicial review.[46] Even the scope of language rights was narrowed in an attempt to appease provincial opposition. For instance, in the 4 July draft Charter, section 10(1) stated that "English and French are the official languages of Canada, having the status and protection set forth in this Charter."[47] In the 22 August draft Charter, the application of the official languages section had been narrowed in section 18(1) "to their use in all institutions of the Parliament and government of Canada."[48] As most provincial governments were opposed to the language rights provisions in the 4 July draft Charter, section 18(1) was an important concession to address provincial concerns.

The trend toward a weaker Charter designed to increase the amount of discretion available to the first ministers was not a uniform characteristic of the 22 August draft, as a number of provisions were strengthened, such as legal rights and non-discrimination rights. For instance, under section 6(c) of the 4 July draft Charter, everyone had the right not to be detained or imprisoned "except on grounds provided by law and in accordance with prescribed procedures." This meant that established police procedures would be constitutional, suggesting that the qualification on this right undermined its effectiveness. In the 22 August draft, this legal right was expanded to protect against arbitrary detention and imprisonment, thus excluding the qualification that existed in the 4 July draft. As well, the right to be informed of the specific charge under section 10(c)(i) was changed to require that individuals were promptly informed of the specific offence under section 11(a). Perhaps most problematic from the provincial perspective was the strengthening of non-discrimination rights in section 17 of the 22 August draft. Though non-discrimination rights were narrowed to include specific grounds for protection, such as race, national or ethnic origin, colour, religion, age, or sex, the language was changed to protect against discrimination and not simply distinction or restriction as in the 4 July draft.[49] Finally, section 17 did not include the qualification from the 4 July draft that held constitutional "any distinction or restriction provided by law that is fair and reasonable having regard to the object of the law."[50] This was a difficult strategy by the federal government, as the concessions to the provincial premiers on the limitation clause and property rights were matched by the strengthened legal and non-discrimination rights. This was not a strategy, therefore, to generate unanimity as a constitutional necessity for entrenchment.

A Provincial Proposal

A provincial proposal was submitted on 28 August 1980 that indicated what rights and level of protections the premiers were willing to accept in the event that a Charter was entrenched in the constitution. This document clearly reveals the premiers' desire to limit judicial review and to preserve the Canadian variant of parliamentary supremacy through deferential language that placed minor constitutional constraints on government. The premiers' defence of parliamentary supremacy is problematic, as it had been distorted by the movement toward institutionalized cabinets in the 1960s and 1970s that effectively marginalized provincial legislative assemblies through changes in the cabinet support system in all jurisdictions.[51] While the premiers became staunch defenders of parliamentary supremacy during the patriation discussions, they were actually attempting to protect their unconstrained power during the summer of 1980.[52] In effect, parliamentary supremacy had been suppressed by executive dominance, and the premiers were reluctant to place constraints on existing parliamentary practices that facilitated their ability to govern from the centre unhindered.

The defence of parliamentary supremacy as understood by the premiers began with the suggested wording of section 1, the reasonable limits clause: "The Canadian Charter of Rights and Freedoms recognizes the following rights and freedoms subject only to such reasonable limits as are generally accepted in a free society living under a parliamentary democracy."[53] Romanow, Whyte, and Leeson have argued that the premiers advanced this approach to section 1 to prevent the courts from ruling provincial acts and regulations unconstitutional: "The idea behind the provincial text was that, if Parliament or a legislative assembly enacted a provision that was thought to infringe rights, it would in most instances, simply by virtue of being enacted, be considered to be generally accepted in a free society living under a parliamentary democracy."[54] Such an approach to section 1 would have effectively undermined the rationale for entrenching rights, ensuring the dominance of parliamentary supremacy in regard to rights and relegating constitutional supremacy to simply a symbolic aspect of the Canadian constitution.

The provincial proposal generally endorsed the least controversial elements of the federal approach to rights, such as fundamental freedoms and democratic rights, and opposed either the inclusion or the wording in the remaining sections of the draft Charter.[55] For instance, the provincial proposal unanimously recommended that section 6, which protected "right to life, liberty and security of the person and right not to be deprived except by due process of law," should not be included in the Charter.[56] Further, the provincial proposal suggested, to varying degrees of consensus, that qualifying provisions should be attached to several legal rights, such as section 7 and the protection against unreasonable searches and seizures. Specifically, the provincial proposal, with New Brunswick and Newfoundland dissenting, wanted section 7 to be qualified by the phrase "except on lawful grounds provided by law and in accordance with prescribed procedures." The protection provided for reasonable bail was unanimously opposed in the provincial proposal, and the provinces narrowed the protection to simply pretrial release, which was qualified in the same manner as section 7. Other important provincial differences include the unanimous recommendation that the word "treatment" be deleted from section 12 (protection against unusual treatment or punishment) and the unanimous suggestion that section 14 of the 22 August draft (right of witness not to be compelled to testify if denied right to consult counsel) should also be deleted. Finally, the provincial proposal unanimously recommended that section 13 (right when compelled to testify not to have evidence used against the witness in subsequent proceedings, except prosecution for perjury or giving contradictory evidence) should be deferred and reworded based on the report of the Evidence Task Force.[57]

The provincial proposal also recommended that non-discrimination rights should be deleted from the Charter, though New Brunswick was in favour of the principle but not the wording of section 17(1) in the latest federal draft. As well, the provinces were unanimous that if mobility rights were included, they should not be in the Charter but in other parts of the constitution. The issue of language rights and official language protection was not addressed, as the provinces felt that further discussions were necessary to decide whether to include these rights in the Charter.[58] Section 25 of the 22 August federal draft was entitled "undeclared rights" and protected those rights not enumerated, such as Native rights; the provincial proposal recommended deleting this section. In only one section did the provincial proposal recommend that the draft Charter be expanded, and this involved the admissibility of evidence. Specifically, the provinces sought to prevent the courts from excluding evidence, and section 22(2) of the provincial proposal read as follows: "Nothing in this Charter affects the admissibility of evidence or the ability of Parliament or a legislature to legislate thereon."[59] Indeed, the attempt to limit judicial review is most evident in the absence of a remedy clause for constitutional violations, as the provincial proposal did not authorize the courts to remedy such infringements, as section 27 of the 22 August federal draft had done.

This proposal, therefore, indicated the premiers' reluctance to alter the status quo on rights and the principles informing the Canadian constitution. In several respects the provincial proposal was marginally better than the *Canadian Bill of Rights,* as the Charter would be entrenched and applicable to both levels of government. However, given the wide discretion available to governments to justify limiting rights in section 1, the provincial proposal was a substantively weaker document than the Bill of Rights. For instance, the *Canadian Bill of Rights* provided protection against discrimination and guaranteed that an individual could only be deprived of life, liberty, and security of the person in accordance with the due process of law. Both of these important provisions were included in the federal drafts but deleted from the provincial proposal of 28 August 1980. The constitutional politics surrounding the Charter and the process of executive federalism, therefore, had produced a constitutional stalemate where provincial autonomy and elite accommodation had weakened the draft Charter in an effort to produce a consensus.

The September 1980 First Ministers' Conference

While the FMC failed to produce a consensus, the draft Charter presented on 3 September 1980 was amended to incorporate elements of the provincial proposal of 28 August 1980. The most significant change was the reasonable limits clause in section 1, which adopted the wording in the provincial proposal with minor revisions: "The *Canadian Charter of Rights and Freedoms* recognizes the following rights and freedoms subject only to such reasonable limits as are generally accepted in a free and democratic society with a parliamentary system of government."[60] Provincial concerns regarding the possibility of incorporating "American jurisprudence relating to due process of law and non-admissibility of illegally obtained evidence"[61] were addressed in this draft, as the wording of section 6 was changed from "due process of law" to "the principles of fundamental justice" in an effort to avoid substantive due process and the excesses of American jurisprudence. Further, in section 25 the revised discussion draft addressed the provincial concern regarding the exclusion of evidence by the courts, reading:

"No provision of this Charter other than section 12 affects the laws respecting the admissibility of evidence in any proceedings or the authority of Parliament or a legislature to make laws in relation thereto."[62]

Despite these changes, the FMC began with statements from a significant majority of the premiers who opposed entrenching a Charter. The strongest opposition came from Premier Sterling Lyon of Manitoba, who defended the principle of parliamentary supremacy and the common law as flexible instruments for the protection of rights.[63] Lyon argued that an entrenched Charter would freeze rights and that parliament and the legislatures were better able to address social and policy issues than the courts.[64] The Charter also came under attack by Allan Blakeney, the NDP premier of Saskatchewan, who viewed litigation as antithetical to democratic decision making and likely to empower corporate interests. He argued that "decisions which are to be determined in the Supreme Court of Canada give an advantage to the rich. Decisions which are determined in Parliament and the legislatures give less of an advantage to the rich."[65] The defence of parliamentary supremacy was also advanced by Peter Lougheed from Alberta, who viewed elected representatives as the best actor to protect rights: "So we come to a conclusion that the better way to protect rights of the citizens of our province, and frankly of the country, is to continue with the way we are doing it today and leave that responsibility to the elected representatives."[66] Only the premiers of Ontario and New Brunswick supported the principle of entrenchment, but this only involved a limited number of rights. Indeed, after polling the premiers on which rights they would support, only fundamental freedoms and democratic rights received near unanimous support, both in principle and in the wording favoured by the federal drafts.[67]

Much of the provincial opposition involved the suggested difficulty in finding precise language to guide judicial review. In his closing remarks, Trudeau identified a contradiction in the premiers' approach, as they were able to find appropriate language for the amending formula, equalization payments, and changes in the division of powers, but unable to find appropriate language for rights:

> Maybe I will tell you tomorrow or the next day why, but right now my conclusion is that we have heard nothing else when it comes to powers of the provinces or powers of the federal government but put it in the Constitution. Suddenly, we get to protect fundamental rights and freedoms of the citizen you say, "Don't put it in the Constitution, the words are too hard to find." Well, I say what is wrong with going to the courts as we have in cases which have been brought before us today, and CIGOL [Canadian Industrial Gas and Oil Ltd.] – we had to go to the courts, we hoped to find an answer so that next time we go to the courts the Province of Saskatchewan could be satisfied in the management of its resources. What is wrong with going to

the courts if we, as legislators or as bureaucrats, or why shouldn't a minority which is adversely affected be able to call us to account in front of the courts?[68]

The stalemate produced by the institutions of executive federalism and convention, which required both orders of government to consent to constitutional changes affecting the division of powers and the federal character of Canada, had once again allowed Canada's colonial status to endure. It would take an enormous effort to change this status and break the Gordian knot of unanimity. Recognizing that patriation would be prevented by the premiers until the division of powers was radically altered in favour of provincial interests,[69] Trudeau argued that

> there were only two ways to solve the conundrum. The government of Canada could accept the "compact theory," recognizing that our country was nothing more than a community of communities, in which fundamental powers (including the power to patriate the constitution) flowed from the provinces that had freely united to form a loose confederation. Or the government of Canada, as the sole governing body empowered to act in the name of all Canadians, could reject the compact theory, hold that Canada was something more than and different from the sum of its parts, and proceed to patriate the constitution unilaterally. We chose the latter course.[70]

On 2 October 1980, in a televised news conference, Pierre Trudeau informed the Canadian public and the premiers that his government would seek to unilaterally patriate the constitution.

The Strategy of Unilateral Patriation

The proposed resolution presented to parliament on 6 October 1980 contained a Charter applicable to both orders of government, constitutional provisions regarding equalization payments, and a domestic amending formula. This constitutional agenda had been dubbed the "people's package" by Trudeau and his federal officials. Unilateral patriation was initially a procedural change designed to entrench the draft Charter that was the product of federal-provincial negotiations in the summer of 1980. What changed the substantive content of the draft Charter was the public's reaction to a document that it considered inadequate and unable to effectively protect rights from legislative encroachment. Peter Russell has described this strategic move by Trudeau as "truly Gaullist in nature. By appealing over the heads of provincial politicians directly to the people, he aimed to forge a popular consensus in support of constitutional changes."[71] Though the premiers did not agree to the draft Charter nor the strategy of unilateral patriation, the draft was designed to appease provincial opposition by incorporating many elements of the provincial proposal of 28 August 1980. In effect, Trudeau may have appealed directly to Canadians to overcome the constitutional impasse created by executive federalism, but he spoke largely with the script that had been the product of federal-provincial negotiations in the summer of 1980.

The draft Charter in the proposed resolution was much weaker than the document rejected by the first ministers in September 1980. This was because the Trudeau government attempted to address provincial concerns outlined in the Tassé report as well as the provincial proposal of 28 August 1980.[72] Like the 3 September draft Charter, the most significant concession to the provincial premiers was section 1, which allowed rights to be limited "in a free and democratic society with a parliamentary system of government."[73] Further, the legal rights protections in sections 7 to 14 were changed to appease the provinces and their concern that the Charter would undermine effective law enforcement and result in substantive due process. In addition to amending the phrase "due process of law" to "the principles of fundamental justice" and including the admissibility of evidence clause (now section 26) from the 3 September draft Charter, several legal rights were weakened to limit the ability of the courts to rule state action unconstitutional. For instance, the right against unreasonable searches and seizures (section 8) was amended to include the following qualification: "except on grounds, and in accordance with procedures, established by law."[74] Similarly, the right not to be detained or imprisoned (section 9) and the right not to be denied reasonable bail (section 11(d)) were qualified in the same manner. Each change, therefore, moved the Charter toward the provincial position that rights should not unduly interfere with the supremacy of parliament or the provincial legislatures and were designed simply to prevent a loss of power for the provincial premiers.

The most significant change was the application of language rights solely to the federal government and parliament. In previous drafts, the language rights guarantees had applied to all governments and legislatures to varying degrees of compliance. Specifically, the right to use English or French in parliamentary debates had applied to parliament and the provincial legislatures, but had been narrowed in the 6 October resolution to simply the Parliament of Canada.[75] In the 3 September draft Charter, section 18 required parliament and the legislatures of Ontario, Quebec, New Brunswick, and Manitoba to print and publish all statutes and records in English and French, and it required the remaining legislatures to comply "to the greatest extent practicable accordingly as the legislature of the province prescribes."[76] This language right was also narrowed to apply only to parliament in the proposed resolution. Further, the right to use either English or French in court proceedings (section 19) was limited to courts established by parliament, whereas it had previously applied to those established by Ontario, Quebec, New Brunswick, and other provinces to the greatest extent possible. Finally, the right to communicate with and receive services from government and legislatures in either English or French was subsequently restricted to parliament and the government of Canada in the 6 October resolution.[77]

There were important changes in minority language education rights that empowered the courts, expanded the rights, and revoked the provincial legislatures' power to determine when numbers warranted the provision of educational services. In previous drafts it was the role of the provincial legislatures, under section 22(2) of the 3 September draft, to decide whether the number of official language minorities in areas of the provinces required "the provision out of public funds of minority language educational facilities in that area."[78] In the 6 October resolution, the drafters empowered the courts to make these determinations. Leaving minority language education rights to provincial legislatures would have reduced this right to a symbolic gesture in the Charter, as it is difficult to understand the process by which minority language groups could establish a rights violation and then seek an acceptable remedy in compliance with the constitution, since both the duty to honour minority language education rights and the remedy for their infringement were solely the prerogative of provincial legislatures. The second significant change in this draft's section 23 (formerly section 22) was the extension of the right to citizens who changed residence from one province to another. This clarified the portability of minority language education rights for Canadian citizens, as it was ambiguous in earlier versions whether citizens moving between provinces could have their children educated in their choice of either English or French.

The application of the Charter was explicitly stated in the proposed resolution in section 29, which had not occurred until this version. For instance, the Charter was limited to all matters within the authority of parliament and the provincial legislatures, as well as the legislatures of Yukon and Northwest Territories. Thus, the Charter would apply to state action, both the acts and regulations passed by parliament and provincial and territorial legislative bodies, and the action of public officials such as the police. The process of executive federalism had weakened the draft Charter, as federal officials attempted to incorporate the principle of parliamentary supremacy in an entrenched Charter to satisfy the objections of the premiers. Indeed, two distinct sets of intentions were evident at this point in constitutional politics surrounding the Charter: the intention of the premiers to preserve the dominance of the executive through a defence of parliamentary supremacy, and the intention of federal officials to entrench a Charter, with the substance of the document sacrificed to elite accommodation.

The combination of these constitutional principles led Tassé to observe that "the result of these three months of discussions was that a rather watered-down draft Charter, one that would not upset the provinces too much, was presented to Parliament."[79] The disappointment with the *Canadian Bill of Rights,* which Tarnopolsky and others have suggested provided the motivation for an entrenched Charter, was not addressed in the 6 October 1980 resolution, as parliamentary supremacy would have been entrenched within this constitutional document at the expense of rights.[80] While this draft avoided several of the limitations of the *Canadian Bill of Rights,* as it would be entrenched and did explicitly authorize the courts to invalidate unconstitutional public policies and practices, the price of appeasing the first ministers would have repeated several mistakes of the *Canadian Bill of Rights.* This Charter was not internally consistent, nor was the commitment by parliamentary actors to place rights beyond routine legislative encroachment clear.

The Special Joint Committee on the Constitution of Canada

This constitutional déjà vu was avoided because the process and the pressures the draft Charter responded to changed from the institutions of executive federalism and the concerns of the first ministers to the parliamentary arena and the involvement of citizens appearing before the SJC.[81] While unilateralism would be a temporary procedural change, as the *Patriation Reference* by the Supreme Court would return the issue to the forum of executive federalism, it resulted in a significant and unexpected strengthening of the draft Charter. Tassé states that the Trudeau government was initially reluctant to televise the proceedings, as the government wanted the SJC to review the proposed resolution for one month so that the British parliament could consider Trudeau's request by January 1981.[82] Trudeau was concerned that televised proceedings would provide the opposition parties with an opportunity to attack the government and its decision to proceed unilaterally and would delay consideration of the proposed resolution by the British parliament.[83] However, as Tassé has observed, "by televising the process the government of Mr. Trudeau unwittingly changed the nature of the process by allowing the people and associations to participate, and this generated great interest in the matter."[84]

As deputy minister of justice and a participant in the CCMC, Tassé was well placed to understand the impact the shift away from executive federalism to the SJC had on the substance of the draft Charter. In this regard, he has suggested that "the public interest helped the government to achieve its constitutional agenda," as the individuals and public interest groups, for the most part, called on the Trudeau government to amend the draft Charter to strengthen the protections and to reduce the amount of deference to cabinet, legislatures, and the police found within much of the proposed resolution.[85] Because of public interest, the Trudeau government's timetable for presenting the proposed resolution to the British parliament was not met. Instead of four weeks of parliamentary hearings, nearly six months were needed to hear from the 104 groups and individuals that appeared as witnesses. Indeed, a total of 914 individuals and 294 groups sent letters, briefs, and telegrams to the SJC, and 106 meetings on fifty-six sitting days, totalling 267 hours of televised proceedings, were devoted to reviewing the proposed resolution that contained the draft Charter.[86]

The work of the SJC occurred in four phases, with the first involving the opening statement by Justice Minister Jean Chrétien on 7 November.[87] The justice minister returned with members of his department on 12-14 November for further questioning by committee members. The second phase occurred 14 November to 9 January and involved individuals and public interest groups that appeared as witnesses. For only the second time in Canadian history, a proposed constitutional amendment had been scrutinized by Canadians, and serious reservations were expressed by groups and individuals that appeared.[88] During the third phase, the justice minister and his officials returned before the SJC on 12 January with a series of suggested amendments that responded to the criticisms of Canadians during the second phase. This new version of the Charter was considered, clause by clause, by the SJC until 9 February. The final phase saw the SJC release its report to parliament on 13 February 1981.[89]

The 12 January 1981 draft Charter would prove to be a turning point. The proposed amendments represented a drastic shift in the importance of constitutional principles guiding the Charter, as constitutional supremacy took centre stage. While the use of the notwithstanding clause in the final Charter allows parliamentary supremacy to be reasserted, it became a second order principle after this date. Until the 12 January draft, parliamentary supremacy was the dominant characteristic of the Charter because of its importance in section 1 and the requirement that rights were to be interpreted by the courts in light of this principle. With the inclusion of the notwithstanding clause in the final Charter, and the rewording of the reasonable limits clause, parliamentary supremacy became a second order principle because it was not the lens through which the Charter was viewed. It became a reaction to constitutional supremacy if parliament and the provincial legislatures decided to override a decision by the courts involving the Charter.

Peter Russell asked whether Canadians can become a sovereign people and provided a mixed answer to this question.[90] I would suggest that Canadians became a sovereign people as a result of the proceedings of the SJC when the draft Charter, which protected the sovereignty of parliament and the provincial legislatures in regard to rights, was rejected by, among others, Canadians who appeared before the committee and refused to accept that constitutional rights should be weakened to accommodate the parliamentary arena. Tassé has observed that "what in fact happened is that pressure groups of all colours and opinions, as well as a number of back-bench Members of Parliament from all three parties with seats in the House, seized upon the process as their opportunity to amend and strengthen the Charter considerably, and when the government ultimately re-introduced its resolution in Parliament the Charter had become unrecognizable."[91]

Thus, constitutional supremacy came to characterize the draft Charter because the federal government, for a temporary but significant number of months, responded to the criticism of Canadians. This formative event allowed the activist intentions of the Trudeau government to overcome provincial opposition and to be realized, as the suggested amendments were entrenched in the final version of the Charter.

Parliamentary Scrutiny of the Draft Charter

Though the proposed resolution containing the Charter would become the focus of criticism by interest groups, it was first subjected to parliamentary scrutiny. During examination of the justice minister and his officials, several parliamentarians criticized the reasonable limits clause as undermining the intention of entrenching rights. James McGrath, MP, argued that the approach to reasonable limits in section 1 repeated the mistakes of the *Canadian Bill of Rights* and rendered the Charter meaningless: "I am saying that your charter is meaningless in light of what is said in Section 1 of Schedule B when you make it subject to reasonable limits as are generally accepted in a free and democratic society with a parliamentary system of government."[92] This criticism of section 1 and the Charter was also advanced by Robinson, MP, when he questioned Jean Chrétien: "However, I want to ask the Minister in particular about clause one of this proposed Charter of Rights and Freedoms because I suggest in its present wording it is a gaping hole in the Charter which really makes the alleged rights and freedoms which are supposed to be protected completely illusory, and in fact if this section one is permitted in its present form that in many ways we will be in a worse position in this country than had this particular Charter not been implemented."[93]

The justice minister's defence of section 1 was rather lukewarm, as he argued that it would be the responsibility of the courts to determine reasonable limitations in a parliamentary democracy.[94] During subsequent questioning by Senator Austin, Chrétien stated that the present section 1 was the result of federal-provincial negotiations that took place the summer of 1980:

> If I can make a comment on that, I do think that when we discussed during the summer with the provinces this general clause number one, that it was at the insistence of the provinces that we made that qualification there, so

that it will not be too strict a proposition of the guarantee of rights and freedoms, that we will restrict too much the activities of, traditional activities of the different levels of government.

It is a very complex problem, and at the insistence of the provinces we put that, I do not know how to describe it, but, not a caveat, but this kind of limitations clause so that it will not limit too extensively the power of the provincial legislature, and of course the National Parliament, to legislate what is considered legitimate in a free and democratic society.[95]

Morton and Knopff have been particularly critical of the suggested influence of interest groups that appeared, such as the Canadian Civil Liberties Association (CCLA), arguing that "the CCLA joined feminists and other rights-advocacy groups in calling for the rewording of section 1 of the Charter, which permits reasonable limits on rights, so as to place a greater burden of proof on governments."[96] The difficulty with their criticism is that these groups would have had no influence if the SJC and the Trudeau government were not favourably disposed toward a stronger Charter. Indeed, the evolution of the draft Charter is an example of legitimate tactics by interest groups that convinced political actors to accept their demands and is not evidence of the illegitimate influence of "special" interest groups on the final version of the Charter. The initial appearance by Chrétien is important, as the reservations of parliamentarians regarding section 1 occurred before similar criticisms were made by interest groups that appeared before the SJC. Tassé argues that "the political leaders and their legal and other advisors had to work directly with Canadians, essentially negotiate with them, through the agency of the Parliamentary Committee, in writing the final version of the Charter. The result is not only a democratic product, but also a very Canadian product."[97]

Citizens and the Constitution

Not all the groups and individuals that appeared supported entrenching rights and expanding the power of the courts in a revised Charter. In addition to the presentations by the premiers of Nova Scotia, Saskatchewan, and Prince Edward Island, the Canada West Foundation (CWF) was not in favour of entrenchment. Specifically, this organization argued that it was better to adopt a statutory instrument because of the flexibility this accorded its future amendment.[98] As well, the CWF opposed entrenchment because it would politicize the judiciary and undermine decision making by politically accountable actors. In his appearance before the SJC, Peter Russell indicated that he did not favour entrenchment because it would result in the politicization of the judiciary and the judicialization of politics. Further, Russell suggested that a fundamental mistake surrounded the ability of a Charter to protect rights: "I believe that a Charter only guarantees a change in the way in which certain decisions are made. It does not guarantee rights or freedoms, it guarantees a change in the way in which decisions are made about rights and freedoms."[99] Russell stated that it would be foolish to view the courts as essential to rights protection and argued that legislatures had historically been more progressive in this area. In several respects, Russell was concerned that the public would equate the protection of rights with the courts, and this would undermine the legitimacy of the political arena as the focus of public policy.[100]

Overall, however, there was a tremendous amount of support from the interest groups for an entrenched Charter, but very little for the version presented to parliament in the proposed resolution of 6 October 1980.[101] The most pointed criticisms of the draft Charter involved section 1 (the reasonable limitations clause),[102] the various legal rights provisions, the exclusion-of-evidence rule, and the non-discrimination rights: in sum, the very sections that had been weakened in an attempt to overcome provincial resistance to an entrenched Charter. In his appearance before the SJC, Gordon Fairweather, the chief commissioner of the Canadian Human Rights Commission (CHRC), argued that the wording of section 1 served to raise questions about the Trudeau government's commitment to rights: "We are troubled by the language of Clause 1 which, in its present form, raises fundamental doubts about just how serious the commitment is to reform. Those are strong words but you will hear them, I am sure, again and again from witnesses that come before this Committee."[103] Fairweather was concerned that section 1 departed sharply from the language used in domestic bills of rights to justify limitations, and that the language was "dangerously broad" and would weaken the protection of rights.[104] Indeed, the National Action Committee on the Status of Women (NACSW) referred to section 1 as the "Mack truck clause" because of its broad wording and clear deference to the principle of parliamentary supremacy in regard to rights.[105] This critique of section 1 was also advanced by the CCLA during the presentation by Tarnopolsky, who said that "section 1 permits Parliament to take away everything that Parliament gives by the rest of the charter."[106] In particular, Tarnopolsky took issue with the phrase "generally accepted" in section 1, as he pointed out that "it would be very difficult to argue that whatever Parliament enacts is not generally acceptable in that society."[107]

Similar critiques of section 1 were made before the SJC by several interest groups.[108] In each presentation, interest groups questioned the value of entrenching a Charter with such a generous limitations clause and called upon parliamentarians to amend section 1 to ensure that the Charter became more than simply a symbolic statement on rights. Beyond simply critiquing the Charter within the proposed resolution, these groups suggested ways to amend section 1 to ensure an effective Charter. Three elements of the reasonable limitations clause were identified: the reference to parliamentary democracy, the standard of generally acceptable, and the actor responsible for demonstrating the reasonableness of an infringement. For instance, the CHRC suggested that Charter rights be "subject only to such limits prescribed by law as are reasonably justifiable in a free and democratic society,"[109] thus dropping the reference to a parliamentary system of government. Similarly, the CCLA recommended that section 1 be modelled on the limitations clause in the *International Covenant on Civil and Political Rights*, to which Canada is a signatory:

> Now, it seems to me that the importance of that is that the onus has to be upon the one who argues that there are restrictions, and that has to be put in terms of being either necessary or demonstrably justifiable or demonstrably necessary; but the onus has clearly to be upon the one who argues in favour of the restriction and, which is important, it has to be prescribed by law, because that – and this is as far as I will go into the question of pluses and minuses of the Bill of Rights; because the most important aspect of the Canadian Bill of Rights is not so much in the invalidation of parliamentary legislation as it is in the control of administrative acts, police acts, and with respect to the limitations that are provided in the international instruments require that they be provided specifically by law.[110]

It is not entirely clear whether the federal government recognized the difficulty that section 1 posed to the Charter and its effectiveness, as Chrétien and his departmental officials were initially taken aback by the criticisms first voiced by parliamentarians over the wording of the reasonable limitations clause. The Canadian Jewish Congress (CJC) clearly articulated the practical limitation of the reference to parliamentary democracy: "If you are going to retain the two supremacies in this Section 1 then the courts are going to have an impossible task to reconcile them."[111] These groups did not create the language that eventually appeared in the final version of section 1, but they suggested to the SJC that the reasonable limitations clause should reflect similar clauses in international agreements that Canada was a signatory to. This was neither a radical request nor the result of questionable practices by interest groups and social movements that appeared before the SJC.

Legal Rights and the Rules of Evidence
Support for legal rights and the exclusion-of-evidence rule in the draft Charter came predictably from the Canadian Association of Chiefs of Police (CACP) and the Canadian Association of Crown Counsel (CACC). These organiza-

tions supported the legal rights provisions because they would entrench the status quo and the crime control approach to law enforcement, as the ability of the courts to interfere with either the rules of evidence or established police practices was compromised by the qualifying language attached to these sections. In regard to the exclusion-of-evidence rule in section 26, Chief Ackroyd stated before the Special Joint Committee that "the association agrees with this section as now written and would be strongly opposed to any change."[112] This statement was in reference to the presentation by the CCLA and its critique of the exclusion-of-evidence rule as being unacceptable. The CACP recommended that the guarantee in section 10(a) to be informed promptly of the reasons for arrest, and that in section 11(a) to be informed promptly of a specific offence, should be replaced with "as soon as practicable," to ensure that police interaction with the accused did not violate the Charter.[113] Just as the provinces did, the CACP sought to limit the Charter's application to its members' activities.

The strongest opposition to the legal rights provisions came from the CCLA, and there were similar objections raised by the CHRC, CJC, and CBA. On a practical level, these groups saw the qualifying language attached to legal rights reinforcing the illusionary aspect of Charter rights that began with the reasonable limits clause. For instance, Fairweather argued that legal rights, particularly sections 8 and 9, "may be seriously circumscribed by the qualification except on grounds and in accordance with procedures established by law."[114] In fact, Alan Borovoy of the CCLA criticized the qualification as "a verbal illustration in the sense that it may pretend to give us something, but in fact, gives us nothing more than we already have. At the moment, there can be no searches and seizures unless they are done in accordance with procedures established by law."[115] A number of presentations recommended that the right against searches and seizures in section 8 should be amended to allow for protection against unreasonable searches and seizures, thus increasing the ability to challenge existing police practices that were not merely unlawful but excessive.[116] Similar criticisms were made against section 9, and it was recommended that the qualification on the right be deleted and the right be extended to protect individuals against arbitrary detention or imprisonment. Finally, the CCLA identified a fundamental limitation in the rights provided under section 10 upon arrest or detention. Specifically, this group argued that for the right to be effective, there should be a constitutional requirement to inform individuals of the right to counsel, whereby this right could be exercised or waived.[117]

The exclusion-of-evidence rule in section 26 drew criticism from the various civil liberties groups because it was considered regressive and likely to greatly reduce the level of protection provided in the legal rights.[118] For instance, Fairweather correctly suggested that section 26 was a late addition to the draft Charter to appease provincial opposition to legal rights and their effect on law enforcement and the rules of evidence: "The section has obviously been drafted by those provincial officials who wish to perpetuate outmoded laws of evidence. It should be re-cast. In its present form it clouds all that part of the charter that deals with legal rights."[119] Several organizations, such as the Canadian Association of Lesbians and Gay Men (CALGM) and the CCLA, called for the elimination of section 26, though recommendations were made for improving the provision to provide a stronger role for the judiciary in determining the rules of evidence.

It is interesting to note that no civil liberties organization called for the approach to the admissibility of evidence that had been developed by the United States Supreme Court, though the CACP erroneously suggested that the adoption of the "poisoned fruit" doctrine had been recommended by the CCLA.[120] The CCLA simply took issue with the wording of the remedy clause in section 25, which limited declarations of unconstitutionality to laws and not to administrative actions. Using the example of *Hogan v. The Queen*,[121] where the issue was not the Criminal Code but the gathering of evidence by the police, Tarnopolsky argued that neither section 25 nor 26 of the proposed Charter would allow the courts to remedy similar police practices in the future. Specifically, the Charter's remedy clause was limited to laws, and section 26 prevented the courts from challenging the admissibility of evidence gathered by the police. For Tarnopolsky, this was problematic because the greatest threat to the rights of citizens did not originate in legislation but in the administrative actions of the police.[122]

The CCLA argued that "section 26 enshrines the rule that evidence, even if illegally obtained, is admissible if relevant," thus constitutionalizing *Hogan* in the draft Charter.[123] This organization endorsed neither the automatic exclusionary rule developed by the United States Supreme Court nor the automatic inclusion of evidence by the Supreme Court of Canada, but called for a remedies clause that allowed the courts the discretion to admit or exclude illegally obtained evidence. Indeed, the CCLA wanted to avoid a rigid exclusionary rule that would automatically exclude all illegally obtained evidence. Instead, the organization called for a balancing test under the discretion of the judiciary, "in which the court could weigh on the one hand the gravity of the offence, the circumstances on the other, the seriousness of the infringement ... and that there are other remedies that might be available."[124] While the Trudeau government would amend the draft Charter based on the critiques presented by civil liberties organizations in regard to the limitations clause, legal rights, the general remedies clause, and the exclusionary rule, it is interesting to note that the balancing test suggested by Tarnopolsky for the exclusion of evidence closely mirrors the test developed by the Supreme Court in *Collins*.[125]

Non-Discrimination Rights and Substantive Equality

The criticism that the proposed Charter would constitutionalize narrow doctrines developed by the Supreme Court in cases such as *Hogan* continued during the analysis of section 15 and the non-discrimination rights by interest groups before the SJC. There was a consensus that the limited approach to equality developed by the Supreme Court in *Bliss* and *Lavell* was reflected in the proposed wording of section 15, as the right was limited to equality before the law and equal protection of the law. In *Bliss v. A.G. Canada* and *Lavell v. A.G. Canada*, the equality rights provisions of the *Canadian Bill of Rights* simply protected the equal administration of the law, and the substance of the law was not subject to considerations of equality.[126] Specifically, as long as the law was equally applied, it was constitutional because the effect of the law would not be considered by the courts. The continuation of this formal approach to equality in the draft Charter resulted in significant criticism by civil liberties organizations. The most important and damning critique would be presented by the CACSW.

Fairweather was critical of section 15 because it provided a very limited set of grounds for protection and it did not address the doctrinal limitations developed by the Supreme Court in *Bliss* and *Lavell*. This criticism was made by several civil liberties organizations, which suggested the grounds of prohibited discrimination should either be expanded to cover more areas, such as physical and mental disability, sexual orientation, and marital status, or, failing this, the Trudeau government should return to its original approach in the 4 July draft, where no grounds were specified and the courts could determine prohibited grounds.[127] In his testimony, Fairweather called upon the Trudeau government to demonstrate its commitment to substantive equality by amending section 15 to ensure that equality rights decisions by the Supreme Court under the Bill of Rights would be overturned by the Charter.[128]

The call for a broader approach to equality was strongly advocated by the CACSW during its appearance. This organization was frustrated that "the wording in Clause 15 is almost exactly the same wording as in the Canadian Bill of Rights and this wording we have found through ten years of testing before the Supreme Court of Canada has not alleviated the discrimination for women at all."[129] Instead of simply restricting equality protection to the administration of the law, and thus repeating the mistakes of *Bliss* and *Lavell*, the CACSW, along with several other civil liberties organizations including the Saskatchewan Human Rights Commission (SHRC) and the CBA, called for an approach that indicated substantive equality and not simply formal equality would be the principle that guided judicial review. According to the CACSW presentation, "the equality that we envision would exist in the law, not merely the administration of the law. Clarity in the drafting of Clause 15 is essential so that there can be no misinterpretation of the directive to the court. It must be clearly understood by the public, by the courts and the legislatures that Canadians intend to enshrine in the Constitution a genuine principle of equality rights."[130]

Mary Eberts was more explicit on this issue during questioning by Pauline Jewett, MP, when she stated that her organization wanted "a guarantee of substantive rights as well as procedural rights and that guarantee be up front as it were in the very first phrase of Subsection 15(1)."[131] In addition to a substantive approach, the CACSW called for a two-tiered approach to equality rights involving enumerated categories and those analogous to the prohibited grounds of discrimination. This was endorsed by the SHRC.[132]

The SJC has been criticized as an orchestrated exercise designed to ensure that the Trudeau government's preference for a stronger Charter would materialize. Romanow, Whyte, and Leeson argue that the SJC only heard evidence from interest groups that supported a strong Charter and did not consider evidence from individuals and groups that opposed entrenchment.[133] In effect, they contend the Trudeau government used interest groups as a resource in constitutional politics to overcome provincial resistance. In an interview with Senator Serge Joyal, who was co-chair of the SJC during his time in the House of Commons, I asked whether the committee had been under the instruction of the Trudeau government. Joyal soundly rejected the argument by Romanow that the SJC had been instrumental in selecting groups and individuals that supported the Charter and were likely to call for a much stronger document.[134] A poll taken during September 1980 indicated that 81 percent of Canadians were in favour of an entrenched document,[135] suggesting that the interest groups that appeared before the SJC were more a reflection of public opinion than actors in a constitutional drama under the direction of the Trudeau government.

This critical position overlooks two important issues. First, the presentations made in support of a stronger document were generally correct that the proposed resolution attempted to entrench two types of supremacy, and this would have had serious implications for the internal consistency of the document and its ability to provide clear signals to the judiciary for its interpretation of rights and freedoms. Indeed, the politics of appeasement by the Trudeau government undermined the effectiveness of the Charter because the qualifications attached to limit its application to provincial governments weakened the document. Second, and perhaps more importantly, this critical position downplays the role of the premiers in creating a constitutional impasse that could only be overcome by challenging the paradigm of executive federalism, which had prevented significant constitutional change since 1927. Both orders of government relied on resources to advance their constitutional agendas and to ensure that their intentions would prevail. In this respect, the premiers' defence of parliamentary supremacy as the justification to block entrenchment of the Charter found its legitimacy in unwritten constitutional practices and not in the constitutional objectives of Canadian citizens, and this would be decisive. The intention of the Trudeau government for a stronger Charter prevailed because the sovereignty of the Canadian state shifted in 1980-81 during the proceedings of the SJC due to citizen participation. Ultimately, this facilitated the emergence of the citizens' constitution despite the premiers' intention to remain the bulwarks of a limited constitution defined by parliamentary supremacy.

The Impact of Parliamentary Scrutiny

The issue of framers' intent and whether the Supreme Court's activism has advanced or departed from this principle will be considered in Chapter 3. The proceedings of the SJC between 12 January 1981, when the minister of justice appeared, and the Trudeau government's return to the institutions of executive federalism after the *Patriation Reference* decision will be critical for this issue, and a fuller analysis is left until then. In this section, the reaction of the Trudeau government to the initial proceedings of the SJC will be considered, as well as the constitutional politics surrounding the premiers' reaction to a strengthened Charter. The proceedings of the SJC were haunted by the spectre of a constitutional challenge by the provinces over the legality of unilateral patriation, as well as the parliamentary filibuster by the official opposition. Both of these challenges to unilateral patriation were suspended after the Trudeau government agreed to seek a reference opinion by the Supreme Court on the issue of unilateral patriation.[136]

From 12 January 1981 to the passage of the final resolution respecting patriation by the Senate on 8 December 1981, there were five additional drafts of the Charter.[137] The most significant revision of the draft Charter occurred between 12 January 1981, when Justice Minister Chrétien appeared with possible amendments based on the testimony of interest groups and individuals, and 13 February 1981, when the Trudeau government submitted a new proposed resolution that incorporated the suggested amendments. Indeed, the Trudeau government made fifty-eight recommendations to the proposed resolution that were accepted by the SJC in the revised resolution of 13 February 1981, and a significant number of the recommendations involved the draft Charter.[138] The importance of the amendments recommended by Chrétien is that they significantly marginalized the intention of the premiers for a weak Charter. In effect, framers' intent changed in the Charter from the qualified rights favoured by the premiers to the activist constitution championed by the Trudeau government with significant public support.

The justice minister indicated that the proposed amendments were largely based on the testimony provided by groups and individuals that rejected the original resolution. In a statement to the SJC on 12 January 1981, Chrétien said: "You have been told by many witnesses that Canadians are not satisfied with the type of compromise which weakens the effectiveness of constitutional protection of human rights and freedoms. I accept the legitimacy of that criticism."[139] The most substantive change involved section 1 and the standards applied to governments for limiting rights. During this testimony, Chrétien acknowledged that the revised limitations clause was generally based on the recommendations made by the CHRC and the CJC, though it was more stringent than requested.[140] The new version of section 1 in the 13 February 1981 resolution now protected rights "subject only to such reasonable limits prescribed by law as can be demonstrably justified in a free and democratic society."[141] In the explanatory notes it was stated that the revision to section 1 narrowed the limitations that could be placed on rights, as the reference to a parliamentary system of government was deleted and the limitation would have to be prescribed by law and "to be both reasonable and capable of being demonstrably justified."[142] Further, the 13 February proposed resolution included the creation of a separate right to freedom of association in section 2(d), a right that had previously been included alongside freedom of peaceful assembly. This change was based on the recommendation of the CBA and was designed to reflect Canada's commitment to the *International Covenant on Civil and Political Rights,* which listed these rights as separate and distinct.[143]

The next significant proposed amendments accepted by the SJC involved substantive changes to the legal rights protections, which came under serious criticism between November 1980 and January 1981. Most of the qualifications on legal rights were removed, and additional safeguards were included, such as the requirement that the police must inform individuals of the right to retain and instruct counsel in section 10(b). Section 8 and the right involving searches and seizures were changed to a test of reasonableness as opposed to being simply authorized by law. Similarly, the protection against detention or imprisonment was changed from being provided for by law to a test of whether it was arbitrary. The minister of justice informed the SJC that "the fact that procedures are established by law will not be conclusive proof that search and seizure or detention is legal. Such procedures and the laws on which they are based will have to meet the tests of being reasonable and not being arbitrary."[144] Additional safeguards were provided for the right to reasonable bail, which could only be limited by just cause instead of the former qualification, which allowed this right to be limited in accordance with procedures established by law.

The non-discrimination rights were renamed equality rights to stress their positive characteristics. Chrétien acknowledged the influential role of the CACSW and endorsed the two-level approach to equality rights, with enumerated and analogous grounds. In addition, the new equality rights provision in the 13 February proposed resolution included mental or physical disability as protected characteristics. Further, section 15 now protected substantive equality as opposed to procedural equality as it had in the 6 October 1980 version, thus signalling to the courts that *Bliss* and *Lavell* would be incompatible with the new equality rights provisions. Indeed, Tassé has argued that "the Department and the Committee had done their utmost to ensure that the text of section 15 would be drafted in such a way that the decisions of the Supreme Court in *Lavell* and *Bliss* would quite simply be reversed."[145] Thus, both the Trudeau government and interest groups were committed to section 15(1) being interpreted by the courts as protecting substantive equality.

The proposed amendments transformed both the form and the substance of the Charter, as the remedies available to the courts for constitutional violations were increased. The general remedies clause in section 25 previously applied only to laws that were inconsistent with the Charter, but in the 13 February resolution this was extended to include administrative action. According to the minister of justice, this change was at the request of the CCLA and the CJC and "would ensure that an appropriate remedy as determined by the Courts would be afforded to anyone whose rights have been infringed whether through enactment of a law or by an action of a government official."[146] The rules affecting the admissibility of evidence were not included in the 12 January consolidated resolution and would result in a completely new approach in the form of section 24(2). The current exclusion-of-evidence rule first appeared in the 13 February 1981 proposed resolution and increased the level of judicial scrutiny, as it allowed the courts to determine whether evidence gathered in violation of certain legal rights should be excluded to protect the reputation of justice. This represents a significant difference from earlier versions of the Charter, where the laws of evidence were not affected by legal rights guarantees.

Several other sections of the draft Charter were amended in the 13 February 1981 resolution based on the recommendations to the SJC by the minister of justice. At the request of the premier of New Brunswick, the language rights provisions were extended to the legislature, government, and courts of New Brunswick. Further, the minority language education rights were also strengthened, as the right now referred to educational facilities instead of simply the provision of instruction. Whereas the previous version of section 23 had protected the right to have all children instructed in the language of the oldest child when the residence changed between provinces, the new version dropped this reference. A new clause was added under section 26 that stated the Charter would be interpreted in a manner to preserve and promote the multicultural heritage of Canadians, and additional safeguards for denominational school rights were added under section 28 of the February resolution that protected these rights from Charter review.

Finally, the 24 April version included the guarantee of gender equality under section 28.

The consolidated resolution tabled by the minister of justice on 23 April 1981 and the Charter that exists today are nearly identical, with the exception of minor changes to democratic rights, the inclusion of the notwithstanding clause, and a further qualification on mobility rights that were added at the November 1981 FMC after the *Patriation Reference* decision. In effect, the critical period in the textual evolution of the Charter occurred between 12 January and 13 February 1981, when the premiers' intention to prevent an entrenched Charter, or at the very least ensure that it did not impact executive-dominated parliamentary democracy, was defeated. Even as late as 16 April 1981, the eight provincial premiers opposed to unilateral patriation released a four-part constitutional accord that called on the federal government to withdraw its proposed joint address. This accord called for rapid patriation, a new amending formula, a three-year period of constitutional renewal based on the new amending formula, and the discontinuation of court action on the Trudeau patriation project by the premiers, but not a charter of rights and freedoms.[147] Presumably, discussions on the Charter would occur during the subsequent constitutional negotiations when Trudeau was no longer prime minister.

Tassé has argued that the evolution of the draft Charter was fundamentally democratic and not orchestrated because of the significant role played by Canadians and the inability of the Trudeau government to anticipate the public's positive reaction to the Charter. Specifically, the government did not originally intend to have the document reviewed by the SJC but did so as a concession to the opposition parties in the House of Commons. Because the Trudeau government conceded to this, it is difficult to conceive how it orchestrated the selection of favourable interest groups. In Tassé's view, the original Charter was quite timid, but through the SJC it "came to look like a radical document capable of making a profound impact on our fundamental institutions and on the future of the country."[148] These radical changes that now favoured the judicial branch at the expense of the legislative branch required one more significant event before they became part of the Canadian constitution.

Judicial Politics and the Charter

This occurred with the release of the *Patriation Reference* decision on 28 September 1981. The Supreme Court ruled, in a majority opinion, that provincial consent was not required as a matter of law but that, as a matter of constitutional convention and practice, substantial provincial consent was necessary before the federal government could seek changes to the *BNA Act* by the British parliament.[149] Russell has argued that the political consequences of this decision were generally positive because it facilitated federal-provincial agreement between Ottawa and nine provinces on patriation.[150] However, this decision served as a significant resource for the Trudeau government because the Supreme Court indicated that if federal-provincial agreement was not obtained, the Trudeau government could proceed with unilateral patriation. The *Patriation Reference* weakened the bargaining position of the provincial premiers, as the decision effectively prevented the first ministers' blocking constitutional change indefinitely and paved the way for an agreement that generally favoured the federal government.

There were a series of substantive changes to the proposed resolution that secured substantial provincial consent. The Trudeau government accepted the amending formula favoured by the provincial premiers, entrenched equalization payments, and accepted section 93(3), which provided the provinces with concurrent jurisdiction over natural resources. The draft Charter was modified to include section 33, the notwithstanding clause, which would apply to sections 2 and 7 through 15 once invoked by a competent legislative body for a renewable five-year period. In addition, mobility rights were amended to include section 6(3), which allowed the provinces to undertake affirmative action programs in depressed regions if the provincial unemployment average was above the national average. In exchange for these federal concessions, the nine premiers agreed to patriation and the application of section 23 (minority language education rights) to their provinces.[151] Perhaps most importantly, the premiers accepted the substantive changes to the Charter at the committee stage, which they had prevented within the institutions of executive federalism.

Before the declaration of unilateral patriation, the practice of executive federalism had prevented the Trudeau government from securing constitutional change. The significance of the *Patriation Reference* decision is that it facilitated change by weakening the principle of unanimity that had allowed the premiers to block patriation. While the Charter would be modified to appease the premiers through the notwithstanding clause and the changes to mobility rights, these concessions would prove to have little effect on the substantive content of the Charter. The focus of Charter review and judicial activism has been in the areas of legal and equality rights and the remedies involving section 1 and section 24(2), the exclusion-of-evidence rule. In effect, the Supreme Court's activism has involved the very sections that were strengthened as a result of the SJC and were not part of the constitutional trade-offs at the November 1981 first ministers' conference that led to patriation.

Conclusion

Two distinct sets of intentions and resources were used by political actors involved in the constitutional politics that surrounded patriation. The

Trudeau government sought to entrench a Charter that principally protected language and education rights. In certain respects, the remaining sections of the Charter were open to negotiation, as the Trudeau government did not initially have a strategy beyond the issue of entrenchment or a clear view of the interpretive approach that it favoured beyond this narrow set of rights. The Charter project was therefore incomplete, as the relationship between the cabinet and the Supreme Court, and the institutional reforms necessary to preserve democratic governance, had not been considered. The underdeveloped nature of legislative activism continues to be the fundamental failure of the Charter project, and this issue is explored in Chapter 7. In contrast, the premiers sought to preserve executive dominance through a defence of parliamentary supremacy and changes in the division of powers that enhanced their responsibilities.

At first the premiers were clearly the dominant actor, as the informal principles structuring constitutional reform, such as unanimity, meant that an entrenched Charter would only be realized if the premiers consented. The relative bargaining strengths of the participants resulted in a constitutional impasse in which the substantive content of the Charter became part of the politics of appeasement that the Trudeau government engaged in to achieve unanimity and to overcome provincial opposition. If the 6 October 1980 resolution had been passed, the intention of the premiers for a weak Charter would have triumphed over the activist intentions of the Trudeau government. Their defence of parliamentary supremacy began with the reasonable limits clause, and the qualified language attached to most rights provided limited grounds to establish a constitutional violation. The remedy of constitutional violations also favoured parliamentary actors, as the determination of minority language education rights was a legislative choice, and the general remedies clause was limited to unconstitutional laws. However, the high degree of deference accorded to parliamentary actors in this draft Charter suggested that few cases would require the courts to remedy Charter violations.

In this chapter, I have argued that the formative event that determined which set of interests triumphed was the opposition parties' demand, after the Trudeau government indicated its intention to proceed unilaterally, that the Charter be reviewed by an SJC. The substantive content of the Charter was not at first directly affected by unilateral patriation, as the resolution advanced the premiers' intention to preserve parliamentary control over rights. It was not until the draft Charter was reviewed first by parliamentarians and then by interest groups and individuals between 14 November 1980 and 9 January 1981 that the balance of power shifted decisively in favour of the Trudeau government. The negative reaction by interest groups acted as an important resource to challenge the dominance of the premiers in constitutional politics, as the public rejected the illusionary and largely rhetorical commitment to rights that federal-provincial negotiations had produced. Seizing upon these criticisms, the activist intentions of the Trudeau government became the dominant and enduring aspect of the Charter after 12 January 1981.

The reliance on public support for a stronger Charter represented a temporary resource for the Trudeau government as the premiers attempted to have unilateral patriation declared unconstitutional by the Supreme Court. Until the *Patriation Reference* decision was released on 28 September 1981, it was unclear whether the Trudeau government would be able to overcome provincial opposition. While the Supreme Court's decision did facilitate a final round of constitutional negotiations, it ultimately ensured that the Trudeau government was able to entrench an activist Charter. The premiers now bargained from a position of weakness, as the reliance on unanimity had been significantly qualified by the Supreme Court. This marked the ascendancy of the Trudeau government in constitutional politics and allowed for patriation in 1982 with a Charter that would provide sufficient protections against legislative encroachment. As a result, the activist constitution emerged, and parliamentary supremacy became the symbolic characteristic of the Canadian constitution.

3
Framers' Intent and the Parliamentary Arena

The framers of the Charter succeeded in entrenching an activist document over the opposition of the premiers. Despite Trudeau's characterization of the Charter "as the culmination of a political endeavour whose purpose was to strengthen Canadian unity through the pursuit of a Just Society based on freedom and equality,"[1] conservative judicial critics continue to argue that the Supreme Court has departed from framers' intent in its understanding of the Charter.[2] This position downplays the political events that preceded the Charter's evolution from a compromise document designed to appease the premiers to Roger Tassé's characterization of it as "a radical document which was capable of making a profound impact on our fundamental institutions and on the future of our country."[3] The Charter is neither a legal nor a judicial revolution, but a formative political and societal event in which the activist intentions of the Trudeau government triumphed, and the power of the judiciary was expanded to protect rights from unconstitutional legislative encroachment.[4]

The issue of framers' intent, and its use by conservative judicial critics, will be explored in this chapter. A central limitation of this position is the assumption that the most significant change has been the Supreme Court's approach to judicial review.[5] Because the Supreme Court has approached Charter review in a far more activist manner, conservative judicial critics contend that the Supreme Court has undermined the legitimacy of Charter review.[6] While there are specific examples where the Supreme Court has departed from the intentions of the Charter's framers, such as its decision to interpret the principles of fundamental justice in a substantive manner,[7] its interpretation has generally been consistent with the activist intentions of the Trudeau government and the interest groups that called for a stronger Charter during the design of the document.

The argument advanced in this chapter is that a new framers' intent characterizes the Charter, and this legitimizes judicial activism by the Supreme Court. Indeed, I am skeptical about the value of comparing judicial deference under the *Canadian Bill of Rights* with judicial activism under the Charter as these are fundamentally different documents with different intentions. To claim that the Supreme Court has violated framers' intent because it has abandoned the deferential approach under the *Canadian Bill of Rights* assigns too much importance to the discretionary choices of the judiciary and neglects to consider the relationship between judicial review and political choices. This activist approach transpired because important political actors rejected the Bill of Rights and judicial deference long before the court rejected its own Bill of Rights jurisprudence.[8] Judicial activism is therefore an appropriate response to the activist intentions of the Trudeau government and its desire that all actors govern with the Charter to better protect rights.[9] Patrick Monahan has suggested that substantive framers intent refers to the specific meaning attached to various constitutional provisions, whereas interpretive intent simply refers to how the framers intended the courts to interpret substantive constitutional provisions.[10] The proceedings of the Special Joint Committee (SJC) demonstrate the absence of substantive intent by the framers outside a narrow set of rights, but indicate an interpretive intent that the Charter was to be read in an activist manner by the courts. Perhaps more importantly, this activist interpretive intent challenges the position that judicial activism is a distortion of framers' intent.

While judicial activism has clearly been contrary to the intentions of a majority of the premiers present during its design, this does not mean that it is necessarily a violation of framers' intent as it relates to the Charter. For judicial activism to be a violation would require undue importance being assigned to the intentions of the premiers who were marginalized during the constitutional politics surrounding the Charter. Thus, I intend to provide an analysis of the individuals who constitute the framers of the Charter and to demonstrate their preference for an expansive approach by the courts. A related objective, which will be addressed first, is to question the use of American theories of judicial review to discredit judicial activism by the Supreme Court of Canada. Conservative judicial critics equate framers' intent with the judicial technique of interpretivism, which is a restrictive approach that requires the courts to respect the substantive intent of constitutional protections. However, given the general absence of substantive intent on the part of the political actors who are the framers of the Charter, the distinction between interpretivism and non-interpretivism holds little value in the Canadian example. With a distinct political culture and the absence of a separation of powers theory, judicial review and its relationship to the broader political system assume a different importance in a parliamentary system.[11]

American Constitutionalism and Framers' Intent

Kent Roach has remarked that the "judicial activism debate that has emerged in Canada since the Charter is an unfortunate example of a branch-plant mentality that ignores the differences between the Charter and the American Bill of Rights."[12] For instance, these critics suggest that the Supreme Court had either to employ an interpretivist approach to the Charter or to move beyond the wishes of the drafters and create the document's meaning through non-interpretivist judicial review.[13] The assumption that framers' intent in Canada must be equated with the restrictive judicial technique of interpretivism is debatable.[14] This presupposes that the framers were suspicious of the judiciary as a potential political rival and drafted the Charter in a manner to restrict the interpretive role of the Supreme Court. While the provincial premiers were surely suspicious, as illustrated by their near unanimous stand against entrenching the Charter and their defence of parliamentary supremacy, they cannot be considered framers of the Charter that was entrenched in 1982. (Later in this chapter, I will explain why the provincial premiers who opposed entrenchment cannot be considered significant framers of the Charter beyond the notwithstanding clause and mobility rights.)

Suspicion of judicial power was not the attitude of the Trudeau government, which had increased access to the judiciary in the 1970s. For instance, the Trudeau government established the Court Challenges Program in 1977 to fund interest group challenges to provincial language policies, and thus attempted to enlist the judiciary and use litigation as a strategy to overcome provincial resistance to increased language protections for linguistic minorities.[15] Janet Hiebert has argued that the Trudeau government's initial approach to rights did not even include a limitations clause, as Trudeau preferred that the determination of limitations be the responsibility of the courts.[16] In essence, the federal government did not view the courts as "the bulwarks of a limited constitution," to cite Alexander Hamilton,[17] or a rival centre of power, but as an important actor that could aid Ottawa in expanding the limited protections provided in the Canadian constitution in the face of provincial resistance before the introduction of the Charter. In Canada, the framers of the Charter intended the courts, along with political and bureaucratic actors, to be the bulwarks against the limited constitution.

The limitations in the Canadian approach to framers' intent have extended to the comparisons between the Bill of Rights and the Charter of Rights. Framers' intent is clearly different in the two documents, as the purpose of the Charter was to overcome the limitations of the Bill of Rights, both institutionally and textually.[18] In fact, the Charter of Rights can be seen as an explicit rejection of the Bill of Rights, as the Charter was intended to be a more substantive statement on rights and freedoms.[19] In effect, the activist constitution replaced the deferential and restrained Bill of Rights, and the framers of the Charter intended this document to offer stronger institutional and textual protections for rights.[20] Lorraine Weinrib has advanced a similar defence of the Supreme Court, arguing that "the fact that the Charter was designed to correct widely perceived failings in the Canadian political system demonstrates the fragility of claims that the judges who find fault with pre-Charter laws are, for that reason alone, off on a frolic of their own."[21] Judicial activism, therefore, is an important characteristic of framers' intent and necessary for the activist constitution to be realized.[22]

The Supreme Court approached the Bill of Rights in a restrained and deferential manner for two important reasons. First, the document was an ordinary statute that simply applied to the actions of the federal government and the police. Second, the language of the Bill of Rights reinforced the restrained tone set by the framers of this document, as the Bill of Rights protected human rights and fundamental freedoms that "exist and continue to exist" in Canada.[23] The same structural factors that required judicial restraint in the Bill of Rights are not present in the Charter, either in the text of the document or the intention of its framers.[24] Charles Epp has suggested that the framers of the Charter rejected interpretivism and legitimized an activist role by the courts: "The final list of rights resulting from the historical struggle is about seven pages long and contains detailed language inserted to discourage the courts from adopting narrow interpretations of its guarantees."[25] More than simply being judge-led, rights activism in Canada is foremost a political exercise in which the judiciary is merely a participant in a broader institutional relationship responsible for protecting rights.[26] Therefore, judicial activism is consistent with the desire of politically accountable actors to strengthen protected rights and the ability of the Supreme Court to effectively protect civil liberties.[27]

The Supreme Court and the Charter Revolution

In a number of important writings,[28] conservative judicial critics such as Morton, Knopff, and Manfredi have sketched out the limitations of what they refer to as the Charter revolution and point to two elements that are said to facilitate judicial supremacy: judicial discretion in interpreting the Charter, which they suggest has allowed the court to infuse the Charter with meaning beyond that intended by the framers;[29] and the emergence of the Supreme Court as an "oracular courtroom" that has increased the policy-making role of the judiciary, "whose primary purpose is to solve social problems by issuing broad declarations of constitutional policy."[30] For these critics, this is a judge-led revolution because neither the text of the Charter nor framers' intent can justify the shift from judicial restraint under the Bill of Rights to judicial activism during Charter review.[31]

In concluding that judicial activism by the Supreme Court is inconsistent with the intentions of the framers, these critics engage in a comparative assessment of the court's approach to the Bill of Rights and the Charter. Simply stated, they favour the deferential approach to judicial review that the Supreme Court applied in its Bill of Rights jurisprudence.[32] Though conservative judicial critics do not explicitly state that framers' intent has remained the same between the Bill of Rights and the Charter of Rights, it is my contention that this is the foundation of their critique. For instance, in earlier work, Knopff and Morton suggested that the protections in the Bill of Rights and the Charter of Rights had not greatly changed in terms of their content:

> What is new about these rights in Canada is not their existence as fundamental principles of the regime, but their constitutional entrenchment. Unless the framers of the Charter clearly intended to change the content or meaning of these rights in the course of entrenching them, judicial decisions that make such changes can be considered non-interpretivist in character. They can be seen as transforming the traditional understanding of the proper scope and limits of rights without warrant in the original understanding of the constitutional provision they rely upon. In this view, such decisions use vague constitutional language, which is usually quite compatible with the right as traditionally understood, to create a new right.[33]

While Morton and Knopff do acknowledge that there are several textual differences between the Bill of Rights and the Charter of Rights, such as in the area of criminal procedure, the broader definition of equality protections in the Charter, and, finally, section 23 and minority language education rights, "this innovation explains relatively little of the Charter revolution."[34] The general position of these critics, therefore, is that the legislative record of the SJC does not provide sufficient evidence that the framers of the Charter intended to change the meaning of rights and freedoms. What has changed, therefore, is the Supreme Court and its approach to rights litigation.

What is more problematic for Morton and Knopff is the transformation of interest group politics and the rise of the Court Party, a term used to refer to a loose coalition of new social movements that attempt to influence public policy through litigation rather than through the traditional lobbying strategies of interest groups. Morton and Knopff say that "the Charter revolution, in other words, is characterized by the rising prominence in Canadian public life of both a policy making institution (the judiciary) and its partisans (the Court Party)."[35] In this view, the Court Party is anti-democratic because it forsakes the political arena for the judicial arena and seeks policy success not through majoritarian politics, but through judicial politics. Perhaps more significantly, the emergence of the Court Party reinforces the position that the Supreme Court has clearly departed from framers' intent in its interpretation of the Charter. Specifically, the equivalent of the Court Party was notably absent during the Bill of Rights, and according to Morton and Knopff, "it was the underdevelopment of such a constituency that helped stunt the 1960 Diefenbaker Bill of Rights."[36] What has created this constituency, therefore, is the transformation of the Supreme Court from deference to activism and the ability of the Court Party constituency to successfully press minority interests onto majoritarian politics through the elitism of judicial politics.[37]

The Charter revolution, according to this view, has become neither the citizens' nor the governments' constitution, but the constitution of special interests and the judiciary under the leadership of the Supreme Court. This is what Manfredi has referred to as the paradox of liberal constitutionalism: "If judicial review evolves such that political power in its judicial guise is limited only by a constitution whose meaning courts alone define, then judicial power is no longer itself constrained by constitutional limits."[38] Indeed, it is claimed that the traditional constraints on judicial power have been consciously ignored by the Supreme Court in its desire for greater political power and influence on public policy. This departure is most explicitly illustrated for these critics in the Supreme Court's early Charter jurisprudence when it decided to ignore its Bill of Rights precedents, such as in *R. v. Big M Drug Mart Ltd.*,[39] where the court reversed its decision that the *Lord's Day Act* was constitutional under the Bill of Rights and ruled that it was unconstitutional under the Charter of Rights as a violation of freedom of religion.

There is a serious limitation in suggesting that the intention of the statutory Bill of Rights and the judiciary's approach were to continue with the entrenchment of the Charter.[40] Quite simply, if Trudeau and the other framers had wanted to continue the Supreme Court's approach to civil liberties, they would have entrenched the Bill of Rights, with the additional guarantees that were central to Trudeau's Charter project.[41] This would have signalled to both the judiciary and to other actors that the only difference between the two documents was the entrenched status of the latter and its application to the provinces. On a more strategic level, this approach would have allowed the Trudeau government to overcome provincial resistance to entrenching rights much sooner than 1981, as the Bill of Rights had been in existence since 1960 and there was little in the court's jurisprudence to concern the provinces or to challenge either parliamentary supremacy or provincial autonomy.[42]

If Trudeau and the other major framers simply wanted to entrench the approach to rights and freedoms under the Bill of Rights, why was so much political and personal capital expended over sixteen years to entrench an approach to civil liberties already in existence? Specifically, the numerous first ministers conferences, starting with Victoria in 1971, demonstrate that the draft Charter and its textual protections for rights and freedoms became stronger during each subsequent constitutional conference. Further, the extraordinary efforts that Trudeau and his officials pursued to secure the entrenchment of the Charter, such as the strategy of unilateral patriation, the subsequent *Patriation Reference* and its split decision rendered by the Supreme Court, and, finally, the conceptualization of the Charter as the "people's package" to overcome provincial resistance, do not represent the actions of political actors intent on maintaining the status quo in the protection of rights.[43] Additionally, the parliamentary record suggests that the legislative status of the Bill of Rights and provincial human rights codes had not seen these documents weakened through legislative amendment. Indeed, the pattern between 1960 and 1982 was for governments to increase the scope of provincial human rights codes and other statutory protections for rights, suggesting that political actors had shown leadership in the area of civil liberties.[44] This is significant, as statutory protections for rights and freedoms had increased since 1960, yet judicial protections had plateaued soon after the enactment of the Bill of Rights. The failure by conservative judicial critics to address why Trudeau and the other framers went to such measures to entrench, as they suggest, the intention of the Bill of Rights undermines their position that the Supreme Court has departed from framers' intent during Charter review.[45]

A New Framers' Intent

It is largely asserted that the Charter and the Bill of Rights contain the same purpose and approach to rights and freedoms, and this assertion is a result of the judge-centred analysis that Morton, Knopff, and Manfredi engage in. According to Weinrib, the critique of judicial activism "disregards the prolonged, well-informed and remarkably participatory debate that led to the *Charter*'s adoption."[46] A more serious limitation is the conservative critics' general approach to the framers of this document, as they fail to identify the actual framers of the Charter and simply use their assumptions about "framers' intent" to attack judicial activism. My approach to framers' intent is not the traditional one, which argues framers' intent is an illusive concept because competing and contradictory positions are generally presented by the framers. This view is only true if all participants involved in the drafting of constitutions are accorded the same status and their views are given equal weight. For framers' intent to have relevance, therefore, levels of importance have to be attached to those individuals and groups that participated in the drafting of the Charter.[47]

This is clearly the approach in the American context, where James Madison and Alexander Hamilton are given primacy of place among the framers of the American constitution. Canadian Charter critics fail to make important distinctions between the individuals involved in the drafting of the Charter, and they dilute the significance of more important figures – such as Trudeau, officials within the Department of Justice (DOJ), and the SJC –

and overstate the importance of the premiers and their officials. This results in an uneven presentation of framers' intent that reduces the activist intentions of the Charter, as the dominant and activist roles played by the individuals responsible for its textual evolution are sidestepped in an effort to provide a more comprehensive, but, in my opinion, a more general and misleading view of the framers of the Charter. There is a further limitation that hinders critics from concluding that a new framers' intent is the political and theoretical foundation of the Charter project: this is the disregard of the fact that Trudeau never appeared before the SJC and the failure to take into consideration the political will and intentions of the individual primarily responsible for the entrenchment of the Charter in 1982.[48] This unfairly reduces the importance of Trudeau's political legacy in ascertaining whether, in fact, the justices of the Supreme Court have approached Charter review in a manner consistent with framers' intent.[49]

A useful approach to framers' intent has been advanced by Tassé, who, as deputy minister of justice, participated in both the drafting of the Charter and the deliberations of the SJC. Tassé argues that four categories of participants should be recognized as constituting the framers of the Charter. First are the federal political leaders under the direction of Trudeau. Tassé remarks that, "as for the federal political leaders, it is obvious that had it not been for Mr. Trudeau's determination and political will there would have been no Charter of Rights. Because of his personal interests in these issues, he personally drafted several of the Charter's provisions."[50] Included in this group is Jean Chrétien, who as minister of justice appeared before the Special Joint Committee and presented the position of the federal government. The second group involves the senior officials within the DOJ. According to Tassé, "the Department of Justice lawyers were the first and last to hold the pen. They prepared the drafts; they prepared the revisions they were asked to do; and finally they prepared the legislation."[51] Tassé suggests that the DOJ played a significant support role for Trudeau and Chrétien, as senior departmental officials conducted negotiations with the provinces, met with interest groups, and, finally, testified before the SJC.[52] The third group is the provincial premiers and their public servants, who, to varying degrees, were opposed to the Charter project. The final group includes the SJC and the interest groups that made presentations during the parliamentary hearings on the draft Charter.[53]

Unlike Tassé, who categorizes all the participants as drafters of the Charter, I reserve the label "framer" for those participants who succeeded in having their intentions entrenched in the Charter. Based on this approach, the provincial premiers would be considered, at best, the least important category of framers because their intention to preserve the principle of executive-dominated parliamentary supremacy and to deny a significant role for the courts was unsuccessful. At worst, the premiers would not even be considered framers of the Charter that was entrenched, but I am reluctant to exclude them because of the inclusion of the notwithstanding clause and changes to mobility rights at their insistence during the first ministers' conference of 2-5 November 1981. With the exception of Premiers Davis of Ontario and Hatfield of New Brunswick, the provincial premiers opposed the Charter project. For instance, the majority of provincial premiers continued to oppose entrenchment, with the strongest opposition coming from Sterling Lyon of Manitoba, who defended parliamentary supremacy and opposed the Charter as a serious erosion of this principle.[54] Indeed, the official record indicates that the premiers' influence on the draft Charter was to weaken it as a statement of rights and freedoms. The intention of the premiers, therefore, was to preserve the status quo in the area of rights and freedoms.

There is a more fundamental reason to relegate the premiers to the second tier of participants, and that is the reality of the Canadian amending procedure prior to 1982 and the implications of the *Patriation Reference* decision that further marginalized the premiers.[55] Because Canada lacked a domestic amending formula, changes to the *British North America Act, 1867*, occurred when the British parliament accepted a legislative resolution passed by the Canadian parliament requesting changes. In effect, Canada's amending formula was decidedly unitary, albeit within a colonial framework that required the British parliament to agree to the requested changes. However, constitutional practice in Canada had established the convention that provincial agreement would be attained before parliament passed a legislative resolution requesting changes to the *BNA Act*, thus allowing an informal role for the premiers in amending the constitution prior to 1982. The *Patriation Reference* temporarily weakened the informal federal characteristics of the amending procedure, as the court decided that constitutional law allowed the federal government to proceed unilaterally, but that, based on constitutional convention, the federal government required "substantial provincial consent" before it could ask the British parliament to amend the Canadian constitution.[56] However, the court qualified the issue of constitutional convention by ruling that a convention was not enforceable in court, suggesting that the federal government could legally patriate without provincial consent. The significance of this decision is that once the draft Charter was submitted to the SJC for consideration, the ability of the premiers to directly influence the content of the Charter was drastically limited, as demonstrated in Chapter 2.

The remaining drafters were committed to entrenching a substantive document and increasing the ability of the judiciary to remedy unconstitutional action.[57] While it is necessary to rely on the testimony of specific individuals, the reality is that a consensus emerged that the Charter was to be an activist document, and the comments of specific individuals are used simply to illustrate the activist intentions of the framers as a whole. Because the Trudeau government realized its constitutional objectives through the proceedings of the SJC, the testimony provided by members of the Trudeau government and officials of the DOJ is particularly relevant to the issue of framers' intent. The return appearance of Jean Chrétien before the SJC on 12 January 1981 and the testimony of senior officials of the DOJ, such as Roger Tassé and Barry Strayer, until 9 February 1981 are therefore critical to understanding the intention of the Charter's principal framers.

Activist Intentions

The testimony before the SJC reveals the importance of political and cultural differences between Canada and the United States in regard to judicial review, as the framers recognized that the Supreme Court would play a significant role in determining the substantive content of rights and accepted this as legitimate in a modern democracy. Monahan has referred to the "modified judicial realism" of Trudeau and the framers, as they recognized that the American experience had demonstrated the significant degree of freedom available to courts when interpreting constitutional protections.[58] The concerns regarding judicial power were generally absent in the testimony of Jean Chrétien and senior members of the DOJ, and a confidence in the complementary nature of rights protection by political, bureaucratic, and judicial actors was revealed. During a clause by clause examination of the Charter, the drafters largely speculated how the judiciary would approach the substantive interpretation of specific sections. Though judicial independence is a significant element of parliamentary democracy, the judiciary is not a separate branch of government and is therefore not a rival centre of power but is complementary to the legislative arena. Because political actors desired to strengthen judicial review in the area of civil liberties, the criticisms of judicial activism are problematic, as is the use of interpretivist and non-interpretivist theories to evaluate the Supreme Court.

The intentions of the framers can be divided into two general objectives: protecting rights and advancing national unity by highlighting what common values exist in Canada as a way to transcend regional identities.[59] Leaving the national unity function aside, the framers intended to strengthen the ability of the courts to protect rights, and they recognized that judicial review would play an important role in defining the scope of Charter provisions. In early writings, Trudeau articulated the new role envisioned for the courts under an entrenched Bill of Rights: "This will confer new and very important responsibilities on the courts because it will be up to the courts to interpret the Bill of Rights, to decide how much scope should be given to the protected rights and to what extent the power of government should be curtailed."[60] Tassé also identifies the expanded power of judicial review as a specific intention of the framers: "This was the original objective of the first advocates of a Charter of Rights entrenched in the Constitution. This move-ment never flagged in finally imposing its vision of things in 1982."[61] The interpretive intent of the framers for an empowered judiciary flies in the face of the criticism of judicial activism by conservative judicial critics.

In addition to its desire for a more activist judiciary, the Trudeau govern-ment also recognized that the DOJ would have to change its approach to rights litigation. In essence, three interrelated forms of activism were neces-sary for the success of the Charter. First, democratic activism on the part of Trudeau and his constitutional agenda, which culminated in the entrench-ment of the Charter. Second, judicial activism that would provide effective protections for civil liberties and avoid the fate of the Bill of Rights. Finally, legislative activism under the leadership of the DOJ, which would change the approach to civil liberties within the federal administrative apparatus.[62] For instance, the fate of the Bill of Rights was not simply the result of the Supreme Court continuing its restrained and deferential approach to judi-cial review. It was also the result of the DOJ continuing its pre-Bill of Rights approach to civil liberties, which, in effect, compounded the effect of judi-cial restraint with bureaucratic restraint. According to a former senior DOJ official:

> Our perception of what had happened under the Bill of Rights was that the Department of Justice had simply taken its traditional approach as the law-yer for the government to argue against almost all applications of the *Cana-dian Bill of Rights* if somebody was trying to use it to get in the way of the administration of federal laws. There was this sort of conflict in Justice be-tween the policy makers and the litigators. The litigators had their way under the Bill of Rights, resisting the application of the Bill of Rights. This was something we wanted to try and turn around because we said that the Charter of Rights and Freedoms was a very important part of government policy, and we were there to advance the policy of the government of Canada.[63]

This is significant, as conservative critics have contended that judicial ac-tivism is largely the discretionary choice of the courts. However, this is a debatable proposition, as other forms of activism preceded judicial activism and can serve as a justification for the court's new approach to rights. Even before the Supreme Court released its first Charter decision in 1984, the cabinet and bureaucratic actors under the direction of former prime minis-ter Trudeau had begun to advance an agenda of rights activism to condition the courts against judicial restraint and to discourage a continuation of the approach to judicial and bureaucratic review that existed under the Bill of Rights.

A Living Document

During the July 1980 meetings of the Continuing Committee of Ministers on the Constitution, Jean Chrétien revealed that the Trudeau government intended to avoid the problem of frozen rights by entrenching a broadly worded Charter that would allow the judiciary to play a decisive role in defining the content of rights as a way to allow for the continual evolution of their meaning: "It is essentially a drafting problem to ensure that entrenched rights will not be 'frozen.' If the Charter casts the rights in broad terms and contains a clause stating that the rights listed in the Charter are not exclusive, courts will have sufficient latitude to interpret the rights flexibly but subject to reasonable limitations."[64] An analysis of the drafters' testimony to the SJC after January 1981 demonstrates that the courts were conceptualized as important actors necessary to facilitate the emergence of a rights culture in Canada, and, from the beginning, the drafters envisioned the importance of complementary centres of rights activism in an effort to govern with the Charter. In my estimation, Russell's definition of judicial activism is therefore most appropriate in Canada, as it is described as "judicial vigour in enforcing constitutional limitations on the other branches of government on constitutional grounds."[65] In Chapter 2 it was suggested that the drafters sought a substantive document that could effectively protect rights in Canada, and the constitutional politics allowed the activist intentions of the Trudeau government to be entrenched at the expense of the interests of a majority of premiers. To ensure that this substantive document would be used effectively, the drafters took steps to ensure that parliamentary, judicial, and legislative actors would be vigorous in their approach to rights. Thus, the intention of the framers can generally be considered to be rights activism by those actors charged with governing with the Charter.

When questioned by NDP MP Svend Robinson about the precise test for determining whether a limitation was reasonable in a free and democratic society, Chrétien replied, during his first appearance before the SJC, "It will be the courts who will decide. The way I understand the courts to operate, the precedents will determine the next move. It will be the court because we are not giving them other tests than these."[66] This position was reinforced by Tassé, in a subsequent exchange with Robinson, when the deputy minister of justice acknowledged that the courts would define the test for reasonableness in section 1 of the Charter: "I would think that in effect the courts will read this as an objective test that is being spelled out in section one and that in effect they would have to address their mind as to whether the restrictions that are being challenged before the courts are generally acceptable ones in a democratic society."[67] This flexible interpretive approach was reiterated during Chrétien's subsequent appearance, when he justified the textual change in the reasonable limitations clause. During questioning by Senator Roblin, Chrétien was clear that the new approach expanded the ability of the courts to review the substantive dimension of legislation. Chrétien suggested the initial approach to section 1 was the result of provincial pressure and was ineffective, as "even if the law were passed – it was a danger before that it was almost impossible for the court to go behind a decision of a Parliament or a legislative assembly."[68] The justice minister informed the committee that the new approach to section 1 avoided the dangers of the *Canadian Bill of Rights* and removed many of the constraints placed on the courts in reviewing the legislative choices of parliament and the provincial legislatures for Charter compliance. Instead of choosing language that would serve to constrain judicial discretion, the framers adopted a general approach that would invariably increase the role of the courts after 1982.[69]

The recognition by the framers that the judiciary would play an activist and constructive role in shaping the Charter's meaning is evident in the testimony provided on the general remedies clause. Though the deputy minister of justice acknowledged that the 12 January 1981 draft Charter was silent on the admissibility of evidence, as the earlier reference to the rules of evidence had been deleted, the drafters did not intend the courts to be silent on this issue. Tassé told the SJC that "section 24 is drafted in such a way that in an appropriate case it would be possible for the court to decide that in effect the just remedy that the section refers to here would require that the evidence that has been illegally obtained be declared inadmissible in the proceedings before it."[70] Thus, the drafters were explicit that judicial discretion would play a legitimate role in constructing the meaning of "just and appropriate remedies," and they did not seek to constrain the interpretive role of the judiciary. The minister of justice was more explicit on the question of exclusion of evidence through section 24 despite the absence of instructive language in the general remedies clause: "We say that the court has the discretion to apply the appropriate remedy. It is up to the court to decide, I am not a judge. We gave the rights to the person to apply to the court and the court can grant a remedy. What kind of remedy I do not know what it might be, it is up to the courts to decide. I do not want to speculate at this moment."[71] Later in his testimony, Chrétien observed that the absence of an explicit exclusion-of-evidence rule did not prevent the courts from determining that evidence should be excluded: "It is up to the court to decide that the evidence has been gained against this, in spite of this provision in the constitution."[72] While the proposed resolution of 17 February 1981 included an explicit exclusion-of-evidence rule, the language employed left it to the discretion of the courts to determine whether the manner in which evidence was obtained brought the justice system into disrepute.

The most obvious example of the framers' demonstrating substantive intent for sections of the Charter is section 7, which covers the principles of fundamental justice. Conservative judicial critics have consistently pointed to the Supreme Court's decision to approach section 7 in a substantive manner as a violation of framers' intent, and they use this specific example to demonstrate the general departure from this principle.[73] In describing why the term "principles of fundamental justice" was adopted instead of "due process of law," the associate deputy minister of justice, Barry Strayer, indicated that the drafters wanted to avoid a substantive approach to section 7, which the American Supreme Court had interpreted "due process" to mean. Thus, the principles of fundamental justice were taken to mean simply administrative fairness, and judicial review involving section 7 was not to evaluate the substantive merits of challenged legislation.[74] In this regard, the critics are correct that the Supreme Court has violated framers' intent by attaching a substantive meaning to section 7 in *B.C. Motor Vehicle Reference*.[75] However, this is simply one example of the Supreme Court ignoring the substantive intent of the framers, and examples do exist of the Supreme Court respecting the specific substantive intent of the framers.

During the parliamentary hearings, the minister of justice was adamant that section 10(b) did not include the right to the provision of legal aid by the provincial governments. In his testimony, Chrétien stated that the drafters did not see this right as imposing a financial obligation on provincial governments, and he limited section 10(b) to simply the right to retain and instruct counsel: "What we are giving is the right, the right to counsel, it is as a basic right. How to pay for counsel, it is either the individual or legal aid and it is not a matter of the Charter, it is a matter of operation after the person accused has been informed of his rights."[76] In *R. v. Prosper*, the Supreme Court considered the claim that section 10(b) provided the right to free and immediate legal aid for those detained. In rejecting the attempt to expand the meaning of section 10(b), the court relied on the legislative record, which demonstrated the right was narrow in scope and excluded the right to legal aid.[77] While one case does not refute the position of conservative judicial critics that the court has ignored framers' intent, the extensive legislative record provides more than enough evidence that the framers sought to prevent a narrow approach to judicial review. Indeed, the minister of justice indicated during his testimony on 15 January 1981 that courts would be under no obligation to strictly adhere to the intention of the framers: "We must not underestimate the importance of this committee. When the courts are called upon to decide what the legislator's intention was, the lawyers and others studying the problem will obviously try to understand the intention of the legislator, but there is no obligation. The discussions we have had will not impose any obligations on them."[78] This statement does not indicate that the drafters were of the view that the courts would be the guardian of the constitution or that judicial actors possessed infallible wisdom. What is revealed are the deeply ingrained principles held by political actors in a parliamentary system that the judiciary is part of the constitutional order and advances the same values as other actors attempting to govern with the Charter in a way that reconciles parliamentary democracy and constitutional supremacy.

The issue of remedies for minority language rights violations by provincial governments further demonstrates the interpretive and policy role for the courts envisioned by the framers. The original approach to minority language education rights had been criticized before the SJC as too restrictive, as it limited the protection to educational facilities and, as late as the 3 September draft, it was provincial governments that determined whether sufficient numbers existed for the provision of minority language educational services out of public funds.[79] Manfredi has suggested that the construction of the sliding-scale approach to section 23(2) in *Mahé v. Alberta*[80] augmented judicial power: "What the 'sliding scale' mandates, however, cannot be known readily without judicial assistance, making possible a significant degree of judicial management of education policy through remedial decrees."[81] The legislative record demonstrates, however, that the framers intended for the courts to determine the remedies necessary to address section 23 violations by provincial governments and alluded to the sliding-scale approach that conservative critics have attacked as simply a judicial creation. Chrétien defended the substitution of the phrase "minority language education facilities" with "minority language instruction" in the 12 January resolution to broaden the educational services available to official language minorities when numbers warranted. He stated that they "wanted to broaden the scope so that minority language education would be offered in every case, either by the construction of schools or by other methods which might be developed."[82]

Conservative judicial critics further criticize the Charter for resulting in a forum shift in educational policy, and have argued that the Supreme Court has become "the de facto national school board for bilingual education."[83] This criticism is problematic because the legislative record indicates that the framers intentionally removed the provision of minority language education rights from the political arena and empowered the courts in this regard:

> The courts will decide and it would be out of the political arena, where the matter is sometimes dealt with by some people who do not comprehend or do not want to comprehend.
>
> I think we are rendering a great service to Canadians by taking some of these problems away from the political debate and allowing the matter to be debated, argued, coolly before the courts with precedents and so on.
>
> It will serve the population, in my judgement very well.[84]

While the provincial premiers disagreed with this assessment of section 23(1), as a majority were opposed to the amendment that saw the courts determine the appropriate remedy for a minority language rights violation, the main drafters of the Charter viewed this section and the increased role of the courts as essential for the effective protection of official language minorities.

During his initial appearance before the SJC, the minister of justice addressed the decision to transfer responsibility for the determination of minority language education services from the provincial legislatures to the courts: "We must have confidence in the courts. Having confidence in the provinces has not proved very satisfactory over time."[85] However, the inclusion of section 23(1) in the final draft, and the "where numbers warrant approach," was not simply imposed on the provincial governments, but was modelled after the intergovernmental agreement on minority language rights reached at St. Andrews-by-the-Sea during the Annual Premiers' Conference.[86] Even the sliding-scale approach to section 23(1), though it required judicial discretion in determining the level of services to provide, was anticipated to be driven principally by political decisions, and judicial leadership would only occur if political leaders failed to provide comparable services.[87] In this respect, the framers expected that the courts would function as a policy actor in minority language education and keep abreast of provincial approaches to section 23(1) in determining the type of services to provide based on the number of official language minorities. As the minister of justice testified on 11 December 1980, "it cannot be reasonably expected that one family should warrant one school so that their children may receive instruction in the language of their choice at prohibitive costs. With this mechanism, Mr. Corbin, the courts will be able to interpret the situation in English Canada based on the situation in Quebec. The more generous Quebec is towards its Anglophone minority, the more often the courts will be able to use the Quebec precedent to impose criteria on French speaking minority groups elsewhere in Canada."[88]

The most criticized element of Charter review by the Supreme Court has been the remedies used by the Supreme Court, and the criticism has focused on the ability of the courts to create tests that advance judicial power and policy discretion. The legislative history demonstrates that the dichotomy between law and politics that has been used to criticize judicial activism by the Supreme Court is problematic, as the major framers were not troubled by the increased policy role required for the courts under the Charter. The framers politicized the judiciary by entrenching a Charter that explicitly invited judicial discretion and policy choices through constitutional remedies for rights violations.

Equality Rights and Substantive Intent

The strongest criticism of the Supreme Court's approach to Charter review has centred on its equality rights jurisprudence. The general criticism is that the Supreme Court has adopted an expansive approach that allows it to directly participate in political debates and to advance its agenda in the area of social policy.[89] Indeed, conservative judicial critics find fault with this approach to section 15(1), suggesting that the court has independently adopted a substantive approach to equality rights jurisprudence.[90] The issue involves the question of whether this approach to section 15(1) is justified either by the text of the Charter or by the intention of its framers. This issue is particularly relevant in the area of the court's equality rights jurisprudence, as judicial amendment of section 15(1) occurred in *Egan v. Canada* when the court recognized that sexual orientation was analogous to the enumerated categories of equality rights protections in the Charter.[91]

Though the court's equality rights jurisprudence has received intense condemnation from these critics, it is suggested here that the strongest defence of judicial activism can be mounted by relying on the court's approach to section 15(1). Specifically, both the intention of the framers and the wording of section 15(1) that gave textual expression to this new approach to civil liberties illustrate that Trudeau and the federal officials under his leadership saw section 15(1), and judicial activism in this particular area, as essential to avoid the fate of the Bill of Rights. Indeed, my argument takes issue with the assumption that it was an independent choice of the court to adopt a substantive approach to equality rights. Rather, the framers of the Charter signalled to the court that the formal approach to equality rights in the Bill of Rights would not be acceptable under the Charter. The decision by the court to recognize sexual orientation as analogous to the enumerated categories of section 15(1), in effect, finds its justification in both the new role envisioned for the court by the framers of the Charter, and the open-ended language of section 15(1) that provided the textual guidance for the court to approach equality rights in an expansive manner.

Earlier in this chapter it was stated that the Charter of Rights can be interpreted as an explicit rejection of the Bill of Rights, both textually and in the framers' preference for a new approach to judicial review. This is particularly true in the case of section 15(1), where the wording was intended to overcome the formal approach to equality rights in the Bill of Rights, which had reduced the value of this statutory protection. For instance, Roger Tassé has articulated the purpose behind section 15(1) that can justify the court's activism in this area: "Take, for example, the equality principles, section 15, where it was very clear; the Department and the Committee had done their utmost to ensure that the text of section 15 would be drafted in such a way that the decisions of the Supreme Court in *Lavell* and *Bliss* would quite simply be reversed."[92] This is significant, as conservative judicial critics have suggested that the decision to move beyond formal equality toward a jurisprudence of substantive equality was a decision made independently by the

Supreme Court. Indeed, these Charter critics reinforce their preference for the restrained and deferential approach to judicial review that characterized the court's Bill of Rights jurisprudence, an approach that is now characteristic of the United States Supreme Court. According to Manfredi, "the US approach to equality under the Rehnquist Court represented a return to the doctrine of formal equality, which the Canadian Supreme Court has abandoned under the Charter."[93] For Charter critics, then, it was the court that made the shift from formal to substantive equality under the Charter, and according to this view, this represents the boldest attempt by the court to shift political power toward itself.

However, the court embraced a substantive approach to equality rights because this was clearly the intention of the document's framers. Specifically, the early draft of the Charter closely mirrored the equality rights protections found in the Bill of Rights, as the initial draft of section 15(1) only protected equality before the law and equal protection of the law, thus continuing the formal approach to equality that existed before 1982.[94] This approach was eventually abandoned in favour of a more substantive one that protected equality before and under the law, and equal protection and equal benefit of the law. Further, the framers of the Charter included very expansive language in drafting section 15(1), as the prohibited grounds of discrimination included both enumerated categories and those analogous to those listed in section 15(1). The significance of this new approach to equality rights is that the language of section 15(1) would require judicial modification and expansion of section 15(1) when the court determined that a basis of discrimination was analogous to those enumerated under equality rights.

The background notes of the federal government delegation for the 5 July 1980 meeting of the Continuing Committee of Ministers on the Constitution indicate that the principal framers intended that this section, like the rest of the Charter, would be flexible enough to allow for judicial expansion of the text and would avoid a "frozen rights" approach. According to Chrétien, the inclusion of the phrase "analogous grounds" was a reflection of the difficulty in creating enumerated categories: "Because it has been very difficult to reach an agreement on a complete enumeration of these grounds, the federal 'discussion draft' includes a general clause rather than a list."[95] In defending the amendment to section 15(1) that saw the federal government accept the wording that is now entrenched in the Charter, Chrétien clearly stated that the framers intended the court to approach equality rights in a substantive manner because "equality relates to the substance as well as the administration of the law," and further, "a provision on 'equality rights' must demonstrate that there is a positive principle of equality in the general sense and, in addition, a right to laws which assure equal protection and equal benefits without discrimination."[96]

Chrétien's comments directly challenge the view that it was an independent decision by the Supreme Court to take a substantive approach to equality rights. Further, the justice minister's discussion of the rationale behind including analogous grounds in section 15(1) reinforces the position that the framers intended that the activist constitution would require an activist court. For instance, in stating that the enumerated grounds for equality rights protections were not exclusive, Chrétien indicated that it would be legitimate for the courts to demonstrate leadership in those areas where legislatures refused to act: "But if legislatures do not act, there should be room for the courts to move in. Therefore, the amendment, which I mentioned, does not list certain grounds of discrimination to the exclusion of others. Rather, it is open-ended and meets the recommendations made by many witnesses before your Committee. Because of the difficulty of identifying legitimate new grounds for discrimination in a rapidly evolving area of the law, I prefer to be open-ended rather than adding some new categories with the risk of excluding others."[97]

During a later discussion of equality rights protections, Roger Tassé elaborated on the important role for the courts envisioned by the framers in expanding the prohibited grounds of discrimination through judicial review: "We also think that, in effect, the way in which the clause is structured, it would be open to the court to add to the list if they were placed before a situation where, in effect, there were any grounds other than those which are specifically mentioned, and they would come to a conclusion that this is an unreasonable distinction, that should not be condoned and it would be open to them to declare that there is discrimination that is not acceptable."[98]

In effect, the drafters of the Charter sanctioned judicial expansion of section 15(1) through the analogous grounds of equality rights protections. What remains to be determined, therefore, is whether this expansive approach to equality rights entrenched by the framers can support the court's decision in *Egan* to extend equality rights protections to sexual orientation.

Judicial Activism and Sexual Orientation

The SJC debated whether to include sexual orientation as an enumerated category for equality rights protections, ultimately rejecting the motion presented by Svend Robinson.[99] This has been taken as conclusive evidence that the framers of the Charter explicitly rejected sexual orientation as a prohibited ground for discrimination, and so the court's decision to interpret sexual orientation as analogous to the enumerated protections is a direct violation of framers' intent.[100] While this position does have merit, two factors suggest that the inclusion of sexual orientation by the Supreme Court can be justified as consistent with the general intent of the framers. First, a closer analysis of the SJC suggests that it excluded sexual orientation largely because it posed a drafting difficulty. Barry Strayer, the same individual conservative critics rely on to demonstrate that the Supreme Court has departed from framers' intent in its approach to section 7, has concluded, "I do not think that *Egan* really commits much damage to section 15(1)."[101] Second, democratic activism in the area of sexual orientation had preceded judicial activism in *Egan, Vriend v. Alberta,* and *M. v. H.,*[102] as most provinces (seven out of ten) had amended their human rights codes to include sexual orientation as a protected ground before the court amended Alberta's human rights code in 1998.[103] Janet Hiebert contends that "governments in most jurisdictions have shown little inclination to introduce legislative reforms until judicial rulings make it clear that the status quo cannot be constitutionally sustained."[104] Indeed, soon after the *Vriend* decision, all provincial human rights codes were amended to include sexual orientation as part of their equality rights protections, thus illustrating Hiebert's point on the necessity of judicial activism in this policy area, as the *Canadian Human Rights Act* was not amended to include protection for sexual orientation until 1996, after the *Egan* decision.

Turning first to the legislative record, the Trudeau government appeared reluctant to include new grounds of discrimination, preferring instead to enumerate traditional categories in section 15(1). Specifically, Chrétien stated that new categories of discrimination could be added to section 15(1) once they matured, both in terms of Canadians' acceptance of these new prohibited grounds and, more importantly for the framers of the Charter, after more precise definitions of these categories emerged:

> There are a lot of rights that will evolve in the society, will mature in the society, and will be capable of precise definition so as to be in a Charter of Rights, but in the meantime, the evolution of these rights will be measured and bring about into Parliament through the Bill of Rights, through the Human Rights Bill that will come outside of the Bill of Rights, because the Human Rights Commission will still be there, will analyze the problems, the evolution of society ... So these things have to mature, to find their place in a Charter of Rights, but in the meantime, the Human Rights Commission will be called upon to follow up the evolution and the drafting and the regulations, and so on, that it will be easier in the future.[105]

This statement by the justice minister is telling and illustrates the interinstitutional relationship for the definition of Charter values envisioned by the main drafters of the Charter. The Trudeau government did not intend the courts to be the guardians of the constitution, but it saw the expansion of Charter rights to be an institutional process whereby human rights commissions, legislative actors, and the courts contributed to the development of rights jurisprudence.

When asked to provide a definition for sexual orientation during a later appearance before the SJC, Chrétien refused to include sexual orientation in the enumerated categories of equality rights protections, not because it was considered an unacceptable basis for protection, but because the framers did not believe that sexual orientation had attained the maturity or level of definition needed for it to be entrenched as an enumerated equality right. Chrétien said, "I am not here as a judge to determine what marital status means, what sexual orientation means. It is because of the problem of the definition of those words that we do not think they should be in the constitution."[106] These statements have been interpreted to mean that the framers rejected sexual orientation as an enumerated category of equality rights protection and that, as a result, the court should have refused to recognize it as an analogous ground in *Egan*. However, as Chrétien's comments suggest, the framers simply intended sexual orientation to be excluded at that time, but they did not foreclose the possibility of updating equality rights to include sexual orientation through judicial review and the analogous grounds approach to section 15(1). In fact, the potential amendment of section 15(1) by the judiciary to include sexual orientation was confirmed by Robert Kaplan, who, as solicitor general of Canada, appeared on behalf of Chrétien. When asked by Svend Robinson whether "it would be open to a court to proscribe discrimination on the grounds of marital status, political belief, sexual orientation and disability,"[107] Kaplan reiterated the Trudeau government's position that the enumerated grounds of equality rights simply represented traditional categories, and that the evolution of Canadian society would justify judicial amendment of the enumerated categories: "I think there might be found a consensus among Canadians that these grounds which are enumerated are those which have the highest degree of recognition in Canadian society as being rights which ought to be recognized and the general statement gives the possibility down the road not only of those on Mr. Robinson's list being recognized, but of others which may not have occurred to him of being included in the future as being unacceptable grounds of discrimination."[108]

An alternative analysis of the SJC and the issue of sexual orientation has been provided by Morton, who, after reviewing the transcripts, concludes that "not only is sexual orientation not protected by section 15, there is a clear legislative history that the framers purposely excluded it."[109] However, the framers of the Charter did not permanently exclude sexual orientation from section 15(1), and the legislative history indicates that both framers' intent and the text of section 15(1) allowed judicial amendment of the Charter. There is, however, an additional justification for judicial activism in the area of equality rights and its extension to include sexual orientation. Specifically, the framers stressed that new categories of protection could be included when more precise definitions emerged and when new grounds attained the necessary maturity to be added to the Charter. The legislative record suggests that a large majority of provinces came to the conclusion that sexual orientation had met both these conditions before the *Egan* decision in 1995. In particular, human rights codes had been amended in seven provinces – all except Alberta, Newfoundland, and Prince Edward Island – to include equality protections for sexual orientation before the Supreme Court recognized it as analogous to section 15(1) in *Egan,* and, subsequently, before the court read sexual orientation into the *Individual's Rights Protection Act (IRPA)* of Alberta in the 1998 *Vriend* decision. In effect, judicial activism in the area of sexual orientation and equality rights followed democratic activism at the political level, suggesting that both framers' intent and subsequent political developments in this policy area provide a justification for the Supreme Court's approach to judicial review in general and its equality rights jurisprudence in particular.

The *Vriend* decision resulted in intense criticism from conservative judicial analysts such as Morton, who has questioned whether the Supreme Court can declare legislative inaction to be unconstitutional. I dispute this interpretation and the suggestion by Morton that the "government, reflecting the public opinion of its constituents, has chosen to remain neutral on the issue of homosexuality. Its laws, including the AHRA, neither punish nor reward homosexual behaviour. They are silent."[110] In December 1992 the Alberta Human Rights Commission (AHRC) decided to investigate the discrimination claims of gays and lesbians, but was soon ordered, by ministerial instruction, to abandon this investigation.[111] The Alberta government, therefore, did not remain silent or neutral on this issue, but prevented the AHRC from investigating claims of discrimination on the basis that the *IRPA* did not recognize sexual orientation. In March 1993 the government of Alberta appointed a new chief commissioner of the AHRC with a mandate to review the act and to make recommendations, a task that was completed in June 1994. In the final report the AHRC recognized the polarizing nature of sexual orientation, but recommended that "sexual orientation be included among the grounds listed in the IRPA on which people are protected against discrimination, and that this protection apply to all areas, i.e. employment, tenancy and public services."[112] Thus, the provincially appointed human rights commission, after soliciting the views of Albertans beyond the constituency that supports the Progressive Conservative Party, foreshadowed the decision by the Supreme Court in *Vriend v. Alberta* that the *IRPA* be amended to include sexual orientation. In a written response to the commission, the Alberta government stated it would wait until the Supreme Court released its decision in *Vriend* before deciding how to reply to the commission's recommendation.[113]

It is questionable, therefore, whether the court's decision in *Vriend* illustrates the dangers of judicial supremacy or the illegitimacy of activist judicial review. Like the AHRC, the Supreme Court was simply reacting to Albertans' desire to increase the scope of the *IRPA* to provide gays and lesbians with the opportunity to challenge discrimination in areas protected by the act, though public opinion was divided on this controversial issue. Perhaps more importantly, the court's activism is legitimate because it satisfies the former federal justice minister's criterion for judicial expansion of section 15(1) – when legislatures refuse to act.[114] Thus, legislative inaction, from the beginning, has been a legitimate area of constitutional review for the Supreme Court. Miriam Smith has concluded that "policy in the area of lesbian and gay rights has been driven by litigation," but this overlooks the important role of the AHRC in its review of the *IRPA* and its recommendation regarding the inclusion of sexual orientation.[115] Indeed, the Supreme Court responded to the recommendation of the AHRC, and this suggests that public consultation and institutions are the driving forces behind the expansion of human rights protections for gays and lesbians. In this sense, the court has not led in this policy field but has followed the recommendations of democratically appointed institutions.

Conclusion

The Charter of Rights, in its design, objectives, and the intention of its framers, was a fundamental rejection of the Bill of Rights, both as a document and in the courts' approach to judicial review involving civil liberties. The legislative record of the SJC does not reveal that the framers sought to restrict either the scope of the Charter or the role of the courts by requiring a precise following of the text by judicial actors. On the contrary, the legislative record reveals that the framers sought a flexible document that would avoid the limitations of the "frozen rights" approach that emerged in the Supreme Court's Bill of Rights jurisprudence. Thus, a central intention of the main drafters of the Charter was to empower judicial actors as part of the inter-institutional activism necessary to ensure that the Charter would become a substantive document. The main limitation of the suggestion that judicial review that has expanded the meaning of the Charter or has resulted in the creation of discretionary judicial tests is a violation of framers' intent is that it cannot, outside very few examples, be supported by the extensive legislative record of the SJC.

In challenging this position of conservative judicial critics, I have argued that they prioritize the views of individuals who do not constitute the main drafters of the Charter. Their position on framers' intent requires an analysis of the Charter and its textual evolution without reference to the political events that preceded its entrenchment. My intention in viewing the entrenchment of the Charter as an exercise in constitutional politics was to understand this project as essentially a political battle in which resources were used by competing actors with differing agendas and where certain interests dominated. After they succeeded in entrenching an activist document, the framers then turned to the role of the courts in interpreting the Charter. Indeed, an implicit assumption that emerged from the SJC was that the courts and activist judicial review would be a necessity to avoid the fate of the Bill of Rights. However, the framers did not envision the courts as the sole guardian of the constitution but as part of the overall process of rights activism that would emerge once political, bureaucratic, and judicial actors recognized the fundamental differences from the Bill of Rights and began to govern with the Charter. The activist constitution required an activist court, and the framers' recognized this during the proceedings of the SJC, where judicial discretion was provided for and legitimized in the final version of the Charter.

Part 2
Judicial Activism and the Supreme Court of Canada

4
The Supreme Court and Police Conduct

The Supreme Court's activist approach to legal rights has been an unexpected element of Charter review, and a development that has generated both praise and tremendous criticism.[1] While the framers of the Charter focused on the importance of entrenching minority language and education rights, equality rights, and mobility rights, these have not been the focus of the court's Charter review, as nearly two-thirds of decisions between 1982 and 2003 have involved legal rights.[2] Further, most of the instances of judicial activism have centred on these rights, and the exclusion of evidence under section 24(2) of the Charter has seen the court emerge as an important policy actor through the creation of a discretionary test that determines whether the gathering of evidence undermines the reputation of justice.[3] The impact of judicial review on the administration of justice, particularly its effect on the police, trial procedures, and the rights of the accused, is a significant aspect of the inter-institutional relationships created under the Charter. The reality is that the Supreme Court is more likely to check the discretionary conduct of unelected actors, such as the police, than it is to challenge the policy preferences of cabinets at the federal or provincial level, as a majority of constitutional challenges involve the conduct of public officials, such as the police and customs officers.[4]

This leads to an important research inquiry that has so far been overlooked in the decision to focus on the cabinet, the Supreme Court, and the pursuit of a rights-based dialogue through legislative responses to invalidated statutes.[5] Specifically, does the implication of judicial activism vary depending on the state actor at the centre of a Charter challenge? Can judicial activism, by checking the discretionary conduct of the police, a largely autonomous state actor, deepen constitutional supremacy by redefining the relationship between citizens and state actors through an activist legal rights jurisprudence? This chapter argues that judicial activism in the area of legal rights has been a significant development that enforces a constitutional requirement under section 52 of the *Constitution Act* that all actors – judicial, political, bureaucratic, and legal – must govern with the Charter. This activist legal rights jurisprudence has deepened constitutional supremacy because it has required those exercising power on behalf of the state to do so in a manner consistent with the Charter.[6] Constitutional supremacy has been advanced by evaluating the actions of the police against an entrenched Charter of Rights that allows for the exclusion of evidence when police officers violate the legal rights of Canadians.[7] Paradoxically, then, activism on the part of an unelected judiciary can serve as a check against another unelected actor and can strengthen the relationship between citizens and the state in a democratic society.[8] However, judicial activism in the area of legal rights does not facilitate judicial supremacy simply because it has challenged common-law constraints on police conduct and the crime control approach to criminal procedure.[9] The movement away from the crime control model was not a judicial choice but the result of political decisions that strengthened the legal rights provisions in the draft Charter.[10] As demonstrated in Chapter 2, the legislative record indicates that the attempt to preserve the crime control model was rejected by the framers through a significant revision of legal rights provisions and the inclusion of an explicit constitutional remedy for excluding evidence, section 24(2), as one of the last amendments to the draft Charter.[11]

The court's approach to legal rights demonstrates its acceptance that it is simply one guardian of the constitution and shares this responsibility with actors and institutions responsible for the proper administration of justice. In this regard, judicial activism in the area of legal rights has not been as revolutionary as commentators have contended.[12] The balanced approach to legal rights has been inherently Canadian and consistent with the intention of the framers to move away from the crime control approach but to avoid the excesses of the American due process model.[13] Indeed, critical commentary has concluded that judicial activism has resulted in a clear shift to due process by focusing on the rights of the accused, and that this has come at the expense of victims' rights, which are best protected under the crime control model, as this model places primary emphasis on the investigative techniques of the police and their efficiency in securing guilty pleas.[14] Under the crime control model, the police, who work in conjunction with Crown prosecutors, are provided with wide- and far-reaching investigative techniques that serve to filter out factually weak cases and secure convictions through guilty pleas during the investigative process.[15] In contrast, the due process model favours the use of "formal, adjudicative, adversary fact-finding processes in which the factual case against the accused is publicly heard by an impartial tribunal."[16] This model emphasizes the importance of procedural rights available to the accused, such as the right to counsel and the right to silence, and emphasizes that the waiving of these rights must be voluntary, and the consequences truly appreciated by an individual, to be valid. In effect, the due process model emphasizes the importance of a fair trial by protecting the accused against self-incrimination and erects a set of procedural safeguards that the police must respect during their investigations.

The Supreme Court has advanced important elements of both models in its legal rights jurisprudence, and this has led Kent Roach to suggest that "due process was at times for crime control and victims' rights."[17] Don Stuart has been more forceful in his contention that this approach severely weakens the level of protection available to the accused.[18] The difficulty with this position is that it advocates a level of judicial activism that would require the court to adopt the American approach to due process and an automatic exclusion-of-evidence rule. The Charter was not intended to create a due process revolution, but to alter the common-law approach that placed minimal procedural requirements on the police when interrogating subjects or investigating crime. Thus, the framers sought to infuse the crime control model with elements of due process, and this has been the outcome of the court's approach to legal rights and judicial remedies under section 24(2) of the Charter, the exclusion-of-evidence remedy. The claims that excessive judicial activism has resulted in a paradigm shift to due process are not correct in the context of the court's balanced approach to legal rights and the judicial remedies under the Charter.[19]

In this chapter, I argue that the balanced approach to legal rights has seen the Supreme Court place important procedural requirements on the police when dealing with suspects but that this has not undermined the legitimate objectives of law enforcement and crime control. More emphasis has been placed on informing individuals of their legal rights, such as the right to counsel and the right against self-incrimination, and judicial activism has been vigilant in preventing the police from circumventing these protections.[20] However, once the police have dispensed these rights, the Supreme Court has been generally supportive of the actions by the police during criminal investigations and has been motivated to provide the conditions necessary for the accused to receive a fair trial.[21] Indeed, the Supreme Court has been willing to accept that the police acted in "good faith" and that minor procedural violations of Charter rights do not warrant the exclusion of evidence under section 24(2) of the Charter. A balanced approach, intended to ensure that the administration of justice is respected and the reputation of justice is protected during criminal investigations, has been the result of judicial review of legal rights since 1982.

Stirred but Not Shaken: Crime Control with Due Process

The distinction between crime control and due process models of criminal procedure is attributable to Herbert Packer and his work forty years ago.[22]

While this distinction endures, it has been criticized as increasingly irrelevant because of its inability to accommodate victims' rights and issues of restorative justice in modern approaches to criminal procedure.[23] Critics arguing that the Supreme Court has ensured a due process revolution by its activist legal rights jurisprudence have focused on the procedural rights provided to the accused through successful challenges to the common-law and Criminal Code provisions dealing with trial procedures in sexual assault cases such as *Seaboyer v. The Queen, R. v. Daviault, R. v. O'Connor, R. v. Carosella* and *R. v. Mills*.[24] In *Seaboyer v. The Queen,* the court ruled that the restrictions in section 276 of the Criminal Code, which prevented the defence from using the complainant's sexual history with third parties, violated the right to a fair trial, as the provision of the Criminal Code had "the potential to exclude otherwise admissible evidence which may in certain cases be relevant to the defense."[25] In *R. v. Daviault,* the Supreme Court ruled that the common-law restrictions on the defence of extreme intoxication for specific intent offences violated the presumption of innocence protected under section 7 and 11(d), as extreme intoxication, in certain cases, may be used as a defence in specific intent offences.[26]

At issue in *R. v. O'Connor* and *R. v. Carosella* was the duty to disclose therapeutic records held by third parties in sexual assault cases, which the court ruled must be made available to protect the section 7 rights of the accused to a full answer and defence.[27] Where the court divided was on the test for determining the rules for disclosure, thus suggesting the emergence of due process principles because of the use of judicially determined rules governing a significant aspect of trial procedures in sexual assault cases.[28] In disputing Hiebert's position that the court has accepted parliament's attempt to re-establish legislative control over the rules of disclosure to protect the victim in sexual assault cases in *R. v. Mills,*[29] Manfredi has argued that the "Court did not defer to legislative judgement in Mills, but merely affirmed a policy that four of its own members had constructed in 1995."[30] While elements of due process have emerged in trial procedures, it would require a fundamental change in the relationship between the police and the accused for a paradigm shift to occur. Indeed, a due process shift in trial procedures may be irrelevant if crime control endures in the relationship between the police and individuals during criminal investigations. The shift to due process, therefore, cannot simply be the outcome of judicially determined tests governing trial procedures, but is more influenced by the impact of judicial review on those sections of the Charter governing the conduct of police officers and other agents of law enforcement.

To demonstrate that the outcome of judicial review involving legal rights has been consistent with framers' intent, as its purpose was to infuse crime control with elements of due process, I will focus on Supreme Court decisions that regulate the conduct of the police through sections 7 to 10 and

24(2) of the Charter, as well as section 11(b) and the requirement that trials be held within a reasonable time. The test for each remedy created by the court incorporates due process and crime control considerations, and balancing these considerations has allowed the Supreme Court to take an approach to legal rights that protects the administration of justice and the rights of the accused. The judicial remedy governing the exclusion of evidence under section 24(2) is a three-part test referred to as the *Collins* test after the decision in which the court established the rules.[31] Under the *Collins* test, the court balances the following considerations: first, the effect of the evidence on the fairness of the trial; second, the seriousness of the Charter violation by the police; and finally, the effect of excluding the evidence on the reputation of justice.

Between 1982 and 2003, the Supreme Court considered the exclusion of evidence in seventy-nine cases where it determined that legal rights had been violated by the actions of the police. However, as shown in Table 4.1, evidence has been excluded in only 44 percent (35 out of 79) of section 24(2) cases in this twenty-one-year period, which challenges the conclusion that judicial activism in legal rights cases has seen a paradigm shift to due process. During the 1993 to 2003 period, the court has only excluded evidence in 38 percent (15 out of 40) of cases, suggesting that the initial activist approach to section 24(2) also coincided with the highly activist approach by the court, which has not proved to be characteristic of the long-term approach to Charter review.[32] Indeed, the *Collins* test is not an automatic exclusionary rule but a flexible test that sees the court consider factors, in addition to the rights violation, that can justify including evidence obtained through a violation of legal rights. The Supreme Court has indicated that the reputation of justice can be undermined by admitting evidence produced by Charter violations but also by excluding evidence in cases that would shock the public. What the empirical evidence suggests, however, is that the court has been more disposed to support the actions of the police when they gather evidence in a manner that infringes the Charter, and this illustrates that crime control has endured but has been modified by elements of due process. As a result, criminal procedure has been stirred but not shaken by the Charter's introduction.

In using the *Collins* test, the court has generally applied due process and crime control considerations depending on the nature of evidence gathered that violates specific legal rights. For instance, the court has ruled that "real evidence" such as narcotics, weapons, and other physical evidence gathered during criminal investigations does not undermine the fairness of the trial, as it exists independent of a rights violation and would normally be discovered by the police.[33] Thus, the principle of inevitable discoverability supports the investigative techniques of the police and advances the objectives of crime control, as the exclusion of real evidence generally occurs

Table 4.1

Exclusion of evidence, 1982 to 2003

Case	Evidence	Category
Evidence excluded		
1 *R. v. Therens*, [1985]	Breath samples	Conscripted
2 *R. v. Trask*, [1985]	Breath samples	Conscripted
3 *Rahn v. The Queen*, [1985]	Breath sample	Conscripted
4 *R. v. Clarkson*, [1986]	Incriminating statements	Conscripted
5 *R. v. Collins*, [1987]	Narcotics	Real
6 *R. v. Pohoretsky*, [1987]	Blood samples	Conscripted
7 *R. v. Manninen*, [1987]	Incriminating statements	Conscripted
8 *R. v. Dyment*, [1988]	Blood samples	Conscripted
9 *R. v. Ross (Leclair)*, [1989]	Police lineup	Conscripted
10 *R. v. Genest*, [1989]	Weapon	Real
11 *R. v. Leduc*, [1989]	Breath sample	Conscripted
12 *R. v. Black*, [1989]	Incriminating statements	Conscripted
13 *R. v. Brydges*, [1990]	Incriminating statements	Conscripted
14 *R. v. Greffe*, [1990]	Narcotics	Real
15 *R. v. Hebert*, [1990]	Incriminating statements	Conscripted
16 *R. v. Kokesch*, [1990]	Narcotics	Real
17 *R. v. Evans*, [1991]	Incriminating statements	Conscripted
18 *R. v. Elshaw*, [1991]	Incriminating statements	Conscripted
19 *R. v. Broyles*, [1991]	Incriminating statements	Conscripted
20 *R. v. Mellenthin*, [1992]	Narcotics	Real
21 *R. v. Dersch*, [1993]	Blood sample	Conscripted
22 *R. v. Borden*, [1994]	Hair and blood samples	Conscripted
23 *R. v. Bartle*, [1994]	Incriminating statements	Conscripted
24 *R. v. Prosper*, [1994]	Breath samples	Conscripted
25 *R. v. Pozniak*, [1994]	Breath samples	Conscripted
26 *R. v. Cobham*, [1994]	Refusal to provide breath samples	Conscripted
27 *R. v. Burlingham*, [1995]	Incriminating statements	Conscripted
28 *R. v. Burlingham*, [1995]	Weapon	Real
29 *R. v. Calder*, [1996]	Incriminating statements	Conscripted
30 *R. v. Stillman*, [1997]	Teeth impressions, hair samples, swabs	Conscripted
31 *R. v. Feeney*, [1997]	Incriminating statements, fingerprints	Conscripted
32 *R. v. Feeney*, [1997]	Bloody shirt, shoes, cigarettes, money	Non-conscripted
33 *R. v. Cook*, [1998]	Incriminating statements	Conscripted
34 *R. v. Law*, [2002]	Photocopies of tax information	Non-conscripted
35 *R. v. Buhay*, [2003]	Narcotics	Non-conscripted

▶

◄ *Table 4.1*

Case	Evidence	Category
Evidence included		
1 *R. v. Sieben*, [1987]	Narcotics	Real
2 *R. v. Hamil*, [1987]	Narcotics	Real
3 *R. v. Tremblay*, [1987]	Breath sample	Conscripted
4 *R. v. Simmons*, [1988]	Narcotics	Real
5 *R. v. Jacoy*, [1988]	Narcotics	Real
6 *R. v. Strachan*, [1988]	Narcotics	Real
7 *R. v. Black*, [1989]	Weapon	Real
8 *R. v. Mohl*, [1989]	Breath sample	Conscripted
9 *R. v. Lamb*, [1989]	Narcotics	Real
10 *R. v. Debot*, [1989]	Narcotics	Real
11 *R. v. Duarte*, [1990]	Electronic surveillance	Conscripted
12 *R. v. Schmautz*, [1990]	Refusal to submit to Breathalyzer	Conscripted
13 *R. v. Thompson*, [1990]	Private communication	Conscripted
14 *R. v. Wong*, [1990]	Electronic surveillance	Conscripted
15 *R. v. Tessier*, [1991]	Breath samples	Conscripted
16 *R. v. Smith*, [1991]	Statements	Conscripted
17 *R. v. Wise*, [1992]	Metal fragments	Real
18 *R. v. Duncanson*, [1992]	Narcotics	Real
19 *R. v. Généreux*, [1992]	Narcotics	Real
20 *R. v. Goncalves*, [1993]	Narcotics	Real
21 *R. v. Erickson*, [1993]	Blood samples	Conscripted
22 *R. v. Grant*, [1993]	Narcotics	Real
23 *R. v. Wiley*, [1993]	Narcotics	Real
24 *R. v. Plant*, [1993]	Narcotics	Real
25 *R. v. Yorke*, [1993]	Cultural property	Real
26 *R. v. I. (L.R.) and T. (E.)*, [1993]	Involuntary statements	Conscripted
27 *R. v. Harper*, [1994]	Voluntary statements	Conscripted
28 *R. v. Colarusso*, [1994]	Blood and urine samples	Conscripted
29 *R. v. Patriquen*, [1995]	Narcotics	Real
30 *R. v. McIntyre*, [1995]	Voluntary statements	Conscripted
31 *R. v. Silveria*, [1995]	Narcotics	Real
32 *R. v. Wijesinha*, [1995]	Tapes	Real
33 *R. v. Harrer*, [1995]	Voluntary statements	Conscripted
34 *R. v. Evans*, [1996]	Narcotics	Real
35 *R. v. Dewald*, [1996]	Breath samples	Conscripted
36 *R. v. Edwards*, [1996]	Narcotics	Real
37 *R. v. Martin*, [1996]	Narcotics	Real
38 *R. v. Goldhart*, [1996]	Narcotics	Real
39 *R. v. Knox*, [1996]	Blood samples	Conscripted
40 *R. v. Keshane*, [1996]	Narcotics	Real
41 *R. v. Belnavis*, [1997]	Clothing	Real
42 *R. v. Soloman*, [1997]	Telephone conversation	Conscripted
43 *R. v. Caslake*, [1998]	Narcotics	Real
44 *R. v. Fliss*, [2002]	Recorded confession	Non-conscripted

when the rights violation has been so flagrant as to necessitate its exclusion to protect the reputation of justice.[34] "Conscripted evidence," on the other hand, is considered to be manufactured through a rights violation, such as when an individual is unable to exercise the right to counsel and the police obtain a confession that leads to conviction. "Conscription" is the "term compendiously describing the process which, contrary to adjudicative fairness, involves an agent of the state, without lawful authority meeting constitutional prerequisites, extracting from a detainee or a 'person charged' evidence which owes its existence to the conscription process. In effect, it is a situation where the detainee or 'person charged' is being compelled to self-incriminate."[35] Examples of conscripted evidence include incriminating statements made by the accused in the absence of counsel, statements made without a valid waiver of Charter rights, Breathalyzer samples, blood samples, and samples of other bodily fluids seized by the police without prior authorization.

This distinction endured until 1997, when, in *R. v. Stillman,* real evidence was reclassified as non-conscripted because the court determined the existing distinction was unsuitable in situations where real evidence, like DNA samples, was taken without consent or by force. In this decision, the majority stated that evidence would be conscripted "when an accused, in violation of his Charter rights, is compelled to incriminate himself at the behest of the state by means of a statement, the use of the body or the production of body samples."[36] Only Justice L'Heureux-Dubé failed to find that Stillman's right against search and seizure was violated and that the sanctity of the person was violated by taking samples by force.

Even when the court decides whether to exclude real/non-conscripted evidence under the second part of the *Collins* test, the determining factor is not the due process rights of the accused but the seriousness of police action that produced the rights violation. The court has refused to exclude real evidence produced by minor rights violation, accepting that the police acted in "good faith" and did not intend to circumvent Charter rights.[37] For the most part, crime control endures under section 24(2) in terms of real evidence, as the court has excluded real evidence gathered in violation of the Charter only nine times between 1982 and 2003 because the rights violations were considered so serious that the reputation of justice required such a remedy. This demonstrates the complexity of the court's approach and how, due to the distinct elements of the *Collins* test, the court assigns different weight to crime control and due process considerations depending on the nature of the evidence and the differing requirements of upholding the reputation of justice.

A very different approach to the exclusion of evidence characterizes the Supreme Court's attitude to conscripted evidence. The court has determined that conscripted evidence undermines the fairness of the trial because it would not be discovered except for the unconstitutional action of the police.[38] Indeed, between 1982 and 2003, 74 percent (26 out of 35) of the cases in which the Supreme Court excluded evidence involved conscripted evidence, and of the forty-four cases in which the Supreme Court did not exclude evidence, conscripted evidence was involved in 39 percent (17 out of 44). The primary impact of the court's activism stemming from section 24(2) has thus been to require the police to place greater emphasis on informing individuals of their Charter protections, and the court has also found some of the more questionable practices employed by the police to be inconsistent with the Charter. For instance, the use of deception in securing convictions, approaching waivers of rights as blanket provisions when an accused voluntarily sets aside Charter protections for a specific offence, seizing blood samples from unconscious suspects, and allowing intoxicated individuals to waive their Charter rights have been found unconstitutional by the court and resulted in the exclusion of evidence as conscripted under section 24(2) of the Charter.

These due process requirements placed on the police are important constraints that have subjected the discretionary power of a state actor to constitutional review and remedy if found to violate the Charter. Because the Supreme Court has not approached the exclusion of evidence as an automatic principle, but has attempted, through the three-part *Collins* test, to balance the rights of the accused with legitimate law enforcement objectives to protect the reputation of justice, the due process revolution has been moderated by important crime control factors. As long as the police have demonstrated an intention to govern with the Charter, the Supreme Court has generally been supportive of the agents of law enforcement.

The Right to Counsel and Silence
The attempt to balance crime control with due process considerations first appeared in *R. v. Therens*, a case involving the question of whether a Breathalyzer sample obtained in the absence of counsel should be excluded.[39] Section 10(b) provides the right to retain and instruct counsel, as well as the obligation that a detainee be informed of this right by an agent of law enforcement. Because the police did not inform Therens of this right under section 10(b), the Breathalyzer sample was excluded by the Supreme Court through section 24(2) of the Charter. The significant aspect of *Therens* involves the dissenting judgment by Justice Le Dain and his discussion of the factors to consider during section 24(2) analysis. Le Dain argued that the seriousness of the rights violation should be considered in light of the seriousness of the criminal charge, and he signalled a moderate approach between these two models: "The relative seriousness of the constitutional violation has been assessed in light of whether it was committed in good faith, or was inadvertent or of a merely technical nature, or whether it was

deliberate, wilful or flagrant. Another relevant consideration is whether the action which constituted the constitutional violation was motivated by urgency or necessity to prevent the loss or destruction of evidence."[40] While Le Dain argued that a different approach to section 24(2) was required in section 10(b) cases because of the importance of the right to counsel, he concluded that the administration of justice would not be brought into disrepute by including the Breathalyzer sample taken from Therens after he crashed his car due to intoxication, despite the violation of his legal rights.

This clearly demonstrates the complex approach to section 24(2) by the Supreme Court and the recognition that the legitimate objectives of law enforcement must be balanced with the rights of the accused.[41] Indeed, this approach to the exclusion of evidence directly influenced the development of the *Collins* test by Justice Lamer, who stated that "section 24(2) of the Charter has rejected extreme answers. No longer is all evidence admissible, regardless of the means by which it was obtained. Nor, on the other hand, is all improperly obtained evidence inadmissible. A middle ground has been chosen."[42] In this regard, Lamer articulated the purpose of section 24(2), which emerged during the proceedings of the Special Joint Committee on the Constitution of Canada (SJC) when the Canadian Civil Liberties Association called for, and the federal government included, an exclusionary rule that changed the practice established under *Hogan* (which rarely excluded evidence) but cautioned against an automatic exclusionary rule like the one that exists in the United States.[43] The implication of judicial activism in these initial cases involving section 10(b) is to place a constitutional obligation on the police to inform suspects of the right to retain and instruct counsel, which is exactly what the proceedings of the SJC and the textual changes to the rights to counsel intended. In *R. v. Brydges,* a unanimous court ruled on the informational component of section 10(b) and whether the failure by the police to inform an accused of the availability of legal aid violated the right to counsel.[44] Speaking for the court, Chief Justice Lamer reconfirmed the decision in *Manninen*[45] and ruled that section 10(b) imposed two duties on the police: "First, the police must give the accused or detained person a reasonable opportunity to exercise the right to retain and instruct counsel." Second, "the police must refrain from questioning or attempting to elicit information from the detainee until the detainee has had that reasonable opportunity."[46] In this case, the accused felt that the right to counsel was contingent on the ability to afford legal advice, and because this impression was not corrected by the police, the court ruled that the accused had not properly exercised his right to counsel, and thus section 10(b) of the Charter was violated.

In its decision, a unanimous court excluded the accused's incriminating statements and restored the acquittal against second-degree murder since the statements used as evidence were conscripted, thus undermining the fairness of the trial. The effect of the decision in *Brydges* was to expand the informational component of section 10(b), and Chief Justice Lamer concluded that *Brydges* required "the police to inform detainees of the existence and availability of duty counsel services and legal aid plans."[47] The court suspended the *Brydges* duty counsel requirement for thirty days to give the police time to conform to the decision and to produce new statements, outlining Charter rights, that would be read to those detained by the police.

In *R. v. Prosper,* the court addressed the related issue of whether section 10(b) of the Charter imposed a substantive constitutional obligation on governments to provide free and immediate legal aid to detainees.[48] In a unanimous judgment, the court ruled that a substantive obligation did not exist and based this judgment on two factors. First, speaking for the court, Chief Justice Lamer concluded that the framers of section 10(b) had rejected the inclusion of free duty counsel as part of the protection, and second, "the fact that such an obligation would almost certainly interfere with governments' allocation of limited resources by requiring them to expend public funds on the provision of a service is, I might add, a further consideration which weighs against this interpretation."[49] This decision is significant because it illustrates the distinction within the court's activism in the area of legal rights between cases that increase the onus on the police and those that place constitutional obligations on cabinet, parliament, and the provincial legislatures. In particular, the court is most comfortable limiting the discretionary powers of police officers by expanding the informational requirements of section 10(b), but clearly less interested in extending its activism in directions that force governments to spend limited resources.

This approach was modified in 1999 when the Supreme Court determined that state-funded counsel must be provided in limited circumstances to ensure that section 7 and the principles of fundamental justice were respected. In *New Brunswick v. G.(J.),* the court ruled that a constitutional obligation exists in cases where the province removes a child from the family home and the parent seeks to challenge the court-ordered custody.[50] Chief Justice Lamer argued that the decision to separate parent and child violated the security of the person by harming the physical and mental security of both individuals, and thus extended section 7 beyond the criminal law context to family law and custody hearings. However, the Supreme Court was explicit that a constitutional obligation to provide legal counsel existed in a very narrow set of circumstances to ensure a fair trial under section 7 in cases where parents possessed neither the financial nor mental abilities to serve as their own counsel. Thus a general constitutional right to duty counsel was not established, and this case is consistent with *Prosper* in establishing the constitutional right to counsel in a very narrow context.

The most significant impact of the court's legal rights jurisprudence has been in the procedural rights available to individuals subjected to police interrogations. Indeed, the Supreme Court has established a very high threshold for the voluntary waiving of Charter rights by the accused, as the court has not accepted as valid the actions of intoxicated detainees who waive their Charter right to counsel, an issue that arose in *R. v. Clarkson* and *R. v. Black*. In *Clarkson*, the court ruled that the incriminating statements by the accused should be excluded as conscripted evidence because the voluntary waiver was made by an individual who did not appreciate the consequences of her actions: "While this constitutional guarantee cannot be forced upon an unwilling accused, any voluntary waiver in order to be valid and effective must be premised on a true appreciation of the consequences of giving up the right."[51] An even more questionable approach arose in *Black*, where the police secured incriminating statements from an intoxicated individual known to the police to be an alcoholic with a Grade 4 education.[52] In this case, the court excluded, as conscripted evidence, the incriminating statements made in connection with a murder investigation, but included the knife found when the police searched the murder scene.[53] The outcome in *Black* clearly illustrates the important distinction between conscripted and non-conscripted evidence and how it influences whether the court favours crime control or due process considerations when using the remedy available through section 24(2). For instance, the court excluded the conscripted evidence in *Black* because it undermined the fairness of the trial, but the court included the non-conscripted evidence, the weapon, because of the principle of inevitable discoverability.

Though the court has established a high threshold for a valid waiver of the right to counsel, it has been clear that this does not require an individual to possess full information on the nature of the criminal investigation. In *R. v. Smith*, an individual was arrested in connection with a shooting and informed of the right to counsel, which the accused explicitly waived.[54] At trial, the defence claimed that the waiving of Charter rights by Smith was not valid because he was not informed that the victim had died as a result of the shooting. In a unanimous decision, Justice McLachlin stated that "it has never been suggested, however, that full information is required for a valid waiver. Indeed, if this were the case, waivers would seldom be valid, since the police typically do not know the whole story when the accused is arrested. Nor is the failure of the police to precisely identify the charges faced in the words of the Criminal Code necessarily fatal."[55] This judgment shows that the rights of the accused are not absolute during criminal procedures, and the due process constraints on the police are not so onerous as to prevent the advancement of law enforcement.

The court has also been willing to accept that the actions of the accused can offset the infringement of the right to counsel and cause conscripted evidence to be admitted. In *R. v. Tremblay,* after being arrested for drunk driving and informed of the right to counsel, the accused telephoned his wife and asked her to call a lawyer.[56] Immediately after he telephoned his wife, the police demanded and were provided with a Breathalyzer sample. During trial, the defence attempted to have the conscripted evidence excluded, arguing that the right to counsel was violated because Tremblay was not given a reasonable opportunity to retain and instruct counsel. The court refused to exclude the conscripted evidence and revised the constitutional principle developed in *Manninen* regarding the duties placed on the police in respect to section 10(b) rights: "If a detainee is not being reasonably diligent in the exercise of his rights, the correlative duties set out in this Court's decision in *Manninen* imposed on the police in a situation where a detainee has requested the assistance of counsel are suspended and are not a bar to their continuing their investigation and calling upon him to give a sample of his breath."[57] In this case, Tremblay's behaviour was the decisive factor, as he was described as violent, vulgar, and obnoxious, and the haste in obtaining a breath sample was the result of this behaviour.[58]

In conjunction with the right to counsel, the Supreme Court has been vigilant in protecting the decision by the accused to remain silent until counsel has arrived.[59] The court has refused to accept as legitimate those investigatory practices that circumvent the right to silence through the use of deception or trickery while an individual is in police custody.[60] In *R. v. Hebert,* the court ruled that the right to silence is infringed when undercover police officers are placed in the cells of individuals and actively solicit confessions of those who refuse to make statements to the police. In a unanimous decision, Justice McLachlin argued that the right to silence was "beyond the narrow formulation of the confessions rule"[61] and that "under section 7, the state is not entitled to use its superior power to override the suspect's will and negate his choice to speak to the authority or to remain silent."[62] In the case at hand, because the evidence used in the conviction was based on the statements made by the accused to the undercover police officer who solicited a confession, the court excluded the statements as conscripted and restored the acquittal against the robbery charges.

This decision was expanded in *R. v. Broyles,* where the court prohibited the use of private individuals to secure incriminating statements while an individual is in police custody.[63] In this case, the police arranged a prison visit between the accused and a friend who wore a wiretap and recorded incriminating statements for use by the criminal prosecution. In a unanimous judgment, Justice Iacobucci concluded that "the right to silence will only be infringed where it was the informer who caused the accused to make the statement, and where the informer was acting as an agent of the state at the time the accused made the statement."[64] Accordingly, the evidence was conscripted and undermined the fairness of the trial proceedings. However, the court has not simply excluded all conscripted evidence produced through the use of undercover police officers, as demonstrated in *Liew*, where an individual confessed to an undercover police officer during a cell block interview that he possessed the cocaine seized during a sting operation.[65] This incriminating statement was not excluded because the court determined that the undercover police officer did not seek a confession; instead, it was volunteered by Liew.[66]

In reaching this conclusion, the court reiterated Justice McLachlin's reasoning in *Hebert* that the right to silence was not absolute and that two functions were performed by undercover police officers: observing the individual and actively eliciting information. Only the latter activity violates the right to silence.[67] In *Liew*, the majority reiterated its attempt to balance crime control and due process considerations in its legal rights jurisprudence by concluding that this approach defines and protects the use of undercover techniques and cell block interviews. The court rejected an absolute right to silence, but noted its disdain for investigative techniques that circumvented this right.[68] More recently in *R. v. Fliss*, the court reiterated that unsolicited confessions to undercover police officers do not require the exclusion of evidence as a remedy for a legal rights violation. In this case, an undercover police officer recorded Fliss's confession to murder, and the Supreme Court ruled that the edited transcripts submitted by the officer for the criminal trial violated the right against unreasonable search and seizure.[69] In its section 24(2) analysis, however, the court determined that the evidence was non-conscripted because the confession was voluntary, the police acted in good faith by securing judicial authorization for the recorded conversation, and excluding the evidence would undermine the reputation of justice because of the brutal nature of the murder.

The court has interpreted the right to counsel and to silence as essential to provide the conditions for a fair trial, and it has been vigilant in excluding evidence that would undermine the reputation of justice. But the court has not simply emphasized the rights of the accused at the expense of police action. It has approached section 10(b) in a fair and balanced manner that has placed important due process constraints on the police. For the police, governing with the Charter has simply meant properly dispensing the right to counsel and giving an individual a reasonable opportunity to exercise this right. In situations where the accused has waived this right, the court has demanded that the waiver be valid and that the accused understand the consequences of such an action, which protects vulnerable or intoxicated individuals from being taken advantage of during criminal investigations. The automatic exclusion of evidence and the due process revolution have not transpired because the police have generally governed with the Charter by informing individuals of their legal rights. When this has not occurred, the evidence suggests that the Supreme Court has been as willing to favour police conduct as it has been to find fault with the police and remedy this through section 24(2), the exclusion-of-evidence rule.

To reformulate Roach's position that due process is for crime control, the experience of twenty-one years of legal rights activism suggests that the proper dispensing of due process has not come at the expense of legitimate police investigatory techniques.[70] In this regard, the Charter, and not judicial activism, has resulted in an important shift in the nature of policing, as Devonshire concludes that "police officers are no longer merely detectors of crime and apprehenders of criminals. Their role has expanded. They have joined the Courts and the legislatures in the protection of rights and freedoms."[71] The court's balanced approach to legal rights demonstrates that it respects the inter-institutional relationships necessary to ensure that all actors govern with the Charter and act as guardians of rights and freedoms. While the Supreme Court is the guardian of the constitution in a purely legal sense, its approach is an acknowledgment that it cannot govern on its own but requires the police to implement legal rights protections to ensure the value of the Charter.

Searches and Seizures

The constitutional standards governing reasonable searches and seizures were established in *Hunter v. Southam* when Chief Justice Dickson ruled that a reasonable expectation of privacy accompanied section 8 and that searches must be authorized by statute or the common law to be constitutional.[72] The standard of reasonable expectation of privacy has tempered the due process revolution because it has factored the context of the search into considerations of reasonableness, with a high expectation of privacy involved for searches that involve bodily integrity and private dwellings, but a much lower threshold for all other searches, particularly those in third-party dwellings, prisons, vehicles, and at border crossings by customs officials. This is significant because the context of a search, coupled with the type of evidence gathered in light of a Charter violation, has seen the court balance both due process consideration and crime control values in the development of the principles surrounding the protection against unreasonable searches and seizures. Because section 8 generally governs physical searches by police or customs officials, it inevitably focuses on real or non-conscripted evidence and the question of whether it should be excluded if gathered in a manner that violates a legal right protected under the Charter. Because the Supreme Court has been reluctant to exclude real or non-conscripted evidence, an unreasonable search or seizure will generally see evidence excluded only if the rights violation is very serious or the invasion of privacy so severe as to require its exclusion to protect the reputation of justice. In this regard, the application of the *Collins* test in conjunction with section 8 has advanced the due process rights of ordinary citizens by protecting them from routine and invasive searches by the police, but it has not protected those engaged in criminal activity where unconstitutional searches result in the discovery of evidence. In this case, the crime control objectives of law enforcement have been the decisive factor in the application of section 24(2) by the Supreme Court.

R. v. Stillman and *R. v. Feeney* are cases that illustrate the complex approach to section 8 and the importance of reasonable expectations of privacy and prior authorization that determine whether police conduct violates the right against unreasonable searches and seizures. In *R. v. Stillman* a seventeen year old was suspected of murder and taken into police custody, where counsel informed the police that he would not consent to providing DNA samples for investigative purposes.[73] Once counsel left, the police obtained DNA samples under threat of force and questioned Stillman in the absence of counsel. Nearly two months later, Stillman was arrested, and more DNA samples and teeth impressions were taken without consent. In a majority opinion written by Justice Cory, the court determined that section 8 was violated because Stillman had a reasonable expectation of privacy. It further determined that most of the evidence should be excluded because it was conscripted and produced as a result of serious rights violations by the police. While a DNA sample would normally be considered real evidence, and the method of obtaining it would not affect the fairness of the trial, the court revised this principle and argued that Stillman's sample was conscripted because of the manner in which it was obtained.[74] David Paciocco has argued that the seriousness of the rights violation and the invasion of privacy are the most significant considerations when the court excludes DNA samples taken without prior authorization.[75]

The first case to see the new classification scheme used was *R. v. Feeney*,[76] and it has been criticized as evidence of the court's preoccupation with the rights of the accused to the detriment of effective law enforcement.[77] While *Feeney* is an example of judicial activism, the new exclusionary rule did not determine the outcome in this case, but a series of procedural violations by the police that necessitated its use did. First, the police did not secure a warrant before entering Feeney's trailer, where they discovered a bloody shirt, shoes, cigarette package, and money. As Feeney was passed out on his couch and in plain view of the police, the possibility of flight was nonexistent, and exigent circumstances, such as the destruction of evidence before a warrant arrived, were minimal. If Feeney had destroyed evidence, the common law would have provided the police with exigent circumstances to enter the dwelling without judicial authorization in order to protect the evidence. Second, the police did not properly carry out the *Brydges* duty counsel requirements upon detaining Feeney, and they failed to cite the availability of free duty council. At this time, the police asked Feeney several questions, which he answered, thus incriminating himself in the murder. Finally, after bringing Feeney to the police station, where he continued to make incriminating statements, the police obtained fingerprints and secured a search warrant for his trailer.[78]

In this case, the majority of judges (five to four) concluded that sections 8 and 10(b) had been violated by the police, and they therefore excluded the conscripted evidence, the fingerprints and the incriminating statements, because it was manufactured as a result of procedural violations by the police. Speaking for the majority, Justice Sopinka ruled that the non-conscripted evidence (the bloody shirt, shoes, cigarettes, and money) must be excluded because of the seriousness of the section 10(b) violation. Sopinka argued that "the fact that the appellant did not speak with a lawyer for 2 days following his detention yet the police did not cease in their efforts to gather information, indicates a lack of respect for the appellant's rights displayed by the police."[79] As a result of the *Feeney* decision, the court ruled that prior authorization was required to enter the dwelling of an individual to gather evidence. In a remedy similar to that in *Stillman*, the Supreme Court did not dismiss the murder charge against Feeney, but ordered a new trial with some of the evidence excluded.

There is a distortion produced, however, by reading *Stillman* and *Feeney* as a trend toward more rigorous constraints on law enforcement (because the court limited the use of warrantless searches) and as evidence of the dominance of due process considerations in criminal procedure. Immediately following the decision in *Feeney*, the Department of the Solicitor General began to construct a new search warrant to address the constraints placed on police by this decision. According to a senior government official, the department recognizes "that cases like *Feeney* will in the short term create problems for effective law enforcement, but *Feeney* is not viewed as having a long-term negative impact."[80] This is an important statement because it indicates that the federal department responsible for law enforcement was confident that it could create new search warrants to minimize the impact of the court's decision in *Feeney*. Hiebert has argued that the legislative response to *Feeney* did not simply codify the judicial requirements that the privacy of an individual outweighed legitimate law enforcement requirements and that prior judicial authorization was needed to enter a dwelling to gather evidence. In 1997, cabinet introduced Bill C-17, which included generous exemptions for the entering of dwellings without prior judicial authorization, allowing the police to enter a residence to prevent imminent bodily harm or death and to prevent the destruction of evidence.[81] As Roach and Hiebert have demonstrated, even when the Supreme Court favours the

due process rights of the accused at the expense of crime control considerations, cabinet has introduced legislative responses to judicial decisions that
redress the balance in favour of law enforcement.[82]

High Expectations of Privacy: Physical Integrity and Section 8

The court's approach to unreasonable searches and seizures has normally
seen the exclusion of evidence if the physical integrity of an individual is
compromised through a serious rights violation. For instance, in *R. v. Greffe*,
an individual was suspected of smuggling heroin and subjected to a strip
search at the Calgary airport, where Canada Customs failed to discover the
contraband substance.[83] After Greffe was arrested for traffic warrants, he
was informed that a body-cavity search would be performed at a hospital.
This search produced the heroin. In its decision, the court excluded the real
evidence because of the seriousness of the Charter breach and the court's
judgment that the police did not have reasonable and probable grounds to
execute a body-cavity search, because it was conducted in connection with
the arrest for traffic warrants. Specifically, the court ruled that the "administration of justice would be brought into greater disrepute if this Court
were to condone, *taking the record as it is given by the police and the prosecution,* the practice of using an arrest for traffic warrants as an artifice to conduct a rectal examination of an accused who the police do not have
reasonable and probable grounds to believe is carrying drugs."[84]

The Supreme Court has not excluded all evidence gathered as the result
of strip searches, because in *R. v. Simmons* it ruled that the expectation of
privacy surrounding section 8 depended on the context of the search. For
instance, Chief Justice Dickson ruled that the approach to section 8 developed in *Hunter v. Southam* did not apply to searches at border crossings,
because there was a much lower expectation of privacy. He distinguished
between three types of searches: routine questioning and searches of bags;
strip or skin searches; and body-cavity searches.[85] The constitutional right
against unreasonable searches and seizures would have a threshold dependent on the nature of the search, and evidence gathered in a way that violated personal integrity, such as the body-cavity search in *Greffe*, would violate
section 8 and would be excluded to protect the reputation of justice.
Devonshire has argued that the initial concern that legal rights would undermine effective law enforcement has been allayed because, "through intensive training, police officers have been made aware of [the Charter's]
provisions and requirements so that guaranteed rights and freedoms are
respected."[86] The *Monney* decision is an excellent illustration of law enforcement learning to govern with the Charter and not repeating the mistakes of
Greffe, as a suspected heroin smuggler was not subjected to a body-cavity
search but was detained until the contraband substance passed through the

suspect's system. In this case, the Supreme Court ruled that section 8 was not violated because the individual had a lower expectation of privacy – the search occurred at a border crossing – and the search was reasonable because the physical integrity of Monney was not compromised.[87]

The seizure of blood samples without prior authorization has been ruled unconstitutional by the court because of the interference with bodily integrity and because of the high level of privacy the court has determined such seizures are to be evaluated against. In a series of cases involving the seizure of blood samples from individuals suspected of drunk driving, the Supreme Court has excluded evidence because it was obtained in a manner that brought the administration of justice into disrepute. In *R. v. Pohoretsky* it was ruled that the police seizure of a blood sample from an unconscious suspect violated section 8 because "they took advantage of the appellant's unconsciousness to obtain evidence which they had no right to obtain from him without his consent had he been conscious."[88] The court ruled that the method of gathering the evidence required it to be classified as conscripted because the police did not act in good faith and wilfully disregarded the privacy rights of an unconscious person.[89] Similarly, in *R. v. Dyment* the court ruled that forwarding blood samples collected for medical purposes to the police also violated section 8 when the samples were collected from an unconscious individual and used for a criminal investigation: "Under these circumstances, the sample was surrounded by an aura of privacy meeting Charter protections. For the state to take it in violation of a patient's right to privacy constitutes a seizure for the purpose of section 8."[90]

This principle was expanded in *R. v. Dersch* when the police received the results of a blood test from medical personnel without a warrant.[91] The court ruled that the police benefited from the misconduct of a medical professional who had been instructed by Dersch not to take a blood sample. Once Dersch became unconscious, the medical professional took a blood sample and forwarded the toxicology results to the police for their criminal investigation. The court ruled that Dersch had a reasonable expectation of privacy, and the forwarding of the medical records to the police was analogous to a search and seizure that violated section 8. The medical records were excluded by the Supreme Court because the medical personnel disregarded the specific instructions of Dersch, and the court emphasized "the importance of guarding against a free exchange between health care professionals and the police" during criminal investigations when unconscious individuals cannot provide consent.[92] Pomerance argues that, as a result of *Dersch*, the police are now accountable for the actions of medical personnel, and this has placed onerous constraints on criminal investigations in the context of medical procedures.[93]

Lowered Expectations: Narcotics, Third Parties, and Surveillance

In cases involving the seizure of bodily fluids, this evidence is conscripted because of the manner in which it was obtained and because of the high constitutional threshold provided to individuals to protect them from state interference with their physical integrity. But the standard of reasonable searches and the expectation of privacy have not been so onerous as to undermine the modified crime control approach that has placed more emphasis on the due process rights of the accused. In the cases considered, there were serious rights violations that compromised the physical integrity of individuals through body-cavity searches or searches of unconscious individuals.

A very different approach to section 8 and privacy considerations has arisen when narcotics are seized in violation of this Charter right. In this context, the court has applied a relaxed standard and has altered several of its decisions to prevent the exclusion of evidence when third parties provide the police with assistance during criminal investigations. Nowhere is the crime control model more evident than when the police seize narcotics in violation of section 8, and the court refuses to exclude this evidence to protect the reputation of justice. In this sense, due process rights are contextually applied depending on the nature of the police investigation, the type of evidence gathered in an unconstitutional manner, and the court's apprehension that the public would be shocked if it excluded evidence gathered in violation of the Charter.

In *R. v. Plant,* the police suspected an individual was cultivating marijuana in his basement and conducted a warrantless perimeter search to gather evidence.[94] During the investigation, the police checked the computerized records of Plant's electricity use to see if the consumption of power was consistent with large-scale marijuana production. In a unanimous decision, the court ruled that the warrantless perimeter search violated section 8 of the Charter, but that the seizure of computerized records was not unreasonable. Specifically, the court ruled that the seizure of the computer records was reasonable because of the lowered expectation of privacy attached to these records and the physical location of the electricity meter outside the house.[95] Indeed, Justice Sopinka stated that the purpose of section 8 was to protect individual privacy against state interference by balancing "the right of citizens to have respected a reasonable expectation of privacy as against state interest in law enforcement."[96] The reduced expectation of privacy occurred because the police obtained computerized records through an agreement with the electricity commission and did not invade "the personal computer records confidentially maintained by a private citizen."[97] In *Plant,* the court found that the search of computerized records was not unreasonable because it was not intrusive and was consistent with the expectation of privacy attached to public records in the keeping of a third party.

The varied approach to section 8 has seen the court reduce the expectation of privacy in a private dwelling if the search produces real evidence. Unanimous decisions in *Plant, R. v. Wiley, R. v. Grant,* and *R. v. Evans* all involved illegal searches against narcotics traffickers at private residences that saw the court admit the evidence despite the Charter violation.[98] The unanimous decisions in these cases are even more surprising because Justice Laforest sat on each decision, and he was a strong advocate of greater privacy protections for individuals. A notable exception to Justice Laforest's acceptance of real evidence produced as a result of an illegal search involving drug traffickers occurred in *R. v. Silveria,* where he was the lone dissenter.[99] In *Silveria,* an undercover operation had located a large cache of narcotics, and the police feared flight and removal of the evidence before a search warrant could be obtained. To ensure the integrity of the crime scene, the police entered the house to protect the evidence until a search warrant arrived. In the dissenting opinion, Justice Laforest rejected the idea that exigent circumstances existed which allowed the police to enter a house without a search warrant: "To expand exigent circumstances to include police created emergencies, whether arising from bad faith or gross ineptitude, is to severely undermine the requirement that judicial authorization is required before entry onto a premises can be made."[100] However, in a decision representing five of seven justices in the majority, Justice Cory accepted that section 8 had been violated by the entry but that the evidence must be admitted under section 24(2). Justice Cory accepted that exigent circumstances prompted the police to enter the dwelling, and that the fairness of the trial would not be affected by admitting real evidence.[101] Perhaps most importantly, the court recognized that the Charter breach was serious, but this was offset by the serious nature of narcotics trafficking. Moreover, the court concluded that the public would not be shocked by the conduct of the police against narcotics traffickers, whereas allowing a narcotics trafficker to escape prosecution by excluding evidence because of a minor rights violation would shock the community's sense of justice.[102]

The court addressed the expectation of privacy at the residence of third parties in *R. v. Edwards,* another case involving a section 8 challenge by a convicted narcotics trafficker.[103] In this case, the police suspected that the accused kept a large supply of narcotics at the residence of his girlfriend. Having arrested the accused on a traffic violation, the police gained entrance to the girlfriend's apartment through deception and were directed to the narcotics. In a majority opinion, Justice Cory dismissed the Charter challenge against an unreasonable search and seizure because it was not the accused's privacy that was infringed but the third party's.[104] Indeed, the court concluded that the expectation of privacy at the residence of a third party was reduced because the accused was an occasional guest who did not contribute to the rent. Moreover, even though the accused had keys to the residence, he had no expectation of privacy at the residence of a third party as the court ruled that "an important aspect of privacy is the ability to exclude others from the premises."[105] As such, the discretion accorded to law enforcement is an important development that reinforces the claim that crime control has been stirred and not shaken since the Charter's introduction because a moderate course has been struck between the two paradigms of crime control and due process.

The court's accepting that Charter violations were not intentional but the result of the "good faith" of the police is important because it distinguishes the Canadian approach to constitutional remedies for evidence gathered in breach of Charter rights from the American approach, which is the epitome of the due process model. In *R. v. Duarte*, the court found that warrantless surveillance of individuals by the police did not infringe the Charter, but the interception of private communications without prior judicial authorization constituted an unreasonable search and seizure.[106] In a majority decision, Justice Laforest admitted the evidence obtained through the interception of private communication because he accepted that the police had acted in good faith and the Charter violation was "in no way deliberate, wilful or flagrant."[107] The court acknowledged that the Criminal Code placed no restrictions on participant surveillance, and the Charter violation by the police stemmed from the assumption that private communication seized during a participant surveillance was valid under section 178.11(2)(a) of the Criminal Code. Because the police were "acting in accordance with what they had good reason to believe was the law," the court accepted that the evidence produced as a result of a Charter violation would not bring the administration of justice into disrepute.[108]

A related issue arose in *R. v. Wong*, where the police installed video surveillance in a hotel room to gather evidence against the appellant, who was suspected of operating an illegal gambling establishment.[109] In a majority decision that produced two concurring majority opinions, four justices concluded that warrantless video surveillance in a hotel room constitutes an unreasonable search and seizure. However, because the Charter violation occurred before the court had clarified the relationship between video surveillance and section 8, and parliament had not yet legislated on this issue, the court admitted the evidence because it accepted that the police "acted in accordance with what they had good reason to believe was the law, and before they had a reasonable opportunity to assess the consequences of the Charter on their established practices."[110] In essence, the court was satisfied that the police governed with the Charter and that it was the responsibility of parliament to clarify the ambiguity in law before the police could adjust their investigative techniques. For Justices Lamer and McLachlin, the Charter was not violated because the appellant used his hotel room for public gambling, which substantially reduced the expectation of privacy and therefore resulted in no search taking place within the meaning of section 8.[111]

To make the claim that judicial review has facilitated a due process revolution would require analysis that focused exclusively on activist decisions to the neglect of the majority of legal rights decisions in which the court has supported the agents of law enforcement. As it has been in the case of the right to counsel and silence, the Supreme Court has been justifiably activist when the police have disregarded Charter obligations and compelled individuals to self-incriminate through the seizure of DNA samples. In this regard, the court has defended the due process rights of the accused in a narrow and important set of circumstances by emphasizing that section 8 must be evaluated against the standard of a reasonable expectation of privacy. But the Supreme Court has been equally and justifiably deferential to the legitimate objectives of law enforcement by refusing to accept that technical or unintentional Charter violations require the exclusion of evidence to protect the reputation of justice. While the determination of reasonableness is discretionary, the decisions of the Supreme Court have confirmed neither the critics' position that a due process revolution would result from activist legal rights decisions, nor the equally critical position that the court's approach to legal rights has simply reinforced the crime control model. The complexity of judicial review by the Supreme Court has prevented either model from dominating criminal procedure in Canada.

Trial Procedures and Victims' Rights

The *Askov* decision, which requires that a trial occur within a reasonable time, has been used as an example of the court's preoccupation with rights of the accused and the dominance of due process considerations. In *R. v. Askov*, the issue of institutional delay saw the court establish a four-part test to determine whether a trial delay was unreasonable and in violation of section 11(b). The test established by Justice Cory sought to balance complex interests, such as the length of the delay, the explanation for the delay, whether the accused waived his rights, and the level of prejudice experienced by the accused as a result of the delay.[112] In its decision, the court ruled that delays between six and eight months, under certain circumstances, could result in an infringement of section 11(b) of the Charter. However, the lower courts interpreted this time frame as a hard rule and did not engage in the complex balancing of factors that Justice Cory intended, with the result that 47,000 charges were stayed between 22 October 1990 and 6 September 1991.[113] This outcome has been roundly criticized by Knopff and Morton, who argue that "had the Court decided only the extreme case actually before it, refraining from the temptation to set more general policy for all cases, a problem of such dimensions would not have arisen."[114] Baar contends that the Supreme Court misused social science evidence in *Askov*, and this led to a regrettable episode of judicial policy making.[115] Russell provides a more positive assessment of *Askov* as "the strengthening of the position of Ontario's Attorney General in securing more resources for the province's justice system and the implementation of management changes in a very badly administered judicial region."[116]

A full assessment of *Askov* is incomplete without reference to the court's approach to section 11(b) in subsequent cases. In *R. v. Morin,* a majority court reflected on the impact of *Askov* and addressed the application of the test by lower courts. There were two fundamental shifts in *Morin* that Chief Justice Lamer expressed profound disagreement with in his lone dissenting opinion. First, the majority decision written by Justice Sopinka shifted the balance in the *Askov* test onto the accused and away from institutional delay, placing primary importance on the accused's demonstrating that an unreasonable level of prejudice resulted from a trial delay.[117] Justice Gonthier further reduced the burden on the Crown to demonstrate the absence of prejudice because "the onus which rests on the Crown may be met by direct evidence or by inference, whether it be to establish the absence of prejudice or its extent or degree."[118] This fundamental shift effectively transformed the *Askov* test from one that largely emphasized the due process rights of the accused to one that considers the institutional pressures on the judicial system and the crime control objective of factual guilt.

The principal impact of the shift in *Morin* has been to drastically reduce the ability of Charter claimants to demonstrate that a trial delay has been unreasonable.[119] Since *Askov,* the court has supported the Charter claimant in less than 10 percent (2 out of 22) of the cases in which the defence argued that a trial delay infringed section 11(b). Moreover, the average delay accepted as reasonable by the court since *Askov* has been sixteen months, a period double the acceptable delay suggested by Justice Cory.[120] The court's acceptance of longer delays stems from the greater emphasis placed on the accused's demonstrating prejudice, the degrees of prejudice experienced in various offences, as well as the recognition by the court that the judicial system's ability to respond quickly was determined by complex factors. In *R. v. Frazer,* the court noted that "legal and social conditions can increase the volume of work to such an extent that longer delays are inevitable. The legal system cannot be expected to adjust immediately to meet sudden or short term increases in the volume of cases."[121] For instance, in *R. v. Potvin,* a unanimous court found that a twenty-six-month delay was reasonable for an individual charged with criminal negligence causing death. In a concurring opinion, Justice McLachlin suggested that the remedy for a section 11(b) violation must be appropriate to the crime committed to ensure that individuals charged with serious crimes do not escape appropriate punishment merely because of the length of delay.[122] The significance of the shift between *Askov* and *Morin* is that the court has emphasized important crime control objectives in the context of a trial, where the length of a delay has been downplayed, the seriousness of the charge has been emphasized, and the level of prejudice is now balanced with the nature of the crime.

In contrast to the assumption that the rights of the accused have been the focus of the Supreme Court's legal rights jurisprudence stands a body of evidence in which societal interests have reduced the legal rights protections available to the accused. For instance, the Supreme Court has supported reverse-onus provisions in the Criminal Code that create specific bail provisions for narcotic traffickers.[123] The court has accepted the underlying premise of such provisions, which is to maintain the effectiveness of the bail system by protecting the public from narcotic traffickers who would continue to engage in illegal activities while out on bail. This was the basis of the court's decision in *R. v. Pearson,* where in a majority decision the constitutionality of section 515(6)(d) of the Criminal Code was affirmed, which required an accused to show why the denial of bail was unjustified for those charged with trafficking.[124] The court's low tolerance for narcotics offences continued in *Morales,* where the court found that denying bail to traffickers on the basis of protecting the public interest was too vague, but that denying bail on the basis of public safety was constitutional.[125] *Pearson* and *Morales* demonstrate an important facet in legal rights: the court does not simply evaluate whether the Charter has been infringed, but also engages in a balancing of interests, where societal concerns can offset the limitations experienced by the accused. Recently in *R. v. Hall,* the court upheld section 515(10)(c) of the Criminal Code, which authorizes the denial of bail to "maintain confidence in the administration of justice," as constitutional, but it did sever the provision that permitted detention "on any other just cause being shown" as inconsistent with the principles of fundamental justice.[126]

The interests of society play a pivotal role in modifying the Charter rights of prisoners and dangerous offenders, and the admissibility of pretrial psychiatric assessments leading to an individual being classified as a dangerous offender was raised in *R. v. Jones.*[127] In this case, the defence advanced the position that admitting pretrial mental health assessments without advising the accused that this could be used to determine future dangerous offender status violated the right to counsel. The court's decision produced an important division that highlights the competing issues balanced in legal rights cases. The majority placed primary importance on protecting society from a convicted sexual predator, whereas the minority viewed section 755 of the Criminal Code, which relates to the admission of evidence at dangerous offenders' proceedings, as being too broad and inconsistent with the principles of fundamental justice. By a narrow majority (five to four) the court upheld the admissibility of the psychiatric assessment because the accused consented to the evaluation in the presence of counsel and the loss of liberty was insignificant in comparison to the potential threat posed to the community at large: "To exclude clear psychiatric evidence of the dangerousness of the accused would be to ask other young girls in society to bear the risk that this information might not emerge in the post trial psychiatric evaluation."[128]

The international reputation of Canada has also served as an important consideration in cases where serious criminals have attempted to use the Charter to escape extradition to countries that impose the death penalty. This issue was raised in *Kindler v. Canada* and *Reference Re Ng Extradition,* where the defence argued that returning individuals under section 25 of the *Extradition Act* without first obtaining assurances that the death penalty would not be imposed violated the principles of fundamental justice.[129] The majority decision by Justice Laforest rejected this argument because the appellants had committed the "worst form of murder" in the United States, and extraditing these individuals to face the death penalty "could not be said to shock the conscience of the Canadian people nor be in violation of the standards of the international community."[130] An overriding consideration for the majority in this decision was not the fate of the individuals facing extradition and the death penalty, but the impact on Canada's international reputation. As Justice Laforest said in the majority decision, "I find that it is reasonable to believe that extradition in this case does not go beyond what is necessary to serve the legitimate social purpose of preventing Canada from becoming an attractive haven for fugitives."[131] Indeed, the interests of Ng and Kindler were outweighed by more important societal objectives and the reciprocal integrity of extradition with other nations. This approach was revisited in *United States v. Burns,* when the Supreme Court ruled that the failure by the minister of justice to seek assurances that the death penalty would not be sought violated the principles of fundamental justice.[132] In *Burns* the court endorsed the balancing approach to extradition cases defined in *Kindler,* but it argued that the balance now favoured extradition with assurances that the death penalty would not be sought. Specifically, the court argued that the previous ten years had revealed the institutional limitations associated with the use of the death penalty in the United States, and the suspension of this punishment in several states required the minister of justice to seek assurances against the use of the death penalty. As both Burns and Rafay were Canadian, the court determined that the public would be shocked by sending citizens to a foreign jurisdiction to face execution.

The attempt to protect children from re-victimization through court proceedings challenges the position that the court has generally emphasized the due process rights of the accused. In *R. v. L.(D.O.),* the defence challenged section 715.1 of the Criminal Code as an infringement of the right to a fair trial because the Crown was allowed to substitute a videotaped statement by a young complainant in a sexual assault case instead of direct testimony. The court accepted parliament's goal of "the protection of child witnesses and the attainment of truth through the mechanism of video-taped statements" because the challenged section balanced the needs of the defence by allowing the trial judge "to set aside, edit, disallow such state-ments if their prejudicial effects outweigh their probative value."[133] With-out allowing for special provisions to facilitate the testimony of vulnerable victims, the court was concerned that victims of sexual assault might be unwilling to face the accused during a trial, and this would be detrimental to addressing a serious crime committed against children.[134]

The same concern for protecting young victims of sexual assault was raised in *R. v. Levogiannis.*[135] Under section 486(2.1) of the Criminal Code, a young complainant is permitted to testify behind a screen in the courtroom and does not have to directly face the accused. This section was challenged as an infringement of sections 7 and 11(d) of the Charter, but Justice L'Heureux-Dubé, for a unanimous court, refused to accept that a physical barrier sepa-rating the accused from the complainant, where the defence was still permitted to cross-examine the complainant, violated the Charter: "The slight alteration provided for by Parliament by the impugned section is aimed, simply, in enabling the young complainant to be able to recount the evidence, fully and candidly, in a more appropriate setting, given the cir-cumstances when facing the elicitation of the truth."[136] The court's accep-tance of section 486(2.1) was grounded in the belief that the court system was failing children by not being sensitive enough to accommodate the needs of vulnerable victims, "especially those who have been victims of abuse, who are then subjected to further trauma as participants in the judi-cial process."[137] In essence, the court viewed the limitation placed on the accused as a reasonable balance that considered both the need to conduct an effective defence and the larger societal objective of protecting children from the trauma of directly facing their attacker during a trial.[138] The para-digm shift to due process, therefore, is debatable given the complex ap-proach to legal rights and the balancing of interests the court engages in when determining whether a constitutional infringement has occurred.

Conclusion

The evidence clearly demonstrates that after twenty-one years of legal rights decisions, the crime control model has been stirred but not shaken by the Charter's introduction, as the court has constructed a flexible and moderate jurisprudence. The significance of this approach is that the court has not acted as the guardian of legal rights by simply emphasizing the rights of the accused to the exclusion of law enforcement objectives. By considering both due process and crime control in the construction of the *Collins* and *Askov* tests and in its general approach to legal rights, where searches are evalu-ated against a reasonable expectation of privacy and individuals have a

reasonable opportunity to exercise the right to counsel but also the responsibility to be diligent in exercising it, the court has primarily emphasized
the constitutional requirement that the judicial system and the agents of
law enforcement govern with the Charter. This moderate and balanced approach has been criticized by those who advocate the principles of due process or crime control and evaluate legal rights against their preferred approach
to criminal procedure. However, a fair analysis of the court's legal rights
jurisprudence must be free of advocacy and must assess what the court has
done and not what it should do. Neither the due process revolution nor the
crime control counter-revolution has been the outcome of legal rights rulings by the Supreme Court, but rather a modified crime control model that
emphasizes the procedural rights of the accused during criminal investigations. The concerns of both the victim and the accused have been considered during trial procedures, and the court has been even-handed in its
approach to section 24(2), as technical Charter violations have not resulted
in the exclusion of evidence and the court has accepted that the police
acted in good faith, despite a rights violation. Evidence has generally been
excluded when the actions of the police resulted in serious rights violations
that interfered with the physical integrity of individuals, and this remedy is
necessary to protect the reputation of justice. Thus, the requirements of an
appropriate and just remedy have varied, and the Supreme Court has balanced competing interests and objectives in its legal rights jurisprudence.

The proceedings of the Special Joint Committee on the Constitution reveal the framers' intention to avoid the excesses of the American due process model, but they also demonstrate the intention to address aspects of
criminal procedure that were inadequate constraints on the police. In essence, the framers sought a moderate course that attempted to balance the
procedural rights of the accused with the need for effective law enforcement. The initial drafts of the Charter provided weak legal rights guarantees
that allowed crime control to endure, as many legal rights were protected
"except on grounds, and in accordance with procedures, established by
law."[139] Further, the draft Charters maintained legislative control over the
rules governing evidence and would have entrenched the crime control
approach to criminal procedure had the intentions of the provincial premiers dominated the constitutional politics surrounding entrenchment. The
crime control approach was not totally discredited by the proceedings of
the SJC, nor was due process endorsed as the natural alternative to common-law constraints on police conduct. The wording of the legal rights
provisions, as well as the remedies for unconstitutionally obtained evidence,
indicate that the framers sought a compromise position between the two
approaches. By applying the legal rights guarantees in a manner consistent
with the interpretive intent of the framers, the Supreme Court has governed with the Charter and has not ruled the administration of justice

through judicial activism. It has shared this responsibility with the actors responsible for the proper administration of justice in Canada. The next chapter considers whether this shared responsibility has continued when the inter-institutional relationship between the cabinet and Supreme Court emerges during Charter challenges to statutes and regulations.

5
Guardians of the Constitution

The Charter dialogue debate centres on the attempts by the Supreme Court and the cabinet to govern with the Charter in a way that advances constitutional supremacy. This defence of judicial review is so significant that the Supreme Court adopted the dialogue metaphor in *Vriend v. Alberta,* when Justice Iacobucci defended the court's decision to read sexual orientation into the *Individual's Rights Protection Act (IRPA)* as evidence of "more dynamic interaction between the branches of governance."[1] Supporters of this notion conclude that a successful partnership has been constructed and that the democratic value of this inter-institutional relationship is the defining characteristic of the Charter,[2] whereas the critics contend that a court-structured monologue advancing judicial power is the outcome of this dialogic relationship.[3] My position is that the focus on invalidated statutes is very limited and presents an incomplete assessment of the court's general acceptance of legislative judgments and the need to accommodate cabinet decision making and institutional capacity within its Charter jurisprudence. This is particularly significant as the Supreme Court has found far more statutes to be constitutional than unconstitutional, and the reasoning reveals a court conscious of its institutional limitations and accepting of the cabinet's attempt to balance competing demands in legislative schemes.

While the review of statutes centres on the Supreme Court and its institutional capacity, the complexity of its Charter jurisprudence demonstrates a responsible actor that recognizes a well-functioning constitutional system cannot be imposed by the courts but requires all actors to govern with the Charter. Brian Slattery referred to this as the coordinate model, which "lays stress on the equal responsibilities of the various branches of government to carry out the *Charter's* mandate and the reciprocal nature of their roles."[4] Coordinate constitutionalism, as the last chapter demonstrated, is the defining characteristic of the administration of justice and the relationship between courts and the police. This has extended to the interaction between the Supreme Court and the cabinet in regard to enacted statutes, as a sophisticated approach has not come at the expense of constitutional supremacy nor seen the court act as the principal guardian of the constitution, contrary to the view of the critics who see the court's articulation of this role in *Hunter v. Southam* as a clear indication of a dangerous overconfidence that has compromised constitutional supremacy.[5] Like the Charter dialogue metaphor, the guardian role has been equated with rights and their protection through judicial invalidation of statutes. This role, however, is far broader than the Charter and the actions of the Supreme Court.

Guarding the constitution is not simply about judicially protected rights, but is also about advancing the essential characteristics of the constitution – federalism, parliamentary democracy, and constitutional supremacy – through reciprocal relationships.[6] While the court has articulated the importance of coordinate constitutionalism, the academic debate has focused on the confrontational relationship between these institutional actors when the Supreme Court strikes down acts of parliament or the provincial legislatures. The rest of this book contends that the essential elements of the constitution have been protected by varied institutional actors mandated to govern with the Charter under section 52 of the *Constitution Act*. The court has advanced these essential elements through activist decisions but also through deferential judgments that accept parliamentary actors did indeed reach principled policy decisions when drafting legislation. The growing acceptance of constitutionality cannot be explained solely by changes in the court's approach to section 1 and the *Oakes* test, as the changes have not been significant enough to account for declining rates of invalidation or the growing acceptance of cabinet decisions by the Supreme Court.[7] Institutional changes in the development of public policy, and the emergence of more principled processes that link Charter values with legislative objectives, are the principal causes and will be explored in the last part of this book.

In this chapter, I begin with an analysis of statutes invalidated by the Supreme Court and suggest that judicial activism is not simply a discretionary decision by the court but a reaction to limitations in the drafting of legislation. The cabinet-centred approach is extended to judicial decisions by looking at the characteristics of the statutes nullified, such as the date a statute was enacted or last amended. The most significant feature of invalidated statutes is that a large number used to demonstrate the growth of judicial power were enacted or last amended before the Charter's introduction. Thus, the court may be activist today, but it is generally activist against policy decisions of the past and the legislative choices of the cabinet enacted in different policy contexts with different constitutional requirements. Even when the court invalidates legislation, its approach to constitutional remedies still advances coordinate constitutionalism by a growing use of suspended declarations of unconstitutionality as the remedy to rights violations in statutes. As the Supreme Court has become more disposed in recent years to suspending its judgments in Charter cases, this provides the responsible cabinet with an opportunity to introduce amendments to establish the constitutionality of offending provisions before the suspended declaration of unconstitutionality by the Supreme Court expires. There is no clearer demonstration of coordinate constitutionalism or multiple guardians of the constitution, therefore, than the inter-institutional relationships that exist during suspended judgments that result in political responses by the cabinet or its provincial counterparts.

The Supreme Court and the Cabinet

The guardian of the constitution metaphor has been used by the Supreme Court to justify the invalidation of legislation as a way to protect Charter rights. It has also been used to discredit judicial activism and to argue that the court has acted in a way that causes a paradigm shift to judicial supremacy, both claims rejected in this study. The guardian role exists in two distinct forms, each with very different implications for coordinate constitutionalism: the constitutional (formal) and the political (informal). As a matter of constitutional law, the Supreme Court is the guardian of the constitution, but this formal role is overshadowed by the reality of Charter politics and the informal functioning of the constitution within the political arena, which are characterized as reciprocal relationships. Both the application of section 1 of the Charter, the reasonable limits clause, and the remedies employed when statutes are invalidated demonstrate that the formal dimension of the guardian role is rarely relied upon by the Supreme Court. The emerging approach to declarations of invalidity has seen the increased use of suspended decisions to allow the competent legislative body an opportunity to introduce amendments to better tailor policy objectives with constitutional obligations. Both the supporters and critics of judicial activism have applied the guardian metaphor solely as a matter of constitutional law and have neglected the fact that, as a matter of constitutional practice, the Supreme Court shares this responsibility with the cabinet and its provincial counterparts.[8] This is a significant characteristic of activist decisions that questions whether the invalidation of legislation is as problematic as the critics contend, or as necessary to advance Charter rights as the supporters contend.

The evolution of section 1 of the Charter, the *Oakes* test, for determining whether a limitation on a Charter right is reasonable illustrates both the emergence of coordinate constitutionalism in Canada and the transition from the formal to the informal guardian role and its application by the Supreme Court. I contend that the court's changing conception of reasonable limits is a clear indication of its commitment to coordinate constitutionalism and its acceptance that alternative policy approaches may not constitute a minimal impairment but can still be considered a reasonable limitation that establishes the constitutionality of challenged acts of parliament and the provincial legislatures. There are notable examples where the Supreme Court has rejected coordinate constitutionalism and invoked the formal guardian role, such as *RJR-Macdonald Inc. v. Canada* and the *Reference Re Provincial Court Judges* of 1997.[9] However, a few extremely activist decisions do not demonstrate a general pattern of subordinate constitutionalism, as the critics contend, in which the court uses the Charter and disregards the legislative choices of the cabinet. While it is dangerous to rely on a few cases to establish a general principle, the ones chosen for analysis are reflective of general patterns in the court's approach to section 1 and its attempt to respect the difficult task facing legislative bodies in balancing competing interests in public policy. Indeed, evidence of the court's attempt to govern with cabinet under the Charter is the evolution of the *Oakes* test, characterized by a movement away from minimal impairment and an acceptance of a range of possible legislative alternatives that satisfy section 1. These shifts have not established judicial hegemony but have attached greater weight to the policy context that cabinet and its provincial counterparts operate within when attempting to advance their legislative agendas, supported by the bureaucracy.

In *R. v. Oakes*, the Supreme Court established the test to determine whether legislation that violates the Charter is constitutional because it represents a reasonable limitation demonstrably justified in a free and democratic society.[10] Under the *Oakes* test, there are principally two requirements on governments attempting to establish the reasonableness of a Charter violation. The first is that the challenged legislation advances a pressing and substantial objective that warrants infringing a Charter right. The second part is referred to as the proportionality test and involves the following considerations: first, there must be a rational connection between the law and the policy objectives advanced; second, the law must represent a minimal impairment on a right; and finally, the law must be proportionate and not have a severe effect on an individual who suffers a rights limitation. Unlike the *Collins* test, in which the court balances the effect of evidence on the administration of justice, the *Oakes* test, in theory, is a far stricter standard, and the government must satisfy each distinct requirement to justify a limitation. However, the *Oakes* test has come down to the requirement of minimal impairment, as Hogg has argued that the Supreme Court rarely refuses to accept that a limitation is motivated by a pressing and substantial objective.[11] Indeed, the notable exception to this approach is *Vriend,* where the Supreme Court did not consider the Alberta cabinet's decision to exclude sexual orientation as a protected category under the IRPA a pressing and substantial policy objective.[12] Instead, as Hogg has suggested, "the requirement of least drastic means has turned out to be the heart and soul of section 1 justification."[13]

The initial approach to minimal impairment made it very difficult for governments to establish a reasonable limitation, as the court only accepted two of the first ten section 1 defences between 1984 and 1987.[14] In this initial approach to section 1, which corresponded to the court's highly activist Charter jurisprudence, the Supreme Court used the *Oakes* test to act as the formal guardian of the constitution, as it demanded that pressing and substantial legislative objectives had to be a minimal impairment on a protected right. This was problematic because it contradicted the rationale behind section 1 and the view that rights were not absolute: by accepting only a minimal impairment, the court focused on the right and not on the policy context of the challenged legislation. Patrick Monahan has suggested that it was nearly impossible during this period to demonstrate that less restrictive means were not available.[15] Though the court in *Oakes* cautioned against a rigid application, the high threshold robbed the *Oakes* test of its flexibility.

Beginning in *R. v. Edwards Books and Art Ltd.*, and clearly emerging in *Irwin Toy v. A.G. Quebec*, the Supreme Court revised the *Oakes* test and attached more sensitivity to the policy context of challenged legislation.[16] In essence, the court signalled its recognition that the complexity of, and the need to balance, competing interests required it to relax the standard of minimal impairment to truly respect the efforts by cabinet and the Department of Justice to draft legislation consistent with the Charter. In *Edwards Books*, the *Retail Business Holiday Act* in Ontario, which provided for a secular day of rest on Sunday, was challenged as a violation of freedom of religion because it required Saturday Sabbatarians to respect the Christian Sabbath. In a majority decision, five justices of the Supreme Court ruled that the act did violate freedom of religion because it had an unconstitutional effect despite a constitutional purpose of establishing a common day of rest. The significance of this judgment is the section 1 analysis by Chief Justice Dickson and Justice Laforest, who rejected a rigid approach and established that a range of possible approaches to the issue of Sunday shopping could be justified as a reasonable limitation. Perhaps more importantly, the majority opinions articulated coordinate constitutionalism and the need by the court to respect the attempt by the Ontario cabinet to balance complex issues, as Dickson stated that "the courts are not called upon to substitute judicial opinions for legislative ones as to the place at which to draw a precise line."[17]

In his concurring decision, Justice Laforest articulated a contextual approach to section 1 that would be fully developed in *RJR-Macdonald*. This movement away from minimal impairment signals the shift to the informal guardian role, as the reality of governing with the Charter necessitated a flexible approach to constitutional review. As Laforest noted, "it must be remembered that the business of government is a practical one. The Constitution must be applied on a realistic basis having regard to the nature of the particular area sought to be regulated and not on an abstract theoretical plane."[18] Further, Laforest stated that different policy contexts required a flexible approach to section 1: "A legislature must be given reasonable room to manoeuvre to meet these conflicting pressures. Of course, what is reasonable will vary with the context. Regard must be had to the nature of the interest infringed and to the legislative scheme sought to be implemented."[19] For Laforest, the complexity of the policy context and the limited institutional capacity of the court in this area were significant factors that required deference to legislative judgments.[20]

The softening of section 1 of the Charter continued in *Irwin Toy* with the creation of the bifurcated *Oakes* test that applies a different standard for reasonable limitations depending on the policy context of a challenged statute. In *Irwin Toys*, the court considered the constitutionality of sections of Quebec's *Consumer Protection Act* that banned advertising directed at individuals under the age of thirteen. While the court, in a majority decision, found that the act violated freedom of expression, it determined the limitation to be reasonable. In the majority opinion by Dickson, Lamer, and Wilson, a distinction was made between policy contexts where the competent legislature balances competing interests and distributes limited resources, such as social policy, and criminal policy, where the state acts "as the singular antagonist of the individual whose right has been infringed."[21] The court stated that the balancing of interests in social policy required it to apply a more flexible approach, as cabinet and the bureaucracy were better suited than courts to evaluate social science evidence when drafting legislative schemes. In this regard, the judgment used the argument of institutional capacity to defend judicial rigour in section 1 cases involving criminal policy, as "the courts can assess with some certainty whether the 'least drastic means' for achieving the purpose have been chosen, especially given their accumulated experience in dealing with such questions."[22]

Though the bifurcated approach has been criticized as unstable because criminal policy can involve a balancing of interests between the rights of the accused and the victim, it is an attempt to construct an approach that emphasizes the institutional capacity of the Supreme Court and the cabinet, supported by the bureaucracy, in distinct policy contexts. Roach has remarked that "section 1 is not a toothless tiger – courts will invalidate measures if the state has not explained the need for the most drastic approach – but its teeth are much less sharp than they used to be."[23] This is generally a welcomed development and essential for constitutional supremacy, as the initial *Oakes* test, if it had continued to be the approach to reasonable limits, would have made section 1 irrelevant. Most statutes found to infringe a right would have been ruled unconstitutional, and the *Oakes* test, therefore, would have functioned as an automatic finding of unreasonable policy choices by competent legislative bodies. Indeed, a balancing of interests is essential for the functioning of coordinate constitutionalism. Further, the lesser standard demanded in policy contexts that balance competing interests is particularly significant for policy diversity and provincial autonomy, as the jurisdictional responsibility of provincial governments generally involves non-criminal policy issues. By focusing on the guardian role as simply involving rights, those who are critical of policy sensitivity by the court ignore the broader constitutional framework that is affected by Charter review.

In addition to the bifurcated approach to *Oakes* and the movement away from minimal impairment, the establishment of the "tailoring approach" to section 1 in *RJR-Macdonald* advanced coordinate constitutionalism and multiple guardians of the constitution. In *RJR-Macdonald* the Supreme Court struck down restrictions on tobacco advertising in the *Tobacco Products Control Act* by a five to four decision, ruling that the restrictions were an unreasonable limitation on freedom of expression. The majority decision by Justice McLachlin refused to accept that a total ban on advertising was a reasonable limitation on the expression of tobacco companies. The decision is significant because it demonstrates the discretionary nature of the bifurcated *Oakes* test. The majority viewed the policy context as the state acting as singular antagonist against the tobacco companies and demanded a stricter standard, whereas the minority position called for a relaxed standard because the federal cabinet had attempted to balance competing interests: the advertising rights of tobacco companies and the need to protect young Canadians from the effects of tobacco advertising. The majority decision has been criticized as an example of the general limitation in the court's approach to section 2(b). Hiebert has argued that this case should not have been dealt with under the Charter as "at no stage in the debate did it seem to matter that the 'fundamental' Charter right at stake – tobacco advertising – was not a right in any philosophical sense but a right created by judicial decree."[24] I also agree that freedom of expression should be limited to the essential conditions necessary for a political community to be self-governing and should not be at the disposal of corporate interests. In my estimation, this is the most problematic area of the court's Charter jurisprudence.

The majority opinion advanced the formal guardian role, and McLachlin argued that "Parliament does not have the right to determine unilaterally the limits of its intrusion on the rights and freedoms guaranteed by the *Charter*. The Constitution, as interpreted by the Court, determines these limits."[25] This is clearly an activist decision and a difficult one to reconcile with coordinate constitutionalism, but the court did alter the *Oakes* test in a significant way with the "tailoring approach" and acceptance that a range of possible legislative schemes could satisfy section 1. In *RJR-Macdonald,* however, the majority simply concluded that this approach did not apply to the *Tobacco Products Control Act*. Justice McLachlin articulated the court's view that a rigid approach to section 1 was unworkable and recognized the difficult task confronting legislative bodies in governing with the Charter: "The tailoring process seldom admits of perfection and the courts must accord some leeway to the legislator. If the law falls within a range of reasonable alternatives, the courts will not find it overbroad merely because they can conceive of an alternative which might better tailor objective to infringement."[26] The constitutionality of a range of acceptable alternatives is a clear rejection of the original *Oakes* test and has informed the court's approach since this decision, as demonstrated by Chief Justice McLachlin's use of the tailoring approach in *R. v. Sharpe,* a case involving Criminal Code restrictions on the possession of child pornography.[27] In this decision, the court upheld most of the provisions that restricted child pornography and remedied the offending sections by reading-in a number of exceptions involving self-created expressive materials and private recordings of lawful sexual material.

The *Sharpe* decision was criticized because the court did not completely endorse the federal cabinet's approach, but this overlooks important nuances and the balanced use of section 1, as only the peripheral elements of the statute were invalidated and then remedied by the court through the process referred to as "reading-in." Chief Justice McLachlin acknowledged that, after *Oakes,* the court's position was that any limitation not absolutely a minimal impairment would fail section 1, but "this Court has rejected that notion. The language of the third branch of the *Oakes* test is consistent with a more nuanced approach to the minimal impairment inquiry – one that takes into account the difficulty of drafting laws that accomplish Parliament's goals, achieve certainty and only minimally intrude on rights."[28] As Chief Justice McLachlin remarked on section 1, "some laws may fail. I, for one, do not find this appalling."[29] The reality is that even with this flexible approach to section 1, some legislation will fail to be considered a reasonable limitation. This is to be expected in a constitutional system that legitimizes judicial review and the invalidation of legislation that violates the Charter, as nearly one-third of challenged statutes do.

Judicial Activism and Invalidated Statutes
The introduction of the Charter has significantly altered the standards against which legislation is evaluated for constitutionality, and this has resulted in sixty-four statutes being invalidated, in whole or in part, between 1982 and 2003.[30] The frequency of judicial invalidation and the empirical basis of judicial supremacy, therefore, are slightly more than three statutes a year during the first twenty-one years of Charter review by the Supreme Court. In

assessing the first decade of Charter review, Peter Russell argued that "none of the key economic and social policy interests of government – monetary and fiscal policy, international trade, resource development, social welfare, education, labour relations, environmental protection – have been significantly encroached upon by judicial enforcement of the Charter."[31] This pattern continues, as legal rights represent 44 percent (28 out of 64) and fundamental freedoms cases are 27 percent (17 out of 64) of the statutes invalidated.

Before we turn to the statutes invalidated, we must consider the context of the court's activism, as a central weakness in the debate lies in the failure to consider the characteristics of the statutes nullified. There is no distinction in the academic debate between the statutes' dates of enactment and whether the Supreme Court has focused on recent statutes or those enacted or last amended before the Charter's introduction. Thus, judicial activism is prioritized and the characteristics of statutes downplayed in the judicial-centred approach to understanding the relationship between the Supreme Court and the cabinet. Because the framers of the Charter intended the introduction of the document to fundamentally change the policy process and conceptions of what was constitutional under an entrenched Charter, it should not be considered necessarily problematic when the court invalidates legislation enacted or amended before the Charter's introduction as inconsistent with the new constitutional standards established by political actors in 1982. This earlier legislation was designed in a policy context that placed less emphasis on protected rights and did not consider whether the legislation, if challenged in a court, would be considered a reasonable limitation if found to violate the Charter.[32] The analysis provided by departments of justice before 1982 focused on whether the proposed legislation was constitutional in terms of the division of powers, and limited emphasis was placed on the few language rights in the *BNA Act,* Canada's original constitution. In essence, rights analysis was not a significant part of the policy context before 1982, and it is unfair to evaluate the court's activism under the Charter against statutes enacted before the Charter because of this significant procedural difference in the drafting of legislation.

The sixty-four statutes invalidated by the Supreme Court are presented in Table 5.1, which includes information about Charter section, the basis of the failed section 1 defence, the remedy employed by the Supreme Court, the date the statute was enacted or last amended, and the date the statute was invalidated by the Supreme Court. In terms of the date of enactment, a significant number of the statutes were proclaimed into law before the entrenchment of the Charter, as 31 percent (20 out of 64) of the invalidated statutes were enacted between 1970 and 1982. As forty-four of the sixty-four statutes invalidated were proclaimed into law after 1982, the Charter revolution rests on an even narrower empirical foundation, as slightly more than two statutes a year have been invalidated in a twenty-one-year period.

Table 5.1

Judicial invalidation and Charter review, 1982 to 2003

Case[1]	Government	Section 1	Remedy	Statute[2]	Decision[3]
Legal rights					
Hunter v. Southam	Federal	N/A	Nullification	1970	1984
Singh	Federal	Unreasonable	Nullification	1976	1985
Motor Vehicle Act Reference	BC	Excessive	Nullification	1982	1985
Oakes	Federal	Excessive	Nullification	1970	1986
Smith	Federal	Excessive	Nullification	1970	1987
Vaillancourt	Federal	Excessive	Nullification	1976	1987
Morgentaler	Federal	Excessive	Nullification	1970	1988
Thibault	Quebec	Unreasonable	Nullification	1982	1988
Martineau	Federal	Excessive	Nullification	1985	1990
Logan	Federal	Excessive	Nullification	1985	1990
Nguyen	Federal	Total	Nullification	1987	1990
Swain	Federal	Overbreadth	Suspended	1970	1991
Seaboyer	Federal	Total	Nullification	1985	1991
Sit	Federal	Excessive	Nullification	1983	1991
Bain	Federal	Unreasonable	Suspended	1985	1992
Généreux	Federal	Unreasonable	Prequel	1985	1992
Morales	Federal	Overbreadth	Nullification	1985	1992
Baron; Kourtessi	Federal	Unreasonable	Nullification	1986	1993
Heywood	Federal	Overbreadth	Nullification	1985	1994
Laba	Federal	Unreasonable	Nullification	1985	1994
Campbell	Alberta	Unreasonable	Suspended	1985	1997

▲

▼ *Table 5.1*

Case[1]	Government	Section 1	Remedy	Statute[2]	Decision[3]
Provincial Court of PEI	PEI	Unreasonable	Suspended	1994	1997
Provincial Judges Association	Manitoba	Unreasonable	Read-down	1990	1997
Burns	Federal	Overbreadth	Read-in	1999	2001
Ruzic	Federal	Excessive	Nullification	1985	2001
Mackin	NB	Unreasonable	Suspended	1995	2002
Hall	Federal	Overbreadth	Read-down	1997	2002
White, Ottenheimer & Baker	Federal	Unreasonable	Nullification	1985	2002
Fundamental freedoms					
Big M. Drug Mart Ltd.	Federal	Total	Nullification	1970	1985
Ford	Quebec	Total	Nullification	1983	1988
Devine	Quebec	Total	Nullification	1983	1988
Edmonton Journal	Alberta	Excessive	Nullification	1980	1989
Rocket	Ontario	Total	Nullification	1980	1990
Committee for the Commonwealth of Canada	Federal	Total	Nullification	1979	1991
Osborne	Federal	Overbreadth	Read-down	1985	1991
Zundel	Federal	Overbreadth	Nullification	1985	1992
RJR-Macdonald Inc.	Federal	Total	Nullification	1988	1995
Libman	Quebec	Unreasonable	Nullification	1981	1997
Thomson Newspaper Company	Federal	Total	Nullification	1985	1998
Lucas	Federal	Overbreadth	Read-down	1985	1998
U.F.C.W., Local 1518 v. Kmart Canada	BC	Overbreadth	Suspended	1992	1999
Little Sisters Book and Art Emporium	Federal	Unreasonable	Read-down	1985	2002
Sharpe	Federal	Overbreadth	Read-in	1993	2001
Dunmore	Ontario	Total	Suspended	1997	2001
Ruby	Federal	Unreasonable	Read-down	1985	2002

Equality rights

Case	Jurisdiction				
Andrews	BC	Total	Nullification	1979	1989
Tétreault-Gadoury	Federal	Total	Nullification	1985	1991
Schacter	Federal	Total	Prequel	1980	1992
Miron	Ontario	Total	Read-in	1980	1995
Benner	Federal	Excessive	Nullification	1985	1997
Eldridge	BC	Unreasonable	Suspended	1996	1997
Vriend	Alberta	Total	Read-in	1990	1998
Corbiere	Federal	Total	Suspended	1985	1999
M. v. H.	Ontario	Total	Suspended	1990	1999
Trociuk	BC	Total	Suspended	1996	2003
Nova Scotia v. Martin	NS	Total	Suspended	1995	2003

Minority language education rights

Case	Jurisdiction				
Protestant School Boards	Quebec	Total	Nullification	1977	1984
Mahé	Alberta	Unreasonable	Declaration	1982	1990
Reference Re Public Schools Act	Manitoba	Unreasonable	Declaration	1987	1993
Arsenault-Cameron	PEI	N/A	Declaration	1990	2000

Mobility rights

Case	Jurisdiction				
Black v. Law Society	Alberta	Overbreadth	Nullification	1980	1989

Democratic rights

Case	Jurisdiction				
Sauvé (1993)	Federal	Overbreadth	Nullification	1985	1993
Sauvé (2002)	Federal	Overbreadth	Nullification	1993	2002
Figueroa	Federal	Total	Suspended	1993	2003

1 Complete case citations are listed in the Bibliography.
2 Date act introduced or last amended, as reported in *Supreme Court Reports*.
3 Date Supreme Court heard case.

Focusing on the forty-four invalidated statutes introduced after 1982 reveals that much of the court's activism involves statutes enacted immediately after the Charter's entrenchment, as thirty-two statutes were proclaimed into law in the 1983 to 1990 period. Most were enacted in 1985 (twenty-one statutes). Few statutes enacted after 1990 have been invalidated by the Supreme Court; only twelve statutes enacted in this period were determined to be inconsistent with the Charter. Indeed, one of the most recent statutes found unconstitutional on Charter grounds was enacted in 1996. This was the *Vital Statistics Act (British Columbia)*. The court ruled in *Trociuk v. British Columbia* that the act, which allowed a mother to decide whether to include the name of her child's biological father on the birth certificate, violated the Charter's equality rights provisions.[33]

If the limited number of statutes enacted after 1982 that have been nullified by the Supreme Court is not a serious enough reservation on the judicial supremacy thesis, then a broader consideration of the statutes reviewed by the Supreme Court is. A total of 175 statutes have been reviewed at the level of the Supreme Court for their relationship to the Charter, and 111 have been found constitutional (see Table 5.2). In addition to the Criminal Code provisions involving the possession of child pornography, added in 1993, that were partially invalidated in *Sharpe,* and amendments to the *Canada Elections Act* in 1993 that restricted the voting rights of prisoners, which were invalidated in *Sauvé v. Canada*,[34] very few statutes reviewed by the Supreme Court were enacted in the post-1990 period.[35] It is significant that very few statutes enacted in a policy environment that places greater emphasis on reconciling legislation with Charter values are reviewed by the

Table 5.2

Rates of invalidation and the Charter, 1982 to 2003[1]

	Constitutional		Unconstitutional		
	Number	%	Number	%	Total
Federal government					
Charter decisions	73	65.18	39	34.82	112
Non-Charter decisions	1	100.00	0	0.00	1
Total decisions	74	65.49	39	34.51	113
Provincial governments					
Charter decisions	38	60.32	25	39.68	63
Non-Charter decisions	9	37.50	15	62.50	24
Total decisions	47	54.02	40	45.98	87

1 This table includes cases where the Supreme Court of Canada has used a number of remedies in addition to judicial nullification of statutes, such as suspended decisions, determining constitutional obligations, reading-in, or reading-down definitions by the court.

Supreme Court. The Supreme Court has control over its docket and can select which cases to review, so it is the pool of cases that the court chooses from that is significant. The important empirical study by Charles Epp also neglects the date of enactment and focuses simply on the year in which the court invalidated legislation, as well as the volume of cases, as evidence of the Charter's importance.[36] However, what matters is the date a statute is enacted or last amended and not when it is invalidated, as judicial activism may be an irrelevant empirical consideration if the court simply invalidates statutes enacted in a pre-rights policy context or those in the immediate aftermath of the Charter's entrenchment.

A number of hypotheses exist to explain the limited number of statutes proclaimed into law after 1990 that have been reviewed by the Supreme Court. First, governments have not appealed lower-court invalidations of recently enacted legislation. This hypothesis has been advanced by Morton and Knopff, who contend that the federal government has simply refused to appeal lower-court victories by gay-rights organizations against federal statutes and suggest that a number of provincial governments use this strategy as well.[37] However, as Roach has noted, governments remain the largest repeat players, retain an automatic right of intervention, and "represent the first eight of the top ten list of interveners in *Charter* cases before the Supreme Court."[38] This hypothesis, therefore, is not empirically borne out, unless one accepts that governments are selective about which defeats to appeal as a general strategy to advance a policy agenda indirectly through judicial invalidations. A more reasonable explanation for a docket with few statutes enacted after 1990 is the general success of Charter vetting by departments of justice during the pre-legislative development of legislation, as I have argued elsewhere.[39] Even if the Supreme Court uses its discretion to choose cases in which it wants to be a strategic actor, as Manfredi claims with regard to abortion politics and gay rights,[40] its choices are limited by the importance of legislative activism, which has generally contained judicial activism to older statutes enacted in a less demanding policy context.

Legislative Precision and Coordinate Constitutionalism

This section begins with a basic question and provides potential answers before turning to a deeper analysis of invalidated statutes. The question is: Why are statutes nullified by the Supreme Court? This is essentially the heart of the judicial-review-and-democracy debate in Canada, and there are two obvious answers. First, the statute is inconsistent with the policy preferences of the Supreme Court and is nullified to preserve judicial power and autonomy. Second, the act in question is unconstitutional and requires its invalidation. Generally, the first answer suggests a judicial-centred approach that sees invalidation as a calculated choice of a strategic policy actor, and the second advances a cabinet-centred understanding of judicial invalidation as a reaction to the limitations of an executive-dominated policy process. Manfredi advanced the idea of a strategic policy actor in his analysis of the Chrétien court when he argued "the Supreme Court is a political institution. It makes policy not as an accidental by-product of its legal function, but because its justices believe that certain legal rules will be socially beneficial."[41] There is evidence for the strategic actor argument, such as the issue of judicial independence protected by section 11(d) of the Charter. In this regard, the Supreme Court has clearly established judicial hegemony over the meaning of judicial independence and rejected the coordinate constitutionalism model.

In the *Judicial Independence Reference* of 1997, the Supreme Court ruled that the attempt by three provinces to address their budgetary deficits by reducing the salaries of provincial court judges violated judicial independence and was not a reasonable limitation on section 11(d).[42] In the *Reference Re Provincial Court Judges*, Chief Justice Lamer ruled that provincial governments can change the salaries of judges, but only after seeking the recommendations of an independent judicial compensation committee charged with submitting non-binding reports to each provincial legislature. In effect, the court determined both the process for establishing judicial salaries and the institutional structure that the judicial compensation committees must take to satisfy section 11(d). For instance, the members of the judicial compensation committee must have security of tenure and serve for fixed terms to prevent political interference by the legislative branch.[43]

The significance of this decision is that the court expanded both the content and the meaning of judicial independence beyond the three core characteristics – security of tenure, financial security, and administrative independence – that it established in *R. v. Valente*.[44] While the court provided for a non-binding report to be submitted to those provincial actors responsible for setting judicial salaries, the court narrowed the manoeuvrability of these actors in such a way that the report issued by the judicial compensation committees, for all intents and purposes, is a binding report. Specifically, if a provincial legislature rejects the recommendation, "it must be prepared to justify this decision, if necessary, in a court of law."[45] Clearly, the discretionary power of provincial legislatures to reduce judicial salaries as part of a general program of spending has been limited by the *Provincial Court Judges Reference* and the mandated creation of independent judicial committees. In doing so, the court has adopted a confrontational stance with provincial cabinets that suggests judicial supremacy and hegemony over section 11(d).

The implications of the *Provincial Court Judges Reference* were evidenced in *Mackin v. New Brunswick* when the Supreme Court determined that the elimination of supernumerary judges in New Brunswick violated judicial independence.[46] In 1987, New Brunswick created the office of supernumerary judge to replace that of deputy judge. At the age of retirement, a judge had three choices: retire, continue to sit as a full-time judge, or become a supernumerary judge and perform duties assigned by the chief justice. The supernumerary judge continued to receive a salary and benefits equivalent to the salary of a full-time judge but was expected to perform 40 percent of the caseload of a full-time judge. The position of supernumerary judge was eliminated in 1995 and replaced with a panel of retired judges who would be paid on a per diem basis. In *Mackin,* the Supreme Court ruled that the unilateral decision by the New Brunswick legislature to eliminate the position of supernumerary judge violated the conditions of judicial independence established in *Valente* and was unconstitutional because the decision was not made by an independent judicial compensation committee, as mandated by the court in *Provincial Court Judges Reference:*

> Any change made to the remuneration conditions of judges at any given time must necessarily pass through the *institutional filter* of an independent, effective and objective body so that the relationship between the judiciary, on the one hand, and the executive and legislative branches, on the other, remain depoliticized as far as possible. That is a structural requirement of the Canadian Constitution resulting from the separation of powers and the rule of law. By failing to refer the question of the elimination of the office of supernumerary judge to such a body, the government of New Brunswick breached this fundamental duty.[47]

Because the court considered the decision by the legislature a serious attack on judicial independence, the rigorous application of the *Oakes* test was adopted in this case. The court considered the legislature's failure to justify circumventing the judicial compensation committee to be a serious breach and not a reasonable limitation on section 11(d). The trend since *Valente,* therefore, has been growing judicial control over the determination of section 11(d) and the emergence of the court as a strategic policy actor in determining the parameters of judicial independence.

Like Manfredi, Peacock contends that strategic choice, in the form of judicial rationalism over the meaning of the Charter's equality rights, explains the invalidation of acts by the Supreme Court.[48] However, the limitation with the judicial-centred approach is that it implies that legislation, once passed by competent bodies, is constitutional and, further, that the constitutionality of acts is simply determined by judicial choices and not legislative choices. My approach advances a cabinet-centred analysis that focuses on the characteristics of the statutes nullified and not simply the judicial reasoning leading to declarations of unconstitutionality, though this is an important dimension nonetheless. Much of the legislation found to violate the Charter suffers from both vagueness, in the definition of activities it seeks to regulate, and from overbreadth, by attempting to regulate vaguely defined activities in an excessive manner. It is these inherent flaws in impugned legislation that account for judicial invalidation, as most such statutes do not marginally exceed minimal impairment of a Charter right, but generally constitute excessive limitations or total limitations of rights. Thus, it is the lack of proportionality that is the primary cause of judicial activism, and not the discretionary decisions of judicial actors. Judicial activism can therefore be interpreted as a signal to the parliamentary arena, dominated by the cabinet, to draft legislation in a more precise manner in order to reconcile statutes with the Charter. As a result, judicial activism may be less problematic than normally contended, as invalidation rarely prevents governments from legislating in a particular policy area. Rather, legislative precision as an emerging principle of Charter review can be offered as a justification for judicial activism that allows it to be consistent with constitutional supremacy.

This analysis of judicial activism is premised on the assumption that it is more appropriate for political scientists to understand judicial invalidation as a legitimate reaction to the deficiencies of an executive-dominated policy process. Thus, the responsibility for invalidated statutes does not rest with the Supreme Court, outside of the limited cases where it does act as a strategic policy actor, but with the cabinet and its provincial counterparts, who have primary responsibility for drafting legislation. The limited scrutiny of legislation by parliamentary committees, the ability of the governing party to defeat amendments proposed by standing committees, the decline of an effective opposition, and the concentration of power within the office of the prime minister suggest a policy process that can withstand judicial scrutiny in an age of rights, but at the price of parliamentary democracy.[49] These limitations are surely replicated within the legislative process and within the design of statutes that eventually become the focus of Charter review by the Supreme Court because of the absence of formal and effective scrutiny of the cabinet's legislative agenda.

These characteristics of the parliamentary arena help to explain why statutes that were enacted before, or shortly after, the Charter's introduction have been invalidated, as the political executive monopolized the legislative process, and constitutional advice was limited to compliance with the division of powers. My overall conclusion, however, is not a pessimistic one regarding the health of Canadian parliamentary democracy. What the judicial-centric analyses overlook is the Charter's potential reformist influence on the legislative process, and the way in which cabinets of the federal and provincial orders of government have responded by incorporating greater legislative precision into the development of public policy, though the process is no less executive-dominated.[50] The political and bureaucratic response to legislative precision illustrates a central argument advanced in this book

Table 5.3

Rejected section 1 defences by limitation, 1982 to 2003

Nature of the limitation	Characteristics	Number[1]	Percentage
Unreasonable	Marginally exceeds section 1	17	27.4193548
Overbreadth	Vague and imprecise	13	20.9677419
Excessive	Total lack of proportion	11	17.7419355
Total limitation	Limitation constitutes a denial	21	33.8709677

1 The total is 62 cases and not 64 because 2 cases did not include a section 1 analysis: *Hunter v. Southam* and *Arsenault-Cameron v. PEI.*

– the secondary components of rights activism are a response to democratic activism and serve to limit the potential for judicial supremacy by ensuring the proper functioning of constitutional supremacy in Canada.

The Supreme Court has refused to accept that infringements on Charter rights constitute a reasonable limitation in two-thirds of cases, as outlined in Table 5.3, which shows that sixty-two section 1 defences have been rejected between 1982 and 2003. The court's use of section 1 has been taken as a gauge of judicial discretion and the state of constitutional supremacy. For instance, the court's acceptance that a limitation is reasonable is considered compatible with constitutional supremacy, whereas the court's refusal to accept that a limitation is reasonable is far more problematic and can raise questions about the legitimacy of judicial review.[51] This dichotomous approach by the court is too imprecise to indicate why statutes fail the reasonable limits test, and it reinforces the faulty assumption that the constitutionality of statutes is a judicial determination and not the result of policy decisions by political actors – by applying this dichotomous approach, the judiciary either accepts or rejects a claim by government that a limitation is justifiable.

In Table 5.4, failed section 1 defences are organized into four categories based on the amount the infringement exceeded minimal impairment and the range of acceptable alternatives that would justify an infringement. The first category, unreasonable limitation, includes statutes whose constitutionality is determined by judicial discretion because minimal impairment is marginally exceeded and these statutes could easily have been found constitutional. The second category, overbreadth, is characterized by provisions that attempt to regulate specific activities through vague and imprecise legislative instruments: in essence, the provisions cover a broad area of regulation and interfere with legitimate action as a result. The third, excessive limitations, displays a total lack of proportionality between the legislative means chosen and the infringement, while the fourth category contains statutes that represent a total limitation and generally constitute a denial of

Table 5.4

Section 1 and the nature of the limitation, 1982 to 2003

Unreasonable	Overbreadth	Excessive	Total
1 Singh	1 Swain	1 B.C. Motor Vehicle Act	1 Nguyen
2 Thibault	2 Morales	2 Oakes	2 Seaboyer
3 Bain	3 Heywood	3 Smith	3 Big M. Drug Mart Ltd.
4 Généreux	4 Burns	4 Vaillancourt	4 Ford
5 Baron; Kourtessi	5 Hall	5 Morgentaler	5 Devine
6 Laba	6 Osborne	6 Martineau	6 Rocket
7 Campbell	7 Zundel	7 Logan	7 Committee for the Commonwealth of Canada
8 Provincial Court of P.E.I	8 Lucas	8 Sit	8 RJR-Macdonald Inc.
9 Provincial Judges Association	9 U.F.C.W., Local 1518	9 Ruzic	9 Thomson Newspaper Company
10 Mackin	10 Sharpe	10 Edmonton Journal	10 Dunmore
11 White, Ottenheimer & Baker	11 Black	11 Benner	11 Andrews
12 Libman	12 Sauvé (1993)		12 Tétreault-Gadoury
13 Little Sisters Book and Art Emporium	13 Sauvé (2002)		13 Schacter
14 Ruby			14 Miron
15 Eldridge			15 Vriend
16 Mahé			16 Corbiere
17 Reference Re Public Schools Act			17 M. v. H.
			18 Protestant School Boards
			19 Figueroa
			20 Trociuk
			21 Nova Scotia v. Martin

Note: Complete case citations are listed in the Bibliography.

a Charter right. As a failed section 1 defence progresses along this spectrum, the legislation in question grows increasingly less precise in the attempt to link policy objectives with legislative instruments for their implementation. In effect, the overly broad regulation of vaguely defined activities is a deficiency in the drafting process that requires the Supreme Court to find that invalidated statutes exceed minimal impairment. This characteristic is legislative and not judicial, though it is identified by the Supreme Court when it determines that statutes cannot be justified as a reasonable limitation.

Applying an approach that looks at the characteristics of the statutes and not simply the judicial reasoning demonstrates that only a small number of statutes marginally exceed minimal impairment and most suffer substantive internal limitations. In essence, judicial discretion determines unconstitutionality in a limited number of cases, as 72 percent (45 out of 62) of the failed section 1 defences involve statutes that are fundamentally flawed, and the largest category are those that represent a total limitation (21 out of 62). Simply stated, the determination of constitutionality is more the result of the discretionary choices of cabinets and bureaucratic actors, reflected in legislative schemes, than the result of discretionary judicial choices. This is significant as it questions whether section 1 is a highly discretionary judicial instrument or whether statutes that are nullified are so seriously flawed that it would be unreasonable for the court to uphold their constitutionality through a section 1 analysis. The lack of legislative precision in invalidated statutes, and the inability of the court to uphold such legislation as a minimal impairment, are discussed below. Understanding constitutional invalidation of statutes should not begin and end with a judicial-centred analysis but must incorporate elements of the cabinet-centred focus because of the near hegemonic position of the cabinet and bureaucratic actors in the development of legislation. To do otherwise is to assign too much importance to judicial decisions and to devalue the role of political decisions in the constitutional evaluation of statutes by the Supreme Court, as Robert Martin has done in his recent book.[52]

Minimal Impairment Marginally Exceeded
It is probably easiest for the competent legislative body to re-establish the constitutionality of statutes that marginally exceed minimal impairment because the basis of invalidation is generally the result of a procedural limitation in the statute, whereas statutes failing section 1 for other reasons are generally invalidated on substantive grounds. While the determination of constitutionality is at the discretion of the court, the ability of the competent body to re-establish constitutionality through a legislative response demonstrates that the determination of constitutionality is also within the competence of the cabinet. The analysis below will be limited to four cases that illustrate the narrow basis of many invalidations and the ability of

competent legislative bodies to re-establish the constitutionality of offending statutes; *Singh v. Minister of Employment and Immigration, Libman v. Quebec, Little Sisters Book and Art Emporium v. Canada,* and *Eldridge v. British
Columbia.*[53]

In *Singh,* the court concluded that appeal procedures available to an individual denied convention refugee status under section 71(1) of the *Immigration Act* violated the principles of fundamental justice under section 7 of the
Charter because an oral hearing was not part of the appeal process. Under
section 71(1) of the *Immigration Act,* a negative decision was appealed in
writing to the Immigration Appeal Board which decided, on the basis of the
transcript submitted under oath during the initial determination of refugee
status, whether an appeal hearing should occur.[54] In a unanimous decision,
the Supreme Court ruled that section 71(1) was unconstitutional, with equal
numbers of judges finding the declaration of unconstitutionality on the
basis of the Charter or the 1960 *Canadian Bill of Rights.* The finding of unconstitutionality as a violation of section 7 of the Charter was the basis of
Justice Wilson's decision, which took issue with the inability of individuals
appealing a decision to challenge the case against them. Wilson argued that
"a refugee claimant may never have the opportunity to make an effective
challenge to the information or policies which underlie the Minister's decision to reject his claim," and this violated the principles of fundamental
justice because Justice Wilson did not foresee how "a successful challenge
to the accuracy of the undisclosed information upon which the Minister's
decision is based could ever be launched."[55] The limitation on section 7 was
not considered reasonable, largely because the federal government justified
the absence of an oral hearing on utilitarian grounds, arguing that the limited financial resources of the Immigration Appeal Board could not sustain
such an appeal process.

The section 1 analysis by Justice Wilson is significant, as the court recognized the difficult task it faced in determining whether limitations were
reasonable: "If too low a threshold is set, the courts run the risk of emascu-
lating the *Charter.* If too high a threshold is set, the courts run the risk of
unjustifiably restricting government action. It is not a task to be entered
upon lightly."[56] Thus, the court recognized that its approach had to balance
rights and responsible parliamentary government and is an early indication
of the emergence of coordinate constitutionalism in its Charter jurisprudence. Further, the court rejected the idea that financial concerns could
justify a limitation, saying that "the guarantees of the *Charter* would be
illusory if they could be ignored because it was administratively convenient
to do so."[57] This decision is important in another sense, as it illustrates the
Diceyan principle that judicial legislation should be considered as secondary legislation subject to parliamentary modification. Because the *Immigration Act* was invalidated on narrow procedural grounds, the federal cabinet

introduced amendments in 1986 that included an oral hearing as part of the appeal procedure.[58] This decision has been criticized on financial grounds by conservative judicial critics, who suggest the Supreme Court "forced" this amendment on the cabinet.[59] This downplays whether the *Immigration Act*, passed in 1976 and drafted in a policy environment where administrative efficiency was prioritized at the expense of administrative fairness, could be considered constitutional after 1982. As the legislative response was minimal and the judicial decision did not challenge the substantive characteristics of the policy, judicial invalidation proved to be a constitutional hurdle that the cabinet easily overcame in its legislative response to *Singh*.

The invalidation of sections of Quebec's *Referendum Act* in *Libman* illustrates the marginal unconstitutionality of a large number of statutes and the importance of judicial discretion in determining compliance with the Charter. At issue in *Libman* was section 404 of the *Referendum Act*, which limited third-party spending by individuals or groups not willing to be affiliated with an official committee to $600. This spending limitation was challenged as a violation of freedom of expression and association, both claims accepted by the Supreme Court. Turning to the section 1 analysis, the Supreme Court accepted that spending restrictions were necessary to ensure equality in the positions presented by the "Yes" and "No" committees during a referendum, but it questioned the reasonableness of severe spending restrictions on third parties. During the minimal impairment analysis, the Supreme Court suggested that alternatives existed to advance the objectives of the *Referendum Act* and recommended a spending restriction of $1,000, as suggested by the Lortie Commission.[60] However, the Supreme Court refrained from establishing the spending limit that could ensure the constitutionality of section 404, saying that it would "be up to the legislature to make the appropriate amendments."[61]

The decision in *Libman* can be criticized on the grounds that the difference between constitutionality and unconstitutionality for section 404 was $400, and it is reasonable to ask whether the offending provisions of the *Referendum Act* should have been invalidated for such a marginal amount. The restrained remedy by the Supreme Court, and its insistence that the National Assembly in the city of Québec city should decide an appropriate spending restriction, reinforce the principle of coordinate constitutionalism that underlies much of the Supreme Court's Charter jurisprudence. As well, the narrow basis of the invalidation allowed the Quebec cabinet to easily amend the *Referendum Act* to ensure the constitutionality of spending restrictions. In the lead-up to the 1998 Quebec election, Lucien Bouchard recalled the National Assembly for one day to amend the *Referendum Act* in order to ensure its compliance with both the Canadian Charter and the *Quebec Charter of Human Rights and Freedoms*, as the Supreme Court determined the spending restrictions were in violation of both documents.

In *Eldridge,* the Supreme Court ruled that the absence of sign-language interpreters, when necessary for communication during medical situations, violated the equality rights of the hearing impaired.[62] In rejecting the section 1 argument by British Columbia that the cost of providing sign-language interpreters was prohibitive, Justice Laforest argued that it would cost $150,000 a year, a figure disputed by Manfredi and Maioni, who question Laforest's analysis of the social science evidence.[63] What is significant, however, is the legislative response to *Eldridge.* The British Columbia government initially set up a twenty-four-hour toll-free phone number that hearing impaired people could call for help with essential medical services. It also instituted a formal policy whereby the hearing impaired or medical personnel could request sign-language interpreters for hospital or physician visits.[64] While the Supreme Court ruled on the constitutionality of the *Hospital Insurance Act,* the responsibility for remedying the invalidation was at the discretion of the British Columbia cabinet, and, in reality, only a minor policy adjustment was needed to re-establish the constitutionality of the offending provisions.

In *Little Sisters,* a reverse-onus provision in the *Customs Act,* which prohibited the importing of material determined obscene by customs officials, was invalidated by the Supreme Court as a violation of freedom of expression. In this case, a Vancouver bookstore that catered to the gay and lesbian community imported material from the United States and had experienced undue delays and regular classification of its material as obscene for nearly fifteen years. Under the *Customs Act,* if officials determined that imported material was obscene, the onus was on the importer to disprove the classification that prevented the material from entering Canada.[65] This is a significant decision because it reveals the Supreme Court's dichotomous approach to state actors during Charter review. In this case, the court accepted the premise of the *Customs Act* and its regulation of obscene material and found fault simply with the reverse-onus provision. Further, the court continued its activist approach to the conduct of public officials, finding fault with the actions of customs officials, but supported the actions of the cabinet by accepting the substantial objectives of the statute. The most problematic aspect of the *Customs Act,* in the court's estimation, was not the substance of the legislation but its application by customs officials, which resulted in the constitutional violation because of the officials' poor training and inability to evaluate the artistic merit of material classified as obscene. In its remedy, the Supreme Court read-down this provision and placed the onus on the Crown to demonstrate that material was obscene.[66]

Overly Broad Statutes
Once failed section 1 defences move beyond marginally exceeding minimal impairment, the emphasis on legislative precision in the court's judgments

becomes more pronounced. Unlike cases in the first category, where judicial discretion generally determines the finding of unconstitutionality and the difference between constitutionality and unconstitutionality is marginal (as *Libman* demonstrates), the invalidation of statutes in the remaining categories on the grounds that the limitation is not reasonable is generally the result of the policy instruments chosen by the cabinet to achieve its legislative agenda and not judicial decisions by the Supreme Court. The lack of proportionality in legislative schemes that are vague or imprecise about the activities to be controlled results in judicial determinations of unconstitutionality by the Supreme Court. This was evident in *Osborne v. Canada*, where section 33 of the *Public Service Employment Act*, which prohibited "partisan political expression and activity by public servants under threat of disciplining action including dismissal from employment," was found to be in violation of freedom of expression.[67] The legislative objective of the act was legitimate, as it sought to ensure a neutral public service, but the legislative scheme lacked proportionality and was overly broad as it applied to the entire public service.

The majority opinion by Justice Sopinka did not consider the broad application of the ban as a minimal impairment because, the justice wrote, "to apply the same standard to a Deputy Minister and a cafeteria worker appears to me to invoke considerable overkill and does not meet the test of constituting a measure that is carefully designed to impair freedom of expression as little as reasonably possible."[68] In its remedy, the court considered reading-down section 33 to include only politically sensitive public servants, but rejected this approach because "it is Parliament that should determine how the section should be redrafted and not the Court ... Parliament will have available to it information and expertise that is not available to the Court."[69] Again the theme of coordinate constitutionalism emerges in activist Charter decisions, where the court leaves it to the discretion of parliament to fashion a legislative response to a constitutional invalidation. Though it cautioned against reading-down the act to include politically sensitive public servants only, the Supreme Court did narrow the ban on partisan political activity to deputy ministers.

Sections of the Criminal Code that provide for indeterminate incarcerations or blanket provisions prohibiting certain activities cannot be justified as a reasonable limitation, according to the Supreme Court, because this approach suffers from overbreadth and is therefore inconsistent with the principles of fundamental justice. Several cases demonstrate this concern with precision as a necessary condition to satisfy the Charter. In *R. v. Swain*, for example, the court ruled in a majority decision that section 542(2) of the Criminal Code, which allowed the Crown to indefinitely detain a person found not guilty by reason of insanity, to be in violation of sections 7 and 9 of the Charter.[70] In its section 1 analysis, the majority applied the stringent application of the *Oakes* test, and section 542(2) fell because it was not deemed to represent a minimal impairment on both sections 7 and 9 of the Charter. Chief Justice Lamer concluded that section 542(2) resulted in an indeterminate period of incarceration that did not conform to minimal impairment because "the *Oakes* test requires that insanity acquittees be detained no longer than necessary to determine whether they are currently dangerous due to their insanity."[71] In reaching this conclusion, the chief justice referred to other sections of the Criminal Code, which "provided for remands of a fixed duration for psychiatric observations," to demonstrate the lack of proportionality within section 542(2).[72]

In a majority decision in *R. v. Heywood,* Justice Cory ruled that section 179(1)(b) of the Criminal Code, which prohibited convicted sexual offenders from loitering in public places, was also inconsistent with the principles of fundamental justice as it was drawn too broadly and applied "without prior notice to the accused, to too many places, to too many people with no possibility of review."[73] Thus, because of the characteristics of overbreadth in the definition of public loitering and the lifetime ban, the majority rejected section 179(1)(b) as a minimal impairment on the right to liberty of convicted sexual offenders. This decision, however, was somewhat of a moot issue because the federal cabinet had created, and parliament had enacted, section 161 of the Criminal Code, which Justice Cory considered "a good example of legislation which is much more carefully and narrowly fashioned to achieve the same objective as s.179(1)(b)."[74]

The court's decisions in *Swain* and *Heywood* illustrate several limitations in concluding that the invalidation of legislation necessarily facilitates judicial supremacy. Recognizing that nullifying section 542(2) of the Criminal Code in *Swain* would release insanity acquittees en masse into the general public, the court suspended its decision for six months to allow the cabinet time to reflect on the inadequacy of the section and instruct the Department of Justice to rewrite the offending Criminal Code provisions to conform with the Charter.

The clearest example of legislative precision being incorporated into the policy process is found in the legislative sequel to *Swain,* which was challenged in *Winko v. B.C. (Forensic Psychiatric Institute).*[75] In response to the court's decision in *Swain,* the cabinet amended the Criminal Code to provide for the periodic review of those incarcerated but found not criminally responsible (NCR) because of mental disorder. This amendment was designed to overcome the procedural limitations identified by the *Swain* decision, namely the absence of review procedures to determine how long an individual found NCR should be held in custody. In *Winko,* the Supreme Court upheld the constitutionality of the legislative response to the *Swain* decision because the cabinet had carefully tailored its objectives in the area of criminal law with precise legislative instruments drafted by the Department of Justice. In a concurring unanimous judgment representing seven justices on a nine-member panel, Justice McLachlin concluded that the challenged section of the Criminal Code was constitutional because it was "carefully crafted to protect the liberty of the NCR accused to the maximum extent compatible with the person's current situation and the need to protect public safety."[76] The significance of the two decisions in *Swain* and *Winko* is that legislative precision has emerged as an important aspect of coordinate constitutionalism in Canada, with the court identifying the limitations in the design of legislation and the cabinet recognizing the importance of greater precision in the development of public policy and in its legislative response to judicial activism.

This explains the different outcomes in *Keegstra* and *Zundel,* which involved challenges to sections of the Criminal Code that restricted hate speech.[77] In *Keegstra,* the court, in majority (four to three), found that section 319(a) of the Criminal Code violated freedom of expression but that the section constituted a reasonable limitation.[78] The court accepted that section 319(a) was a minimal impairment on freedom of expression because the prohibition was well-crafted and created "a narrowly confined offence which suffers from neither overbreadth nor vagueness."[79] Moreover, the section excluded private communication, required public communication to target an identifiable group, and allowed an individual to defend this form of expression within section 319(a).[80] However, in *Zundel* the majority (four to three) determined that section 181 of the Criminal Code, which prohibited "the wilful publication of false statements or news that a person knows is false and is likely to cause mischief and harm," did not constitute a reasonable limitation because it suffered from overbreadth. The majority decision by Justice McLachlin contrasted sections 319(a) and 181 to demonstrate the proportionality in section 319(a) and the lack thereof in section 181: "The broad range of expression caught by s.181 – extending to virtually all controversial statements of apparent fact which might be argued to be false and likely do some mischief ... make it impossible to say that s.181 is appropriately measured and restrained having regard to the evil addressed."[81] Thus, the different legislative approaches in *Keegstra* and *Zundel* explain the different judicial outcomes and findings of constitutionality. While the principle of legislative precision characterizes the judicial decisions, it has been incorporated into the policy process, demonstrating both coordinate constitutionalism and the continued dominance of the legislative process by cabinet despite the ability of the courts to invalidate legislation.

The invalidation of sections of the British Columbia *Labour Relations Code (LRC)* that prohibited unions from distributing leaflets at secondary picketing sites in *UFCW, Local 1518 v. Kmart Canada* demonstrates the central role that cabinet decisions play in constitutional infringements.[82] The *LRC* definition of picketing was overly broad, regulated legitimate activities by organized labour, and prohibited the distribution of leaflets at secondary sites, even if they were distributed in a manner that did not interfere with the economic activities of secondary sites. In defending the definition of picketing, the attorney general of British Columbia argued that the overly broad approach under the *LRC* was rational because "conventional picketing and leafleting are indistinguishable."[83] The unanimous court argued that there was an important difference between picketing and leafleting, as picketing generally restricted access by consumers, but leafleting allowed the consumer to decide whether to accept and to read the information provided in a peaceful manner. Because the definition of picketing under section 1(1) of the *LRC* prohibited this legitimate action, it violated freedom of expression.[84]

The British Columbia cabinet's decision to include leafleting under the definition of picketing was not a minimal impairment because it prohibited legitimate constitutional activity in its attempt to prevent the harmful effects of secondary picketing, which the court accepted as a legitimate legislative objective. It was simply the broad approach to the definition of picketing that failed the section 1 test, as the court was concerned that the attorney general did not show that a partial ban limited to conventional picketing "would be less effective in achieving the government objective."[85] The remedy employed in this case is consistent with coordinate constitutionalism, as the Supreme Court suspended its decision for six months to allow the cabinet to introduce amendments to the *LRC*. The narrow basis of the invalidation suggests a minor legislative amendment would be needed to ensure the constitutionality of the definition of picketing by excluding leafleting as a restricted activity.

Despite the problematic nature of certain statutory provisions in *Osborne, Swain, Heywood, Zundel,* and *UFCW,* the narrow basis of the invalidations left the respective cabinets with sufficient flexibility to amend the offending sections to ensure their constitutionality. The court did not challenge the policy objectives of the cabinet and its provincial counterparts in any of the cases but simply argued that procedural limitations in legislative schemes violated Charter rights. The legislative response to *Swain,* and the subsequent finding of constitutionality in *Winko,* challenge the finality of invalidation that critics associate with judicial activism and the suggested loss of policy capacity for the cabinet, supported by the bureaucracy. Only in *Sauvé* was the legislative response to an earlier invalidation of section 51(e) of the *Canada Elections Act,* which prohibited prisoners serving more than two years from voting in elections, subsequently invalidated as inconsistent with democratic rights protected under section 3 of the Charter.[86] Cabinets generally do retain sufficient policy discretion to respond to judicial invalidation in an independent manner.[87] This is a development that is consistent, therefore, with coordinate constitutionalism and the reciprocal relationships that are required under the Charter.

Excessive Limitations

The common characteristic in statutes that fail section 1 because the legislative scheme is an excessive limitation is the lack of proportionality between the objective and the statutory means chosen to advance it. The central limitation in the judicial-centred approach is that it absolves the legislative arena of responsibility for invalidated statutes by focusing on the discretionary choices made by judicial actors. This is the major fault with Robert Martin's recent book, in which he states that "the Supreme Court has acted so as to undermine the essential structure and to subvert the processes of Canadian constitutional democracy."[88] Further, this approach factors out the inherently political aspect of decision making by the cabinet and discounts that policy decisions which are legitimate, based on the nearly hegemonic structure of the process in a parliamentary democracy with strong majority governments, may not be legitimate once subjected to other evaluative processes such as constitutional review. Parliament's decision to disenfranchise certain prisoners is an example of a politically motivated policy decision that lacked a constitutional basis because there is no ambiguity in the interpretation of the Charter's democratic rights.

The *Oakes* decision is an excellent illustration of the general lack of proportionality in statutes that excessively limit rights. In this case, a reverse-onus provision of the *Narcotics Control Act* was invalidated as a violation of the presumption of innocence protected by sections 11(d) and 7 of the Charter. Under section 8 of the *Narcotics Control Act,* individuals convicted of possession of narcotics were presumed to be engaged in trafficking and were convicted of the more serious crime unless they could prove otherwise.[89] In the case of Oakes, he was unable to dispense the reverse-onus provision and was convicted of trafficking based on the possession of eight grams of hashish oil. Under the act, therefore, an individual could be imprisoned for trafficking narcotics when the quantity seized did not suggest such an activity. Because the crime carried the possibility of life imprisonment, section 8 of the *Narcotics Control Act* was not a proportional response to the legitimate objective of drug enforcement because it could result in recreational drug users being indefinitely incarcerated. Further, before the Supreme Court invalidated section 51(e) of the Canada Elections Act in *Sauvé* in 1993, an individual convicted of trafficking on a small amount of narcotics would also lose the right to vote. While the court did invalidate this section of the *Narcotics Control Act,* the responsibility for the finding of unconstitutionality is with the cabinet, which decided to consider possession, regardless of the quantity, as evidence of the act of trafficking narcotics.

Most of the offending provisions that excessively limit rights are from the Criminal Code and involve the cabinet's attempt to restrict the rights of the accused. For instance, in *R. v. Martineau* the majority decision (six to one) found section 231(a) of the Criminal Code infringed sections 7 and 11(d) of the Charter because it "expressly eliminates the requirement for proof of subjective foresight" in a murder conviction.[90] Relying on the judgment in *R. v. Vaillancourt*,[91] Justice Lamer for the majority stated that it was a principle of fundamental justice "that before a person could be convicted of murder there must be proof beyond a reasonable doubt of at least objective foreseeability of death"[92] and that "a special mental element with respect to murder is necessary before a culpable homicide can be treated as murder."[93] More importantly, the majority did not consider section 213(a) to be a minimal impairment on section 7. In reaching this conclusion, the majority argued that convicting someone of murder "who did not intend or foresee death unnecessarily stigmatizes and punishes those whose moral blameworthiness is not that of a murderer, thus it unnecessarily impairs the rights guaranteed by s.7 and s.11(d)."[94] Similarly in *R. v. Logan,* the court considered the constitutionality of section 21(2) of the Criminal Code, which allowed for the conviction of parties who knew or "ought to have known" the outcome of an unlawful purpose.[95] This unanimous decision was delivered the same day as *Martineau,* and the court found section 21(2) to be constitutional except for a few offences. In particular, the court reiterated *Vaillancourt's* ruling that the state must prove guilt beyond a reasonable doubt for murder and extended the requirement of subjective foresight of death to attempted murder.[96]

Some might question whether it is a valid concern that the rights of the accused are excessively limited, and they could argue that the Supreme Court has simply advanced its agenda at the expense of victims' rights. Such a position is problematic because it demands the same hegemonic decision-making capacity for the cabinet that it derides for the Supreme Court as unsustainable under constitutional supremacy. Further, if the standard of assessment for the Supreme Court is that of an arbitrary actor, then surely this standard can be applied in evaluating the decision making of the cabinet in the area of criminal policy that constitutes excessive limitations of rights. Indeed, my approach is not to assess whether the policy decisions are reasonable, which they surely are in majoritarian institutions, but whether these majoritarian decisions are reasonable in light of constitutional guarantees. The decision in *R. v. Morgentaler* illustrates how majoritarian decisions in a parliamentary setting can be legitimate but arbitrary and inconsistent with constitutional protections.[97] Section 251 of the Criminal Code provided that abortions, to be legal, had to be authorized by a therapeutic abortion committee at an institution accredited by the minister of health in each province. Further, section 251 carried a maximum penalty of life imprisonment for individuals who performed an unauthorized abortion, and a maximum prison term of two years for the woman undergoing the procedure.[98]

The decision in *Morgentaler* may be one of the most misunderstood and has been used by Flanagan as an illustration of the ability of judicial decisions to prevent legislative responses to invalidated statutes.[99] According to Flanagan, the judicial decision framed the future legislative response and resulted in the limited policy manoeuvrability of the cabinet that prevented a response to *Morgentaler*. While Manfredi has suggested that there are unintended consequences of the invalidation of section 251 for federalism, as the provinces are free to determine the delivery of abortion services,[100] the importance of this decision is found in the court's commitment to coordinate constitutionalism in the judgments of Dickson and Beetz. Chief Justice Dickson argued that the procedures established for a legal abortion were arbitrary and unfair, and the limited access to the services at accredited hospitals violated the principles of fundamental justice. Dickson stated that section 251 contained "so many potential barriers to its own operation that the defence it creates will in many circumstances be practically unavailable to women who would prima facie qualify for the defence, or at least would force such women to travel great distances at substantial expense and inconvenience in order to benefit from a defence that is held out to be generally available."[101] Additionally, the chief justice argued that the absence of criteria to determine when a pregnancy endangered the health of the women was problematic, and "in the absence of such a definition, each physician and each hospital reaches an individual decision on this matter. How the concept of health is variably defined leads to considerable inequity in the distribution and the accessibility of the abortion procedure."[102] For Beetz, section 251 violated the security of the person for pregnant women because the procedural delays resulted in higher mortality rates, as a therapeutic abortion would be performed later in the pregnancy.

The court's analysis of the deficiencies of section 251 is suspect but is not evidence of a strategic actor seeking to determine the contours of a policy area. As a political scientist, I focus my analysis on the criminalization by the federal government of a policy area that is under provincial control – in this case, the medical procedure of abortion and the delivery of this service by the provinces. In *Morgentaler,* the judgments by Dickson and Beetz stated that section 251 had created undue delays in the delivery of abortion services, and this violated the principles of fundamental justice. The problematic nature of this decision is the court's assumption that a federal statute had caused delays in a medical procedure under the jurisdiction of the provinces. The delays and access difficulties were not caused by section 251, but by the reluctance of some provincial cabinets to establish therapeutic abortion committees, as authorized by the Criminal Code.[103] This was the

implementational limitation of section 251, as it placed a voluntary requirement – but not a constitutional duty – on provincial cabinets to provide
this medical procedure at accredited hospitals. The delays are documented
in the Badgley Report, which outlined that in 1977 only 271 hospitals had
established therapeutic abortion committees, and this had declined to 250
by 1985. Further, 18 percent of the hospitals that had therapeutic abortion
committees performed no abortions in 1984.[104] It was the complexity of
this policy context, and the court's lack of understanding of the relationship between section 251 and the division of powers, that led to the determination that the provision violated section 7 of the Charter.

In essence, the court found that a federal statute violated the Charter
because it was not implemented equitably by provincial governments: the
constitutionality of section 251, therefore, was caught in the vise of federalism.[105] Beyond this issue, *Morgentaler* was a narrow decision because Justices
Beetz and Wilson indicated that the Charter violation was excessive but
could easily be amended to ensure the constitutionality of section 251. Perhaps more importantly, they indicated that it was the responsibility of parliament, because of institutional capacity and legitimacy, to address the
limitations. For instance, Justice Wilson accepted the trimester approach to
the issue of abortion, in which the personal autonomy of a woman would
be absolute during the initial stages of a pregnancy, but the state would
have a compelling interest to protect the foetus in the latter stages. Consistent with coordinate constitutionalism, this compelling interest would be
decided by parliament, but more accurately cabinet, as Wilson stated the
"precise point in the development of the foetus at which the state's interest
in its protection becomes 'compelling' I leave to the informed judgment of
the legislature which is in a position to receive guidance on the subject
from all the relevant disciplines."[106] Justice Beetz reviewed the comparative
approaches to the state having a compelling interest to regulate abortion
services and considered whether these approaches could ensure the constitutionality of section 251. However, he refrained from articulating an appropriate legislative response as, he stated, it was "possible that a future
enactment by Parliament along the lines of the laws adopted in these jurisdictions could achieve a proportionality which is acceptable under s.1."[107]
The cabinet, therefore, would have to craft its response to the *Morgentaler*
decision.

The legislative responses introduced by the Mulroney government failed
to pass, as the first attempt was defeated in the House of Commons and the
second was defeated by a tie vote in the Senate.[108] Flanagan's assessment
that the *Morgentaler* decision prevented a legislative response because it narrowed the policy manoeuvrability of the cabinet is disputed because neither motion addressed the limited access to therapeutic abortions that
violated section 7. Even if the cabinet's response to *Morgentaler* had been

passed into law, it would have been invalidated in a subsequent Charter challenge because the constitutionality of criminalizing abortion was not dependent on this response but on the provincial cabinets accrediting hospitals, and on therapeutic abortion committees allowing the procedure to take place. As the cabinet's response did not – and could not – require provincial action to ensure the constitutionality of an amended section 251, the policy status quo endured because of the inability of the federal Criminal Code to compel provincial implementation of abortion services. The arbitrary decision by provincial cabinets to limit the number of accredited hospitals, and the arbitrary decision by some therapeutic abortion committees to not provide this medical procedure, violated section 7 of the Charter, therefore, and not the Supreme Court acting as a strategic policy actor or the formal guardian of the constitution.

Total Limitations

The distinction between a limitation and a denial of a Charter right emerged in *Attorney General (Quebec) v. Protestant School Boards* when the Supreme Court ruled that the restrictions on English education in Quebec violated section 23(1)(b) of the Charter and its guarantee of minority language education rights.[109] At issue were sections 72 and 73 of chapter 8 of Bill 101, the *Charter of the French Language,* which limited English education to the children of anglophones educated in Quebec. This conflicted with the Charter's guarantee of education for children in either official language when speakers of that language represented a minority in a province. The Quebec government did not challenge the fact that Bill 101 violated minority language education rights, but it argued that this was a reasonable limitation because of the need to protect the French language and culture. As other free and democratic societies, such as Switzerland and Belgium, had adopted stricter language polices subsequently upheld by the Swiss and European courts, Quebec reasoned that this policy would be upheld through section 1 of the Charter.[110]

The decision by the Quebec cabinet to deny educational instruction in English to the children of Canadian citizens educated in English outside of Quebec was not a reasonable limitation but a total limitation of section 23 outside of the anglophone community educated in Quebec. A fuller analysis of *Protestant School Boards* will be provided in Chapter 6, as this decision contains important federalist implications for provincial autonomy, but, briefly, Bill 101 was a legislative scheme that removed access to English education for Canadian citizens who had previously qualified before Bill 101 was enacted in 1977. As Manfredi has argued, the judgment was "less controversial than one might expect because it did not create any new rights, but simply restored rights that English-speaking Quebecers had enjoyed prior to Bill 101."[111] The court's decision in *Protestant School Boards* did not interfere with the substantive policy objective of preserving the French language, because it only privileged Canadian citizens educated outside Quebec who moved to Quebec. As the demographic strength of francophones was not threatened by interprovincial immigration but bolstered by French-speaking immigrants from la Francophonie, the invalidation of sections of the *Charter of the French Language* had no practical impact beyond providing a strong rhetorical tool for critics of the Charter and the 1982 constitutional settlement, such as Guy Laforest.[112]

Manfredi contends that *Protestant School Boards* was the only time the Supreme Court refused to consider a section 1 justification because the legislative scheme was determined to be a denial, but many of the failed section 1 analyses the court has conducted closely mirror this decision and approach.[113] For instance, in a number of cases involving the total prohibition of forms of expression, legislative schemes that essentially deny expressive activity have not been upheld as a reasonable limitation by the Supreme Court. In *Ford v. Quebec,* the Quebec cabinet conceded that sections 58 and 69 of the *Charter of the French Language,* which prohibited the use of languages other than French on public signs, violated freedom of expression, but argued it was a reasonable limitation.[114] In contrast to its approach in *Protestant School Boards,* the court abandoned the denial versus limitations approach to section 1, the reasonable limits clause, and determined whether the challenged sections of the *Charter of the French Language* were a reasonable limitation on freedom of expression. The issue of legislative precision emerged in the *Ford* decision, as the important policy objectives of the *Charter of the French Language* were not carefully tailored to the legislative means chosen. In its decision, the court indicated that whereas "requiring the predominant display of the French language, even its marked predominance, would be proportional to the goal of promoting and maintaining a French '*visage linguistique*' in Quebec and therefore justified under the *Quebec Charter* and the *Canadian Charter,* requiring the exclusive use of French has not been so justified."[115] The language policy of the Quebec government, therefore, was reasonable in terms of majoritarian decision making, but it was not a reasonable limitation in light of the Canadian Charter, as well as being inconsistent with the Quebec Charter, which was independently adopted by the Parti Québécois before the 1982 constitutional settlement.

The lack of legislative precision is evident in statutory schemes that ban expressive activity, and this issue arose in several cases, including *Rocket v. Royal College of Dental Surgeons of Ontario,* though the discussion here will be limited to *Thompson Newspapers Company v. Canada.*[116] In *Thompson Newspapers,* the court determined, in a majority decision (five to three), that section 322.1 of the *Canada Elections Act,* which banned polling data from being published three days before an election, to be a violation of freedom of expression. The majority decision by Justice Bastarache accepted the legislative objective of section 322.1, which was to prevent the publication of inaccurate public opinion polls that could have an undue effect on the voter and thus cause an uninformed decision on election day.[117] In its approach to section 1 of the Charter, the majority decision did not adopt a deferential approach because the cabinet was not mediating between competing groups, nor was it attempting to protect vulnerable groups or individuals, as the Quebec cabinet had been doing in *Irwin Toys* with regard to children and advertising restrictions, or as the federal cabinet had done in *Keegstra*, when it sought to protect targeted groups from hate speech.[118] In essence, the majority did not accept that the cabinet was motivated to protect vulnerable voters from the ill effects of polling data. The challenged section of the *Canada Elections Act* was not a reasoned response because it prevented the public from being exposed to accurate polling that could allow a rational voter to make an informed decision. Thus, section 322.1 lacked precision because in its attempt to prevent the publication of methodologically suspect polling data in the period immediately before an election, it banned "all those polls which would meet the usual standards of accuracy."[119]

Once again, the court did not challenge the substance of the legislation but, in the words of Justice Bastarache, the "crude instrument" that cabinet had chosen to advance its legislative objective. The narrow basis of the invalidation, however, provided the federal cabinet with sufficient room to respond to *Thompson Newspapers* and advanced coordinate constitutionalism because the court clearly stated: "This is not to say that there is no possibility for Parliament to legislate with regards to the dangers that represent bad polls."[120] It may have been reasonable for cabinet to introduce a blackout period when it introduced section 322.1 in 1985, but this approach did not constitute a reasonable limitation on freedom of expression in the post-Charter period.

The court's concern that partisan political considerations influenced the structure of the *Canada Elections Act* continued in *Figueroa v. Canada* when it ruled that the requirement that political parties must field at least fifty candidates to qualify for registered party status, and the benefits derived from this status, violated the Charter's democratic rights. The main benefits associated with registered party status are the ability to issue tax receipts for donations and to have party affiliation listed with candidates' names on election ballots.[121] Sections 24(2) and (3) and 28(2) of the *Canada Elections Act* were not minimal impairments because benefits were denied to nonestablished parties.

The temporary state of judicial invalidation and the importance of coordinate constitutionalism are evident in the legislative responses in two legal rights cases that denied certain defences for the accused. In *R. v. Nguyen*, a majority decision (five to two) ruled that section 146(1) of the Criminal

Code, which prohibited sexual intercourse with a female under the age of fourteen, violated the principles of fundamental justice because "the provision expressly removes the defence that the accused bona fide believed that the female was 14 years of age or older."[122] Speaking for the majority, Justice Wilson did not accept that section 146(1) was a minimal impairment because it did not make a distinction between the "mentally innocent and mentally guilty" and "at a minimum the provision must provide for a defence of due diligence."[123] In *R. v. Daviault*, the majority decision (six to three) stated that the common-law rule that the mental element of general intent cannot be negated by extreme drunkenness violated both sections 7 and 11(d) of the Charter.[124] For the majority, Justice Cory reiterated the position that eliminating the mental aspect of a crime violated the principles of fundamental justice, and, thus, the common-law rule could not be considered a reasonable limitation, for "to deny that even a minimal mental element is required for sexual assault offends the Charter in a manner that is so dramatic and so contrary to the principles of fundamental justice that it cannot be justified under section 1 of the Charter."[125]

In both cases the federal cabinet amended the Criminal Code to address the court's rulings. In response to *Nguyen*, the cabinet revised the Criminal Code, replacing the term "rape" with "sexual assault" and restricting the "mistaken belief" defence to those who took all the necessary steps to discover the age of the complainant. For *Daviault*, the cabinet introduced Bill C-72, which effectively reversed the court's decision as section 33.3(1) once again denies the defence of extreme intoxication in sexual assault cases. The revision states that "it is not a defence to an offence referred to in subsection (3) that the accused, by reason of self-induced intoxication, lacked the basic intent or voluntariness required to commit the offence, where the accused departed markedly from the standard of care as described in subsection (2)."[126] *Nguyen* and *Daviault* illustrate the court's stringent approach to section 1 in legal rights cases and its refusal to accept as reasonable the state's denial of an avenue of defence for the accused. More importantly, they illustrate that judicial legislation is secondary legislation and that the cabinet can effectively respond to and reverse judicial invalidation on Charter grounds.

The decision in *Dunmore v. Ontario* is similar to that in *Protestant School Boards*, as the issue involved the constitutionality of rescinding a provision previously granted by a legislature.[127] In *Dunmore*, it was the decision by the Ontario cabinet in 1995 to rescind the decision by the previous NDP government to extend the right to organize to agricultural workers. Section 3(b) of the *Labour Relations Act (LRA)* was determined to be a violation of freedom of association protected under section 2(d) of the Charter because it purposefully excluded a vulnerable group, and by "extending the statutory protection to just about every class of worker in Ontario, the legislature has essentially discredited the organizing efforts of agricultural work-ers."[128] The Ontario cabinet justified the under-inclusion of the act as an attempt to protect the family farm and its economic productivity, which the court accepted as pressing and substantial legislative objectives.

However, the *LRA* did not constitute a minimal impairment, according to the majority opinion (eight to one) authored by Justice Bastarache, because the Ontario cabinet did not attempt to balance competing interests and simply excluded all agricultural workers irrespective of the labour context. For instance, the court questioned the "family farm" justification for ex-cluding all agricultural workers, as this model was no longer the dominant one for the industry and was "rapidly assuming a less important role in the agricultural sector, as evidenced by increases in non-family farm incorpora-tions, hired farm labour, seasonal workers and average labour cost."[129] The lack of precision in defining categories of agricultural workers based on the economic organization of a farm was not a reasonable limitation on free-dom of association, Bastarache argued, and refused to accept Ontario's ar-gument that "distinguishing various sectors of agriculture requires an impossible line-drawing exercise which the legislature should have the dis-cretion to reject."[130] As several provinces had excluded agricultural workers who truly worked on family farms from labour relations acts, the court reasoned that the family farm could be protected without having to deny the freedom of association of all agricultural workers. In its remedy, the court did not nullify the offending provision of the *LRA* but suspended its decision for eighteen months to allow the Ontario cabinet the opportunity to amend section 3(b). While the objectives were reasonable in the *LRA*, the legislative approach was unconstitutional, and the court stated that the Ontario cabinet could exclude categories of agricultural workers, but not all, to protect the family farm.

The issue of under-inclusion arose in both *Vriend v. Alberta* and *M. v. H.* when the exclusion of gays and lesbians from legislative schemes was chal-lenged as a violation of equality rights protected under section 15(1) of the Charter. In *Vriend*, which was analyzed in Chapter 3, the absence of sexual orientation as a protected ground under the *Individual's Rights Protection Act* was ruled a violation of section 15(1) that could not be considered a reason-able limitation. The Alberta cabinet was not silent on this issue, as Macklem contends it was.[131] The political decision of the Alberta cabinet to order the Alberta Human Rights Commission (AHRC) to stop investigating discrimi-nation claims by gays and lesbians, as well as the cabinet's refusal to accept the recommendation of the AHRC to amend the *IRPA* to include protection for gays and lesbians, preceded the *Vriend* decision. The Alberta cabinet was decidedly activist on this issue and simply excluded gays and lesbians from equality protections under the *IRPA*.[132] In its remedy, the court judi-cially amended the *IRPA* by reading sexual orientation into the grounds for protection. While it was possible in a legislature dominated by Progressive Conservatives to disregard the recommendation of the AHRA to extend protection to gays and lesbians under the *IRPA* because of the political strength of the party's rural constituency, the exclusion of these vulnerable groups could not be justified under the Charter once the act was subjected to judicial review. Because the Alberta cabinet refused to offer a pressing and substantial legislative objective advanced by this exclusion, its decision appeared arbitrary and unprincipled.

Similarly in *M. v. H.*, the Ontario cabinet had amended the definition of spouse in the *Family Law Act (FLA)* in 1990 to include heterosexual couples, either married or unmarried and living together for at least three years or those who had a relationship of permanence through a child.[133] The purpose of the *FLA* was to provide for the distribution of property and resources accumulated by spouses in relationships that had dissolved. Because section 29 of the *FLA* made a distinction between heterosexual and homosexual couples and only provided opposite-sex couples with a legal claim to property, the Supreme Court, in a majority decision (eight to one), ruled that the distinction resulted in discrimination because it denied a benefit to same-sex couples and promoted the view that "individuals in same-sex relationships generally, are less worthy of recognition and protection."[134] The equality rights violation in the *FLA* was not a reasonable limitation for the majority because it denied same-sex partners an equitable division of property accumulated during the relationship.

Speaking for six members of the majority, Justices Cory and Iacobucci accepted that the *FLA* advanced pressing and substantial objectives to provide for the equitable division of assets between spouses and to ensure that the state would not have to financially support individuals when relationships ended: both objectives, it was claimed, were designed to protect children.[135] Cory and Iacobucci refused to accept that a rational connection existed in section 29 of the *FLA* by excluding same-sex couples from the *FLA*, as "the *inclusion* of same-sex couples in section 29 of the FLA would better achieve the objectives of the legislation while respecting *Charter* rights of individuals in same-sex relationships."[136] In considering whether the *FLA* constituted a minimal impairment on the equality rights of gays and lesbians, the majority opinion rejected the need for deference as "no group will be disadvantaged by granting members of same-sex couples access to the spousal support scheme under the FLA," and the Ontario cabinet, therefore, was not distributing scarce resources among competing groups.[137] Because the exclusion of same-sex couples from the *FLA* and its spousal-support system was absolute, the limitation on equality rights of same-sex couples was not a minimal impairment on section 15(1).

In his analysis of *M. v. H.*, Manfredi is critical of what he perceives as judicial hubris and the suggestion by Justice Cory that the cost of leaving this issue undecided would be high. In response, Manfredi contends that a vigorous debate on extending same-sex benefits occurred under the Rae government in Ontario, and Bill 167, which would have granted these benefits, was defeated in a free vote in the Ontario legislature.[138] This analysis has been challenged by Martin Overby, who contends that it was only a free vote in theory. He claims that partisan considerations influenced the voting patterns of the opposition Liberals, who were key to passing Bill 167, as twenty-one members of the assembly abstained from voting and the bill carried on first reading by a vote of fifty-seven to fifty-two, with ten members of the NDP government voting against the measure. According to Overby, "With public opinion polls showing their party with 50 per cent support and likely to win enough seats in the coming election to form a majority government, Liberals apparently did not want to risk alienating the public by supporting a highly controversial measure, especially since Tory leaders had promised to make the 'same-sex' bill an issue in the upcoming election."[139] The empirical analysis by Overby contends that partisanship, and not conscience, was the decisive factor that saw the near defeat of Bill 167 on first reading and its eventual defeat on second reading by a vote of sixty-eight to fifty-nine.[140]

The analysis by Manfredi illustrates the central point advanced here about standards of evaluation – the decision by the Ontario cabinet to deny same-sex benefits was reasonable from a political perspective, particularly that of the opposition Liberals, as well as being legitimate based on majoritarianism, but it was clearly problematic from a constitutional perspective because it denied the possibility of spousal benefits to same-sex couples. Indeed, by changing the definition of spouse in 1976, first in order to incorporate non-traditional heterosexual relationships such as common-law relationships, the Ontario cabinet weakened its ability to defend the exclusion of same-sex couples as a reasonable limitation in the 1990s. In contrast to the argument in *Dunmore,* where the attorney general claimed that it was an "impossible line-drawing exercise" to distinguish between agricultural workers under the *Labour Relations Act,* it appeared possible to distinguish between categories of relationships that met the definition of spouse under the *FLA.* This arbitrary exercise, therefore, could not meet the test of minimal impairment because the denial of spousal benefits to same-sex couples stood in stark contrast to the inclusion of common-law couples under the *FLA.* The Ontario cabinet drew the line but simply stopped short, because of political considerations and an impending election, of including homosexual and lesbian couples within the meaning of spouse. This political decision, once subjected to constitutional standards, could not be sustained as reasonable in a free and democratic society.

The invalidation of legislation has generally been the focus of critical analysis of the Supreme Court. In reviewing statutes that have failed the reasonable limits test of the Charter, I focused on the characteristics of the statutes nullified instead of simply the act of invalidation by the Supreme Court. This approach directly challenges critical analyses of the court because many of the statutes invalidated were enacted before the Charter's introduction or shortly after 1982. Further, many of the invalidated approaches or definitions do not marginally exceed minimal impairment but suffer from overbreadth or vagueness in the description of activities they legitimately seek to restrict. These are drafting limitations that are the responsibility of the cabinet at the federal and provincial levels, supported by their public bureaucracies. The policy outcome of invalidation is not the result of discretionary judicial choices but a reaction to discretionary choices by cabinets that lack precision or are under-inclusive in their application. Cabinet retains the ability to respond to judicial invalidation and to prevent its occurrence through the legislative process. The emerging approach to judicial remedies by the court illustrates the ability of the cabinet to introduce legislative sequels that overcome constitutional invalidations. The institutionalization of Charter scrutiny within the legislative arena, which is discussed in Chapters 6 and 7, demonstrates that the cabinet governs with the Charter and is not ruled by judicial actors through Charter decisions.

Judicial Remedies and Legislative Responses

If the emergence of coordinate constitutionalism is not evident in the reasons why the Supreme Court invalidates legislation, then it surely is in the increasing tendency to use the remedy of suspended declarations of invalidity in Charter decisions.[141] As shown in Table 5.5, during the first decade of Charter review the Supreme Court generally nullified statutes as the remedy for Charter violations. This approach was used in 81 percent (25 out of 31) of statutes invalidated. However, the second decade saw a sharp decline in the use of nullification; it was used in only 33 percent (11 out of 33) of cases. The use of other remedies has dramatically increased in the second decade. For example, judicial amendment of offending statutes by reading-in or reading-down legislative schemes, which was used only once in the first decade, was used nine times in the second decade. Nearly half of the instances of judicial amendment involve violations of fundamental freedoms, where the Supreme Court has read-down legislative schemes that unduly restrict freedom of expression, such as *Osborne* and *Little Sisters*. Further, in *Miron v. Trudel,* the Supreme Court amended the *Insurance Act* in Ontario to include common-law couples in the definition of spouse to provide benefits to an individual injured in an automobile accident, and the court read sexual orientation into Alberta's *IRPA* in *Vriend.*

The increased use of suspended declarations of invalidity, the second important remedy from the second decade, clearly illustrates the court's commitment to coordinate constitutionalism. Suspended remedies are important

Table 5.5

Judicial remedies in Charter cases, 1982 to 2003[1]

Remedy	1982 to 1992		1993 to 2003		Total	
	Number	%	Number	%	Number	%
Read-in or read-down	1	3.23	9	27.30	10	15.60
Prequel	2	6.45	0	0.00	2	3.13
Nullification	25	80.60	11	33.30	36	56.30
Suspended	2	6.45	11	33.30	13	20.30
Declaration	1	3.23	2	6.06	3	4.69
Total	31	100.00	33	100.00	64	100.00

1 Refers to the year the remedy was used and not when the statute was enacted or last amended.

because they allow an invalidated legislative scheme to continue for a period of time, which provides an opportunity for the responsible cabinet to establish the scheme's constitutionality through amendments. This remedy was used only twice during the first decade, most obviously in *Swain*, when the absence of review procedures for individuals indefinitely held in custody was ruled a violation of the principles of fundamental justice, but the declaration of invalidity was suspended for six months. However, this remedy has become quite common during the second decade, increasing from 6 percent (2 out of 31) to 33 percent (11 out of 33) between 1993 and 2003. This judicial remedy has intensified since 1997, with twenty-six statutes being invalidated between 1997 and 2003, and a suspended decision used in 42 percent of cases (11 out of 26). This trend was most pronounced in 2003, as the court invalidated three statutes – in *Figuero, Trociuk,* and *Nova Scotia v. Martin* – suspending the declarations of invalidity for twelve months in the first two cases and six months in the last case.

The use of suspended decisions in important policy areas is particularly striking and further challenges the position that judicial activism allows the court to determine policy outcomes by restricting the legislative responses available to the cabinet at either level.[142] The type of remedy employed directly influences whether the Supreme Court functions as a de facto third chamber of parliament, as suggested by Morton and Knopff, or whether the court sees the Charter as a shared responsibility between itself and the cabinet, which is the hallmark of coordinate constitutionalism. The growing frequency of suspended decisions in sensitive policy areas such as labour relations in *Dunmore* or *UFCW*, the provision of health services in *Eldridge*, or same-sex relationships and the definition of spouse in *M. v. H.* does require the parliamentary arena to respond to judicial invalidation of existing legislation, but the precise response still remains the prerogative of the cabinet. It is unclear how the Supreme Court functions as a third chamber of parliament if policy responses to judicial decisions are designed and implemented by the cabinet, supported by the bureaucracy.

Conclusion

The Supreme Court's commitment to coordinate constitutionalism is most evident in cases where it upholds the constitutionality of statutes without recourse to section 1 of the Charter. The vast majority of Charter challenges against legislation are not successful, and the court has generally accepted the constitutionality of legislative intentions by the cabinet and its provincial counterparts. It is not necessary to review these cases but to reinforce a simple point: the criticisms of judicial activism focus on a limited aspect of Charter review, as most challenges involve conduct cases and not the constitutionality of statutes and legislative intentions. Within this narrow framework, invalidated statutes constitute an even more limited dimension of Charter review by the Supreme Court, as less than a third of challenged statutes are found to breach the Charter. My intention in this chapter has been to suggest that the court's commitment to coordinate constitutionalism is evident in the characteristics of statutes invalidated through the evolution of the *Oakes* test and the court's emerging approach to remedies. Rarely does the court refuse to accept that legislative objectives are pressing and substantial, and most failed section 1 defences result because of the lack of proportionality between the objectives and the legislative instruments chosen by the responsible cabinet. This contextual approach has allowed the Supreme Court to guard an essential element of the constitution, but not at the expense of parliamentary democracy.

The principal legislative response to the Charter has not been the introduction of amendments to overcome judicial invalidation, as suggested by the Charter dialogue theorist, but has largely involved the introduction of Charter-vetting processes within the pre-legislative stage of policy development. Coordinate constitutionalism, therefore, is much broader than simply judicial remedies that leave policy discretion to cabinets during legislative responses to judicial activism. It has generally manifested itself in the cabinets' commitment to a reformed policy process that explicitly links policy objectives with Charter values. Thus, the cabinets' attempt to govern with the Charter and coordinate constitutionalism is vastly more advanced than the Supreme Court's commitment to this principle, yet judicial activism continues to dominate conceptions of Charter politics at the expense of legislative activism.

The relationship between the Charter and Canadian federalism is the focus of the next chapter and presents another aspect of coordinate constitutionalism, namely the implications of a national statement on rights for provincial policy autonomy and diversity. This has represented the second line of attack by judicial critics, with the assumption that federalism has been weakened through Charter review by the Supreme Court. This position is challenged, as, like the Charter, federalism has been a shared responsibility of the cabinet, the Supreme Court, and legislatures, both through court decisions that accommodate federalism and through Charter-vetting at the provincial level that protects against judicial invalidation of legislation. Judicial and legislative actors, therefore, have guarded this essential element of the constitutional order, as intended by the framers of the Charter.

Part 3
Legislative Activism and the Policy Process

6
The Charter and Canadian Federalism

The relationship between judicial review and constitutional supremacy is significant in Canada because of the federal nature of the constitution and the potential tension between a national statement on rights and the principle of diversity. This tension is amplified because the Supreme Court, as a national institution and the formal guardian of the constitution, is solely appointed by the Governor General on the advice of the prime minister without formal provincial consultation. On the question of federalism and provincial autonomy, it has been argued that the Supreme Court has not governed well with the Charter because the invalidation of statutes imposes national standards in provincial areas of jurisdiction. The centralization thesis is a dominant but contested view of the relationship between rights and federalism. Peter Hogg has argued that "where guaranteed rights exist, there must be a single national rule."[1] Guy Laforest echoes a similar reservation by concluding that "the Charter would work towards the unification of the nation by homogenizing policies across the country."[2] These analyses occur within a judicial-centred paradigm, as they argue that the relationship between rights and federalism is dependent on the willingness of the Supreme Court to invalidate provincial statutes, prioritize "national" Charter values at the expense of provincial values, and narrow the policy autonomy of provincial governments.

The assumption that provincial autonomy is largely shaped by judicial activism is problematic and highlights the fundamental limitation of the judicial-centred paradigm as an adequate framework for analyzing the relationship between rights and federalism. The protection of policy diversity and federalism has been a shared responsibility between the Supreme Court and the cabinet since the Charter's introduction, and this essential constitutional principle has been advanced through judicial and legislative efforts. A federalist jurisprudence structures the court's approach to Charter review, and the reasonable limits clause of section 1 has functioned as a margin of appreciation for policy diversity between governments.[3] The court has protected this essential constitutional principle by accepting the need for provincial governments to address policy in distinct ways. This is significant, because it means the court does not require one legislative approach to protect rights but has accepted the multiple answers produced by a federal system.

The complexity of the Charter as a document extends beyond the reasonable limits clause, as section 33 allows governments to override unfavourable judicial decisions and advance diversity by asserting the reasonableness of legislation found to violate the Charter. Additionally, the less-than-complete application of section 23 of the Canadian Charter to the province of Quebec has tempered the pan-Canadian nature of minority language education rights, thus ensuring an asymmetrical application of the Charter in the one province that has yet to sign the *Constitution Act, 1982.*[4] This sensitivity to diversity and the structural requirements of a federal system was first identified in the scholarship of Janet Hiebert and Katherine Swinton, who noted the Supreme Court's willingness to accept as constitutional provincial variation in the application of federal laws.[5] I contend in this chapter that a complex federalism jurisprudence exists in the Charter decisions of the Supreme Court and that this challenges both the normative and empirical bases of the centralization thesis associated with Charter review. This federalism jurisprudence has existed since the beginning of the court's Charter jurisprudence and represents a serious challenge to the centralization thesis and to those who view the relationship between rights and federalism solely within a judicial paradigm.

Because federalism is foremost a political arrangement to protect diversity, it is folly to view the courts as the predominant institution in the management of federal diversity and provincial autonomy. The protection of federalism centres on the parliamentary arena because federal and provincial cabinets have guarded this essential element of the constitutional system by reforming the policy process to ensure that entrenched rights are advanced during the legislative design of public policies. Legislative activism serves a dual purpose: the cabinet guards against judicial review eroding parliamentary democracy, and it protects federalism through a policy process that explicitly advances Charter values by cabinets at the provincial level. These reciprocal relationships demonstrate the emergence of coordinate constitutionalism in Canada and the complexity of the guardian role, as although the court may be the legal guardian of the constitution through section 52, the reality of governing with the Charter is that no actor monopolizes this role.[6] Coordinate constitutionalism has a deeper significance, therefore, as legislative activism acts as a bulwark against judicial encroachment on provincial autonomy.

This chapter advances the argument that a reconciliation between rights and federalism is the result of efforts by the Supreme Court and the cabinet at the provincial level, supported by departments of justice, to advance federal diversity within the framework of rights compliance. Legislative efforts are prioritized because the cabinet remains the centre of public policy, and greater judicial acceptance of the constitutionality of challenged provisions is a response to these legislative efforts. The Supreme Court is a significant institutional actor, but I caution against overestimating the impact of judicial decisions on Canadian federalism or underestimating the central importance of political efforts by provincial cabinets to secure this same end. Therefore, the negative implications drawn by critics are challenged by identifying judicial efforts to advance this principle in the court's Charter jurisprudence. Institutional reforms within the machinery of government at the insistence of provincial cabinets are identified as causal factors precipitating judicial acceptance of policy variation by provincial governments. Governing with the Charter, therefore, is not the sole domain of the Supreme Court, nor is the management of federal diversity principally a judicial responsibility.

This chapter is divided into three sections. The first section evaluates the centralization thesis and considers the evidence used to demonstrate that Charter review by the Supreme Court has undermined federalism and provincial autonomy. After finding the empirical evidence less than convincing, the second section demonstrates that the Supreme Court has been sensitive to federalism in its Charter jurisprudence. This federalism jurisprudence has been advanced by the emerging approach to judicial remedies, as a notable difference exists in the remedy adopted when the Supreme Court invalidates provincial statutes. The court is more likely to suspend a declaration of invalidity when a provincial statute is found unconstitutional than it is for federal statutes, and this has important implications for federalism and provincial autonomy. The final section considers legislative activism at the provincial level and the bureaucratic vetting of legislation that has guarded against judicial invalidation of provincial statutes as inconsistent with the Charter. While this process is executive centred and under the direction of provincial departments of justice, it does ensure that Charter values are advanced within the legislative arena and reinforces the importance of rights dialogue outside the judicial arena.

The Charter and the Centralization Thesis
The primary assumption of the centralization thesis is that the nullification of statutes during Charter review reduces provincial autonomy by validating Canadian values and imposing national standards in provincial jurisdictions.[7] Critics view the nation-building intentions of the Charter as an attempt by Pierre Elliott Trudeau to transfer citizen loyalty to the national community and to reduce provincial diversity by requiring the provinces to conform to the national values in the Charter.[8] Indeed, the explicit

exemption of minority language education rights (section 23) from the scope of the Charter's notwithstanding clause confirms the centralizing intention of the document to Charter critics and especially to Quebec intellectuals.[9] In surveying the impact of section 23 on Quebec language and education policy, Yves de Montigny expressed a widely held belief among Quebec intellectuals that "the Charter has destroyed whole sections of the language regime gradually adopted by the province over the years."[10] This sentiment is shared by Guy Laforest, who concludes that the Charter has injected national standards into Quebec's language and cultural policies.[11]

Morton and Knopff have expressed a related concern about changes in interest group politics, which they refer to as the "Court Party" because of the use of litigation to achieve desired policy outcomes. The Court Party, they argue, facilitates the judicialization of politics because it advances its reformist agenda through litigation. Perhaps what is most damaging for Morton and Knopff is the relationship between the Court Party and Ottawa. Many of the interest groups that fall within the Court Party are funded by the federal government and are encouraged to pursue litigation strategies that challenge provincial legislation as inconsistent with the Charter. Morton has written that the Court Party advances centralization and federal interests because the "Charter has thus allowed the federal government to achieve indirectly what it could not have achieved directly."[12] Thus, judicial activism is doubly problematic because it imposes national values when it strikes down provincial legislation and has given rise to litigation strategies that indirectly advance Ottawa's agenda.

Despite the normative claims of the centralization thesis, the empirical evidence is not convincing, and the suggested reduction of provincial policy autonomy is based on the invalidation of twenty-five statutes between 1982 and 2003. A list of these statutes is presented in Table 6.1. In 1994, Morton described Quebec as the jurisdiction experiencing the greatest loss of policy autonomy because it had suffered the most nullifications of any province, and these nullifications had occurred in vital areas of Quebec's language and cultural policies.[13] In *Attorney General (Quebec) v. Protestant School Boards*, for example, the Supreme Court of Canada invalidated sections of the *Charter of the French Language* that limited educational opportunities in English in Quebec.[14] Similarly, in *Ford v. Quebec,* the court invalidated the "Sign Law" sections of the *Charter of the French Language* as an infringement of freedom of expression (s.2b) and ruled that the infringement could not be considered a reasonable limitation under section 1 of the Charter because the exclusive use of French on commercial signs was not proportionate to the objective sought, this being the preservation of Quebec's *visage linguistic.*[15] Since Morton's initial analysis, the focus of judicial invalidation has been quite even, with Quebec, Alberta, and British Columbia experiencing the nullification of five statutes by the Supreme Court, and Ontario seeing

Table 6.1

Invalidation of provincial statutes on Charter grounds, 1982 to 2003

Case[1]	Government	Statute[2]	Decision[3]	Remedy
Protestant School Boards v. Quebec	PQ	1977	1984	Nullification
Reference Re Motor Vehicle Act	BC	1982	1985	Nullification
Thibault v. Corp. Professionel Médicins du Québec	PQ	1982	1988	Nullification
Ford v. Quebec	PQ	1983	1988	Nullification
Devine v. Quebec	PQ	1983	1988	Nullification
Edmonton Journal v. Alberta	AB	1980	1989	Nullification
Black v. Law Society	AB	1980	1989	Nullification
Andrews v. Law Society	BC	1979	1989	Nullification
Rocket v. Royal College of Dental Surgeons of Ontario	ON	1980	1990	Nullification
Mahé v. Alberta	AB	1982	1990	Declaration of rights
Reference Re Public Schools Act	MB	1987	1993	Declaration of rights
Miron v. Trudel	ON	1980	1995	Read-in
Libman v. Quebec	PQ	1981	1997	Nullification
R. v. Campbell	AB	1985	1997	Suspended (1 year)
Reference Re Provincial Court Judges	PEI	1994	1997	Suspended (1 year)
Manitoba Provincial Judges Association v. Manitoba	MB	1990	1997	Read-down
Eldridge v. British Columbia	BC	1996	1997	Suspended (6 months)
Vriend v. Alberta	AB	1990	1998	Read-in
M. v. H.	ON	1990	1999	Suspended (6 months)
UFCW, Local 1518 v. Kmart Canada Ltd.	BC	1992	1999	Suspended (6 months)
Arsenault-Cameron v. Prince Edward Island	PEI	1990	2000	Declaration of rights
Dunmore v. Ontario	ON	1997	2001	Suspended (18 months)
Mackin v. New Brunswick	NB	1995	2002	Suspended (6 months)
Trociuk v. British Columbia	BC	1996	2003	Suspended (1 year)
Nova Scotia v. Martin	NS	1995	2003	Suspended (6 months)

1 Complete case citations are listed in the Bibliography.
2 Year the statute was enacted or challenged provisions last amended, as reported in *Supreme Court Reports*.
3 Year the Supreme Court of Canada invalidated the statute.

four statutes invalidated as inconsistent with the Charter in this twenty-one-year period. In simple empirical terms, the federal government has been the focus of judicial activism, as thirty-nine statutes have been invalidated. This is a much higher total than that of any provincial jurisdiction and represents 61 percent (39 out of 64) of the total invalidations on Charter grounds.

While the court has been activist in striking down sections of Quebec's language and education policy on Charter grounds, the impact has been offset by the structure of the Charter itself. In the case of *Ford* and *Devine*,[16] the Quebec government of Robert Bourassa used the notwithstanding clause to override judicial nullification of the Sign Law.[17] Indeed, a Charter section was used to enhance the autonomy of Quebec within a core area of provincial jurisdiction. While this is a rare occurrence,[18] it is an important illustration of the structural features of the Charter that can protect provincial autonomy when legislatures decide to act in response to Charter decisions. Similarly, what has been overlooked in the aftermath of *Protestant School Boards* is that this decision has not interfered with the policy objective of limiting access to English schools in an effort to address the demographic decline of francophones in Quebec. This position is contrary to that advanced by Guy Laforest, who contends that the Canadian Charter has established national language and education standards and, therefore, has curtailed the legislative prerogatives of the Quebec National Assembly.[19] Indeed, Peter Russell has commented that "section 23 of the Charter even provides for Quebec's distinctiveness by leaving discretion over the language regime for the schooling of Quebec immigrants to the government and legislature of Quebec."[20] In particular, section 23 applies to citizens of Canada whose first language is either French or English, so the decision in *Protestant School Boards* would only apply to anglophones immigrating to Quebec who had been educated in English in Canada, and not to new immigrants to Quebec, who generally arrive from French-speaking nations. Given provincial immigration patterns in Canada, this is unlikely to affect the broader policy objective of Bill 101 and its attempt to preserve the demographic stability of francophones in the province.

In addition to the structure of the Charter, an important dynamic that can further marginalize the negative implications of Charter review for provincial autonomy involves legislative sequels that advance Charter dialogue between the Supreme Court and provincial cabinets.[21] Hogg and Bushell developed the original Charter dialogue concept and have suggested that dialogue exists when legislative sequels follow judicial nullifications of statutes and regulations, a practice suggested to exist for two-thirds of nullified statutes. Along with Christopher Manfredi, I have challenged this approach by suggesting that not all legislative sequels are evidence of Charter dialogue. Instead, we argue that positive action by parliament and the provincial legislatures is essential to advance dialogue, and that legislative sequels must constitute minor amendments of existing statutes and regulations.[22] For instance, repealing and replacing offending sections of statutes or entire acts does not advance dialogue but is simply legislative compliance with Charter decisions. Further, the increasing use of suspended decisions by the Supreme Court is central to the development of dialogue between courts and legislatures, as this remedy allows the responsible cabinet an opportunity to reflect on the constitutional limitations of statutes and to propose amendments independent of the judicial decisions. This is the most recent dimension to emerge and the one that clearly facilitates an inter-institutional dialogue on the meaning of constitutional protections.

With these caveats aside, Charter dialogue has seen positive legislative sequels or provided for their potential in 68 percent of cases of invalidated provincial statutes (17 out of 25). This is a significant feature of Charter review because it suggests that, even when judicial activism potentially advances national values, certain legislative responses by provincial cabinets can reassert constitutionality and safeguard provincial autonomy against pan-Canadian rights. In both *Ford* and *Devine,* the Quebec National Assembly invoked the notwithstanding clause to override the Supreme Court's decision and preserve the legislative autonomy of Quebec and the constitutionality of the *Charter of the French Language.* In *Libman v. Quebec,* the Quebec cabinet introduced a minor legislative amendment to the *Referendum Act* and increased the spending limits of third parties to ensure the act's constitutionality,[23] and in *Protestant School Boards,* the complexity of the policy context and the reality of immigration patterns offset the implications of this decision for Quebec's control over language and education. These are generally the cases used to demonstrate the homogenization of public policy under the Charter, but the ability of provincial legislatures to minimize the effects of judicial activism is very real and is evidence that courts and legislatures govern with the Charter.[24]

Invalidated Provincial Statutes

Before examining in greater detail the twenty-five provincial statutes used to demonstrate the centralization thesis, there are a number of significant characteristics to consider that raise questions about whether these cases do in fact indicate a loss of autonomy for provincial cabinets under the Charter. In the broadest terms, invalidation does represent a loss of policy autonomy, but this assessment needs to be based on more than simply the act of invalidation by the Supreme Court. To show that provincial autonomy was compromised, the date a statute was enacted and the remedy employed by the Supreme Court must be assessed. As argued in Chapter 5, judicial activism as an empirical indicator is irrelevant if the analysis focuses on the yearly rate of activism, as this overlooks a far more significant characteristic:

the year a statute was enacted or last amended by the responsible provincial cabinet. In focusing on rates of activism, the danger lies in equating all invalidations as a loss of policy autonomy under the Charter, regardless of the fact that many statutes invalidated were enacted before the Charter was entrenched and before the policy process was changed to respond to the new policy demands resulting from a constitutional statement on rights. Such a comparative context is skewed, as the pre-Charter policy environment placed fewer demands on reconciling rights, and policy objectives and statutes enacted in this period are more likely to be invalidated as inconsistent with the Charter. As Barry Strayer observed, after serving as assistant deputy minister of justice during the drafting of the Charter, "some of the substantive laws struck down by the courts, though their demise has caused more anguish in certain quarters, were nevertheless living on borrowed time."[25]

This is still an accurate characterization, as Table 6.1 reveals that 40 percent (10 out of 25) of invalidated provincial statutes were enacted before 1982 or during the year the Charter was entrenched. Thus, in twenty-one years between 1983 and 2003, the Supreme Court determined slightly more than half a provincial statute a year enacted in the post-Charter policy environment exceeded the Charter (15 out of 25), and judicial power, as it relates to provincial autonomy, comes to rest on a very small number of cases. Turning first to invalidated statutes that were enacted before 1982, what is striking is their limited importance, as most were peripheral to significant areas of provincial responsibility, such as education, health, and social policy. For instance, judicial invalidation of provincial statutes affected appeal procedures in *Thibault v. Corp. Professionel Médicins du Québec;* in *Edmonton Journal v. Alberta* the court removed publication restrictions in cases involving matrimonial disputes and in pretrial civil proceedings; in *Andrews v. Law Society (B.C.)* the court struck down the citizenship requirements in the *Barristers and Solicitors Act (B.C.)* as violating section 15(1); and in *Black v. Law Society (Alberta)* it nullified sections of the rules that prohibited the operation of interprovincial law firms.[26] Finally, in *Rocket v. Royal College of Dental Surgeons,* an Ontario regulation that prevented dentists from advertising was invalidated as a violation of freedom of expression.[27] However, this invalidation was quickly reversed through a legislative sequel, as the Ontario cabinet, pursuant to the *Dentistry Act (1994),* narrowed the restrictions on advertising by dentists to situations where the advertising was deceptive and nonfactual in nature.[28] Undoubtedly, these cases do reduce provincial autonomy, but given the limited importance of the statutes invalidated, they cannot be said to limit the ability of provincial cabinets to achieve substantive elements of their legislative agendas. Peter Russell reminds us that "with the exception of Quebec's language policy, social and economic policies of central importance to elected governments have not been significantly affected by the Charter."[29] This conclusion stands despite the invalidation of provincial statutes as inconsistent with the Charter, as the Supreme Court has generally focused on legal rights and criminal procedures.[30]

A far more relevant inquiry is whether statutes enacted in a policy environment that places greater requirements on ensuring that policy objectives explicitly advance protected rights are invalidated under the Charter. The fifteen invalidated statutes that were enacted after 1982 do represent significant areas of provincial jurisdiction and provide a stronger empirical basis for the centralization thesis, as the policies affected are core provincial responsibilities. For instance, the Supreme Court found the under-inclusion of agricultural workers in Ontario's *Labour Relations Act* violated freedom of association, and the restrictions on picketing in British Columbia's *Labour Relations Code* also violated section 2(d) of the Charter.[31] In 2003, the Supreme Court ruled that the exclusion of chronic pain attributable to work-related injuries in Nova Scotia's *Workers' Compensation Act* violated the Charter's equality rights provision because it drew a distinction based on disability that resulted in discrimination involving an enumerated category of protection.[32] Several provincial statutes were found to violate section 15(1), such as the *Individual's Rights Protection Act (IRPA)*, which under-included sexual orientation *(Vriend v. Alberta)*, and Ontario's *Family Law Act (FLA)*, which contained a definition of spouse that violated equality rights because it did not apply to same-sex couples *(M. v. H.)*.[33] In *Eldridge v. British Columbia*, the lack of sign-language interpreters, which were to be provided under the *Hospital Insurance Act* for hearing-impaired people in hospital emergency rooms, was determined to be an equality rights violation that could not be considered a reasonable limitation.[34]

In the area of education policy, the Supreme Court found that several provincial governments had not provided adequate services for official language groups, and this resulted in section 23 of the Charter being violated. Though the Supreme Court did not invalidate provincial legislation in *Reference Re Public Schools Act (Manitoba)* or *Arsenault-Cameron v. Prince Edward Island*, it did declare that minority language education rights had been violated and placed a constitutional obligation on the governments in question to address the violation.[35] The court has been extremely activist in protecting judicial independence, and this resulted in several provincial statutes being invalidated because they were in violation of section 11(d) of the Charter in a decision referred to as the *Judicial Independence Reference* of 1997.[36] In this reference decision, the Supreme Court removed the determination of judicial salaries from the parliamentary arena and mandated that judicial compensation committees must be established to ensure that judicial independence was not compromised. Section 11(d) was placed firmly under judicial control in *Mackin v. New Brunswick* when the Supreme Court ruled that it was unconstitutional for governments to abolish temporary judicial offices created by legislatures.[37]

Many of these invalidations were discussed in Chapter 5, and the Supreme Court's reasons for rejecting section 1 defences were analyzed. While these cases are important for understanding the emergence of coordinate constitutionalism in Canada, they have a deeper meaning because they are, foremost, provincial statutes that have been invalidated as inconsistent with the Canadian Charter. A practical consideration would be to ask whether the invalidation of fifteen statutes is enough to compromise provincial autonomy. Basing an argument on this small number of cases is a real limitation of the centralization thesis, and a problem for those who use judicial activism to demonstrate the decline of provincial autonomy. What distinguishes the court's approach to judicial review involving post-1982 statutes is the remedy used when statutes are found unconstitutional. The most intrusive remedy is the practice of reading-in or reading-down statutory schemes to ensure their constitutionality. When the Supreme Court employs this remedy, it clearly acts as a policy actor, as statutes are amended by the court. This method was employed in *R. v. Sharpe* when protections were read into Criminal Code sections regulating child pornography to ensure that a provision that offended freedom of expression was constitutional.[38] This remedy was also used in *Little Sisters Book and Art Emporium v. Canada* when the Supreme Court read-down the reverse-onus provision in section 163(8) of the Criminal Code that required the importers of erotic material to demonstrate the material was not obscene.[39] The court ruled that this provision violated freedom of expression and could not be justified as a reasonable limit on section 2(b) of the Charter. The least intrusive remedy is the use of suspended decisions, in which the Supreme Court rules that a statutory scheme violates the Charter but suspends the declaration of

Table 6.2

Judicial remedies and Charter decisions for statutes proclaimed into law from 1983 to 2003

Remedy	Federal		Provincial	
	Number	%	Number	%
Nullification[1]	18	62.070	2	13.33
Suspended	3	10.340	9	60.00
Read-in or read-down	7	24.140	2	13.33
Prequel	1	3.448	0	0.00
Declaration of rights	0	0.000	2	13.33
Total	29	100.000	15	100.00

1 The nullification of two provincial statutes in *Ford* and *Devine* was reversed with section 33 of the Charter.

invalidity for a period of time. By employing this remedy, the Supreme Court is clearly advancing coordinate constitutionalism and acting as a legal actor, as the court simply determines constitutionality and leaves it to the discretion of the responsible cabinet to address the shortcomings of statutory schemes that offend the Charter.[40]

There is a distinct difference between the treatment of federal and provincial statutes that demonstrates the higher degree of activism against the federal government. Table 6.2, which focuses on statutes enacted or last amended in the 1983 to 2003 period, shows that the Supreme Court has nullified twenty-nine federal statutes and fifteen provincial statutes, but the remedy employed has been quite different for the two orders of government. Federal statutes are more likely to be nullified; this remedy has been used in 62 percent of cases (18 out of 29) by the Supreme Court, followed by reading-in or reading-down statutory provisions to ensure their constitutionality, which occurred in 24 percent of cases (7 out of 29). The provincial experience is quite different, as suspended decisions have been used in 60 percent of cases (9 out of 15), and the remaining remedies were used equally by the Supreme Court. Indeed, when the remedy of declaring rights is used in cases involving section 23 of the Charter, where the court does not nullify provincial statutes that violate minority language education rights but simply places a constitutional obligation on governments to provide adequate services, the use of remedies that facilitate legislative responses accounts for nearly three-quarters of invalidated provincial statutes enacted after 1983. Perhaps more importantly, in the two instances where the Supreme Court used the remedy of nullification (*Ford* and *Devine*), the court's decisions were reversed when the Quebec National Assembly invoked the Charter's notwithstanding clause, raising the potential of independent legislative responses to 87 percent (13 out of 15) of provincial statutes found to violate the Charter. In this regard, the centralization thesis suffers because the Supreme Court has invalidated more federal statutes enacted after 1982 than provincial statutes and has used far more activist remedies against federal legislation.

One of the more controversial uses of reading-in occurred in *Vriend* when the Supreme Court determined that Alberta's failure to protect sexual orientation in the provincial human rights code violated the Charter's equality rights protections.[41] Instead of suspending its declaration of invalidity, the Supreme Court read sexual orientation into the provincial human rights code as a characteristic protected against discrimination. The *Vriend* decision has been criticized as an example of pan-Canadian values threatening provincial autonomy and the distinct policy choices reflective of the values of provincial societies. The strong disagreement with the Supreme Court's decision saw the Klein government enter a debate over whether to use the notwithstanding clause to overrule the decision and thus assert the primacy of provincial values.[42] In the end, Alberta did not use the notwithstanding clause and allowed the court's decision to stand, despite opposition from rural Alberta and a significant number of Progressive Conservative caucus members.[43]

This decision is significant because it illustrates the structural features of the Charter that allow rights and federalism to co-exist. The debate over section 33 facilitated a dialogue, as Albertans and their government discussed whether the Supreme Court had undermined essential provincial values by reading sexual orientation into the provincial human rights code. The outcome ultimately supported the extension of the provincial human rights code to include protections for gays and lesbians, as the Klein government consulted different sectors of society before deciding how to react to the *Vriend* decision.[44] As argued in Chapter 3, this was not a decision forced on the Alberta cabinet by the Supreme Court, but was originally a recommendation of the Human Rights Commission to amend the *IRPA* to include sexual orientation. This recommendation was rejected by the Klein government. Morton and Knopff conclude that the court's decision narrowed the manoeuvrability of the Klein government and required it to abandon its preference for the policy status quo.[45] This conclusion is debatable because of the extensive public hearings held by the AHRC and its recommendation that the *IRPA* should be amended before the court read-in sexual orientation, as well as the extensive rights dialogue within the Progressive Conservative caucus and society at large after the *Vriend* decision. Had the Klein government used the notwithstanding clause, it would have been the Alberta government, and not the Supreme Court, that thwarted local preferences over local affairs. Indeed, a poll in the *Edmonton Journal* nearly a year after *Vriend* demonstrates that local preferences had triumphed in this instance, as 76 percent of Albertans supported the court's decision to extend protections to gays and lesbians.[46] Without considering the legislative history of this policy decision, observers might come to the wrong conclusion about the Supreme Court's decision to read sexual orientation into the *IRPA*, assuming the Charter has undermined provincial autonomy and transformed the court into an aggressive policy actor, using the most activist remedy at its disposal.[47]

While the Supreme Court has invalidated significant provincial statutes that were passed after 1982, invalidation has been tempered by the use of suspended decisions, as this remedy allows for independent provincial responses. For instance, the court suspended its judgment for six months in *Mackin* when it determined that New Brunswick's decision to eliminate the post of supernumerary judge violated judicial independence. In both cases of provincial labour relations acts found to violate the rights of organized labour, *Dunmore* and *UFCW, Local 1518*, the Supreme Court suspended its judgment for eighteen months and six months respectively. As well, the finding in *Nova Scotia v. Martin* that Nova Scotia's *Workers' Compensation Act* violated the Charter's equality rights was suspended for six months to give the cabinet the opportunity to introduce amendments to address the section 15(1) violation. In *Trociuk v. British Columbia,* the Supreme Court suspended its judgment for twelve months when it determined the discretion given mothers under the *Vital Statistics Act* to decide whether to name a child's father violated the equality rights of fathers.[48]

Eldridge and *M. v. H.* demonstrate the danger in suggesting that judicial invalidation directly leads to a reduction of provincial autonomy by structuring legislative responses to honour court-mandated constitutional requirements. In *M. v. H.* the Supreme Court suspended for six months its judgment that the definition of spouse in the *FLA* violated equality rights of gays and lesbians. While this judgment did place a constitutional obligation on provincial cabinets to amend acts involving the definition of spouse, Janet Hiebert notes the varied approaches to the recognition of spousal rights of gays and lesbians by provincial governments in response to the court's decision.[49] In one sense, this decision had a centralizing effect, as Miriam Smith notes that it did compel all governments to recognize same-sex relationships.[50] But the decision allowed individual jurisdictions to decide how to respond to *M. v. H.* and which benefits to extend to same-sex couples. Interviews that I conducted with provincial policy actors reinforce Hiebert's analysis of the varied responses to this decision, as all provinces recognized they must extend benefits to gays and lesbians but felt they retained discretion in choosing how to respond, as a range of legislative responses existed to satisfy the constitutional principle advanced.[51]

The same dynamic characterizes *Eldridge v. British Columbia,* where the court's decision established a macro-level obligation to provide sign-language interpretation to the hearing impaired in emergency rooms. Manfredi and Maioni suggest that this case reduces the policy autonomy of provincial governments because it establishes national standards in health care policy.[52] The difficulty with this position is that it does not consider the micro-level responses by provincial cabinets, which saw significant variation in the legislative responses to this incursion into provincial jurisdiction. If provincial cabinets can choose how to respond to a judicial decision, this seems to undermine the centralizing implications of judicial invalidation beyond the requirement of having to respond in some manner. Indeed, Kent Roach has argued that, "outside of British Columbia, governmental responses to *Eldridge* have been more uneven and less positive. It appears that a number of provinces have not taken steps to comply with the decision."[53] In certain respects, those advocating the centralization thesis overplay the policy role of the Supreme Court and the path-dependent nature of judicial rulings that restrict provincial autonomy. As the Supreme Court cannot ensure what form legislative responses to its decisions take, governments retain significant degrees of autonomy despite judicial decisions establishing the obligation to respond. This ultimately raises questions about the centralization thesis as a valid characterization of the impact of judicial invalidation on provincial governments and Canadian federalism. There are simply too few examples of judicial invalidation establishing national standards in provincial areas, and too much discretion available to provincial cabinets, to sustain this analysis of the Charter and Canadian federalism.

Reconciling Rights and Federalism

The issues of federalism and provincial diversity are an important aspect of the Supreme Court's jurisprudence involving the division of powers, yet there is an assumption in the centralization thesis that the court forgot these significant features when it began to interpret the Charter. This is particularly problematic because the court began its tenure as the highest court in 1949 as the umpire of Canadian federalism and saw the interpretation of the Charter as simply an extension of this role.[54] The use of suspended decisions is the clearest illustration of Dicey's contention that judicial legislation is secondary legislation because of the ability of the cabinet to respond to judicial rulings. The Charter's interpretation by the Supreme Court has not been neutral but has reconciled rights and federalism since the beginning of this aspect of judicial review. The ability of the Charter to accommodate policy diversity was questioned at the time of entrenchment, as Peter Russell argued that "the Charter will likely have a strong centralizing impact, especially where it affects policies over which provincial governments normally have primary control."[55] This has not occurred, because of the Supreme Court's sensitivity to provincial autonomy in its interpretation of the Charter. Further, the evolution of section 1 of the Charter and the creation of a margin of appreciation have important implications for federalism, as the movement away from minimal impairment has seen the court accept a range of legislative approaches when governments attempt to justify a limitation on a Charter right as reasonable in a free and democratic society.[56]

The attempt to protect provincial autonomy is evident in a complex jurisprudence that structures the court's approach to the Charter. The first dimension is the *Constitution Act*, which acts as a shield. The court uses the division of powers to dispose of Charter challenges against provincial statutes.[57] Second, there is an explicit dimension, where the court frames a Charter challenge within a federalism framework by deferring to the structural requirements of a federal system or dismissing a Charter challenge by invoking the importance of policy variation among provincial governments. Finally, there exists an implicit dimension because of the hidden relationship between federalism and legal rights in Canada. Indeed, this implicit discourse is hidden within the court's legal rights jurisprudence and escapes notice because criminal law is a federal responsibility, thus giving the illusion that a large element of the court's Charter jurisprudence avoids the question of provincial autonomy. The *Constitution Act* gives the federal government responsibility for criminal law and procedure, yet it assigns the provinces responsibility for the administration of justice. In effect, criminal policy in Canada is a concurrent jurisdiction in the guise of a divided responsibility between the two levels of government. The broader question that follows is whether the focus on legal rights has established national standards in the administration of justice at the provincial level. This scenario has yet to unfold because the court has largely refused to place substantive constitutional obligations on provincial governments in situations where the court has supported the Charter claimant in legal rights cases.

This implicit federalism jurisprudence also includes decisions in which the court upholds the constitutionality of challenged provincial statutes. If judicial invalidations reduce provincial autonomy, then decisions that uphold the constitutionality of challenged statutes advance federalism and provincial autonomy. While the court does not articulate its approach to judicial review as an exercise that advances federalism, this is the outcome. Between 1982 and 2003, the Supreme Court reviewed a total of sixty-three provincial statutes for their relationship to the Charter, invalidating twenty-five statutes and finding thirty-eight to be constitutional. The principal limitation of the centralization thesis and its focus on the invalidation of provincial statutes is evident when the statutes found consistent with the Charter are reviewed. Specifically, the statutes upheld by the Supreme Court deal with significant areas of provincial jurisdiction and have involved several challenges to education acts, elections acts, labour relations acts, and child welfare acts. These statutes, however, continue to be ones that were passed into law before 1990, as very few statutes enacted after Charter vetting was institutionalized as part of the legislative process have been reviewed by the Supreme Court.

While it is a normative claim to suggest that provincial statutes found constitutional are substantively more important than those determined to violate the Charter, there is evidence to support this position, as indicated by Table 6.3. Those statutes touching on the core areas of provincial responsibility, such as labour policy (ten cases, one of which reviewed three statutes), educational policy (four cases), social policy (six cases), elections acts (three cases), and motor vehicle acts regulating public safety (five cases), have been found constitutional by the Supreme Court. For instance, provincial education acts have been found consistent with the Charter, as the court turned aside constitutional challenges to the *Education Act* (Ontario) in *Adler v. Ontario* and *Eaton v. Brant County Board of Education* and supported the constitutionality of the *School Act* (Alberta) in *R. v. Jones*.[58] The court has supported the constitutionality of labour relations acts in several

Table 6.3

Provincial statutes upheld by the Supreme Court, 1982 to 2003

	Year[1]	Statute
Labour policy[2]		
1 *Skapinker v. Law Society*	1984	*Law Society Act*, R.S.O. 1980, c. 233, s. 28(c)
2 *R. v. Edwards Books and Art Ltd.*	1986	*Retail Business Holidays Act*, R.S.O. 1980, c. 453, s. 3(4)
3 *Reference re PSERA*	1987	*Public Service Employee Relations Act*, R.S.A. 1980
4 *Reference re PSERA*	1987	*Labour Relations Act*, R.S.A. 1980
5 *Reference re PSERA*	1987	*Police Officers Collective Bargaining Act*, S.A. 1983
6 *RWDSU v. Saskatchewan*	1987	*The Dairy Workers Act*, S.S. 1983-84, c. D-1.1
7 *McKinney v. University of Guelph*	1990	*Human Rights Code*, 1981, S.O. 1981, c. 53, s. 9(a)
8 *Stoffman v. Vancouver General Hospital*	1990	Medical Staff Regulation 5.04
9 *Lavigne v. OPSEU*	1991	*Colleges Collective Bargaining Act*, R.S.O. 1980, c. 74, s. 53
10 *Pearlman v. Law Society*	1991	*Law Society Act*, R.S.M. 1987, c. L100, s. 52(4)
11 *Walker v. PEI*	1995	*Public Accounting and Auditing Act*, RSPEI 1988, c. P-28, s. 14(1)
12 *R. v. Advance Cutting & Coring Ltd.*	2001	*Act Respecting Labour Relations*, R.S.Q., c. R-20, ss. 28, 32
Education policy		
13 *R. v. Jones*	1986	*School Act*, R.S.A. 1980, c. S-3, ss. 142(1), 143(1)
14 *Ontario Home Builders' Association v. York Region*	1996	*Education Development Charges*, R.R.O. 1990, Reg. 268
15 *Adler v. Ontario*	1996	*Education Act*, R.S.O. 1990, ss. 1(1), 14(1), (2)
16 *Eaton v. Brant County Board of Education*	1997	*Education Act*, R.S.O. 1990, c. E-2, s. 8(3)
Social policy		
17 *Reference re Workers' Compensation Act, 1983*	1989	*Workers' Compensation Act*, 1983, S.N. 1983, c. 48, ss. 32, 34
18 *Irwin Toy Ltd. v. Quebec*	1989	*Consumer Protection Act*, R.S.Q., c. P-40.1, ss. 248, 249
19 *B.(R.) v. Children's Aid Society of Metropolitan Toronto*	1995	*Child Welfare Act*, R.S.O. 1980, c. 66, ss. 21, 27, 28(1), (10), (12), 30(1)(2), 41
20 *Winnipeg Child and Family Services v. K.L.W.*	2000	*Child and Family Services Act*, S.M. 1985-86, c. 8, s. 21(1)

	[1]	[2]
21 Nova Scotia v. Walsh	2002	*Matrimonial Property Act*, R.S.N.S. 1989, c. 275, s. 2(g)
22 Gosselin v. Quebec	2002	*Regulation Respecting Social Aid*, R.R.Q. 1984, c. A-16, r.1, s. 29(a)
Elections and voting		
23 MacKay v. Manitoba	1989	*Elections Finances Act*, S.M. 1982-83-84, c. 45
24 Reference re Provincial Electoral Boundaries	1991	*Electoral Boundaries Commission Act*, S.S. 1986-87-88, c. E-6.1, ss. 14, 20
25 Harvey v. New Brunswick	1996	*Elections Act*, R.S.N.B 1973, c. E-3, s. 119(c)
Motor vehicle policy		
26 R. v. Hufsky	1988	*Highway Traffic Act*, R.S.O. 1980, c. 198, s. 189a(1),(2)
27 R. v. Ladouceur	1990	*Highway Traffic Act*, R.S.O. 1980, c. 198, s. 189a(1)
28 R. v. Goltz	1991	*Motor Vehicle Act*, R.S.B.C. 1979, c. 288, s. 88(1)(c)
29 R. v. Pontes	1995	*BC Motor Vehicle Act*, s. 92
30 R. v. Richard	1996	*Provincial Offences Procedure Act*, S.N.B. 1987, c. P-22.1, s. 16
Gaming policy		
31 Lovelace v. Ontario	2000	*Ontario Casino Corporation Act, 1993*, S.O. 1993, c. 25
32 Siemens v. Manitoba	2003	*Gaming Control Local Option (VLT) Act, 1999.*
Judicial administration		
33 Ruffo v. Conseil De La Magistrature	1995	*Justice Act*, R.S.Q., c. T-16, ss. 96, 263, 265
34 Therrien (Re)	2001	*Courts of Justice Act*, R.S.Q., c. T-16, s. 95
35 Moreau-Berube v. New Brunswick	2002	*Provincial Court*, R.S.N.B. 1973, c. P-21
Environmental policy		
36 Ontario v. Canadian Pacific	1995	*Environment Protection Act*, R.S.O. 1980, c. 141, s. 13(a)
Miscellaneous		
37 Comité paritaire de l'industrie de la chemise v. Potash	1994	*Collective Agreement Decrees*, R.S.Q., c. D-2, s. 22(e)
38 B.C. Securities Commission v. Branch	1995	*Securities Act*, S.B.C. 1985, c. 83, s. 128(1)

1 Year the Supreme Court delivered its judgment.
2 Complete case citations are listed in the Bibliography.

Table 6.4

The Supreme Court's three-part federalism jurisprudence

	Year[1]	Significance
Constitution Act as shield[2]		
1 *Reference Re Bill 30*	1987	Charter cannot be used to alter denominational school rights in *Constitution Act*.
2 *New Brunswick Broadcasting Company v. Nova Scotia*	1993	Charter does not apply to inherent privileges of members of legislatures.
3 *Haig v. Canada*	1993	The federal *Referendum Act* cannot apply to disenfranchised Quebec voters.
4 *Ontario Home Builders' Assocation v. York Region*	1996	Section 93(1) is immune from Charter challenges.
5 *Adler v. Ontario*	1996	Non-funding of Jewish schools is constitutional and immune from Charter challenge.
6 *Ell v. Alberta*	2003	Alberta act advances judicial independence protected by preamble in *Constitution Act*.
Explicit dimension		
7 *R. v. Jones*	1986	Provinces must possess adequate discretion in education policy.
8 *R. v. Edwards Books and Art Ltd.*	1986	Different provincial responses to Sunday shopping constitutional.
9 *R. v. Lyons*	1987	Provincial variation in the application of the Criminal Code desirable in a federation.
10 *R. v. Turpin*	1989	Provincial variation in trial procedures constitutional.
11 *R. v. S.(S.)*	1990	Different application of federal laws by provinces advances diversity.
12 *R. v. Askov*	1990	Askov test provides provinces with flexibility in the administration of justice.
13 *McKinney v. University of Guelph*	1990	Provincial mandatory retirement policy variation a reasonable limitation.
14 *Stoffman v. Vancouver General Hospital*	1990	See *McKinney*.
15 *Haig v. Canada*	1993	Provincial differences do not automatically cause a presumption of discrimination.
16 *Therrien (Re)*	2001	Provinces provided flexibility in procedures for removing judges.
17 *Dunmore v. Ontario*	2001	Court reviews provincial labour relations acts and accepts distinct legislative schemes.

18 *R. v. Advance Cutting & Coring Ltd.*	2001	Court invokes federalism as a significant contextual factor for proper section 1 analyses.
19 *Nova Scotia v. Martin*	2003	Court reviews chronic pain regimes in several provinces and rejects a blanket exclusion.
Implicit dimension		
20 *R. v. Morgentaler*	1988	Nullification of Criminal Code section facilitates diversity in abortion services.
21 *R. v. Brydges*	1990	Access to free duty counsel determined by provinces.
22 *R. v. Morin*	1992	Askov test redesigned to place less emphasis on insitutional delay by provinces.
23 *R. v. Bartle*	1994	Informational component of section 10(b) based on legal services provided by provinces.
24 *R. v. Prosper*	1994	No constitutional obligation to provide free duty counsel under section 10(b).
25 *R. v. Pozniak*	1994	See *Bartle.*
26 *R. v. Matheson*	1994	Absence of 24-hour duty counsel in PEI cannot result in section 10(b) violation.
27 *R. v. Cobham*	1994	See *Bartle.*
28 *R. v. Latimer*	1997	Absence of toll-free number for duty counsel in Saskatchewan not a s. 10(b) violation.

1 Year the Supreme Court delivered its judgment.
2 Complete case citations are listed in the Bibliography.

provinces, turning aside challenges to three separate Alberta statutes in *Reference Re Public Service Employee Relations Act* and upholding the restrictions on dairy workers in *RWDSU v. Saskatchewan.*[59]

Turning to social policy, the Supreme Court supported the constitutionality of the *Workers' Compensation Act* in a reference case involving Newfoundland's act and upheld the restrictions on child advertising in *Irwin Toy Ltd. v. Quebec.*[60] More recently, in *Gosselin v. Quebec*, the constitutionality of Quebec's social assistance scheme, which paid reduced benefits to those under thirty who refused to participate in work-training programs, was challenged as a violation of equality rights but was determined by the Supreme Court to be constitutional.[61] Other significant social policies, such as Ontario's *Child Welfare Act* and Manitoba's *Child and Families Services Act*, have been challenged on Charter grounds but upheld as constitutional.[62] As well, the court concluded that the right to vote was not infringed in *Reference Re Provincial Electoral Boundaries (Sask.)*, despite the discrepancies in size between urban and rural ridings, and it turned aside challenges to electoral finance laws that provided public funding to candidates and parties in *McKay v. Manitoba.*[63] Finally, provincial highway traffic acts that promote public safety through random roadside testing have been upheld as constitutional in *R. v. Hufsky* and *R. v. Ladouceur.*[64] Focusing solely on invalidated provincial statutes is problematic because it fails to consider the significant provincial policies that are found to be consistent with the Charter and requires one to accept that the nullification of a handful of statutes in marginal areas has weakened provincial autonomy.

The Constitution Act as a Shield

The first dimension in the Supreme Court's federalism jurisprudence sees the court use the *Constitution Act* as a shield to protect provincial statutes against Charter challenges. This strategy was used in six cases between 1982 and 2003, as outlined in Table 6.4. It has been used to preserve provincial education policy when the court has turned aside Charter challenges to section 93 of the *Constitution Act* and the public funding of denominational schools. In *Reference Re Bill 30*, the court considered whether the Ontario cabinet's decision to extend full funding for Catholic schools was consistent with denominational school rights protected in section 93 of the *Constitution Act, 1867*, and whether Bill 30 was consistent with the Charter.[65] The Charter issues involved the potential infringement of equality rights and freedom of religion, as the extension of public funding was limited to the Catholic school board to the exclusion of all other denominations.

The decisions by Justices Estey and Wilson are important, as they identified the equal status of the Charter and the *Constitution Act* and confirmed that original constitutional guarantees cannot be expanded to other religious groups through Charter victories. In certain respects, section 29 of the

Charter anticipated the tension between section 93 of the *Constitution Act* and the Charter, as section 29 protects denominational school rights from the very challenge that occurred in *Reference Re Bill 30*.[66] In this reference opinion, Justice Wilson stated that "the rights or privileges protected by s.93(1) are immune from *Charter* review under s.29 of the *Charter*," effectively closing Charter litigation as a strategy to expand the original constitutional compromise on religious instruction.[67] Justice Estey was clearest on this point as he rejected a hierarchical relationship, in which the Charter could be used to broaden denominational school rights beyond their original purpose and scope in the *Constitution Act*: "This legislative power in the province is not subject to regulation by other parts of the Constitution in any way which would be tantamount to its repeal."[68] The *Constitution Act*, therefore, can act as a shield that protects provincial acts from Charter scrutiny.

This judicial strategy continued in *Ontario Home Builders' Association v. York Region Board of Education*, where the creation of a common educational development fund was challenged as prejudicially affecting denominational school rights protected under section 93(1) of the *Constitution Act*, as well as a violation of freedom of religion and equality rights. In a unanimous decision, the court disposed of the challenge solely on the section 93(1) issue, as Justice Iacobucci ruled that the common fund did not prejudicially affect denominational school rights because the public and separate school boards had equal access to the funds. However, the most significant aspect of this decision, and evidence of the court using the *Constitution Act* as a shield, is found in Justice Iacobucci's justification for not addressing the Charter issues raised in the appeal. Because the court framed the constitutional issue as falling within the scope of section 93(1), the legislation in question was "immune from Charter scrutiny."[69] In essence, the original federal bargain of 1867 protected Ontario's *Education Act*, and the policy discretion of all provincial governments in a core area of their jurisdiction, from Charter review. Similarly, in *Adler v. Ontario* the court dismissed an attempt by Jewish groups to expand the meaning of denominational school rights in section 93(1) to include public funding for Jewish schools. The court did not accept that the denial of funding violated either the Charter's equality rights protections or freedom of religion, because "given that the appellants cannot bring themselves within the terms of s.93 guarantees, they have no claim to public funding for their schools."[70]

In using the constitution as a shield, the Supreme Court has relied upon the written and unwritten elements to protect provincial autonomy. Recently in *Ell v. Alberta*, amendments to the *Justice of the Peace Act*, which required all judges to meet the qualifications decided upon by the provincial judicial council, were challenged as a violation of judicial independence protected in the *Constitution Act*'s preamble and section 11(d) of the Charter.

The Supreme Court did not address the Charter issue and ruled that the act was constitutional because it was consistent with judicial independence derived from the preamble's statement that Canada would have a constitution similar in principle to that of the United Kingdom.[71] While this particular approach has been employed in a limited number of cases, it is potentially the most expansive because it allows both the written and the unwritten elements of the *Constitution Act* to protect provincial acts against the potential centralizing force of the Charter.

Explicit Dimension

The ability of the provincial cabinets to approach similar problems differently has informed the court's federalism jurisprudence since 1982. In *Jones*, the appellant contended that section 142(1) of the *Alberta School Act*, which required that home instructors hold a certificate of efficient instruction issued by the local school board, infringed both freedom of religion (s.2a) and the principles of fundamental justice (s.7). In this decision, a majority of justices found that section 142(1) infringed freedom of religion but represented a reasonable limitation on this protected right. The significance of this decision is found in Justice Laforest's analysis of the relationship between section 142(1) and the principles of fundamental justice. He stated that provincial governments must be provided with sufficient flexibility in choosing administrative structures to advance their distinct policy objectives. Indeed, Justice Laforest contended that provincial policies would be consistent with section 7 as long as legislative schemes were not so manifestly unfair as to undermine the principles of fundamental justice.[72] Thus, the court articulated two important principles in this decision that inform its federalism jurisprudence: first, it is reasonable for provincial governments to approach shared policy problems differently; and, second, flexibility must be accorded to these governments because of different social contexts.

These principles clearly emerged in *Edwards Books and Art Ltd.*, in which the court considered whether mandatory Sunday closings in the *Retail Business Holiday Act* (Ontario) infringed freedom of religion (s.2a), right to liberty (s.7), and equality rights (s.15) of Saturday sabbatarians.[73] The majority judgments (four to three) by Chief Justice Dickson and Justice Laforest concluded that the act had infringed freedom of religion, but this was simply the effect, as the purpose was to create a common day of rest. In concluding that the infringement on freedom of religion was reasonable, the majority judgment engaged in a comparative assessment of Sunday-closing policies in Canada. In particular, both Dickson and Laforest analyzed various provincial regulations intended to create a common day of rest, and refrained from establishing a uniform standard that must be met to satisfy the reasonable limits clause. Instead, the court allowed a range of different provincial responses to satisfy section 1, illustrated most clearly by Justice Laforest's comparative analysis of provincial legislation, which led him to conclude "the simple fact is that what may work effectively in one province (or part of it) may simply not work in another without unduly interfering with the legislative scheme. And a compromise adopted at a particular time may not be possible at another."[74] In both *Jones* and *Edwards Books,* the court demonstrated sensitivity to the social contexts that structured provincial policies, and, in doing so, advanced an explicit federalist jurisprudence that acknowledged diversity and protected provincial autonomy.

Charter challenges in *R. v. S.(S.), R. v. Turpin,* and *R. v. Lyons* involved the different application of federal statutes (the Criminal Code and the *Young Offenders Act [YOA]*) by the provinces.[75] Of these, *R. v. S.(S.)* is the most important for its explicit statement on federal diversity and Charter review.[76] In *R. v. S.(S.),* sections of the federal *YOA* that allowed provinces to design alternative measures to trial procedures when dealing with young offenders were challenged as a violation of equality rights because the Ontario cabinet had failed to establish alternative measures, thus causing variation in the treatment of young offenders by the provinces.[77] In a unanimous judgment, Justice Lamer offered an analysis of the relationship between federal diversity and judicial review, particularly regarding equality rights:

> Obviously, the federal system of governance demands that the values underlying s.15(1) cannot be given unlimited scope. The division of powers not only permits differential treatment based on province of residence, it mandates and encourages geographic distinction. There can be no question, then, that unequal treatment which stems solely from the exercise, by provincial legislatures, of their legitimate jurisdictional powers cannot be subject to a s.15(1) challenge on the basis that it creates distinctions based on province of residence ... To find otherwise would be to completely undermine the value of diversity which is at the foundation of the division of powers.[78]

Justice Lamer concluded that there was no Charter violation because "it is necessary to bear in mind that differential application of federal law can be a legitimate means of forwarding the values of a federal system."[79] The principles of Charter review that developed from these cases are significant because the issues clearly illustrate the tension between uniformity and diversity that is at the heart of the rights and federalism debate in Canada. By accepting variation in the application of federal laws, the court did a great service to provincial autonomy: it recognized the tension between competing notions of community and attempted to balance them in a federalist jurisprudence designed to minimize the centralizing potential of Charter review.

These principles were further expanded in two cases in 1990 that challenged mandatory retirement policies in universities and hospitals as age-based discrimination and thus inconsistent with equality rights protections in section 15(1) of the Charter. In both *McKinney v. University of Guelph* and *Stoffman v. Vancouver General Hospital*,[80] the court found that if the Charter applied, mandatory retirement provisions would violate section 15(1) but would be saved by section 1 of the Charter.[81] The most poignant illustration of this explicit federalist jurisprudence is captured in Justice Laforest's analysis of different human rights codes at the provincial level. He said that "the fact that other jurisdictions have taken a different view proves only that the legislature there adopted a different balance to a complex set of competing values."[82] Further, his justification for the reasonableness of the infringement is identical to his judgment in *Edwards Books*, where he argued, for the majority opinion, the reality and necessity of policy variation in a federal system. By upholding diverse provincial responses to a shared policy problem, the court advanced federal diversity by sanctioning difference as an acceptable principle in Charter review related to provincial legislation.

An explicit statement on the value of diversity in a federal system occurred in *Haig v. Canada*, three years after the court upheld provincial mandatory retirement policies.[83] At issue in *Haig* was the federal *Referendum Act*, enacted for the referendum on the Charlottetown Accord, and whether the act's inability to accommodate disenfranchised voters in the Quebec referendum violated the right to vote (s.3), freedom of expression (s.2b), and equality rights (s.15). The majority decision (seven to two) written by Justice L'Heureux-Dubé relied heavily on the institutional requirements of a federal system to overturn the challenge to the act. For instance, Justice L'Heureux-Dubé concluded that allowing those who had resided in Quebec for less than six months to participate in the federal referendum would "require enumerators to operate extraterritorially in a province for which no federal referendum writ was issued."[84] The court recognized that this would violate the jurisdictional integrity of Quebec and be inconsistent with the federal character of Canada.[85] In dispensing the section 15(1) challenge against the act, the court expanded the approach developed in *Lyons* and *Turpin* that said federal legislation did not have to be uniformly applied to the provinces to be consistent with section 15(1): "Clearly, in a federal system, province-based distinctions do not automatically give rise to a presumption of discrimination. Section 15(1) of the Charter, while prohibiting discrimination, does not alter the division of powers between governments."[86]

The importance of policy variation was advanced in two significant judgments in 2001 involving provincial labour policy. In *Dunmore*, the Supreme Court ruled that Ontario's *Labour Relations Act (LRA)* violated freedom of association and did not represent a reasonable limitation because it excluded agricultural workers. The section 1 analysis is significant, as the Supreme

Court failed to accept that all agricultural workers needed to be excluded under the *LRA* and compared the Ontario cabinet's approach to other provinces' more reasonable attempts to protect the family farm, which was Ontario's justification for the exclusion of agricultural workers. In reviewing the equivalent legislation in New Brunswick, Quebec, and Alberta, which only excluded agricultural workers who actually worked on family farms, the Supreme Court rejected the Ontario cabinet's claim that the categorization of agricultural workers was impossible: "The fact that some legislation includes exceptions for smaller or family-run farms, most notably labour codes in New Brunswick and Quebec, as well as the *ALRA* itself, suggests that such an exercise is eminently possible, should the legislature choose to undertake it."[87] While this case did establish a minimal standard, it did not establish a national standard beyond the fact that all agricultural workers could not be excluded from provincial acts governing labour relations. The Supreme Court accepted that provincial variation existed in this policy sector and simply determined that the complete denial of all agricultural workers was not a reasonable response to the need to protect the family farm.

A poignant discussion of provincial variation occurred in *R. v. Advance Cutting & Coring Ltd.,* which involved a constitutional challenge against the requirement in Quebec's construction legislation that workers must be members of one of five listed union groups to obtain competency certificates.[88] The challenge involved whether the requirement of membership violated freedom of association, which the court dismissed in a majority decision (five to four). Speaking for three members of the majority, Justice Lebel accepted the policy rationale because of the history of conflict in the construction industry and the unique structure of the labour industry in Quebec. This judgment was sensitive to the complex policy context of labour relations and the limited capacity of the court in this area, stating that "the relevant political, social and economic considerations lie largely beyond the area of expertise of courts."[89] Though Lebel found the act consistent with freedom of association, a section 1 analysis was conducted nonetheless.

The significance of this analysis is the importance of federalism in determining whether a limitation on freedom of association would be reasonable. Justice Lebel elaborated on the contextual factors structuring the Oakes test, saying that "provincial differences must be factored into any proper analysis of the concept of minimal impairment, when assessing the validity of provincial legislation."[90] Further, the judgment embraced the importance of diversity when the court evaluated whether provincial statutes satisfied section 1 of the Charter: "The principle of federalism means that the application of the Charter in fields of provincial jurisdiction does not amount to a call for legislative conformity. It expresses shared values, which may be achieved differently, in different settings."[91] The deferential nature of this judgment is important, as the court accepted that provincial governments were best positioned to structure labour relations because of the complex policy context in each jurisdiction. Federalism and the institutional capacity of provincial governments, therefore, directly influenced the finding of constitutionality by the Supreme Court.

The court's acceptance of different provincial responses to shared problems demonstrates that Charter review does not necessarily ensure uniformity, even when provincial statutes are determined to violate the Charter. In *Nova Scotia v. Martin*, the Supreme Court found section 10(b) of the *Workers' Compensation Act* and the Functional Restoration Program Regulations unconstitutional because the exclusion of chronic pain coverage infringed the equality rights protections of disabled workers. The court considered whether the blanket exclusion of chronic disability under the act was a reasonable limitation on section 15(1). The only defensible legislative objective, in the opinion of the court delivered by Justice Gonthier, was the attempt to avoid fraudulent claims.[92] However, the court determined this objective could be advanced within the *Workers' Compensation Act* without having to exclude all sufferers of chronic pain, and, further, that the chronic pain regimes in other provinces demonstrated that this objective could be achieved without a blanket provision: "The Act already provides that benefits may be limited, suspended or discontinued if the worker fails to mitigate losses, does not comply with medical advice or fails to provide the Board with full and accurate information regarding his or her claim (ss.84 and 113 of the Act)."[93]

The court reached this conclusion by examining the chronic pain regimes in Alberta, British Columbia, Quebec, and Ontario, which provided for coverage by changing the method of assessment to accurately determine each claimant's degree of disability.[94] Justice Gonthier acknowledged that the Nova Scotia cabinet had the constitutional authority to choose from a range of possible approaches to chronic pain regimes, but that "it is impossible to conclude that the blanket exclusion it enacted was necessary to achieve a principled response to chronic pain and avoid fraudulent claims."[95] In essence, provincial standards determined that Nova Scotia had infringed the equality rights of disabled workers in an unreasonable manner, and not the national standards attributed to the Supreme Court's Charter review. Federalism is a significant element of Charter review, as the Supreme Court considers how different provincial cabinets approach shared problems and recognizes that distinct policy contexts and historical experiences caution against the drive for uniformity in public policy. This has been a significant part of the court's Charter jurisprudence, which has reconciled rights and federalism and protected provincial autonomy.

Implicit Dimension

Christopher Manfredi and Ian Urquhart identified an early example of the implication this implicit dimension of Charter review has for provincial autonomy in *R. v. Morgentaler,*[96] where the consequences of striking down Criminal Code restrictions on abortion services were greater policy diversity because the provincial cabinets were able to determine the level of services to provide in the absence of a national abortion policy.[97] There is, however, a more implicit jurisprudence involving the conduct of public officials. What emerge from an analysis of the court's approach to legal rights are constitutional standards that the police must comply with during criminal investigations and, for the most part, an absence of substantive obligations on provincial governments for the administration of justice.[98] This facilitates provincial variation in the administration of justice, as many of the constitutional obligations placed on the police are directly related to the services provided in each province.

In a number of cases involving the informational component of section 10(b) of the Charter, the right to retain and instruct counsel without delay, the court has established standards with which the police must comply when an individual is taken into custody. In a unanimous judgment in *R. v. Brydges,* the court ruled that failure to inform the accused of legal aid resources in Manitoba violated section 10(b). The effect of this decision was to require the police in all jurisdictions to update the informational component of section 10(b), the statement they read to people taken into custody, to include reference to legal aid services available to those people who cannot afford a lawyer.[99] However, the court advanced an implicit federalist jurisprudence in this decision because it accepted that the informational component of section 10(b) was determined by what legal aid services existed in specific jurisdictions. Moreover, the court recognized and accepted that provincial variation existed in legal aid plans, so the outcome in *Brydges* did not set a national standard in the provision of legal aid plans but simply placed a procedural requirement on the police under section 10(b) to inform of existing services.[100]

The principle that the police must inform detainees of the availability of specific legal aid resources as part of section 10(b) informed the court's decisions in *R. v. Bartle, R. v. Wozniak,* and *R. v. Cobham,* of which *Wozniak* is representative.[101] *Wozniak* involved a toll-free phone number that Ontario had established for detainees to use outside normal working hours to access free legal advice. The police informed the accused of the availability of legal aid in Ontario, but did not refer to the toll-free number, which the court concluded had violated section 10(b).[102] The outcome of *Wozniak* was to expand the informational component of section 10(b) to include "whatever system for free and immediate, preliminary legal advice exists in the jurisdiction at the time of detention and how such advice can be accessed."[103] As in *Brydges,* the win for the Charter claimant contained an implicit federalism jurisprudence because the court structured the content of section 10(b) to reflect the legal aid plan in existence in specific jurisdictions. Because the Ontario cabinet had established a toll-free number, the police were obligated to include reference to this when dispensing their section 10(b) requirements. However, the support for the Charter claimant in this case did not lead to conformity in provincial legal aid plans, because other provinces were not required to establish toll-free numbers to be used outside of normal working hours for free legal advice.

The ability of provincial cabinets to independently determine the content of legal aid plans and, thus, the right to counsel was clarified in *R. v. Prosper*, where the court denied that a substantive constitutional obligation to provide free and immediate preliminary legal advice existed under section 10(b).[104] The majority decision did not impose a constitutional obligation, in part because of the financial burden such an obligation would impose. Chief Justice Lamer wrote in his ruling, "The fact that such an obligation would almost certainly interfere with governments' allocation of limited resources by requiring them to expend public funds on the provision of a service is, I might add, a further consideration which weighs against this interpretation."[105] Lamer also said that "an effective duty counsel does not need to be an elaborate one. For instance, it need not consist of anything more than a basic service accessed by dialling a 1-800 number."[106] However, the content and the existence of a duty counsel system were left to the discretion of provincial cabinets, despite the court's support for the Charter claimants. This principle was modified in 1999, when the Supreme Court ruled that a constitutional obligation to provide state-funded legal counsel existed in a very specific context. In *New Brunswick v. G.(J.)*, the court decided that in cases where the province attempted to remove a child from the family home, if the removal was challenged by a parent who lacked the financial resources to challenge the decision, a constitutional duty existed on the part of the province to provide legal counsel.[107]

In *R. v. Matheson* and *R. v. Latimer*, the court addressed whether the absence of a system of duty counsel undermined section 10(b).[108] Consistent with its approach in *Wozniak*, it concluded that the informational component was determined by the services in each province. In *Matheson*, the court considered whether the absence of a system of duty counsel in Prince Edward Island violated section 10(b), whereas in *Latimer*, the absence of a twenty-four-hour toll-free number to access free duty counsel informed the section 10(b) issue before the court. Chief Justice Lamer concluded in *Latimer* that "the proposition which emerges from these cases is that the nature of the information provided pursuant to s.10b depends on the actual services available in a jurisdiction."[109] In each case, the court found that section 10(b) was not infringed because the police had properly dispensed the informational component of section 10(b) as it existed in Saskatchewan and Prince Edward Island. The court's approach to section 10(b) is significant because it recognizes that provincial variation in the provision of legal aid exists and that such services are at the discretion of provincial cabinets and are not constitutionally mandated. By approaching Charter review in legal rights cases in such a fashion, the court has advanced an implicit federalist jurisprudence because provincial autonomy in the administration of justice has not been compromised by Charter victories in section 10(b) cases.

Provincial Responses to the Charter

The unfortunate element of the Charter dialogue metaphor put forward by Hogg and Bushell is their conception of legislative responses to the Charter and which actor initiates a rights-based dialogue. The primary assumption is that it is initiated when courts identify constitutional violations in challenged statutes and the responsible cabinet decides whether to amend the offending legislation.[110] In effect, in this view, a legislative response is simply the cabinet's reaction to judicial invalidation, and Charter dialogue is judicial centred and initiated. The preceding discussion of the attempts by the Supreme Court to reconcile rights and federalism should not be taken as confirmation of the Charter dialogue approach by Hogg and Bushell. While the Supreme Court has been instrumental in protecting provincial autonomy when reviewing statutes, the primary responsibility is legislative, as this objective has been principally advanced by the development of a rights culture within government.[111]

The institutionalization of Charter vetting during the development of legislation in each province has advanced this objective, as legislative activism has acted as a bulwark against judicial invalidation of statutes on Charter grounds. I have elaborated on the importance of legislative activism elsewhere, but it is a significant development for provincial autonomy and illustrates how efforts to govern with the Charter through a reformed policy process have reconciled rights and federalism.[112] The institutional response by the cabinet at both levels of government questions the assumption by Hogg and Bushell that Charter dialogue begins at invalidation and that the courts are the principal guardian of the constitution. The principal reaction to Charter review is not the cabinet's response to judicial activism but judicial responses to legislative activism when the Supreme Court reviews statutes for their constitutionality. This is a central limitation with judicial-centred approaches as the analysis focuses on the Supreme Court and yearly rates of activism. While the Supreme Court has discretion over the cases it hears, legislative activism directed by the cabinet has a direct influence on the statutes that proceed to the court and are reviewed for their relationship to the Charter.

An argument advanced throughout this book is the importance of a cabinet-centred approach to the Charter and the need to evaluate the inter-institutional relationships between the Supreme Court and the cabinet at

Table 6.5

Provincial statutes reviewed by the Supreme Court, 1982 to 2003

Year[1]	Unconstitutional	Constitutional	Total
1973	0	1	1
1977	1	0	1
1979	1	1	2
1980	4	6	10
1981	1	2	3
1982	3	1	4
1983	2	4	6
1984	0	5	5
1985	1	1	2
1986	0	1	1
1987	1	2	3
1988	0	4	4
1989	0	1	1
1990	4	5	9
1992	1	0	1
1994	1	0	1
1995	2	0	2
1996	2	2	4
1997	1	1	2
1999	0	1	1
Total	25	38	63

1   Year a statute was enacted or last amended, as reported in the *Supreme Court Reports*.

the federal and provincial levels of government. The ability of provincial cabinets to protect federalism is revealed in Table 6.5, which presents yearly statistics on the statutes reviewed. Only eleven provincial statutes enacted after 1990 have been reviewed for their relationship to the Charter, which represents only 17 percent of the provincial statutes considered by the Supreme Court (11 out of 63). Before presenting legislative activism and Charter vetting by provincial governments as the explanation for the lack of post-1990 statutes reviewed by the court, alternative explanations must be considered. A possible explanation is that post-1990 statutes are being invalidated by lower courts, and provincial cabinets are not appealing to the Supreme Court. Thus, cabinets are filtering out provincial statutes enacted between 1990 and 2003 by accepting judicial invalidation by lower courts. Alternatively, post-1990 statutes may not yet have progressed through the judicial system for review by the Supreme Court, and their absence is explained by a lengthy appeal process. These explanations are flawed because the Supreme Court does, in fact, review a large number of statutes enacted

Table 6.6

Courts of appeal, Charter decisions, 1982 to 2003

Court of appeal	Pre-1982[1]			1983-1989[2]			1990-2003[3]			1983-2003[4]			Pre-1982-2003			1993-2003		
	C	%	UC	C	%	UC	C	%	UC	C	%	UC	C	%	UC	C	%	UC
Alberta	6	54.5	5	3	100.0	0	4	100.0	0	7	100.0	0	13	72.2	5	0	0.0	0
British Columbia	7	63.6	4	5	62.5	3	14	77.8	4	19	73.1	7	26	70.3	11	6	67.0	3
Manitoba	3	75.0	1	3	75.0	1	2	100.0	0	5	83.3	1	8	80.0	2	1	100.0	0
New Brunswick	4	100.0	0	6	100.0	0	0	0.0	1	6	85.7	1	10	90.9	1	0	0.0	1
Newfoundland	2	100.0	0	1	100.0	0	2	66.7	1	3	75.0	1	5	83.3	1	0	0.0	1
Nova Scotia	7	77.8	2	3	42.9	4	4	100.0	0	7	63.6	4	14	70.0	6	2	100.0	0
Ontario	19	67.9	9	9	64.3	5	19	76.0	6	28	71.8	11	47	70.1	20	7	78.0	2
Prince Edward Island	3	100.0	0	2	66.7	1	3	100.0	0	5	83.3	1	8	88.9	1	3	100.0	0
Quebec	2	40.0	3	6	100.0	0	4	80.0	1	10	90.9	1	12	75.0	4	2	100.0	0
Saskatchewan	2	50.0	2	2	40.0	3	3	75.0	1	5	55.6	4	7	53.8	6	3	75.0	1
Total	55	67.9	26	40	70.2	17	55	79.7	14	95	75.4	31	150	72.5	57	24	75.0	8

Notes: C = Constitutional (court of appeal upholds statute); UC = Unconstitutional (court of appeal invalidates statute); % = percentage of statutes ruled constitutional on Charter grounds.

1 Statutes enacted into law or last amended before 1982, as reported in the *Dominion Law Reports*.
2 Statutes enacted into law or last amended from 1983 to 1989, as reported in the *Dominion Law Reports*.
3 Statutes enacted into law or last amended from 1990 to 2003, as reported in the *Dominion Law Reports*.
4 Statutes enacted into law or last amended from 1993 to 2003, as reported in the *Dominion Law Reports*.

in the post-Charter era. The difference is the outcome: statutes enacted in a post-Charter policy environment are less likely to be nullified.

Table 6.6 summarizes provincial statutes challenged on Charter grounds in each provincial court of appeal (note that in Newfoundland and Prince Edward Island the provincial Supreme Court serves this function). A total of 207 provincial statutes have been reviewed by courts of appeal in relation to the Charter, and the rate of invalidation between 1982 and 2003 was 28 percent (57 out of 207). Focusing on the year of enactment reveals that the statutes were largely proclaimed into law after 1982 and that rates of activism vary considerably. For instance, the total Charter jurisprudence of the courts of appeal is divided into three periods: (1) statutes enacted before 1982; (2) statutes enacted from 1983 to 1989; (3) statutes enacted from 1990 to 2003. In terms of the composition of Charter cases reviewed by the appeal courts, pre-1982 statutes represent 39 percent of the cases (81 out of 207), the statutes enacted or last amended between 1983 and 1989 account for 28 percent (57 out of 207), and statutes enacted between 1990 and 2003 represent 33 percent (69 out of 207). While nongovernmental actors can appeal lower-court rulings supporting the constitutionality of challenged statutes, only governments have an automatic right of intervention when a case is reviewed by the Supreme Court. This is significant, as Roach contends that eight of the top ten interveners in Supreme Court decisions involving the Charter are governments.[113] The Supreme Court, therefore, is considering a limited number of post-1990 statutes, even though a significant number have been reviewed at the appeal court level, because few statutes enacted in this period are being invalidated and appealed to the Supreme Court by provincial governments.

Focusing on the last time period demonstrates that the limited number of statutes reviewed by the Supreme Court is the result of a high rate of constitutionality at the courts of appeal in each province. The overall rate of constitutionality under the Charter is 72.5 percent (150 out of 207), as only 57 provincial statutes have been invalidated by appeal courts (from 1982 to 2003) as violating protected rights. There is, however, a notable increase in Charter consistency, with statutes enacted before 1982 constitutional in 67.9 percent (55 out of 81) of cases, followed by 70.2 percent (40 out of 57) for statutes enacted from 1983 to 1989, and 79.7 percent (55 out of 69) for the remaining provincial statutes. What is the reason for the increasing rates of constitutionality? One explanation might be judicial deference associated with a relaxing of constitutional standards and a greater acceptance by the provincial appeal courts that statutes represent a reasonable limitation when Charter rights are infringed. This is not convincing because judicial review in any given year involves statutes enacted before and after 1982. As there are notable differences in rates of constitutionality based on year of enactment, changes in judicial review cannot account for the higher rates of constitutionality of statutes enacted after the Charter's introduction.

Perhaps a more cynical explanation is that governments are simply responding to judicial decisions and incorporating judicial values into the legislative process, what Vallinder referred to as judicialization from within.[114] Choudhry and Hunter recently referred to this as "government learning," and said that incorporation of judicial interpretation of the Charter into the legislative process shows how "governments that are strategically minded learn to conform both their legislation and their arguments in *Charter* cases to the Court's jurisprudence."[115] This faulty assumption is the same as that of the Charter dialogue theorist who views legislative responses as simply the cabinet's reaction to judicial determination of the Charter. It is embedded within the limitations of the judicial-centred approach to the Charter and devalues the independent and central role of cabinets and departments of Justice in establishing the parameters of Charter review and determining judicial responses to legislative activism.

In order to test the importance of Charter vetting during the legislative process as an explanation for the limited number of provincial statutes invalidated at the level of the Supreme Court, the analysis factors out statutes enacted before 1982 because they were created in a different policy environment, where the constitutional constraint was the division of powers and not consistency with the Charter. Further, a distinction is made among post-1982 statutes to allow the analysis to consider statutes enacted immediately after 1982 and those after 1990. The reality is that provincial cabinets, like their federal counterpart, did not immediately incorporate Charter vetting into the development of legislation to ensure that policy objectives and Charter values were assessed within legislative schemes. The development of a rights culture, and institutional reform of the policy process to facilitate this objective, therefore, were delayed and became a prominent policy exercise after 1990. Indeed, the marginal differences in rates of constitutionality between pre-1982 statutes (67.9 percent) and statutes enacted between 1983 and 1989 (70.2 percent) indicate no discernable differences in the legislative process or evidence of its importance, whereas the statutes enacted after 1990 with the benefit of Charter vetting are constitutional in nearly 80 percent of court of appeal decisions involving provincial statutes. This is a rate of constitutionality nearly 10 percent over statutes enacted immediately after the Charter's introduction, and it suggests that the efforts to govern with the Charter have been successful, as fewer provincial statute are being invalidated at the appellant level and even fewer are progressing to the Supreme Court for consideration.

Legislative Activism and Provincial Departments of Justice

The legislative responses to the Charter at the provincial level bear certain similarities to the federal response, as the provincial departments of Justice have been responsible, to varying degrees, for reviewing legislative exercises for their relationship to the Charter.[116] The importance of legislative activism and the general imbalance between its bureaucratic and parliamentary dimensions are explored in Chapter 7, but the provincial efforts at rights vetting are the principal reason why provincial statutes are constitutional when reviewed by the Supreme Court in Charter cases. The one major difference is the institutionalized nature of the review by the federal Department of Justice and by the corresponding departments in larger provinces such as Ontario, British Columbia, and Quebec, and the informal review by the departments of Justice in smaller provinces. However, I would caution against interpreting the informal development of Charter vetting as a lack of commitment to the development of a rights culture within government or as resistance to governing with the Charter by legislative actors. Based on the interviews conducted in every province, the attempt to ensure the constitutionality of legislation is evident at the provincial level, and the values of the Charter permeate the policy process.[117] Justice officials are committed to providing client departments with informed opinions on the relationship between Charter values and the requests for legislation, and they attempt to work with the client department to minimize the risk of constitutional invalidation. The informal nature of Charter review in some jurisdictions is more a reflection of the small size of government and the close working relationships that develop between client departments and the departments of Justice. In truth, a highly institutionalized Charter review process would potentially prove to be unworkable in smaller provinces because of the limited capacity of government and the closer working relationships this has facilitated between client departments and the provincial departments of Justice.[118]

In the remainder of this chapter, two distinct approaches to the provision of Charter advice in provincial governments will be outlined: the institutionalized model in Ontario, Quebec, and British Columbia; and the informal Charter review model in the remaining provinces. Both models have generally ensured that provincial statutes are subjected to a thorough Charter review, but there are important trade-offs in both approaches. Institutionalized review occurs in jurisdictions where the Department of Justice has emerged as a central agency because of organizational characteristics, such as the absence of line responsibilities and the clear mandates of the branches within Justice. These jurisdictions have sufficient fiscal and human resources to conduct a rigorous and formalized Charter review and devote extensive resources to reviewing the constitutional implications of policy drafts by client departments. Informal Charter review is evident in provinces where the Justice department has important line responsibilities, such as correctional services and the police, and thus does not function principally as the government's law firm. While the Justice department in these jurisdictions cannot be said to be a central agency, all have branches that perform central agency functions across government.

With the exception of Quebec, where legislation is drafted by the legal service units (LSUs) situated in the client department, and Nova Scotia, where it is the responsibility of the Office of Legislative Counsel, all legislation is drafted by the Legislative Counsel Office in departments of Justice. This office ensures that the drafting instructions provided by client departments, once presented to the legislative assembly in the form of legislation, are written to advance Charter values and to demonstrate the cabinet commitment to rights protections.[119] In preparing draft legislation, however, this is the last stage of the Charter vetting process within the bureaucratic arena, as LSUs within client departments or legal services branches within departments of Justice provide constant Charter advice to client departments throughout a policy exercise. Constitutional law branches, where they exist in departments of Justice, provide additional Charter advice and scrutinize policy objectives and draft legislation when consulted by LSUs and legal services branches. Charter vetting is a constant process that begins once a client department develops policy objectives and seeks legal advice to transform these policy objectives into legislation, as the role of the Department of Justice is to ensure Charter compliance throughout all stages of the policy process.

Institutionalized Rights Vetting

At the provincial level, bureaucratic activism is most institutionalized in Ontario, British Columbia, and Quebec, as the respective departments of Justice have responsibility for a formalized Charter review of the policy activities of client departments.[120] What makes this formalized Charter review possible is the structure of these departments of Justice as well as their size. For instance, the Ontario Ministry of the Attorney General (OMAG) and the Quebec Ministry of Justice have organizational structures similar to those of the federal Department of Justice, as LSUs are seconded to client ministries. While several provinces have LSUs within client ministries, such as Alberta, which has four seconded solicitor divisions,[121] Ontario and Quebec are the only provinces that have modelled their organizational structure after the federal Department of Justice.[122] In Ontario, though the LSUs are present within the client ministry and provide general legal advice to a specific client, they remain the line authority of OMAG and report to an assistant deputy minister for Legal Services.[123] In Quebec, the LSUs report to the director general of Legal and Legislative Affairs at the Ministry of Justice.[124] In both cases, the LSUs allow OMAG and the Quebec Ministry of

Justice to participate in the development of policy by client ministries and to ensure that Charter issues are properly addressed and identified at the earliest stages of a policy exercise.[125]

Beyond the provision of constitutional advice through seconded legal services, the constitutional law branches in Ontario, Quebec, and British Columbia provide more specialized legal advice for client ministries when called upon by LSUs or legal services branches, and they represent the government in constitutional cases. In Ontario, when a lawyer within the Constitutional Law Branch provides a written opinion for an LSU, the opinion is reviewed by senior members of the branch.[126] At this stage, the draft policy of a client department has been subjected to three distinct Charter reviews by OMAG. The objective of this review exercise is to ensure that the client ministry can achieve its desired policy in a manner consistent with the Charter. Perhaps more importantly, the client ministry is required by OMAG to seek legal advice during the development of policy. This formal requirement has been critical in the emergence of a rights culture within the Ontario public service.[127] The provision of legal advice is further formalized during the development of a cabinet submission by the client ministry, as the memorandum to cabinet specifies that the legal and constitutional implications of the proposed policy must be assessed. This task is performed by the LSU in tandem with OMAG.[128]

While the client department does write this part of the cabinet submission, it must be approved by the director of the LSU that participated in the provision of legal and constitutional advice. In effect, this section of the cabinet submission assesses the potential for judicial invalidation and the relationship between the proposed policy and the Charter. Once the cabinet approves the submission by the client ministry, the involvement of OMAG continues, as the client ministry provides Legislative Counsel Services with drafting instructions to create legislation for the proposed act. Thus, legislative counsel perform a final and vital Charter review of draft legislation and may seek further legal advice from the LSU and Constitutional Law Branch to better reduce the risk of judicial invalidation once the legislation is proclaimed into law. Therefore, the provision of legal advice is institutionalized in Ontario, and the participation of OMAG is present throughout the development of policy by a client department. Finally, in the event that a statute administered by a client ministry is challenged as unconstitutional, the Ministry of the Attorney General has the responsibility to defend the statute if requested by cabinet.

There are notable differences in the vetting of legislation in Quebec that suggest it is *une province pas comme les autres*. These are the result of the institutional differences in the Quebec state, the quasi-constitutional status of the *Quebec Charter of Human Rights,* and the significant role of the Quebec Human Rights Commission in the vetting of legislation. In this regard, it is more accurate to discuss rights vetting in Quebec because all legislation is reviewed for its relationship to the Canadian Charter and the Quebec Charter. There is a more comprehensive approach because of the quasi-constitutional status of the Quebec Charter, which is not accorded to any other human rights code in Canada.[129] Turning first to the structure of the Quebec Ministry of Justice and its place within the administrative state, the one notable difference is the greater autonomy that LSUs have in their relationship with client departments. In Quebec, the LSU drafts legislation, while in other jurisdictions this is the role of the legislative council office that is normally within the Department of Justice.[130] However, all legislation drafted by the LSU is reviewed by the Government Legislation Directorate located within the General Directorate of Legal and Legislative Affairs at Justice and by the Legislation Secretariat in the Ministry of the Executive Council.[131]

An elaborate vetting of legislation occurs under the direction of the Ministry of Justice, as several units work in tandem. This has elevated Justice to the level of a central agency in Quebec despite greater autonomy of the LSUs, as a central unit within the Ministry of Justice supervises the draft legislation by the LSUs. For instance, the Government Legislation Directorate provides drafting training for LSUs and scrutinizes all draft legislation for its consistency with the Canadian and Quebec Charters. Before any draft bill is submitted to the Legislation Committee of the Executive Council, it is reviewed by the General Directorate of Legal and Legislative Affairs to ensure that outstanding Charter issues have been addressed.[132] Thus, the Quebec Ministry of Justice has both a coordination and control function over the activities of line departments in ensuring that policies developed are consistent with both the Canadian and Quebec Charters. The vetting of legislation continues when a draft bill is submitted to the Legislation Committee of the Executive Council, as it acts as an additional check for Charter and constitutional coherence before a bill is introduced into the National Assembly. The Legislation Committee has the discretion to seek further legal advice from the Ministry of Justice.[133] Once introduced into the National Assembly, any amendment to a bill is reviewed by the Legislation Secretariat at Executive Council, which then seeks the advice of the Ministry of Justice on its consistency with the Quebec and Canadian Charters.[134]

When a bill is tabled in the National Assembly and a parliamentary committee is struck, the Quebec Human Rights Commission (QHRC) receives a copy of the draft bill and prepares a brief that evaluates the bill's consistency with the Quebec and Canadian Charters. This brief is presented before the parliamentary committee and allows the QHRC to participate directly in the development of legislation and its scrutiny from a rights perspective.[135] This is not a common practice in Canada, as provincial human rights commissions generally investigate individual complaints and perform an educational role: in essence, their participation is after the legislation is passed into law.[136] In Quebec, a review of legislation is performed by the Research and Planning Department, which is a branch of the Legal Department of the QHRC. This review function is established in section 71(6) of the Quebec Charter. No other provincial human rights code authorizes a vetting role during the design of legislation for a human rights commission.[137] In 2003 the QHRC reviewed approximately 130 bills and presented nine written briefs to the Quebec National Assembly that critically assessed the constitutionality of draft bills. During my interviews with members of the QHRC, officials indicated that approximately 60 percent of its recommendations to improve the constitutionality of draft legislation were accepted by the National Assembly.[138] The vetting of legislation in Quebec, therefore, is very complex and under the direction of the Quebec Ministry of Justice. In turn, the Ministry of Justice interacts with the client department to ensure compliance with the Quebec and Canadian Charters and liaises with the Ministry of the Executive Council once the draft bill is presented to cabinet for consideration. This process is complemented by the work of parliamentary committees in the National Assembly and by critical examination performed by the QHRC.

Since the introduction of the Quebec Charter in 1975, legislation has been vetted from a rights perspective by bureaucratic, legislative, and quasi-judicial bodies such as the QHRC. In certain respects, legislative activism is most balanced between its bureaucratic and cabinet dimensions in Quebec, and rights scrutiny has a longer history here than in any other jurisdiction. The attempt to govern with rights is most pressing in Quebec because of the potential tension between the Quebec Civil Code and the Canadian Charter. As the Supreme Court's treatment of Quebec statutes has not been noticeably different from its treatment of statutes from other provinces, with a similar number of statutes invalidated,[139] the thoroughness of this scrutiny explains Quebec being *une province comme les autres* during Charter review by the court. This is the case because Quebec has governed with rights unlike the others.

British Columbia's Ministry of Attorney General (BCMAG) has a more traditional organizational structure, as all government solicitors are located within the ministry and the practice of seconded legal services was discontinued in 1991,[140] but the involvement of BCMAG in the development of legislative exercises by client ministries has been formalized since 2000 and conforms to the practices in Ontario and Quebec. In *Guide to Preparing Drafting Instructions for Legislation*, the Office of Legislative Counsel at BCMAG has instructed client ministries to involve their government solicitor as well as the Constitutional and Administrative Law Branch during the development of a request for legislation (RFL).[141] As well, the Office of Legislative Counsel functions as a final review of the constitutional implications of RFLs by client ministries and can request additional reviews by specialized branches within BCMAG.[142] Further, a series of internal consultations must occur before a minister may sign an RFL, and the comments of the Office of Legislative Counsel in consultation with the departmental solicitor and the Constitutional and Administrative Law Branch must be attached to the RFL in Appendix A: Legislative Counsel Comments.[143] The RFL also specifies that internal consultation must take place with the staff of Treasury Board, another traditional central agency.[144]

In each jurisdiction, the cabinet support system has been changed to formalize a process that scrutinizes cabinet proposals submitted by client ministries. This review is the sole responsibility of OMAG, BCMAG, and the Quebec Ministry of Justice, and as a result of the highly institutionalized rights review these departments perform, they have emerged as central agencies because of the importance of ensuring that legislation passed has been thoroughly reviewed for its relationship to the Canadian Charter and, in Quebec, the *Charter of Human Rights and Freedoms*.

Charter Vetting in Small Provinces

All provincial cabinets have increased the responsibilities of departments of Justice in vetting the Charter implications of legislative exercises of client departments.[145] The departments of Justice in the remaining provinces are unlikely to emerge as central agencies because there is no formal Charter review in these jurisdictions and these departments perform important line responsibilities as well. However, these departments all perform essential central agency functions across government, thus suggesting a mixed organizational structure that stands between a line department and a central agency. The absence of a formal Charter review by the department of Justice is generally the result of limited human and fiscal resources, as many government solicitors are unable to begin a Charter review at the earliest stages of a policy exercise because they are responsible for multiple clients and, in many cases, are the only government solicitor assigned to a client department.[146] In contrast, both the federal Department of Justice and the OMAG have LSUs in client departments that resemble mid-sized law firms, with nearly thirty lawyers assigned to Ontario's Ministry of the Environment and more than thirty assigned to Environment Canada. Thus, an institutionalized Charter review from the beginning of a policy exercise is possible in larger jurisdictions because of the availability of legal counsel, which clearly is overstretched in smaller jurisdictions.

While line departments are advised to seek legal counsel on the Charter implications of a policy exercise from the earliest stages,[147] the reality is that Charter vetting occurs much later and is generally initiated by legislative counsel when drafting legislation on the instruction of client departments.[148] At this stage, legislative counsel will seek constitutional advice from the departmental solicitor and from the Constitutional Law Branch. This process is the reverse of the institutionalized model, in which a series of formal Charter reviews of policy exercises occurs before legislative counsel is requested to draft legislation by the client department. Thus, bureaucratic activism does take place in these smaller jurisdictions, but the attempt to govern with the Charter is impeded by fiscal constraints and the need to allocate limited resources.[149] Though the Charter vetting process is more ad hoc and generally relies on the ability of legislative counsel to identify potential Charter breaches in the drafting instructions provided by client departments, few significant provincial statutes enacted after the introduction of Charter scrutiny by provincial departments of Justice have been invalidated by the Supreme Court.

Conclusion

Pierre Trudeau remarked that "the Charter was not intended to subordinate the provinces to the federal government through judicial interpretation of the document, but to act as an instrument of national unity by highlighting what Canadians have in common, not by limiting how the provinces could act."[150] The clearest illustration of the attempt by the cabinet and Supreme Court and legislatures to govern with the Charter centres on the relationship between the Charter and Canadian federalism. In this chapter, the importance of judicial review has not been disputed, but the assumption that the impact of the Charter on provincial autonomy is judicially determined and centred has been challenged. The principal agent protecting policy diversity and provincial autonomy is not the Supreme Court but provincial cabinets that protect their jurisdictional autonomy through a reformed policy process that reconciles policy objectives with Charter commitments made by parliamentarians in 1982. The question of the Charter and federalism reinforces the central limitation of the judicial-centred approach, as it is a paradigm that focuses on judicial reaction to policy decisions by parliamentarians and neglects the attempts by cabinets to govern with the Charter through a reformed policy process directed in the bureaucratic sphere by departments of Justice. Rights and federalism have been reconciled, therefore, principally by the sustained attempts by governments to act as the bulwarks against judicial power. This in turn has been aided by the Supreme Court and its sensitivity to the structural requirements of a federation in its Charter jurisprudence.

The value of the cabinet-centred approach is that it places the attempts to govern with the Charter in the correct order. It begins with the cabinet response to the Charter, considers the judicial response to these attempts to reconcile rights and policy objectives, and ends with the cabinet response to unfavourable judicial decisions. As this chapter demonstrated, there are few instances of significant provincial statutes enacted (or last amended) after 1982 being invalidated by the Supreme Court, which is a testament to the ability of legislative activism to structure the court's approach to judicial review. Courts are essentially reactive institutions. This fact has, unfortunately, been lost in the judicial-centred approaches to understanding the Charter. In a response to the critics of the Judicial Committee of the Privy Council, Alan Cairns remarked that "it is impossible to believe that a few elderly men in London deciding two or three constitutional cases a year precipitated, sustained, and caused the development of Canada in a federalist direction the country would otherwise not have taken."[151] The underlying argument in this chapter has been that it is impossible to believe that nine members of the Supreme Court deciding two or three Charter cases a year involving provincial statutes have caused the centralization of Canadian federalism and the decline of provincial autonomy. To do so would be to participate in the further flight from politics that informs much of the Charter debate.

7
Governing with the Charter of Rights

The cabinet has governed with the Charter through legislative activism and its attempt to develop a principled process that explicitly links Charter values with policy goals. This has occurred independent of judicial activism, as the institutionalization of rights vetting by the Department of Justice (DOJ) preceded a complementary review by the Supreme Court and represents the principal legislative response to the Charter.[1] Legislative activism suggests that Charter dialogue is present throughout a policy exercise and originates within the legislative arena before it becomes part of the inter-institutional dialogue between the Supreme Court and the cabinet.[2] Perhaps more importantly, legislative activism structures the later dialogue between these actors when statutes are reviewed for their constitutionality. As most statutes are never reviewed in the judicial arena, this dialogue on rights is overshadowed by the cabinet's attempts to comply with the Charter. The protection of rights is fundamentally a legislative responsibility because of this reality.

This chapter analyzes the institutionalization of Charter vetting in the legislative process at the federal level and the leading role of the DOJ in scrutinizing the policy objectives of line departments to ensure compliance with the Charter. The DOJ has emerged as a central agency because the cabinet has prioritized the importance of governing with the Charter, and this has facilitated the emergence of a rights culture within the legislative process and the machinery of government. Donald Savoie's conclusion that the centre of government remains unchanged is challenged, as the institutionalization of rights vetting has seen the DOJ enter the centre because it alone coordinates rights scrutiny across the administrative state.[3] In the 1960s, the political responses to bureaucratic power saw the strengthening of central agencies to control line departments and to rationalize the machinery of government to advance the cabinet's legislative agenda.[4] The same institutional response characterizes the cabinet's approach to judicial power, which has facilitated the emergence of the DOJ as a central agency as the legislative process has been streamlined through the paradigm of rights compliance. The macro- or inter-institutional conclusion presented in this chapter contends that the cabinet and the Supreme Court collectively guard the constitution, and this challenges the claim of a democratic deficit associated with judicial activism by the Supreme Court.[5] The institutionalization of Charter vetting in the legislative arena reinforces the importance of coordinate constitutionalism in Canada and the value of a cabinet-centred but executive-dominated approach because it places primary responsibility for ensuring rights compliance with the actors who develop legislation. The claim that there is a democratic deficit is incorrect because it assumes that courts rule with the Charter through judicial decisions. This development has not transpired, because of concerted efforts by the DOJ, on the instruction of the cabinet, to scrutinize the policy objectives of line departments and to recommend changes that reconcile policy objectives with the Charter before legislation is proclaimed into law.

The concern, therefore, is not whether the parliamentary arena has remained the centre of public policy, which it surely has despite the ability of the judiciary to invalidate legislation.[6] Rather, I am concerned with *how* political actors have governed with the Charter, as it has led to a further marginalization of parliament as an institution and deepened prime-ministerial government. The result is a democratic deficit that is not the result of the Supreme Court's interpretation of the Charter but of the prime minister's decision to govern with the Charter from the centre.[7] This is the intra-institutional paradox of legislative activism: it has contained judicial power but has further weakened parliament as an institution at the hands of the cabinet. Where the democratic critique has merit is in regard to the distribution of power within the parliamentary arena, which has been altered by the cabinet's response to the Charter. There is a serious imbalance that prioritizes bureaucratic scrutiny by the DOJ. Instead of instituting parliamentary scrutiny of legislation to counterbalance the DOJ and to act as a further constraint on judicial power, the political response to the Charter has been to strengthen the policy capacity of the cabinet, albeit dominated by the prime minister, by instituting bureaucratic review to ensure the constitutionality of the cabinet's legislative agenda.

Charter vetting has been extremely significant in ensuring that the cabinet's legislative agenda is a principled attempt to link Charter values with policy objectives. The evidence for this is the limited number of statutes enacted or last amended since the institutionalization of Charter vetting that have been invalidated by the Supreme Court. It is not suggested, however, that Charter vetting by the DOJ can prevent judicial invalidation, nor should the judiciary ruling that statutes violate the Charter be taken as the weakness of rights scrutiny. The cabinet ultimately decides whether to proceed with a legislative proposal that has been scrutinized by the DOJ, and the political dimension of the policy process remains significant.[8] A policy of questionable constitutionality may be central to a government's core constituency and may therefore be implemented despite the advice of the DOJ. The former Harris government's decision in Ontario to revoke the rights extended to agricultural workers under the previous NDP government of Bob Rae, and the subsequent invalidation of the *Labour Relations Act* in *Dunmore*, are an illustration of the importance of political choices and, at times, the secondary importance of constitutional advice by the DOJ. Additionally, the constitutionality of a legislative proposal may not be clear at the time of implementation, and the government may believe that it represents a minimal impairment of a Charter right at the very least. The invalidation of statutes, therefore, is not evidence of judicial power but is testimony to the political process and policy decisions remaining the prerogative of parliamentary actors. Policy decisions are based on more than constitutional considerations, and judicial invalidation may simply highlight the continued importance of politics – and the cabinet – in parliamentary democracies despite the entrenchment of the Charter.

This chapter is divided into three sections. The first two sections consider the inter-institutional relationship between the Supreme Court and the cabinet and critically assess legislative activism and the institutionalization of Charter vetting by the DOJ. The first section considers the role of central agencies in the machinery of government and their use by the cabinet to offset bureaucratic power. With the need to govern with the Charter, the central agency rationale has moved beyond bureaucratic power and now must also address the potential for judicial power.[9] The second section considers the issue of bureaucratic activism and the institutionalization of rights vetting during the legislative process. The introduction of the Charter did not see the DOJ initially emerge as a central agency, as institutional changes were needed and political leadership required to create a rights culture within government. The institutionalization of Charter scrutiny occurred when the clerk of the Privy Council, on the instruction of the prime minister, directed line departments to consult the DOJ. From this period, therefore, Charter scrutiny became a routine element of policy design across government by the DOJ. The importance of bureaucratic activism will be demonstrated empirically, as well as the ability of the cabinet to design legislation that advances the Charter and protects rights. The primary legislative response to the Charter, therefore, is not legislative reaction to judicial activism but the institutionalization of a principled attempt to reconcile rights and policy objectives during the legislative process. The final section considers the implications of legislative activism and the dominance of bureaucratic scrutiny on behalf of the cabinet. A cabinet-centred approach has emerged in Canada, and it has generally excluded parliamentary input. The deepening of executive supremacy and not judicial supremacy, therefore, has been the principal outcome of the cabinet's attempt to govern with the Charter.

Beyond Bureaucratic Power

A central agency is a bureaucratic structure that engages in the management of government on behalf of the cabinet and the officials nearest cabinet.[10] These agencies have a direct and legitimate role in the affairs of line departments and attempt to structure policy proposals at the departmental level to reflect the policy priorities established by the prime minister and cabinet. In effect, central agencies are formally created and abolished by the prime minister and are engaged in the management of government by performing coordination and control functions that constrain the policy autonomy of line departments and allow the legislative priorities of the cabinet to emerge during a policy exercise. As a member of the centre, the Department of Finance (DOF) specifies the total resources available in the expenditure budget for each line department, and thus limits the instruments of government available for the realization of specific policy objectives.[11] Similarly, the Treasury Board Secretariat (TBS) constrains and shapes the policy agendas of line departments through the allocation of resources to established programs administered by line departments.

Within this cabinet support structure the Privy Council Office (PCO) performs an important control function that complements the DOF and the TBS. In particular, the PCO controls access to the coordinative machinery of government and determines whether memoranda submitted to cabinet by line departments are consistent with the broader policy framework established by the cabinet. Thus, the PCO performs a control function because it gives formal authority to policy initiatives that are proposed by line departments. However, unlike the DOF and the TBS, the PCO does not limit its role to a gatekeeper function, but also engages in a coordination function that sensitizes policy proposals to the prime minister's legislative agenda. This latter coordination function is also performed by the Prime Minister's Office (PMO), which infuses the policy process with sensitivity to the political objectives of the prime minister and his government.

In *Governing from the Centre*, Donald Savoie suggests that the composition of the centre has remained consistent over the last thirty years but that the distribution of power has become concentrated in the hands of the prime minister and his advisors.[12] In effect, Savoie focuses on the weakening constraints on prime ministerial power *within* the machinery of government; conceptualizes the centre as the officials within the Langevin Block (i.e., the PMO and PCO), the DOF, and the TBS; and suggests that the executive, regardless of the distribution of power among its elected and appointed officials, maintains a monopoly, subject to parliamentary ratification, on the policy process. This study, however, does not consider whether the entrenchment of the Charter has created competing centres of power that challenge the cabinet's ability to govern from the centre. This limitation extends to our understanding of the machinery of government because the discussion of central agencies continues to be limited to the PCO, the PMO, the TBS, and the DOF.[13] This suggests that the centre remains unchanged despite the introduction of the most significant constitutional change since the founding of Canada and, further, that in a policy environment that places greater emphasis on rights, the DOJ continues to remain on the outside looking in at the centre of government. This undervalues the wider effects of the Charter on the constitutional system and the machinery of government, and it fails to appreciate that the policy process has institutionalized Charter scrutiny within the legislative process.[14]

Given that bureaucratic scrutiny involving the Charter across government has been under the leadership of the DOJ, the suggestion that the centre has remained unchanged stands as a questionable conclusion. The attempt to generate greater democratic control of the policy process by strengthening the decision-making capacity of the cabinet through central agencies contains a paradox that has accentuated the decline of parliament as an effective policy forum.[15] Specifically, the strengthening of the centre further marginalized parliament within the policy process because the organizational changes to the machinery of government increased the decision-making capacity of the cabinet and weakened parliament as an effective constraint on the ministry, or more accurately, on the prime minister.[16] The difficulties facing central agencies in their relationship with line departments are analyzed by Savoie, who suggested that "the strengthening of the centre has not meant that the federal government is better able to articulate a comprehensive policy agenda."[17] There is, however, a more damaging limitation of the traditional central agency that undermines its effectiveness in the new policy environment. The institutional rationale of these organizations is to offset bureaucratic power and allow the cabinet to advance its legislative agenda in the parliamentary arena. The policy requirements introduced by the Charter have challenged the cabinet's ability to govern from the centre, as judicial invalidation can prevent the cabinet from legislating in a particular policy sector or can determine the policy context when the judiciary uses the remedy of reading-in or reading-down.[18]

There are strategies available to the cabinet to offset judicial power in the new policy environment, such as section 33 of the Charter, but its use has proven to be very unpopular with the electorate, and governments have been reluctant to use this explicit check on judicial power as a result.[19] In addition to the lack of explicit instruments available to overcome judicial constraints during Charter review, the movement to a horizontal policy environment has undermined the ability of the established central agencies to generate political space in the new policy environment. Specifically, the control functions employed by central agencies require a hierarchical relationship within government to be effective. The existing conception of the centre of government is therefore ill-equipped to confront judicial power and to ensure that the policy exercises of line departments are designed in compliance with an environment that places greater emphasis on the relationship between rights and the cabinet's legislative agenda.

Entering the Centre of Government

There are primarily two explanations that account for the DOJ's emergence into the centre of government and transformation into a central agency after the Charter's introduction in 1982: a macro-level explanation that considers the necessary preconditions to generate political space, and a micro-level explanation that considers the new roles and responsibilities assumed by the DOJ as a result of bureaucratic activism. The macro-level explanation examines whether the cabinet can achieve its legislative agenda by offsetting bureaucratic centres of power at the department level and, after 1982, judicial power associated with Charter review. In addition to the limitations facing the traditional central agencies in generating political space, there exists a structural imbalance between judicial actors and the traditional central agencies that complicates the cabinet's ability to govern from the centre. Simply stated, none of the traditional central agencies can compete with the judicial arena in a policy environment that requires legislative proposals to be evaluated against the Charter. Further, when policy is found to contravene the Charter, the traditional central agencies do not possess the institutional expertise to ensure future Charter compliance through a legislative response that allows the cabinet to ultimately achieve its policy agenda.

The present conception of the centre is incompatible with the new policy environment and the preconditions necessary to ensure that the cabinet can govern from the centre. For instance, the institutional requirements under a rights culture include the ability to offset both bureaucratic and judicial power and the need to ensure that the cabinet's legislative agenda is

Table 7.1

Central agencies in comparative perspective

Central agency	Role(s)	Power centre offset
Privy Council Office	Coordination and control	Bureaucratic
Prime Minister's Office	Coordination	Bureaucratic
Treasury Board Secretariat	Control	Bureaucratic
Department of Finance	Control	Bureaucratic
Department of Justice	Coordination and control	Bureaucratic and judicial

consistent with the Charter through rights vetting. Table 7.1 compares the traditional central agencies and the DOJ in terms of the roles performed in the new policy environment and the centres of power that must be offset to advance the cabinet's legislative agenda. This brief survey reveals that the DOJ is well positioned to enter the centre of government in the new policy environment because it can act as a complementary executive-support agency to the existing conception of the centre. As the DOJ monopolizes legal advice within the federal government, and because it possesses specialized knowledge that is conducive to the new policy environment and its emphasis on greater protections for rights in legislation, it is an agency that can be deployed by the cabinet to challenge judicial power and facilitate its role as a guardian of the constitution.[20] In particular, Justice can coordinate an extensive Charter review at the departmental level, and by sensitizing policy exercises to the values and purposes contained in the Charter, it can greatly reduce judicial invalidation as a potential constraint on the cabinet's ability to achieve its agenda.

In addition to the theoretical considerations that require a broadening of the centre to include the DOJ, there are important institutional changes within the legislative process that have moved the DOJ into the centre of government. In an initial analysis of the Charter's impact on the DOJ, Patrick Monahan and Marie Finkelstein concluded that Justice had become a central agency because of its increased importance in the development of public policy. Monahan and Finkelstein highlighted the introduction of Charter screening processes, the creation of the Human Rights Law Section (HRLS) within Justice, and the insistence by the clerk of the Privy Council that Justice be consulted early in the development of policy as evidence for this claim.[21] Turning to the unique institutional structure of the DOJ, the presence of legal service units (LSUs) at the departmental level allows Justice to begin a Charter screening process at the earliest stages of a policy exercise. This allows it to overcome the limitations a traditional central agency faces when dealing with operating departments. In particular, Justice resides in departments at the level where policy expertise is found, and the DOJ's Charter expertise matches a department's unique policy expertise at a level where central agency regulation can be most effective. The LSUs allow Justice to facilitate a horizontal Charter vetting exercise at the departmental level, and this happens parallel to the horizontal policy process at the departmental level. Further, Justice is a direct participant in this horizontal policy exercise via its LSUs. In contrasting Justice's ability to regulate the activities of line departments to that of the DOF, a senior official remarked that only the DOJ has hundreds of people deployed in line departments working in partnership with departmental officials.[22] The emerging partnership thesis between Justice and its client departments, facilitated by LSUs, is conducive to central agency regulation in the new policy environment, as it allows the DOJ to play a formative role in the development of policy at the department level during the initial stages of a policy exercise.

Bureaucratic Activism and the Department of Justice

While the DOJ began a review of legislation from a Charter perspective from the moment the document was entrenched into the constitution, this scrutiny was directed at existing legislation; the institutionalization of rights vetting of new legislation was not part of the initial approach to bureaucratic activism. The entry of the DOJ into the centre of government was a gradual process that saw Justice slowly acquire the roles and responsibilities of a central agency.[23] This transformation occurred in the early 1990s, when the DOJ ended its retrospective approach and followed the instruction of the cabinet to institutionalize a screening process of all new legislation to ensure Charter compliance.[24] Bureaucratic activism in the form of Charter scrutiny by the DOJ has exhibited two distinct dimensions, both of which are essential to the emergence of Justice as a central agency.[25] The initial approach to Charter scrutiny saw the DOJ perform neither control nor coordination functions, as the machinery of government was cast in a reactive stance and the department simply evaluated older statutes against the new standards under the Charter.[26] This reactive approach is not characteristic of a central agency as it is an institutional structure that disciplines line departments to carry out the cabinet's existing legislative agenda and ensures a coordinated approach across government. In effect, central agencies play an important role in the development of *new* policy initiatives and not the retroactive review of older statutes. Only when Charter scrutiny turned away from older statutes and became a standard approach to policy development did the DOJ enter the centre of government, because it controls and coordinates the activities of line departments through Charter vetting.[27]

During the initial approach to bureaucratic activism, the DOJ engaged in a two-part Charter exercise: a review of existing statutes, and an educational campaign to overcome bureaucratic resistance to the Charter.[28] The introduction of the *Human Rights Act* in Britain saw a similar approach, with the Lord Chancellor's Department creating a series of guidance documents to help policy actors as well as emphasizing the importance of creating a rights culture within the legislative process.[29] In Canada, the initial attempt at Charter scrutiny consisted largely of the DOJ reviewing existing statutes to identify potential conflicts with the Charter, excluding equality rights, which did not come into force until 1985.[30] To coordinate this retrospective exercise to ensure the Charter compliance of existing statutes, the DOJ created the HRLS as an important institutional response to the Charter.[31] This process is important because the technical review of legislation by Justice began to move toward a substantive review of policy on Charter grounds, a significant event in the emergence of Justice as a central agency.[32]

As well, this process saw the beginning of a cooperative relationship between the DOJ and line departments, an exercise that was directed to ensuring that existing statutes conformed to the new environment introduced by the Charter.

This process lasted roughly three years, and then Justice introduced omnibus legislation that contained the amendments to all existing statutes agreed to by the sponsoring department in consultation with the DOJ. In 1985, parliament passed the omnibus legislation into law.[33] At the end of this exercise, the DOJ began a similar process in relation to the Charter's equality rights.[34] In 1988, parliament passed an act sponsored by the DOJ that amended statutes identified to be in conflict with the equality provisions of the Charter.[35] This coordinated review of legislation by the HRLS was an important exercise, but it did not see Justice perform an essential central agency role: the DOJ was not a participant in the development of policy at the departmental level. Indeed, Justice has always had the responsibility for legislative drafting once the cabinet approves a memorandum to cabinet. The creation of the HRLS clearly shifted this legislative drafting function from a technical review of policy proposals to a substantive review for Charter compliance, but it was confined to existing legislation and did not have an impact on the development of new policy.

Overcoming bureaucratic resistance to the Charter both within the DOJ and throughout the broader administrative state was an important function of the first phase of bureaucratic activism. Line departments originally resisted the attempt by the DOJ to screen their legislative proposals for Charter compliance, as it was seen to be an interference with the policy autonomy of the sponsoring department.[36] Line departments viewed Charter scrutiny as an attempt by the DOJ to enlarge its own jurisdiction, and this often resulted in line departments resisting the attempt by Justice officials to review departmental proposals for potential Charter violations.[37] To temper resistance to the Charter by line departments, the DOJ began an intensive educational campaign within the administrative state to emphasize the importance of Charter vetting.[38] Justice organized a series of seminars and workshops for policy makers immediately after the November 1981 first ministers' conference, and this exercise was directed to sensitizing policy actors to the new policy environment.[39] The campaign extended to the rank of deputy minister, with the deputy minister of justice attempting to educate this community about the importance of the Charter in all policy exercises.

This educational exercise by the DOJ had several objectives, with the principal one being the creation of a rights culture within government and the acceptance of Charter scrutiny as a necessary part of the legislative process.[40] Further, the DOJ sought to demonstrate to line departments that the Charter was a policy framework and a legal document and to further emphasize that the Charter was a very different document from the *Canadian Bill of Rights*.[41] This debate between Justice and line departments was replicated within the DOJ itself. In the first phase of bureaucratic activism, Justice was internally divided between those advocating an orthodox approach to the Charter, with the role of Justice being to defend the state against Charter challenges, and an activist wing that saw a substantive policy role for the DOJ under the Charter. Under the *Canadian Bill of Rights*, the litigators had been dominant and were successful in resisting an activist approach by policy makers to this federal statute. However, senior DOJ officials were determined to resist a conservative approach to the Charter by bureaucratic actors, arguing that the Charter was an important part of government policy and that former Prime Minister Trudeau had intended the Charter to be an activist document.[42]

Savoie suggests that a necessary precondition for the federal government to successfully articulate a comprehensive policy agenda is "a powerful outside element [that] comes into play which forces it to act. When this occurs, the various organizational cultures and even outside forces are held in check by a consensus that something must be done."[43] The initial activist approach by the Supreme Court represents this powerful outside force that helped the DOJ transcend bureaucratic resistance to Charter scrutiny and convince the cabinet that it must govern with the Charter from the centre. Judicial victories in cases such as *Singh v. Minister of Employment and Immigration, R. v. Askov,* and *Schacter v. Canada*[44] by 1990 had placed financial burdens on both levels of government, and in an important way the DOJ benefited from judicial activism because the Supreme Court clearly outlined the consequences if Charter scrutiny was not a standard part of the legislative process.

The first phase of bureaucratic activism saw minor institutional modifications to the DOJ. Perhaps what is more important is that the development of policy within the administrative state remained unchanged despite the introduction of the Charter. Except for the creation of the HRLS, the institutional structure of Justice did not change. Further, the function of the HRLS was not to engage in Charter review of new policy, but to modify existing federal statutes to the contours of the Charter.[45] The presence of LSUs within line departments gave Justice a unique opportunity to sensitize the administrative state to the new policy environment and to play a role in the development of policy at the departmental level. However, the LSUs were not employed in such a fashion during the initial phase of bureaucratic activism. The effectiveness of an LSU was undermined by departmental resistance to a Charter review of its activities and by Justice's emphasis on reviewing existing legislation for Charter consistency. Indeed, this variant of Charter scrutiny performed by the HRLS saw the LSU continue to provide technical support to clients, so a substantive review of policy proposals for Charter consistency did not take place. The absence of an institutionalized Charter scrutiny by the DOJ prevented the department from entering the centre of government in the first phase of bureaucratic activism and emerging as a central agency.

Charter Scrutiny at the Centre of Government

Under the leadership of John Tait as deputy minister, the institutionalization of Charter scrutiny during the legislative process occurred, and this effectively transformed the DOJ into a central agency.[46] In this period, the DOJ acquired both coordination and control functions over the policy objectives of line departments, and through a horizontal and hierarchical relationship with line departments, it came to embody the characteristics of a central agency.[47] Charter scrutiny shifted from its focus on older statutes to the development of legislation that would be filtered through an extensive Charter review by the DOJ. This transition to an activist Charter scrutiny of new policy exercises did not require any institutional modifications to the DOJ. The shift to a forward-looking Charter scrutiny invigorated the HRLS as a centre of Charter expertise and advice for LSUs, and this shift produced a corresponding emphasis on client services by the DOJ, as the HRLS began setting guidelines to be followed by line departments in new policy exercises to ensure Charter consistency. The LSU's relationship with both the line department and the HRLS is central to an institutionalized Charter scrutiny by the DOJ. The LSU is a bridge between the line department and the DOJ, it sensitizes Justice to the policy goals of the line department, and as a direct participant in a policy exercise at the departmental level, it sensitizes the line department to the reality of policy under the Charter. Thus, the LSU conditions both the line department and the DOJ to the reciprocal policy objectives of the other. This ensures that a policy exercise reflects the concerns of the department and it also is consistent with the framework that policy must conform to under the Charter.

The institutionalized Charter scrutiny at the centre is outlined in Table 7.2, which lists the changes in the development of policy with respect to both the DOJ's relationship with line departments and the development of policy at the departmental level in collaboration with LSUs, which provided the momentum for the transition to a proactive Charter review. In preparation for the shift to client-driven services and a proactive Charter scrutiny at the departmental level, the HRLS created the Charter checklist.[48] The purpose of the checklist is to provide LSUs with a tool to identify potential Charter conflicts in the policy proposals of line departments.[49] The checklist is a comprehensive manual, updated by the HRLS every six months, that allows LSUs to provide consistent Charter advice to all operating departments.[50] This is an important consideration, given that much of the Charter screening process is the responsibility of the LSUs, and this decentralized process

Table 7.2

Charter scrutiny at the centre

Actor	Instrument	Role	Description
Human Rights Law Section	Charter checklist	Coordination and control	Consistent Charter advice to LSU Resolve Charter conflicts in proposals
Legal service units	Charter advice to clients	Coordination	Begin a Charter review of proposals within line departments
Legislative counsel	Draft all government bills	Coordination and control	Transform drafting instructions into legislation Ensure that legislation is Charter compliant
Assistant deputy attorney general (Civil litigation)	Charter Litigation Committee	Coordination and control	Resolve Charter issues not resolved by HRLS or LSUs Determine whether to appeal lower-court defeats Decide on litigation strategies
Senior general counsel	Departmental executive committee	Coordination	Raises Charter concerns at weekly line department meetings
Minister of Justice	Memorandum to cabinet	Coordination and control	Must perform a Charter scrutiny of all memoranda to cabinet and assess Charter risk Must sign off on all memoranda to cabinet
Minister of Justice	Charter certification to parliament	Coordination and control	Certifies to parliament that draft legislation is Charter compliant
Attorney general of Canada	*Department of Justice Act*, s. 4.1	Coordination and control	Required to notify parliament of any legislation that contravenes the Charter

could lead to the provision of inconsistent advice. In terms of structure, the checklist is divided to correspond with sections of the Charter, and it summarizes important cases and jurisprudential changes for the LSUs.[51] In addition to the Charter checklist, the HRLS supports the LSUs by providing advanced Charter advice to the line department in a policy exercise.[52] Thus, an LSU is not autonomous from the DOJ, but works in close contact with the HRLS to best ensure that a client's policy objective can be structured in a way that is consistent with the Charter. This minimizes the risk of judicial invalidation and demonstrates the importance of Charter scrutiny to ensure that the cabinet can sustain its legislative agenda outside the parliamentary arena.

At the insistence of the deputy minister of justice, the clerk of the Privy Council, Paul Tellier, wrote to all deputy ministers in 1991 to stress that Charter scrutiny must begin at the earliest stages of a policy exercise.[53] The deputy minister of justice was instrumental in securing changes to the memorandum to cabinet to incorporate a Charter analysis, and line departments were required to consult with Justice to review the Charter implications of policy proposals.[54] The Tellier Memorandum called for a Charter analysis to be incorporated into the memorandum to cabinet, and "the analysis had to include an assessment of the risk of successful challenge in the courts, the impact of an adverse decision, and possible litigation costs."[55] The Tellier Memorandum is important for many reasons, as it advanced the transition of Justice to a central agency. The changes in the memorandum to cabinet legitimized a role for the DOJ in the activities of line departments. This is a significant departure from the type of client services provided by the DOJ before the Tellier Memorandum: previously, it did not evaluate the substantive implications of policy proposals, but only ensured that the proposal was consistent with the division of powers. A Charter review is principally a policy exercise performed by the DOJ in collaboration with client departments. Thus, the Tellier Memorandum legitimized a proactive Charter review at the departmental level, which, because of the type of review performed, saw Justice play a substantive role in the development of new proposals. More importantly, the particular structure of the DOJ is significant as it gives the department multiple access points in the policy process.

What stands out in the institutional evolution of Justice is the positive role played by traditional central agencies that required line departments to be participants in Charter scrutiny performed by the DOJ and its LSUs. The clerk of the Privy Council changed the procedural requirements of a cabinet document to require Charter scrutiny by the DOJ.[56] In *A Guide to the Making of Federal Acts and Regulations,* the DOJ, with the support of the PCO, specifies the participation by Justice legal advisors in the development of policy by line departments: "Departmental legal advisers play a crucial role throughout the legislative process. Departmental officials should consult them in the initial stages of policy formulation and particularly when preparing the Memorandum to Cabinet. Their participation will allow the legal advisers to develop a sound understanding of the subject-matter and its ramifications early on in the process. This understanding is essential for the preparation of an effective Act. The participation of departmental legal advisers should continue throughout the process of obtaining Cabinet approval, drafting of the bill and enactment by Parliament."[57]

As well, the TBS has a vested interest in a thorough Charter review at the departmental level because it shares the cost of litigation with line departments. To ensure that this cost structure does not create a disincentive for a department to be Charter sensitive, the TBS monitors litigation expenses generated by individual line departments. As the TBS is responsible for the expenditure budget, this important resource effectively disciplines line departments to the seriousness of a Charter review under the direction of the DOJ.[58] The actions of senior officials at the centre of government are significant, as the cabinet recognized the cost of successful Charter challenges against its legislative agenda and, using the power and influence of established central agencies, reorganized the machinery of government to admit the DOJ into the centre of government.

These macro changes in the policy process are significant because they facilitated micro changes at the departmental level that have enhanced the status and the role of the DOJ in policy development. This is an ironic development, given that the emphasis on Charter scrutiny by LSUs appears to work against a centralized review coordinated by the DOJ. This is not the case. An analysis of the interaction between the LSU, the line department, and the DOJ will demonstrate that a diffused Charter screening process has not resulted in a decentralized exercise. Indeed, the particular institutional structure of the DOJ has led to a thorough and rigorous Charter screening process, where a proposal is filtered through the lens of the Charter at various stages of a policy exercise. Unlike the traditional central agencies, which have a limited but important role in the activities of line departments, the DOJ has a constant and close working relationship with departmental actors. It is this close proximity and the development of a policy partnership between Justice and line departments that allowed the DOJ to institutionalize Charter scrutiny and facilitate a rights culture within government.[59]

The LSU represents the earliest and most important access point for the DOJ to structure a department's policy objectives to the contours of the Charter. The LSU is integrated into a policy exercise at the earliest stage, and its function is to engage in a risk analysis of the policy objectives of a line department. By assessing the risk of judicial invalidation, the LSU can identify potential conflicts during the formative stages of a policy exercise and resolve such conflicts in partnership with line departments. The Charter checklist serves as a valuable tool in performing the task of risk analysis, so this early Charter review takes place within the parameters determined by the HRLS. The LSU enforces the Charter policy of the DOJ within a line department, and this advances consistent Charter advice. The close working relationship between the LSU and the line department is central to the success of Charter scrutiny as it facilitates a principled approach to the client's policy goals designed in compliance with the Charter.

There is a tendency to view the LSU as an outsider at the departmental level, simply enforcing the parameters of a Charter review established by the HRLS. In fact, locating the LSU within the line department has acted as a mechanism to reduce conflict between the line department and the DOJ and to overcome departmental resistance to Charter scrutiny. Specifically, the perception of the LSU by the line department is central to the emergence of a partnership and not a competitive relationship. Policy actors within the department view the LSU as part of the policy team that provides unique access to the DOJ and acts as a positive contributor during a policy exercise that attempts to advance the objectives of the line department in a way that respects entrenched rights and freedoms.[60] There are tremendous benefits, therefore, derived from the presence of LSUs at the departmental level. As well, the presence of LSUs within a department allows Justice to overcome an important limitation faced by traditional central agencies, which Richard Schultz has identified.[61] Because Justice resides at the same level as policy expertise in a department, Charter experts interact with policy experts during a policy exercise. This allows the DOJ, through the LSUs, to offset the strategic location of expertise within the department and to counterbalance departmental experts with Charter experts. As the new policy environment requires a meshing of both policy and Charter considerations, the DOJ is well positioned to condition the policy process to this new environment.[62]

A clear example that line departments realize the important support function performed by the LSU is the elevated position they have given the senior general counsel (SGC), who heads the LSU, since 1994. At the insistence of all deputy ministers, the SGC now sits as a member of a department's executive committee. The deputy minister heads this committee, and its membership consists of all assistant deputy ministers, directors general of all policy directorates, the minister's executive assistant, and the senior general counsel. The executive committee meets weekly to review ongoing issues and to set the policy direction for the department.[63] The presence of the SGC on this committee is significant because it provides a forum where the head of an LSU can raise Charter concerns about the policy proposals of line departments.[64] Thus, the LSU can engage in an advanced Charter review with senior managers at the departmental level to resolve policy conflicts. The inclusion of the SGC on the senior committee of a line department is evidence that the initial resistance to Charter scrutiny has been overcome and that departments recognize how important it is that policy conforms to the Charter. More importantly, it demonstrates the emerging partnership between line departments and the DOJ in a rights-based policy context.

There is a protocol between the DOJ and line departments that says the LSUs will be called upon first to begin a Charter review during a policy exercise. It is only when the LSU is unable to resolve conflicts between policy objectives and the Charter that a more advanced review takes place with the HRLS.[65] This clearly illustrates the unique central agency roles performed, as the DOJ does not attempt to block or veto policy proposals but seeks to restructure the legislative proposal to ensure greater conformity with entrenched rights. Charter scrutiny is a multilayered exercise directed to meshing the objectives of the department in a policy framework that is respectful of the Charter. The LSU functions as the DOJ's liaison with the HRLS during this advanced stage of Charter scrutiny. Normally, most Charter conflicts will be resolved at the departmental level, and the HRLS is rarely a direct participant in a policy exercise.

The committee system within the DOJ was recently streamlined, and the Charter Committee, which had a mandate to resolve outstanding Charter issues at the departmental level, was folded into the Charter Litigation Committee.[66] The assistant deputy attorney general (Civil Litigation) chairs this committee, which is made up of senior members of the DOJ.[67] This committee principally performs two roles: it provides advanced Charter advice to HRLS and LSUs to resolve outstanding Charter issues in the policy exercises of line departments, and it assesses litigation strategies when the DOJ defends the constitutionality of challenged statutes before the courts.[68] This committee is significant because it fuses the DOJ's policy role with its traditional role as the litigator for the government. Specifically, the Charter Litigation Committee relies on the work of the HRLS and the LSUs as part of its litigation strategy when it attempts to defend legislation as a reasonable limitation on a Charter right. While the LSU does not have a litigation function, it is evident that the substantive policy role it performs can become a critical aspect of a litigation strategy when the DOJ must defend legislation. At this advanced stage in a Charter review, however, the Charter Litigation Committee shifts to considerations of section 1 defences for the proposed legislation. Indeed, given that a policy has been filtered through an extensive screening process, the Charter Litigation Committee begins to prepare for possible Charter challenges in the future, and the LSU begins to document the various policy approaches considered by the line department. If the DOJ comes to defend a challenged statute via section 1 of the Charter, this exercise is critical in demonstrating that the approach taken is a reasonable limitation in a free and democratic society.

The significance of this extensive Charter review is the limited involvement of the traditional central agencies before a policy exercise is formalized in a memorandum to cabinet. At this stage in a policy exercise, the
Charter risk of a proposed policy has been thoroughly assessed, and significant energy has been devoted to reconciling the department's policy objectives with the Charter. Once a policy exercise is formalized as a cabinet
document, however, the involvement of the DOJ does not end. In fact,
there are several avenues still available to the DOJ to influence the design of
the proposed policy. When the PCO reviews a cabinet submission from a
line department, Charter issues have been identified by the DOJ and addressed through Charter scrutiny on behalf of the cabinet. At this stage, the
decision to proceed is the prerogative of the cabinet. There are times when
Justice would prefer the department not go ahead, but the minister of a
department may want to test the policy in the courts.[69] Once a memorandum to cabinet is approved and the DOJ certifies its Charter consistency,
the Legislative Services Branch at the DOJ is responsible for drafting the
legislation, a role that has taken on added significance with the Charter.
Drafting legislation is the sole responsibility of the DOJ, and it is an important step in structuring a policy proposal to conform to the Charter. Indeed,
in situations where the cabinet has approved a submission about which
Justice has serious reservations, the drafting function serves as a final step
in Charter scrutiny before the legislation is introduced into parliament.

What stands out from this extensive Charter scrutiny process is the increased importance of the DOJ in the activities of line departments, and the
subtle way Justice exploits its new influence. It is clear from the preceding
discussion that the DOJ exhibits the characteristics of a central agency identified by Paul Thomas.[70] In particular, the DOJ has a continuing and legitimate authority to intervene in the activities of line departments, it has
multiple access points during a policy exercise to influence the development of a proposal, and, finally, its increased status has been encouraged by
the traditional central agencies and by the cabinet. The imperatives of governing with the Charter and the need to develop a rights culture at the
departmental level, therefore, saw the DOJ enter the centre of government
at the request of the prime minister to directly confront judicial power.

Governing with the Charter

It has been argued throughout this book that the standard evidence used
to demonstrate that the Charter has resulted in stronger protection for
human rights, if true, would actually demonstrate the limited value of the
Charter and the underdevelopment of a rights culture. For instance, this
evidence assumes that political institutions have not attempted to reconcile policy objectives with constitutional commitments and that the judiciary is necessary to ensure the development of a rights culture from without,

and not from within the cabinet, as this book contends.[71] More critical positions – such as Ran Hirschl's argument that the judicialization of politics is a calculated act by political elites to preserve their hegemonic position by transferring power to a similarly positioned judicial elite – continue the judicial-centred approach that dominates the bill of rights debate.[72] The difficulty with the judicial-centred approach to the rights revolution is that it is an imprecise measure and discounts the positive-sum relationship between judicial and legislative activism. If judicial activism is the evidence of the strength of human rights in Canada, then judicial deference would suggest the inability of the courts to discipline the cabinet to the importance of rights. As the Supreme Court has generally been activist against policy decisions of the past, this approach would lead to the conclusion that the court has been able to control past parliaments and not present parliaments, as few statutes enacted after 1990 have been invalidated by the Supreme Court.

The supporters of judicial activism have identified a successful rights revolution in courts that find constitutional violations in the legislative process, which is a debatable method of evaluating whether rights are properly protected. A highly activist court would demonstrate a failed rights revolution because it would indicate the absence of attempts by the cabinet to develop legislation that advances Charter values. The benefit of legislative activism, and the evidence that a rights culture has taken hold, is the general absence of statutes enacted after the institutionalization of Charter scrutiny that have been invalidated by the Supreme Court. Table 7.3 provides an empirical overview of federal statutes challenged before the Supreme Court between 1982 and 2003. In this period, a total of 112 federal statutes have been challenged on Charter grounds, and the Supreme Court has been activist in 35 percent of the cases (39 out of 112). This table is organized by the year in which a statute was enacted or last amended, and not the year in which the Supreme Court reviewed the statute. As argued in previous chapters, the yearly rate is not a precise indicator of judicial activism (or the failure of legislative activism) as the rates of activism in any year may reflect the Supreme Court's invalidating a large number of pre-Charter statutes.

Breaking the data down into distinct periods demonstrates that judicial activism continues to focus on statutes enacted without the benefit of Charter scrutiny by the DOJ, as 85 percent of the statutes reviewed by the Supreme Court (95 out of 112) were enacted between 1970 and 1988. Indeed, only five statutes enacted by the federal parliament after Charter scrutiny was institutionalized in the legislative process have been invalidated by the Supreme Court. This represents 13 percent (5 out of 39) of the total federal statutes found to violate the Charter. If the analysis focuses on the post-1993 period, very few statutes have been reviewed at the level of the Supreme Court for their constitutionality (nine statutes) and the rate of activism has been muted, at 22 percent (2 out of 9) of statutes enacted or last amended

Table 7.3

Summary of federal statutes reviewed by the Supreme Court, 1982 to 2003

Year[1]	Unconstitutional	Constitutional	Total
1970	6	8	14
1972	0	3	3
1976	2	0	2
1977	0	1	1
1978	0	1	1
1979	1	0	1
1980	1	1	2
1983	1	2	3
1984	0	2	2
1985	20	41	61
1986	1	2	3
1987	1	0	1
1988	1	0	1
1992	0	5	5
1993	3	0	3
1995	0	2	2
1996	0	2	2
1997	1	3	4
1999	1	0	1
Total	39	73	112

1 Year the statute was enacted or last amended, as reported in the *Supreme Court Reports*.

between 1994 and 2003. Perhaps what is most revealing about the ability of legislative activism to reach principled decisions that reconcile policy objectives with Charter commitments and make judicial activism less important is the fact that only two statutes enacted in the post-1993 period has been declared unconstitutional. In *R. v. Hall*, the Supreme Court ruled that denying bail in certain cases in order to maintain confidence in the legal system was unduly vague and was not a reasonable limitation on the right to be granted bail without just cause and the presumption of innocence.[73]

A review of the remaining activist statutes in Table 7.4 raises questions about the overall impact of judicial activism. For instance, in *Sauvé v. Canada* the Supreme Court ruled, by a vote of five to four, that section 51(e) of the *Canada Elections Act*, which had been amended to temporarily deny the right to vote to prisoners incarcerated for more than two years, was unconstitutional. The majority decision written by Chief Justice McLachlin argued that the denial of voting rights to prisoners was not a reasonable limitation and lacked proportionality, though McLachlin accepted that the government had a pressing and substantial reason to limit prisoner voting

Table 7.4

Federal Statutes reviewed by the Supreme Court, 1982 to 2003

Case	Decision[1]	Statute[2]
Unconstitutional Statutes		
1 *Hunter v. Southam Inc.*	1984	1970
2 *Singh v. Minister of Employment and Immigration*	1985	1976
3 *R. v. Big M. Drug Mart Ltd.*	1985	1970
4 *R. v. Oakes*	1986	1970
5 *R. v. Smith*	1987	1970
6 *R. v. Vaillancourt*	1987	1976
7 *R. v. Morgentaler*	1988	1970
8 *R. v. Martineau*	1990	1985
9 *R. v. Logan*	1990	1985
10 *R. v. Nguyen*	1990	1987
11 *R. v. Swain*	1991	1970
12 *Seaboyer v. The Queen*	1991	1985
13 *R. v. Sit*	1991	1983
14 *Committee for the Commonwealth of Canada v. Canada*	1991	1979
15 *Osborne v. Canada*	1991	1985
16 *Tétreault-Gadoury v. Canada*	1991	1985
17 *Schacter v. Canada*	1992	1980
18 *R. v. Bain*	1992	1985
19 *R. v. Généreux*	1992	1985
20 *R. v. Morales*	1992	1985
21 *R. v. Zundel*	1992	1985
22 *Baron v. Canada; Kourtessi v. M.N.R.*	1993	1986
23 *Sauvé v. Canada (1993)*	1993	1985
24 *R. v. Heywood*	1994	1985
25 *R. v. Laba*	1994	1985
26 *RJR-Macdonald Inc. v. Canada*	1995	1988
27 *Benner v. Canada*	1997	1985
28 *Thomson Newspaper Company v. Canada*	1998	1985
29 *R. v. Lucas*	1998	1985
30 *Corbiere v. Canada*	1999	1985
31 *United States v. Burns*	2001	1999
32 *R. v. Ruzic*	2001	1985
33 *R. v. Sharpe*	2001	1993
34 *Ruby v. Solicitor General of Canada*	2002	1985
35 *R. v.Hall*	2002	1997
36 *White, Ottenheimer & Baker v. Attorney General of Canada*	2002	1985
37 *Little Sisters Book and Art Emporium v. Canada*	2002	1985
38 *Sauvé (2002) v. Canada*	2002	1993
39 *Figueroa v. Canada*	2003	1993

▶

◄   *Table 7.4*

Case	Decision[1]	Statute[2]
Constitutional Statutes		
1 *P.S.A.C. v. Canada*	1987	1983
2 *R. v. Lyons; R. v. Milne*	1987	1977
3 *R. v. Thomsen*	1988	1985
4 *R. v. Corbett*	1988	1970
5 *R. v. Holmes*	1988	1972
6 *R. v. Whyte*	1988	1985
7 *Canadian Newspapers Co. v. Canada*	1988	1970
8 *Thomson Newpapers Ltd. v. Canada*	1990	1970
9 *R. v. McKinlay*	1990	1970
10 *Ref. Re ss. 193 & 195.1(1)(c); R. v. Skinner*	1990	1985
11 *R. v. Schwartz*	1988	1970
12 *R. v. Simmons*	1988	1970
13 *Slaight Communications Inc. v. Davidson*	1989	1978
14 *R. v. Turpin*	1989	1985
15 *United States of America v. Cotroni*	1989	1970
16 *R. v. Lee*	1989	1985
17 *R. v. Duarte*	1990	1980
18 *CBC v. New Brunswick (AG)*	1996	1985
19 *R. v. Skalbania*	1997	1985
20 *R. v. Lucas*	1998	1985
21 *R. v. S.(S.)*	1990	1985
22 *R. v. Arkell*	1990	1984
23 *R. v. Chaulk*	1990	1985
24 *Kindler v. Canada*	1991	1985
25 *R. v. Furtney; R. v. Jones*	1991	1985
26 *CBC v. Lessard*	1991	1985
27 *R. v. Butler*	1992	1985
28 *Canada (Minister of Employment and Immigration) v. Chiarelli*	1992	1984
29 *R. v. Downey*	1992	1985
30 *R. v. Nova Scotia Pharmaceutical Society*	1992	1986
31 *R. v. DeSousa*	1992	1985
32 *R. v. Rube*	1992	1970
33 *R. v. Pearson*	1992	1985
34 *R. v. Sawyer*	1992	1985
35 *Haig v. Canada*	1993	1992
36 *R. v. Creighton*	1993	1985
37 *Finlay v. Canada*	1993	1985
38 *R. v. Naglik*	1993	1985
39 *Rodriguez v. British Columbia*	1993	1985
40 *Young v. Young*	1993	1985
41 *R. v. L.(D.O.)*	1993	1985
42 *R. v. Levogiannis*	1993	1985

►

◀ *Table 7.4*

Case	Decision[1]	Statute[2]
43 *R. v. Osolin*	1993	1985
44 *Symes v. Canada*	1993	1972
45 *International Longshoremen's and Warehousemen's v. Canada*	1994	1986
46 *R. v. Finta*	1994	1985
47 *R. v. Brown*	1994	1985
48 *R. v. S.(R.J.); R. v. Jobin*	1995	1985
49 *Egan v. Canada*	1995	1985
50 *Thibaudeau v. Canada*	1995	1972
51 *Canadian Egg Marketing Agency v. Richardson*	1998	1997
52 *R. v. Rose*	1998	1985
53 *Law v. Canada*	1999	1985
54 *Vancouver Society of Immigrant and Visible Minority Women v. M.N.R.*	1999	1985
55 *Del Zotto v. Canada*	1999	1985
56 *Winko v. British Columbia; Orlowski v. British Columbia; R. v. Le Page; Bese v. British Columbia*	1999	1985
57 *R. v. Mills*	1999	1997
58 *Delisle v. Canada*	1999	1985
59 *Granovsky v. Canada*	2000	1992
60 *R. v. Morrisey*	2000	1995
61 *R. v. Darrach*	2000	1992
62 *R. v. Latimer*	2001	1995
63 *United States of America v. Kwok; United States of America v. Shulman*	2001	1992
64 *Smith v. Canada*	2001	1985
65 *R. v. Pan*	2001	1985
66 *Lavallee, Rackel and Heintz v. Canada; R. v. Fink*	2002	1985
67 *Lavoie v. Canada*	2002	1985
68 *Suresh v. Canada; Ahani v. Canada*	2002	1992
69 *R. v. S.A.B.*	2003	1997
70 *R. v. Clay*	2003	1996
71 *R. v. Malmo-Levine*	2003	1996

Note: A total of 73 statutes were found constitutional in 71 decisions by the Supreme Court of Canada.
1 Year the Supreme Court decided the case.
2 Year statute was enacted or last amended, as reported in the *Supreme Court Reports.*

rights.[74] The chief justice argued that the right to vote was removed from the political arena when the Charter was enacted, and this placed "prisoners under the protective umbrella of the *Charter* through constitutional limits on punishment. The *Charter* emphatically says that prisoners are protected citizens, and short of a constitutional amendment, lawmakers cannot change this."[75] This is very different from the minority decision written by Gonthier, who found the policy to be both reasoned and rational: it was not a blanket provision applying to all prisoners but only those serving serious crimes and incarcerated for more than two years, and further, this limitation on citizenship only applied during incarceration.[76]

Beyond the merits of this decision, the practical policy effects are rather limited, as it is unclear how many prisoners formerly disenfranchised will actually exercise this right and whether these votes will have any impact, as they are counted in the riding where the individual last had a permanent residence. As in *Attorney General (Quebec) v. Protestant School Boards,* the impact of judicial activism in *Sauvé* may be largely symbolic because the target audience is small and accounts for only a handful of votes in each federal constituency at election time. Similarly in *R. v. Sharpe,* the effects of judicial activism have been overstated, as only a small part of the Criminal Code restrictions on the possession of child pornography was invalidated by the Supreme Court. For instance, the majority decision (six to three) written by Chief Justice McLachlin found the restrictions on child pornography in section 163.1(4) of the Criminal Code constitutional except for their application to private writings or expressive material of imaginary individuals held by the accused.[77] For the majority, parts of section 163.1(4) were overly broad and violated freedom of expression because they applied to material that would not normally be considered child pornography. Thus, the vast majority of the restrictions on child pornography were upheld by the Supreme Court and the court remedied the problematic elements of section 163.1(4) by reading-in two exemptions that applied to self-created expressive material and private recordings of lawful sexual activity.[78]

The invalidation, in *Figueroa v. Canada,* of sections of the *Canada Elections Act* that limited tax benefits to political parties that ran at least fifty candidates in a federal election is an excellent illustration of the partisan nature of policy decisions that are not necessarily consistent with the Charter. The restrictions on public financing to political parties that met the fifty-candidate rule clearly benefited the political parties in parliament that drafted the act, as the practical effect of the fifty-candidate rule was to make it increasingly difficult for new political parties to receive public financing and to elect members to parliament.[79] The effect of the court's activist decision was to challenge the ability of established political parties in parliament to unilaterally determine the rules governing public financing.

It is growing increasingly difficult to make the case for judicial supremacy, and critics are assuming a historical tone as they rely on examples of judicial activism against policy decisions enacted before Charter scrutiny was institutionalized as part of the development of legislation. The invalidation of statutes is an expected outcome of entrenching rights and subjecting statutes to constitutional challenge and review. As most invalidated statutes were enacted before the Charter was entrenched or before the advent of Charter scrutiny in the legislative process, they should not be a cause for concern and should not be used to demonstrate unbridled judicial power. Invalidated statutes enacted with the benefit of Charter scrutiny also provide little evidence for the judicial power thesis, as many of these statutes were motivated by partisan interests and were highly political decisions presented as public policy. Indeed, this reinforces the point that judicial invalidation may be a testimony to the continuing importance of policy decisions being the domain of politically accountable actors, rather than evidence of the decline of democratic institutions and the emergence of the Supreme Court as a policy actor.

Legislative Activism and the Minister of Justice

There has been a significantly different response to the Charter within the bureaucratic and parliamentary arenas, and this imbalance has reinforced an already executive-dominated policy process, as both responses have been at the discretion of the cabinet. The internal approach to Charter review has principally been the responsibility of the DOJ, and parliamentary scrutiny of legislation for its rights implications has generally been absent in the Canadian context. Unlike the case in the United Kingdom, which engaged in both parliamentary and bureaucratic reform to ensure that the introduction of the *Human Rights Act, 1998,* did not result in a loss of policy autonomy for the British parliament,[80] the Canadian response has generally been one-dimensional within the bureaucratic arena in support of the cabinet's legislative agenda. The British parliament created the Joint Committee on Human Rights in 2001 with an explicit mandate to engage in parliamentary scrutiny of legislation from a rights perspective. However, no standing committee or standing senate committee of the Parliament of Canada has been given such a mandate, and parliamentary scrutiny has been displaced by the minister of justice's executive certification to the House of Commons that proposed legislation is constitutional.[81]

The Canadian approach to parliamentary activism is cabinet-centred because the certification by the minister of justice is, in reality, the most important statement on the relationship between the Charter and legislation by a parliamentarian.[82] When parliamentary scrutiny from a rights perspective has occurred in the committee system, it has been ad hoc and an informal review that cannot challenge the certification of the minister of justice, given the limited resources of the committees in comparison to the review capacity of the DOJ on behalf of the minister of justice. Indeed, when the minister certifies that a legislative proposal is consistent with the Charter, there is no documentation presented to the House of Commons to demonstrate this position.[83] This is in stark contrast to the practice in New Zealand, where former attorney general Margaret Wilson established the practice of making available to the select committees of the House of Representatives the advice provided by the Ministry of Justice and the Crown Law Office, which assess the relationship between draft legislation and the *New Zealand Bill of Rights Act (NZBORA)*.[84] Further, when the attorney general determines that a bill is in breach of the *NZBORA*, under section 7 of the act the attorney general must inform parliament that the bill is not compliant.[85] The significance of the section 7 report is that it provides parliamentarians, at the select committee stage, with an opportunity to debate the merits of the policy and seek amendments to ensure its compliance with the *NZBORA*.[86]

The imbalance within legislative activism in Canada is evident in the *Guide to the Making of Federal Acts and Regulations*, produced by the DOJ to aid departments in the development of legislation. It outlines the Charter certification by the minister of justice, but there is no role for parliament, independent of the Charter vetting performed by the DOJ, to challenge the minister's certification.[87] This reinforces Franks' position that "while the executive took additional measures in pre-vetting to ensure that legislation met the new standards imposed by the charter, parliament did not, itself, add additional procedures or mechanisms to review bills from a rights perspective, as it has with the joint committee on statutory instruments."[88] The certification by the minister of justice is based on the review performed by the DOJ and demonstrates that legislative activism is dominated by the political executive through its control of the machinery of government. The *parliamentary* response to Charter review, therefore, has simply strengthened the cabinet via Charter review performed by the DOJ.

Because of the dominance of party discipline, majority governments, extreme partisanship in the House of Commons, and the undervalued role of the Senate, the parliamentary committee system in Canada is prevented from acting as an adequate check on the legislative agenda of the political executive. Thus, parliamentary scrutiny from a rights perspective is generally absent in Canada during the legislative process, though there are notable examples when the parliamentary committee system has been used by cabinet during the development of legislation, such as Bill C-36, the *Anti-Terrorism Act*. In response to the events of 11 September 2001, the cabinet indicated its desire to fight terrorism through new provisions of the Criminal Code and other acts that empowered the investigative techniques of the police and created new offences to address the international dimensions of terrorism, as well as to limit the fundraising capacities of groups designated terrorist organizations.[89] The events that preceded the granting of royal assent to Bill C-36 on 18 December 2001 represent the most balanced example of legislative activism to date.[90] For instance, the DOJ indicated that, because of the obvious Charter implications and the potential rights violations, Bill C-36 had been subjected to the most rigorous Charter screening and the most intensive episode of bureaucratic activism involving proposed legislation to date.[91]

Once the DOJ had finished the draft legislation, it was introduced into parliament and quickly sent to the Standing Committee on Justice and Human Rights for further scrutiny. Because of the importance of Bill C-36, the cabinet employed the rarely used procedure of pre-study by the Senate, with a Special Senate Committee on the Subject Matter of Bill C-36 scrutinizing the bill in tandem with the Standing Committee on Justice and Human Rights.[92] Thus, parliamentary scrutiny complemented bureaucratic scrutiny and provided a different perspective with which to evaluate whether Bill C-36 was in compliance with the Charter. The testimony before the Standing Committee on Justice and Human Rights, as well as that before the special senate committee, subjected the *Anti-Terrorism Act* to extensive parliamentary and public scrutiny and resulted in important amendments that brought in additional safeguards to better balance the policy objective of greater security with the freedoms provided by the Charter. Indeed, many of the substantive changes to Bill C-36, such as the inclusion of a sunset clause that sees the act expire in five years, a more precise definition of terrorist activity, and an annual report to parliament detailing the operation of the *Anti-Terrorism Act,* were recommendations made by the two standing committees.[93]

While this is the most balanced example of legislative activism in Canada, as the sponsoring minister indicated that the cabinet was open to amendments and saw the parliamentary committee system as essential to reconcile the policy objectives of Bill C-36 with the Charter, it is not the typical approach to governing with the Charter. The structure of the committee system, combined with strong party discipline and the limited resources available to challenge the certification by the minister of justice, limits the effectiveness of parliamentary scrutiny. When the cabinet is not disposed to accept recommendations, the committee system has proven unable to overcome the dominance of cabinet certification by the minister of justice and bureaucratic scrutiny during the legislative process.

Though the merits of parliamentary scrutiny are advanced in this book, parliament only nominally remains the centre of public policy because of the constraints imposed by a cabinet-dominated legislative process.[94] Indeed, parliamentary scrutiny has generally occurred during legislative responses to judicial invalidation of acts by the Supreme Court and thus has been part of the cabinet's legislative strategy following an activist judicial decision, such as the parliamentary response to the invalidation of the *Tobacco Products Control Act* in *RJR-Macdonald Inc. v. Canada,* or the invalidation of Criminal Code restrictions on the sexual history of the victim in *R. v. Daviault.* The use of parliamentary scrutiny in response to judicial activism suggests that the Canadian parliamentary tradition has produced strong executives but weak parliaments,[95] as legislative activism in Canada has seen parliamentary scrutiny eclipsed by executive scrutiny that is supported by bureaucratic review of legislation by the DOJ.

These episodes of parliamentary scrutiny are post-judicial and are exceptional, as the cabinet has generally relied on bureaucratic assessment of the constitutionality of legislative proposals and has not effectively employed parliamentary scrutiny during the development of draft legislation. Indeed, the use of the parliamentary committee system in response to a judicial invalidation may simply be a legislative strategy by the cabinet in anticipation of future constitutional challenges against the amendments. This aspect of Charter politics, whereby the cabinet co-opts parliamentary institutions to overcome judicial invalidation of legislation, is no less executive-dominated than the certification process by the minister of justice during the normal legislative process that precedes judicial review. In truth, during the post-invalidation period, which Hogg and Bushell refer to as a legislative sequel and Hiebert as a shared responsibility, parliament has a constructive – yet orchestrated – role when the cabinet attempts to re-establish the constitutionality of an invalidated statute.[96]

Several legislative responses illustrate that the use of the committee system may be more evidence of Charter politics between the Supreme Court and the cabinet than of the effective functioning of parliamentary scrutiny in Canada. In cases where judicial invalidation saw extensive use of the parliamentary committee system – such as the invalidation of the common law prohibition against the defence of extreme intoxication in *Daviault*, the invalidation of the Criminal Code's rape-shield provisions in *Seaboyer*, and the restrictions on tobacco advertising in *RJR-Macdonald* – parliamentary scrutiny occurred because the cabinet required a strong legislative response in the next round of Charter politics with the Supreme Court. A significant aspect of these legislative responses is the different approaches to rights taken by the cabinet and the Supreme Court. In the case of sexual assault jurisprudence, the Supreme Court advanced a concern that the rights of the accused had been unduly restricted by cabinet in its attempt to protect the victims of crime. Similarly, the Supreme Court invalidated the *Tobacco Products Control Act* because it undermined the freedom of expression of tobacco companies, even though the invalidation denied cabinet's attempt to protect the health of young Canadians by restricting the advertising activities of tobacco companies. In essence, cabinet advanced an agenda of victims' rights, and the Supreme Court invalidated this approach as inconsistent with its agenda, which advanced the rights of the accused.

The cabinet responded by using the committee system to demonstrate to the Supreme Court its dissatisfaction with these Charter decisions that prioritized the rights of the accused. This episode of Charter politics was successful for the cabinet because in *R. v. Mills* the Supreme Court upheld the new Criminal Code provisions that established the rules for judicial disclosure of therapeutic records to the defence, despite the court's assertion that the legislative scheme differed greatly from the direction the court suggested in earlier judgments.[97] In effect, parliament effectively reversed the Supreme Court's decision in *R. v. O'Connor*,[98] which established judicial discretion as the principal criterion that would decide the relevancy of third-party therapeutic records for the defence.[99] In each of these episodes of Charter politics, it was not politically difficult for the cabinet to ensure a strong parliamentary response to the court's invalidation, given that the political optics were favourable because the invalidated legislation sought to protect the victims of sexual assault and the court was perceived as being preoccupied with the rights of the accused. Further, the cabinet was well positioned to exploit the unfavourable optics that suggested the Supreme Court valued the ability of tobacco companies to advertise above the attempt to protect the health of young Canadians. In each instance, the cabinet was able to manufacture a very strong legislative response that refuted the court's interpretation of the Charter. While the parliamentary committee system was employed in these examples of legislative responses, it was clearly used by the cabinet as a legislative strategy to directly challenge the Supreme Court's interpretation in an intense episode of Charter politics.

While legislative activism directly challenges the conclusion of judicial supremacy, at the present time it should not be viewed as evidence of the health of parliamentary democracy in Canada. For the most part, policy decisions remain the responsibility of the cabinet, and important cultural and institutional changes have been implemented to allow this institution to govern in a rights culture. Indeed, the policy process has become more principled and explicit in its attempts to reconcile Charter values with legislative objectives. In this respect, the macro-level conclusion that the Charter has weakened Canadian democracy through a transfer of authority to the courts is questionable. However, it is the micro-level or parliamentary implications of legislative activism that suggest a democratic deficit has appeared since the Charter's introduction. The strengthening of the centre has occurred because the machinery of government has been directed to assessing the Charter implications during the pre-legislative process. Thus, the *parliamentary* response to the Charter has been decidedly nonparliamentary and bureaucratic, as the cabinet support system has been reformed to include Charter vetting by the DOJ, thus confirming Donald Savoie's analysis of the rise of Court Government in his presidential address to the Canadian Political Science Association in 1999: "In the late 1990s, effective power rests with the prime minister and a small group of carefully selected courtiers."[100] While Malloy called for realistic expectations for parliamentary committees, the comparative Commonwealth experience suggests that rights scrutiny committees can provide the niches that enhance parliament and its attempt to govern with the Charter.[101] Unfortunately, the Canadian experience suggests that the niches largely emerge as part of a legislative response to judicial activism and under the direction of the cabinet.

Bridled Parliamentary Scrutiny

The imbalance within legislative activism that favours Charter certification by the minister of justice has placed serious constraints on independent parliamentary scrutiny, and an important check on bureaucratic scrutiny has not emerged in the Canadian setting. An illustration that judicial invalidation may be the result of Charter scrutiny dominated by the cabinet with minimal parliamentary scrutiny is found in the court's decision regarding section 25 of the *Extradition Act* in *United States v. Burns*. At issue was the level of ministerial discretion available in cases involving extradition of Canadians to jurisdictions to face possible execution, and whether the failure by the minister of justice to seek assurances that extradited Canadians would not face the death penalty was inconsistent with the principles of fundamental justice protected by section 7 of the Charter.[102] In a unanimous decision, the Supreme Court ruled that the "Minister's decision to decline to request the assurances of the State of Washington that the death penalty will not be imposed on the respondents as a condition of their extradition, violates their rights under s.7 of the Charter."[103] The judgment reaffirmed the importance of the "balancing process" devised by the court in the *Kindler* and *Ng* cases, whereby the minister would have to balance each case with the relevant principles of fundamental justice.

What led the court to find that the particular balance in *Burns* resulted in a violation of section 7 was the debate in the United States over the use of the death penalty. The court said that "the difficulty in this case is that the Minister proposes to send the respondents without assurances into the death penalty controversy at a time when the legal system of the requesting country is under such sustained and authoritative *internal* attack."[104] Nor did the court consider the section 7 violation to be a reasonable limitation: "In our opinion, while the government objective of advancing mutual assistance in the fight against crime is entirely legitimate, the Minister has not shown that extraditing the respondents to face the death penalty without assurances is necessary to achieve that objective."[105] While the court did not invalidate section 25 of the *Extradition Act,* this decision requires the minister of justice to seek assurances that the death penalty will not be requested in all but the most exceptional cases when Canadians face extradition to foreign jurisdictions.

The critics of judicial activism would view the outcome in *Burns* as evidence of judicial supremacy, as they would claim that the discretionary choices of judges explain the different outcomes in *Kindler* and *Ng* as opposed to *Burns*. What this analysis overlooks is the evidence presented before the Standing Senate Committee on Legal and Constitutional Affairs and the cross-examination of the minister of justice and members of her staff by committee members who questioned whether the discretionary power available to the minister under Bill C-40, which amended both the *Extradition Act* and the *Immigration Act,* was a violation of the principles of fundamental justice. A reconstruction of the testimony before the standing senate committee, which shows the concerns of expert witnesses called and the refusal of the minister of justice to accept the validity of the concerns raised by committee members, illustrates the present limitations of parliamentary scrutiny in Canada. Indeed, the very person who certifies the constitutionality of legislation to cabinet when it is first introduced, the minister of justice, is the same person who defends the constitutionality of legislation at the committee stage in both the House of Commons and the Senate. The problematic aspect of Charter certification is compounded when the ministry sponsoring the legislation is the DOJ, as there is no internal check on bureaucratic scrutiny: Justice monopolizes the process across government, and the minister of justice certifies the scrutiny done by DOJ officials. George Williams has identified the dangers of nonjudicial methods of rights compliance when it is in the hands of the executive: "The weakness in this approach is that it entrusts the responsibility for detecting breaches to the government that has proposed the legislation."[106] Because of the executive-dominated nature of parliament, the reality is that valid constitutional challenges to legislation raised at the committee stage have a marginal chance of resulting in legislative amendments.

Before calling the minister of justice to testify, the standing senate committee heard evidence from members of the DOJ on Bill C-40, focusing in particular on the process by which the requested extradition of Canadians to foreign jurisdictions would take place. Several members of the standing senate committee voiced concern that Bill C-40 allowed the minister of justice to authorize the attorney general to issue a provisional arrest warrant for an individual sought by a foreign country for extradition. Given that the minister of justice *is* the attorney general, the committee was concerned that this was not an adequate check on the discretionary authority of the minister of justice under Bill C-40. Justice official Jacques Lemire outlined the unique relationship in Canada, where the minister of justice and the attorney general are the same person, but he qualified this by stating that "the duties and the considerations at different stages are totally different and handled by different personnel." This led Senator Bryden to inquire whether there were "situations in which the Minister of Justice authorizes the Attorney General to take certain actions and vice versa?" and Senator Beaudoin to comment, "That is impossible." After reviewing the changes to the *Extradition Act* in response to the senators' inquiries, Lemire and Donald Piragoff from the DOJ confirmed that, "under the Extradition Act, it is the existing practice." This led Senator Beaudoin to comment to the DOJ: "You have to amend the law."[107]

Much of the DOJ's defence of Bill C-40 was based on the assumption that the court's decisions in *Kindler* and *Ng* confirmed the constitutionality of ministerial discretion to decide whether to seek assurances that execution would not be sought by a foreign jurisdiction. In effect, Anne McLellan, the minister of justice, argued before the standing senate committee that the changes to the *Extradition Act* sought by Bill C-40 did not alter the act in such a way as to bring it into conflict with earlier decisions by the Supreme Court: "Bill C-40 preserves the discretion of the Minister of Justice to decide in each case whether to seek assurances from the requesting state that the death penalty will not be imposed or, if imposed, not carried out. The Supreme Court of Canada, in the *Kindler* and *Ng* cases, found such a discretion to be constitutional."[108] However, the testimony before the standing senate committee from Anne La Forest, dean of the University of New Brunswick Faculty of Law, suggested that Bill C-40 had changed the balance in favour of ministerial discretion and that it was most likely unconstitutional:

Anne La Forest: The general point that I am trying to make before this committee is that the existing decisions of the Supreme Court of Canada were decided in the context of the existing balance between the judiciary and the minister, and in my view that has been altered to some extent by Bill C-40. The consequence of this is that there may be repercussions at both the judiciary and the executive levels that will delay extradition proceedings. At the extradition hearing in particular, I believe there will be challenges in respect of the jurisdiction provision and in terms of the evidence.

The effect of the decision to have all human rights issues addressed at the ministerial level is to invite judicial review, which will result in the courts having the opportunity to again review the extradition process in relation to the Charter. I do not think I need to tell you that many decisions of the Supreme Court of Canada have been close calls. It is, in effect, an invitation to renew judicial scrutiny.[109]

In response to the testimony of Dean La Forest, the minister of justice stated, "after the most intense analysis possible, I believe that, based on the provisions of the Charter and the jurisprudence of the Supreme Court interpreting that Charter and our existing extradition laws, this proposed section withstands constitutional scrutiny under section 7 of the Charter, or potentially even 15, although I think Dean La Forest argued 7 rather than 15 – due process."[110] The certification by the minister of justice that Bill C-40 would survive constitutional scrutiny did not satisfy either Senator Andreychuk or Senator Grafstein, who questioned Yvan Roy, senior general counsel of DOJ's Criminal Law Policy Section, about whether the discretion available to the minister was constitutional:

Mr. Roy: The scheme being proposed by the Minister of Justice requires that the minister start the process. It is the minister who will make the decision as to what country will have the first crack at that person. I would point out that clause 5 states that "A person may be extradited." It is not mandatory, but the minister will have to determine what is the best forum for that person to receive fair treatment and for Canada to be able to discharge its obligations.

Senator Andreychuk: That is the problem I was getting at. It will be decided at the minister's discretion.[111]

Despite the objections of several senators regarding the compatibility of ministerial discretion with the Charter, the Standing Senate Committee on Legal and Constitutional Affairs passed Bill C-40 without amendment. However, two senators abstained from voting.[112] The invalidation of the discretionary authority of the minister of justice in *Burns* occurred after the standing senate committee raised concerns about the level of discretion provided under the *Extradition Act*. A judicial-centred analysis of the Charter would conclude that this episode illustrates the rise of the Supreme Court as a policy actor, but such a conclusion is questionable because of the attempts by parliamentarians to convince the minister of justice that Bill C-40, despite the assurances of the DOJ, conflicted with the Charter. My interpretation of the constitutional invalidation of ministerial discretion in *Burns* is that it highlights the problem of executive supremacy in the policy process and the limitations of parliamentary scrutiny at the present time. The Liberal majority on the standing senate committee, operating under strict party discipline, ensured that the discretionary authority of the minister of justice was not reduced in spite of the evidence presented by legal experts that Bill C-40 faced the strong possibility of constitutional invalidation.

The constraints on Charter certification by ministers of justice are even weaker at the provincial level because of important institutional differences that suggest executive supremacy is much greater.[113] The most significant institutional difference is the unicameral characteristic of provincial legislative assemblies, which has resulted in fewer checks on provincial premiers and cabinets. As a result, legislative activism is far more imbalanced at the provincial level. In addition to the absence of an upper house, the small size of provincial legislative assemblies has resulted in greater dominance by the governing party and, by extension, the premier and cabinet. The emergence of executive supremacy at the provincial level has been little affected by the introduction of the Charter because changes to the machinery of government have simply strengthened an already dominant executive. In effect, a traditional parliamentary function is absent at the provincial level because the role of an upper house is to check the impulses of the lower house, and

Table 7.5

Cabinet in relation to parliament and caucus (as of November 2004)

Province	Parliament	Government	Executive	A[1]	B[2]	C[3]
Alberta	83	63	24	0.76	0.29	0.38
British Columbia	79	77	27	0.97	0.34	0.35
Manitoba	57	35	18	0.61	0.32	0.51
New Brunswick	55	28	18	0.51	0.33	0.64
Newfoundland	48	34	14	0.71	0.29	0.41
Nova Scotia	52	25	15	0.48	0.29	0.60
Ontario	103	71	23	0.69	0.22	0.32
Prince Edward Island	27	23	10	0.85	0.37	0.43
Quebec	125	76	25	0.61	0.20	0.33
Saskatchewan	58	30	17	0.52	0.29	0.57
Provincial total[4]	687	462	191	0.67	0.28	0.41
Canada (House)	308	135	39	0.44	0.13	0.29
Canada (Parliament)	413	199	39	0.48	0.09	0.20
Canada (House)[5]	308	135	67	0.44	0.22	0.50
Britain (House)	659	408	49	0.62	0.07	0.12
Britain (Parliament)	1334	590	49	0.44	0.04	0.08
New Zealand	120	54	27	0.45	0.23	0.50
Australia (House)	150	68	30	0.45	0.20	0.44
Australia (Parliament)	226	99	30	0.44	0.13	0.30

1 Government as a percentage of parliament or the legislature.
2 Cabinet as a percentage of parliament or the legislature.
3 Cabinet as a percentage of the governing caucus.
4 As of 24 November 2004.
5 Executive includes twenty-eight parliamentary secretaries.

this has not been altered by the entrenchment of the Charter. Further, the modern role of an upper house, evident in Britain, Australia, and, to a lesser degree, the Parliament of Canada, is to protect rights by engaging in parliamentary scrutiny from a rights perspective of policy introduced by the cabinet.[114] Neither role, however, is performed at the provincial level.

The composition of provincial legislative assemblies is presented in Table 7.5, and the most startling characteristic is the relative size of the governing party in comparison to opposition members. Specifically, the governing party represents 67 percent of elected members (462 out of 687), which is far higher than in the federal parliament, where the governing Liberals constitute 44 percent (135 out of 308) of the House of Commons. Despite the much smaller size of provincial legislative assemblies, with Prince Edward Island the smallest at 27 seats and Quebec the largest at 125, the cabinet makes up a much higher proportion of the legislative assembly than it does at the federal level. For instance, the federal cabinet constitutes 13 percent (39 out of 308) of the House of Commons, whereas the provincial average is 28 percent (191 out of 687). Even more striking is the composition of the cabinet as a percentage of the government caucus, as the provincial average stands at 41 percent (191 out of 462), while the federal cabinet represents 29 percent (39 out of 135) of the Liberal caucus in the House of Commons and 9 percent (39 out of 199) of its parliamentary caucus. The cabinet as a proportion of the governing caucus is highest in New Brunswick at 64 percent (18 out of 28), and lowest in Ontario (23 out of 71) and Quebec (25 out of 76) at 33 percent. The overall dominance of the provincial cabinet is clear when placed in the comparative Commonwealth experience. Only New Zealand sees the legislature or the governing caucus dominated by the cabinet to the extent it is in the Canadian provinces. In New Zealand, the large size of the cabinet is a reflection of the coalition government produced by a mixed member proportional electoral system, which ultimately reduces the dominance of the cabinet and allows a parliament-centred policy process to emerge.[115]

The provincial cabinet's dominance of the legislative assembly distorts the principle of responsible government to a much larger extent than occurs at the federal level, where a sizeable opposition and a developed committee system in both houses of parliament participate in the legislative process. Though the parliamentary arena at the federal level is executive dominated, the potential does exist for the emergence of parliamentary scrutiny from a rights perspective, whereas the institutional characteristics of provincial legislative assemblies have effectively prevented these institutions from serving a policy or, at the very least, a scrutiny function. For instance, in most provincial assemblies the committee system is underdeveloped, and the committee of the whole is the most important forum for legislative review. Perhaps more importantly, the effectiveness of the committee system is further affected by the small size of the opposition, which is generally divided between two parties. For example, in three provinces the opposition parties hold ten or fewer seats, with only two opposition members in British Columbia and four members in Prince Edward Island. These elected institutions are not structured to effectively scrutinize the legislative agenda of the government or to provide an effective check on the power of the political executive. A democratic deficit exists at the provincial level, but not at the hands of the Supreme Court and its interpretation of the Charter. Public tours of legislative assemblies, which formerly showcased democratic institutions in practice, now resemble museum tours of our parliamentary past. Governing with the Charter at the provincial level has contributed to the decline of parliamentary institutions at the hands of the provincial cabinets.

Conclusion

The principal legislative response to the Charter has been the institutionalization of rights scrutiny by the DOJ. Charter dialogue originates within the cabinet and has ensured the development of a rights culture within the legislative process. When the Supreme Court or lower courts engage in Charter dialogue through judicial decisions, it is a response to legislative activism and does not originate in judicial activism and court decision, as judicial dialogue theorists have contended. It was a political decision to entrench the Charter, and the institutionalization of rights vetting occurred at the insistence of the cabinet to ensure that its legislative agenda conformed to the policy requirements introduced by the Charter. A central limitation of the judicial-centred approach is that it focuses on actors and processes at the periphery of the legislative process and outside the parliamentary arena. The claim that the Supreme Court has emerged as a dominant policy actor would be credible if the legislative process remained unreformed after the introduction of the Charter. Although dominated by the prime minister, the cabinet remains the centre of the policy process because of the institutionalization of Charter vetting by the DOJ. This process of bureaucratic activism directly challenges the claims of judicial supremacy because it precedes and structures Charter dialogue. As a result, judicial actors react to the cabinet's attempt to govern with the Charter; the courts do not lead this process.

The focus on judicial activism, and the assumption that the Supreme Court is the guardian of the constitution, is not surprising, as judicial decisions are the public face of the effort to reach principled policy decisions consistent with the Charter. What I have attempted to demonstrate in this chapter is the nearly invisible aspect of legislative activism within the machinery of government that is rarely exposed to critical commentary when the Supreme Court invalidates legislation. This chapter has attempted to confront the myth of judicial supremacy by offering a critical reappraisal of the empirical evidence used to demonstrate unbridled judicial power since the Charter's introduction. By focusing on the year a statute was enacted or last amended, rather than simply the yearly rate of activism, the benefit of Charter vetting becomes evident as most invalidated statutes were enacted before the institutionalization of bureaucratic activism and rights scrutiny by the DOJ. In effect, it is the absence of post-vetting statutes being reviewed and invalidated by the Supreme Court that demonstrates the emergence of a rights culture within government. This is evidence that the cabinet, supported by the Department of Justice, is governing with the Charter and that it has the ability to prevent unbridled judicial power. A transfer of policy-making authority to the courts has not occurred because parliamentary actors have taken steps to ensure that the Charter remains consistent with its beginnings: a political decision by the Trudeau cabinet to ensure greater protections for rights. The Canadian rights revolution began as, and continues to be, cabinet centred and committed to reaching principled policy decisions that reconcile legislative objectives with Charter commitments. It is legislation, therefore, that is the hallmark of a rights revolution in an advanced Westminster democracy, and not litigation and the legal mobilization support structure contended by Epp.[116]

Unlike in other Westminster democracies that have attempted to govern in a rights culture through parliamentary reform, such as New Zealand and Britain, there has been an absence of similar reforms in Canada. This is the fundamental failure of the Charter project and the reason it remains institutionally incomplete, as constitutional reform must be linked to parliamentary reform for a truly parliament-centred approach to emerge. The focus on the inter-institutional relationship between the cabinet and the Supreme Court has therefore overshadowed the internal response to the Charter, which has resulted in a greater concentration of power with the cabinet and the prime minister. The most significant institutional failure, therefore, has not been the emergence of unbridled judicial power, but the further marginalization of parliament through legislative responses to the Charter.[117] Because of an executive-dominated parliamentary arena, judicial invalidation represents the only external check on unbridled political power in Canada, besides electoral defeat of a government, which, given the long tenure of majority governments in Canada, is a limited constraint on political power.[118] Legislative actors govern with the Charter, but at a noticeable cost to parliament and provincial legislatures as institutions. This is unfortunately the common institutional legacy of the attempts by the federal and provincial cabinets to govern with the Charter.

Conclusion

During the proceedings of the Special Joint Committee on the Constitution of Canada, Peter Russell observed that he believed "a Charter only guarantees a change in the way in which certain decisions are made. It does not guarantee rights or freedoms, it guarantees a change in the way in which decisions are made about rights and freedoms."[1] Unfortunately, this insight was lost during the Charter's first twenty-one years because of the dominance of the judicial-centred paradigm and its focus on the Supreme Court. My decision to advance a cabinet-centred approach is rooted in the position that the Charter has principally changed cabinet decision making as new procedures have been instituted to ensure that policy objectives are explicitly linked to Charter commitments. In turn, this has resulted in an important cultural shift in Canadian society, where the decisions and actions of cabinet, bureaucrats, police, and judiciary have changed to honour the constitutional rights in the Charter.

All of these changes occurred because political actors placed constitutional limits on their power and asked all actors exercising state authority to govern with the Charter. The intention of the framers to ensure greater protection for rights, therefore, has been advanced by the cabinet through Charter dialogue within the machinery of government. The significance of the Charter is not its status as part of the constitution but the reaction to it by the cabinet and the Supreme Court. This is one of the fallacies of the bills of rights debates that occurred in Canada, New Zealand, and Britain: the belief that the status of a charter or bill of rights determines the value of the document.[2] In the Canadian case, if both the cabinet and the Supreme Court had continued to approach rights as they did under the *Canadian Bill of Rights,* the Charter and its entrenched status would not have mattered. The Charter matters because these institutions have demonstrated a commitment to governing with rights and to collectively guarding the constitution and its essential values.

In challenging the judicial-centred paradigm, I questioned the heavy use of American theories of constitutionalism that structure the Canadian debate. Indeed, it was suggested that an uncritical use of American constitutionalism resulted in too much Madison and not enough Dicey in the Canadian debate, and this resulted in a neglect of parliament and the essential principles of Westminster democracy. American constitutionalism is organized to prevent any branch of government from dominating, and a focus on the issue of judicial power is understandable in a political system based on a theory of separation of powers. It is also appropriate in political systems where courts are the bulwark of the limited constitution. As Westminster systems are based on a fusion of power, and the courts are viewed not with suspicion but as a coordinate actor responsible for upholding the rule of law in tandem with parliament, the most basic principle of American constitutionalism is not applicable in Canada. Further, the concern about judicial power, once placed in the broader context of the cabinet response to the Charter, raises questions about the loss of policy autonomy and political authority attributed to judicial review after 1982. As argued throughout this book, the framers of the Charter envisioned that courts, along with parliamentary actors, or more accurately, the cabinet, would be the bulwark against the limited constitution. The Canadian debate has suffered, therefore, by the uncritical application of foreign constitutional principles in the post-Charter era.

Dicey argued that parliament remained supreme because judicial legislation, the term he used to describe common-law rules created by the courts, was secondary legislation that could be reversed by an act of parliament. Judicial legislation in the era of the Charter is still secondary legislation because the cabinet retains the discretion to decide how to respond to judicial findings of unconstitutionality. In arguing this, I have not endorsed the use of the Charter's notwithstanding clause, which surely makes judicial decisions secondary legislation in the most explicit way. Judicial review is a secondary component of Charter review because of the extensive efforts by the cabinet, supported by the Department of Justice, to pass statutes that advance Charter rights. Additionally, the emerging approach to judicial remedies has provided the cabinet with sufficient discretion to determine how to respond to judicial invalidation and re-establish the constitutionality of public policies. This is the clearest illustration of the cabinet and the Supreme Court governing with the Charter, as the Supreme Court identifies violations and the cabinet introduces policy amendments to ensure the continued application of unconstitutional laws. Indeed, this coordinate approach to the Charter reveals that the distinction between law and politics may not be unattainable or as blurred as critics of judicial power contend.

The focus on legislative responses, however useful to understanding the relationship between the cabinet and the Supreme Court, is unconvincing and continues the limitations of the judicial-centred approach, as the critique of the Charter dialogue theory presented by Hogg and Bushell suggested. This is Charter dialogue with a judicial accent, and it overlooks the presence of lower forms within the bureaucratic arena that precede judicial review. Perhaps more importantly, this dialogue on rights within the bureaucracy structures Charter dialogue at the level of the Supreme Court. The analysis of legislative activism demonstrated that judicial invalidation is not required in order for the cabinet and bureaucracy to engage in a dialogue on rights, as Hogg and Bushell argued, but that this dialogue is now an institutionalized part of the development of legislation. Though legislative responses before and after judicial review were used as a framework to demonstrate the shared responsibility of the cabinet and the Supreme Court, I argued that the principal response was the institutionalization of Charter scrutiny within the legislative process, and not simply the cabinet's amendment of statutes identified as unconstitutional by the Supreme Court. Contrary to the claims of either the critics of judicial activism or the Charter dialogue theorists, the cabinet remains the centre of public policy despite the Charter's entrenchment.

My analysis did not begin with the first Charter decision by the Supreme Court in 1984, but with the political decision to seek an entrenched Charter, which intensified in the summer of 1980. The constitutional politics that surrounded the Charter was dominated by the first ministers and not Supreme Court justices, though the Supreme Court played a significant role in the *Patriation Reference* that ended the constitutional stalemate surrounding unilateral patriation by the Trudeau government. While "coordinate constitutionalism" is a term associated with Madisonian democracy, it is, as Brian Slattery demonstrated, a valuable framework for understanding the institutional reaction to the Charter by courts and legislatures.[3] One of the limitations in the Canadian debate is the neglect of the constitutional politics that surrounded patriation. This is a significant period in Canadian history and for the Charter, as the substance of the document was decided upon in the parliamentary arena and not the judicial arena.

The constitutional politics surrounding the Charter, discussed in Chapters 2 and 3, revealed competing agendas and the use of varied resources by the actors who sought to ensure their vision triumphed. At first the Trudeau vision was unsuccessful because of the dynamics of executive federalism and the need to secure unanimous consent from the provincial premiers. The draft Charters during the summer of 1980 demonstrate the influence of the premiers, who sought to prevent an entrenched Charter or, failing this, to produce a weak Charter that placed limited constraints on their power. The principle of unanimity resulted in the Trudeau government's engaging in the politics of appeasement, and the draft Charter presented to parliament after the declaration of unilateral patriation was marginally better than the *Canadian Bill of Rights*. The formative event that allowed the Trudeau vision of an activist constitution to marginalize the wishes of the premiers was the Special Joint Committee on the Constitution of Canada. After the draft Charter was presented to parliamentarians, a consensus emerged that amendments were needed to improve the document. Critical commentary by parliamentarians and interest groups resulted in a significant strengthening of the Charter, and the document that exists today is the product of democratic activism and not judicial activism that followed its entrenchment. Once the *Patriation Reference* decision returned the draft Charter to the institutions of executive federalism, concessions to the premiers were agreed upon, such as the notwithstanding clause. However, the premiers were no longer the dominant actors in constitutional politics during November 1981, as the concessions to parliamentary supremacy had been removed in the draft Charter. Seizing on this shift in relative bargaining strength, the activist intentions of the Trudeau government secured substantial provincial consent, and the Charter became part of the Canadian constitution.

The assessment of the Supreme Court and judicial activism presented in this book departed from the standard approach that focuses on yearly rates of activism. The difficulty with this measure is that a significant number of statutes invalidated by the Supreme Court were enacted or last amended before the Charter was entrenched or shortly after 1982. In effect, this measure of judicial power is empirically irrelevant, as fluctuations in the yearly rates of activism may simply be the by-product of the Supreme Court reviewing a large number of statutes enacted before the Charter, when the legislative process did not require an extensive review to ensure that policy objectives were consistent with Charter commitments.[4] Focusing on the date a statute was enacted or last amended, as shown in Chapters 5 to 7, demonstrates that the Supreme Court has generally been activist against policy decisions of the past, and that statutes enacted in a policy environment where legislation is scrutinized from a rights perspective are largely found constitutional or, perhaps more revealing, are not even reviewed by the Supreme Court. This suggests that the determination of constitutionality is not a judicial choice but a reaction to political decisions and changes in the machinery of government instituted by all cabinets in Canada.

In those situations where the Supreme Court invalidates legislation, an important development that strengthens coordinate constitutionalism is the use of suspended decisions. This is a significant change, as the Supreme Court provides the responsible cabinet with an opportunity to draft amendments to ensure the constitutionality of offending statutes. Legislative activism was prioritized in this book because judicial review is a reaction against the policy choices of the cabinet. It was demonstrated that the institution-alization of Charter scrutiny as part of the legislative process is the principal cause of judicial deference. Perhaps more importantly, the decline of judi-cial activism reveals the central weakness of the judicial-centred paradigm: the assumption that the Charter has value if the courts are activist and willing to protect rights by finding political choices unconstitutional. I dis-agree with this approach because it overlooks the fact that many activist responses to the Charter exist and that judicial deference is the result of a rights culture within the legislative process. The cabinet is the principal guardian of the constitution, and the declining rates of judicial activism are evidence of this.

The emergence of bureaucratic activism is significant, and the role of the DOJ in scrutinizing legislation from a rights perspective has greatly contrib-uted to the improved quality of legislation in Canada. While Charter scru-tiny is most institutionalized at the federal level, comparable processes exist in Ontario and Quebec, and all cabinets have taken steps to govern with the Charter during the legislative process. The importance of the Charter is not its status or the entrenchment of rights, but the cabinets' responses to it, which have changed the legislative processes in Canada. In this book, the relationship between the Charter and provincial autonomy was considered, as an important criticism in 1982 involved the centralization of Canadian federalism that would result from judicial review involving rights. This con-cern has not been borne out, largely due to judicial efforts and the efforts of provincial cabinets to guard the constitution and an essential principle, federal diversity. In an earlier article I considered the relationship between the Charter and federalism using a judicial-centred approach, focusing on the emerging federalism jurisprudence by the Supreme Court to challenge the centralization thesis.[5] I no longer consider this an appropriate approach to this question because of the institutionalization of Charter scrutiny at the provincial level. The reconciliation between rights and federalism is the result of a joint effort by the Supreme Court and provincial cabinets to govern with the Charter, and Chapter 6 argued that this development was further evidence of coordinate constitutionalism in Canada. As provincial cabinets have instituted Charter scrutiny in the legislative process, this has led to fewer provincial statutes being invalidated as inconsistent with the Charter. This attempt to reconcile rights and federalism through legislative changes has been bolstered by the Supreme Court and its sensitivity to pro-vincial autonomy in its Charter jurisprudence.

In challenging the view that the principal institutional effect of the Char-ter has been the empowering of the Supreme Court at the expense of the cabinet, I caution against an overly positive assessment because of the in-tra-institutional implications of the cabinet's attempt to govern with the Charter. While judicial supremacy has not occurred, the prime minister's decision to govern with the Charter from the centre has continued the marginalization of parliament associated with the central agency reforms of the Trudeau and Mulroney governments. The entrenchment of executive supremacy is the most pressing institutional limitation associated with the political response to the Charter. Indeed, judicial power may be the only effective check on unbridled political power in Canada at the present time. The attempts at reform have focused on the process for appointing Supreme Court justices. This is part of Prime Minister Paul Martin's agenda to address the democratic deficit, and appointed Supreme Court justices have been singled out as contributing to this deficit through Charter review.[6] This reform is misguided in a number of respects, not least of which is the perpetuation of the judicial-centred view of the Charter and the assumption that Canadian democracy can be improved by changing the method of appointing justices to the Supreme Court. My concern is that this is a reform borrowed from the American experience, where the public vetting of judges is viewed as democratic and necessary to ensure the integrity of the legislative process. This is the wrong comparative framework, as the Canadian Charter is not a northern and paler version of the *American Bill of Rights* but a constitutional document embedded within the principles of Westminster democracy.

The Commonwealth Model
In recent years, comparative scholars have noted the emergence of the "Commonwealth model" to account for the particular approach to bills of rights by Westminster democracies. Their understanding of this new model is, however, still decidedly judicial centred as scholars have focused on the explicit institutional mechanisms within bills of rights that attempt to "decouple judicial review from judicial supremacy by empowering legislatures to have the final word."[7] The significance of the Commonwealth model is not the originality of notwithstanding clauses and the legislative override in the case of Canada, or the declarations of incompatibility by courts in the United Kingdom as a substitute for declarations of constitutional invalidity,[8] but the attempt to ensure the complementary nature of entrenched rights with the broader constitutional principles of Westminster democracy, of which parliamentary supremacy is important but not the sole principle. At the heart of parliamentary democracy is the belief that the parliamentary arena is the actor principally responsible for the protection of rights. While this has proven to be an unsustainable view of the relationship between rights and political institutions in the modern era, the value of the Commonwealth model is not found in the inter-institutional relationships created between courts and legislatures through bills of rights, but in the intra-institutional attempts to safeguard rights within advanced parliamentary democracies. Interestingly, American scholars such as Tushnet

conceptualize this parliamentary approach to constitutional review as "non-judicial review," but they do conclude that "non-judicial constitutional review stacks up against judicial constitutional review reasonably well."[9]

The Commonwealth model has significant implications for the comparative study of courts and politics because it suggests that the commitment to rights is not predicated on the empowerment of courts through the entrenchment of bills of rights, but on the development of a rights culture within the institutions that formulate public policy. In effect, it is the intra-institutional approach to bills of rights that matters, and not simply the disposition of Supreme Courts to be activist as the means to protect rights against legislative encroachment. For instance, Canada, New Zealand, and Britain have taken varied approaches to the protection of rights, but this does not undermine the importance of the Commonwealth model or question whether a distinct model in fact exists. The value of the Commonwealth model is that it considers the varied institutional configurations within a country that are directed to the protection of rights in the legislative, bureaucratic, and judicial realms. As an example, applying the judicial-centred model to Canada, New Zealand, and Britain would lead to the conclusion that Canada has the strongest institutional approach to rights. In particular, Canada has an entrenched Charter of Rights, whereas Britain has simply incorporated the *European Convention on Human Rights* into domestic law, and in New Zealand, the *New Zealand Bill of Rights Act (NZBORA)* is purely statutory. Further, only the *Canadian Charter of Rights and Freedoms* authorizes courts to invalidate statutes as inconsistent with protected rights, whereas British courts can simply issue declarations of incompatibility, and in New Zealand, under section 4 of the *NZBORA,* the courts are prohibited from invalidating statutes. Under section 6 they are instructed to find interpretations of statutes that ensure their consistency, where possible, with the *NZBORA.*[10] Even in the case of Canada, the notwithstanding clause makes the Commonwealth model potentially weak because political actors can reverse judicial decisions, and the remedies available to the courts to address unconstitutional statutes can be severely reduced as a result. In effect, the status of a bill of rights and the review functions provided to the judiciary are considered the critical factors determining the efficacy of an institutional approach to rights protections.

The complexity of the institutional approaches to protecting rights in Canada, New Zealand, and Britain suggests that the Commonwealth model is perhaps a more effective approach to the protection of rights. Specifically, it prioritizes nonjudicial review in the legislative process and suggests that legislative activism can be sufficient to ensure that legislation conforms to constitutional guarantees. What the Commonwealth model indicates is that the level of protection does not vary between these countries, and that is because of the importance of legislative activism – both in the bureaucratic sphere and the parliamentary sphere. This process is a substitute for robust judicial review in the Commonwealth model and is necessary to preserve the underlying constitutional principles of Westminster democracy. The purpose of the Commonwealth model, therefore, is to design legislation that advances rights guarantees without the need for judicial activism. What may be considered modest models (Canada) or weak models (Britain and New Zealand) may be incorrect assessments because of the importance of legislative activism and the replacement of judicial review with legislative review for rights compliance. Indeed, robust institutional arrangements for the protection of rights exist in these Westminster democracies, but they are in the legislative arena and not the judicial arena. This is the value of the Commonwealth model and its attempt to graft bills of rights onto parliamentary structures.

In the final analysis, whether parliamentary actors govern with the Charter or are ruled by it through unfavourable judicial decisions is ultimately a political choice. Throughout this book I have argued that the Charter has primarily changed cabinet decision making and introduced a rights culture within the judicial and legislative arenas. A cabinet-centred approach to the Charter can be based on the notwithstanding clause, or it can be the result of institutional changes in the legislative process that scrutinize policy from a rights perspective. Both approaches ultimately allow the legislative choices of the cabinet to withstand judicial review, but only one demonstrates a commitment to the Charter and constitutional supremacy. How to govern with the Charter, therefore, is also a political decision.

Notes

Introduction

1 Christopher MacLennan, *Toward the Charter* (Montreal and Kingston: McGill-Queen's University Press, 2003), 109-26.

2 A notable exception to the judicial-centric focus of the debate is found in the most recent work of Janet L. Hiebert, *Charter Conflicts* (Montreal and Kingston: McGill-Queen's University Press, 2002).

3 Hon. Brian Dickson, "The Canadian Charter of Rights and Freedoms: Dawn of a New Era?" *Review of Constitutional Studies* 2 (1994): 13.

4 Peter H. Russell, Rainer Knopff, and Ted Morton, *Federalism and the Charter: Leading Constitutional Decisions* (Ottawa: Carleton University Press, 1990), 19.

5 Lorraine Eisenstat Weinrib, "Trudeau and the Canadian Charter of Rights and Freedoms: A Question of Constitutional Maturation," in Andrew Cohen and J.L. Granatstein, eds., *Trudeau's Shadow* (Toronto: Random House of Canada, 1999), 263-64.

6 Donald J. Savoie, *Governing from the Centre* (Toronto: University of Toronto Press, 1999), 72.

7 At the Commonwealth level, the Australian parliament has a well-developed Senate Standing Committee for the Scrutiny of Bills that reviews all legislation introduced into the Senate for consistency with Australia's domestic and international rights commitments. The committee issues an *Alert Digest* and a *Report* each week the Senate sits. See Parliament of Australia: Senate, "Senate Scrutiny of Bills Committee," http://www.aph.gov.au/senate/committee/scrutiny/cominfo.htm. The State of Victoria has an equivalent structure, the Scrutiny of Acts and Regulations Committee. See Parliament of Victoria, "Role of the Scrutiny of Acts and Regulations Committee," http://www.parliament.vic.gov.au/sarc/role.htm. In Queensland, the Scrutiny of Legislation Committee ensures that legislation pays sufficient regard to the "Fundamental Legislative Principles" that protect basic rights and freedoms. See Queensland Parliament, "Scrutiny of Legislation Committee," http://www.parliament.qld.gov.au/view/committees/committees.asp?area=SLC&LIndex=7&SubArea=SLC, Fundamental Legislative Principles.

8 K.D. Ewing, "The Unbalanced Constitution," in Tom Campbell, K.D. Ewing, and Adam Tomkins, eds., *Sceptical Essays on Human Rights* (Oxford: Oxford University Press, 2001), 114-16. The Joint Committee was established 1 February 2001, and has produced fifteen reports to date (1 July 2002).

9 Grant Huscroft, "The Attorney General, the Bill of Rights, and the Public Interest," in Grant Huscroft and Paul Rishworth, eds., *Rights and Freedoms: The New Zealand Bill of Rights Act 1990 and the Human Rights Act 1993* (Wellington, NZ: Brooker's, 1995) 136-37.

10 John C. Tait, "Policy Development and the Charter," *Perspectives on Public Policy* 7 (1995): 11-16; Patrick J. Monahan and Marie Finkelstein, "The Charter of Rights and Public Policy in Canada," *Osgoode Hall Law Journal* 30 (1992): 509; Kent Roach, *The Supreme Court on Trial* (Toronto: Irwin Law, 2001), 253.

11 Janet L. Hiebert, "Wrestling with Rights: Judges, Parliament and the Making of Social Policy," *Choices* 5 (1999): 6-9; James B. Kelly, "Bureaucratic Activism and the Charter of Rights and Freedoms: The Department of Justice and Its Entry into the Centre of Government," *Canadian Public Administration* 42 (1999): 476-511.

12 Peter H. Russell, "Canadian Constraints on Judicialization from Without," *International Political Science Review* 15 (1994): 169-70.

13 Roach, *The Supreme Court on Trial*, 155-73.

14 Janet L. Hiebert, "A Relational Approach to Constitutional Interpretation: Shared Legislative and Judicial Responsibilities," *Journal of Canadian Studies* 35 (2001): 161-81.

15 Kent Roach, "The Uses and Audiences of Preambles in Legislation," *McGill Law Journal* 47 (2001): 131-32. The Parliament of Canada has employed preambles in legislative responses to the Supreme Court's invalidation of sections of the Criminal Code in cases such as *R. v. Daviault,* [1994] 2 S.C.R. 63, *R. v. Feeney,* [1997] 2 S.C.R. 13, and *R. v. Mills,* [1999] 3 S.C.R. 668.

16 Christopher P. Manfredi and James B. Kelly, "Six Degrees of Dialogue: A Response to Hogg and Bushell," *Osgoode Hall Law Journal* 37 (1999): 513-27.

17 Author interviews with Senator Serge Joyal, Standing Senate Committee on Legal and Constitutional Affairs, 37th Parliament, 22 October 2002, Ottawa, ON; Senator Gérald Beaudoin, Standing Senate Committee on Legal and Constitutional Affairs, 37th Parliament, 22 October 2002, Ottawa, ON; Senator Raynell Andreychuk, Standing Senate Committee on Legal and Constitutional Affairs, 37th Parliament, 23 October 2002, Ottawa, ON; Chuck Cadman, MP (Surrey North), Standing Committee on Justice and Human Rights, 37th Parliament, 23 October 2002, Ottawa, ON; Irwin Cotler, MP (Mont Royal), Standing Committee on Justice and Human Rights, 37th Parliament, 23 October 2002, Ottawa, ON; John Maloney, MP (Erie-Lincoln), Standing Committee on Justice and Human Rights, 37th Parliament, 23 October 2002, Ottawa, ON; John McKay, MP (Scarborough East), Standing Committee on Justice and Human Rights, 37th Parliament, 22 October 2002, Ottawa, ON.

18 Guy Davidov, "The Paradox of Judicial Deference," *National Journal of Constitutional Law* 12 (2001): 145-46.

19 Pierre Elliott Trudeau, *Federalism and the French Canadians* (Toronto: Macmillan, 1968), 55-56.

20 Rainer Knopff and F.L. Morton, *Charter Politics* (Scarborough, ON: Nelson Canada, 1992), 225.

21 F.L. Morton and Rainer Knopff, *The Charter Revolution and the Court Party* (Peterborough, ON: Broadview Press, 2000), 56-59.

22 Christopher P. Manfredi, *Judicial Power and the Charter,* 2nd ed. (Don Mills, ON: Oxford University Press, 2001), 170. Peter Russell provides a similar defence in "Standing Up for Notwithstanding," *Alberta Law Review* 24 (1991): 301. However, Howard Leeson has referred to the notwithstanding clause as a "paper tiger" that has attained the status of the powers of reservation and disallowance: Howard Leeson, "Section 33, the Notwithstanding Clause: A Paper Tiger?" *Choices* 6 (2000): 20.

23 Author interview with former senior DOJ official, 29 September 1997, Ottawa, ON.

24 Tait, "Policy Development and the Charter," 16.

25 Janet L. Hiebert, "Why Must a Bill of Rights Be a Contest of Political and Judicial Wills? The Canadian Alternative," *Public Law Review* 10 (1999): 23-24.

26 Honourable Justice Laforest, "The Balancing of Interests under the Charter," *National Journal of Constitutional Law* 2 (1993): 135.

27 Author interview with the Right Honourable Pierre Elliott Trudeau, PC, QC, 5 September 1997, Montreal, QC.

28 *Canadian Bill of Rights,* 1960, c.44, s.1. Cited in Peter W. Hogg, *Constitutional Law of Canada,* 2nd ed. (Toronto: Carswell, 1985), 895.

29 *Canadian Bill of Rights,* 1960, c.44, preamble.

30 *Constitution Act, 1982,* s.52(1). Cited in Hogg, *Constitutional Law of Canada,* 886.

31 *Canadian Charter of Rights and Freedoms,* s.24(1). The full text is the following: "24(1) Anyone whose rights or freedoms, as guaranteed by this Charter, have been infringed or denied

may apply to a court of competent jurisdiction to obtain such remedy as the court considers appropriate and just in the circumstances."

32 Manfredi, *Judicial Power and the Charter*, 2nd ed., 97-102; Morton and Knopff, *The Charter Revolution and the Court Party*, 39-40.

33 Walter Tarnopolsky, "The Charter and the Supreme Court of Canada," in G. Beaudoin, ed., *The Charter: Ten Years Later* (Cowansville, QC: Les Editions Yvon Blais, 1992), 63.

34 A.V. Dicey, *An Introduction to the Study of the Law of the Constitution* (Indianapolis: Liberty Fund Classics, 1982), 18.

35 Ian Brodie, "Interest Group Litigation and the Embedded State: Canada's Court Challenges Program," *Canadian Journal of Political Science* 34 (2001): 364.

36 Pierre Elliott Trudeau, *A Canadian Charter of Human Rights* (Ottawa: Queen's Printer, 1968), 16.

37 Janet L. Hiebert, "The Evolution of the Limitation Clause," *Osgoode Hall Law Journal* 28 (1990): 106.

38 MacLennan, *Toward the Charter*.

39 James B. Kelly and Michael Murphy, "Confronting Judicial Supremacy: A Defence of Judicial Activism and the Supreme Court of Canada's Legal Rights Jurisprudence," *Canadian Journal of Law and Society* 16 (2001): 6-14.

40 Janet Ajzenstat, "Reconciling Parliament and Rights: A.V. Dicey Reads the Canadian Charter of Rights and Freedoms," *Canadian Journal of Political Science* 30 (1997): 645-62.

41 Dicey, *An Introduction to the Study of the Law of the Constitution*, 18.

42 Patrick J. Monahan, *Politics and the Constitution* (Toronto: Carswell, 1987), 74.

43 Manfredi, *Judicial Power and the Charter*, 2nd ed., 21-24.

44 Peter W. Hogg, "The Charter of Rights and American Theories of Interpretation," *Osgoode Hall Law Journal* 25 (1987): 90-91. Interpretivism is the technique in which the role of the court is simply to apply the constitution. As such, there is no creative role for the courts in construing or creating the meaning of the constitution. This technique has been referred to as the "four corners of the text," as the courts should limit interpretation to the written text and never stray from the intended meaning. The technique of non-interpretivism is generally associated with judicial activism, as it is argued that courts search for the meaning of the text and do not simply apply the text. In essence, the courts view the constitution as a living text that needs to be kept contemporary through judicial review.

45 Hiebert, *Charter Conflicts*, 35.

46 Charles R. Epp, *The Rights Revolution: Lawyers, Activists, and Supreme Courts in Comparative Perspectives* (Chicago: University of Chicago Press, 1998), 56.

47 Ibid., 156. Because Britain has departed from the American model with the limited development of rights advocacy organizations, a generally small and hierarchical legal profession divided between barristers and solicitors, and the dominance of legal education by the firm, Epp concludes that Britain has had simply a "modest" rights revolution. Though Epp contends that India is an ideal environment, he concludes that a very weak rights revolution has resulted because of the limited development of rights advocacy organizations, the small number of large legal firms, and the limited financial resources available to fund progressive cause lawyering.

48 Rodney Brazier, "New Labour, New Constitution?" *Northern Ireland Legal Quarterly* 49 (1998): 2-5.

49 UK Joint Committee on Human Rights, "Memorandum by the Lord Chancellor's Department – Human Rights Policy Implementation," December 2001, http://www.publications. parliament.uk/pa/jt200102/jtselect/jtrights/103/103m02.htm.

50 Stephen Gardbaum, "The New Commonwealth Model of Constitutionalism," *American Journal of Comparative Law* 49 (2001): 707-60.

51 James B. Kelly, "The Supreme Court of Canada's Charter of Rights Decisions, 1982-1999: A Statistical Analysis," in F.L. Morton, ed., *Law, Politics and the Judicial Process in Canada*, 3rd ed. (Calgary: University of Calgary Press, 2002). This study has been updated to include the 2000-2 data.

52 Peter W. Hogg and Allison A. Bushell, "The *Charter* Dialogue between Courts and Legislatures," *Osgoode Hall Law Journal* 35 (1997): 80-81.

53 Manfredi and Kelly, "Six Degrees of Dialogue," 520-21.
54 I thank Rainer Knopff for the term "total limitation."
55 *Ford v. Quebec*, [1988] 2 S.C.R. 712; *Rocket v. Royal College of Dental Surgeons*, [1990] 2 S.C.R. 232; *R. v. Heywood*, [1990] 3 S.C.R. 761; *Osborne v. Canada*, [1991] 2 S.C.R. 69 [*Treasury Board*].
56 Brian Slattery, "A Theory of the Charter," *Osgoode Hall Law Journal* 25 (1987): 701-47.
57 Ibid., 706.
58 Christopher P. Manfredi, *Feminist Activism in the Supreme Court* (Vancouver: UBC Press, 2004); F.L. Morton and Avril Allen, "Feminists and the Courts: Measuring Success in Interest Group Litigation in Canada," *Canadian Journal of Political Science* 34 (2001): 55-84; Ian Brodie, *Friends of the Court: The Privileging of Interest Group Litigants in Canada* (Albany, NY: SUNY Press, 2002), 49-74.
59 Grant Huscroft, "The Attorney General and Charter Challenges to Legislation: Advocate or Adjudicator?" *National Journal of Constitutional Law* 5 (1995): 135-38; Kent Roach, "The Attorney General and the Charter Revisited," *University of Toronto Law Journal* 50 (2000): 21-22.
60 Ian Scott, "Law, Policy, and the Role of the Attorney General: Constancy and Change in the 1980s," *University of Toronto Law Review* 39 (1989): 113.
61 Ibid., 125.
62 Janet L. Hiebert, "Legislative Scrutiny: An Alternative Approach for Protecting Rights," in Joseph F. Fletcher, ed., *Ideas in Action: Essays on Politics and Law in Honour of Peter Russell* (Toronto: University of Toronto Press, 1999), 305-8.
63 Peter H. Russell, "The Effect of a Charter of Rights on the Policy-Making Role of Canadian Courts," *Canadian Public Administration* 25 (1982): 32.
64 Savoie, *Governing from the Centre*.

Chapter 1: Democracy and Judicial Review

1 Joseph F. Fletcher and Paul Howe, "Canadian Attitudes towards the Charter and the Courts in Comparative Perspective," *Choices* 6 (2000): 9.
2 Lorraine Eisenstat Weinrib, "Canada's Constitutional Revolution: From Legislative to Constitutional State," *Israel Law Review* 33 (1999): 37.
3 F.L. Morton and Rainer Knopff, *The Charter Revolution and the Court Party* (Peterborough, ON: Broadview Press, 2000), 33.
4 Kent Roach, *The Supreme Court on Trial* (Toronto: Irwin Law, 2001), 155-56.
5 Weinrib, "Canada's Constitutional Revolution," 23.
6 Michael Mandel, *The Charter of Rights and the Legalization of Politics in Canada* (Toronto: Thompson Educational Publishing, 1994), 455.
7 Judy Fudge, "The Canadian Charter of Rights: Recognition, Redistribution, and the Imperialism of the Courts," in Tom Campbell, K.D. Ewing, and Adam Tomkins, eds., *Sceptical Essays on Human Rights* (Oxford: Oxford University Press, 2001), 339-40.
8 Christopher P. Manfredi, *Judicial Power and the Charter*, 2nd ed. (Don Mills, ON: Oxford University Press, 2001), 88-194.
9 Morton and Knopff, *The Charter Revolution and the Court Party*.
10 Manfredi, *Judicial Power and the Charter*, 2nd ed., 31-38.
11 The term "judicial democrats" comes from Gregory Hein, "Interest Group Litigation in Canada, 1988-1998," *Choices* 6 (March 2000): 19-20.
12 Alan C. Cairns, "The Judicial Committee and Its Critics," *Canadian Journal of Political Science* 3 (1971): 319-20.
13 Miriam Smith, "Ghosts of the Judicial Committee of the Privy Council: Group Politics and Charter Litigation in Canadian Political Science," *Canadian Journal of Political Science* 35 (2002): 4-7. For a reply to Smith, see Rainer Knopff and F.L. Morton, "Ghosts and Straw Men: A Comment on Miriam Smith's 'Ghosts of the Judicial Committee of the Privy Council'," *Canadian Journal of Political Science* 35 (2002): 31-42; Miriam Smith, "Partisanship As Political Science: A Reply to Rainer Knopff and F.L. Morton," *Canadian Journal of Political Science* 35 (2002): 43-48.

14 The work of Robert H. Bork clearly illustrates this point, particularly his analysis of the Canadian case study, which draws heavily on the work of Rainer Knopff, F.L. Morton, and Christopher Manfredi. See Robert H. Bork, *Coercing Virtue* (Toronto: Random House Canada, 2002), 67-105.

15 Allan Hutchinson, *Waiting for Coraf* (Toronto: University of Toronto Press, 1996), 7-12.

16 Allan Hutchinson and Andrew Petter, "Private Rights/Public Wrongs: The Liberal Lie of the Charter," *University of Toronto Law Journal* 23 (1988): 295-96.

17 Torbjörn Vallinder, "The Judicialization of Politics – A Worldwide Phenomenon: Introduction," *International Political Science Review* 15 (1994): 93-94.

18 Lorraine Eisenstat Weinrib, "The Supreme Court of Canada in the Age of Rights: Constitutional Democracy, the Rule of Law and Fundamental Rights under Canada's Constitution," *Canadian Bar Review* 80 (2001): 704.

19 Lorraine Eisenstat Weinrib, "The Supreme Court of Canada and Section One of the Charter," *Supreme Court Law Review* 10 (1988): 495.

20 Lorraine Eisenstat Weinrib, "Learning to Live with the Override," *McGill Law Journal* 35 (1990): 566.

21 Kent Roach, *Due Process and Victims' Rights* (Toronto: University of Toronto Press, 1999), 166; Christopher P. Manfredi and Scott Lemieux, "Judicial Discretion and Fundamental Justice: Sexual Assault Jurisprudence in the Supreme Court of Canada," *American Journal of Comparative Law* 47 (1999): 493-97.

22 Martha Jackman, "Protecting Rights and Promoting Democracy: Judicial Review under Section 1 of the *Charter*," *Osgoode Hall Law Journal* 34 (1996): 663.

23 Guy Davidov, "The Paradox of Judicial Deference," *National Journal of Constitutional Law* 12 (2001): 135.

24 Janet L. Hiebert, "Why Must a Bill of Rights Be a Contest of Political and Judicial Wills? The Canadian Alternative," *Public Law Review* 10 (1999): 24.

25 Patrick J. Monahan and Marie Finkelstein, "The Charter of Rights and Public Policy in Canada," *Osgoode Hall Law Journal* 30 (1992): 502-44.

26 James B. Kelly, "Bureaucratic Activism and the Charter of Rights and Freedoms: The Department of Justice and Its Entry into the Centre of Government," *Canadian Public Administration* 42 (1999): 476-511.

27 Peter W. Hogg and Allison A. Bushell, "The *Charter* Dialogue between Courts and Legislatures," *Osgoode Hall Law Journal* (1997): 75-124.

28 Ibid., 79.

29 Ibid., 79-80.

30 Ibid., 81.

31 Roach, *The Supreme Court on Trial*, 12.

32 Ibid., 176.

33 Ibid., 226.

34 Hogg and Bushell, "The *Charter* Dialogue between Courts and Legislatures," 82.

35 Kent Roach, "Remedial Consensus and Dialogue under the *Charter:* General Declarations and Delayed Declarations of Invalidity," *UBC Law Review* 35 (2002): 218-21.

36 Hogg and Bushell, "The *Charter* Dialogue between Courts and Legislatures," 79.

37 Christopher P. Manfredi and James B. Kelly, "Dialogue, Deference and Restraint: Judicial Independence and Trial Procedures," *Saskatchewan Law Review* 64 (2001): 326-28.

38 John C. Tait, "Policy Development and the Charter," *Perspectives on Public Policy* 7 (1995): 11-12.

39 Monahan and Finkelstein, "The Charter of Rights and Public Policy in Canada," 501-44; Julie Jai, "Policy, Politics and Law: Changing Relationships in Light of the Charter," *National Journal of Constitutional Law* 9 (1996): 1-25; Bernard W. Funston, "The Impact of the Charter of Rights and Freedoms on Policy Development in the Northwest Territories," *Osgoode Hall Law Journal* 30 (1992): 605-11; Mary Dawson, "The Impact of the Charter on the Public Policy Process and the Department of Justice," *Osgoode Hall Law Journal* 30 (1992): 595-603.

40 The committee proceedings of the Standing Senate Committee on Legal and Constitutional Affairs can be found at the following website: http://www.parl.gc.ca/common/committee.asp?Language=E (under "Committee List" then "Legal and Constitutional Affairs" link).

41 *Egan v. Canada*, [1995] 2 S.C.R. 513 [*Egan*]; *M. v. H.*, [1999] 2 S.C.R. 3.
42 *R. v. Mills*, [1999] 3 S.C.R. 668; *R. v. Darrach*, [2000] 2 S.C.R. 443; *Eldridge v. British Columbia*, [1997] 3 S.C.R. 624.
43 Andrew Petter, "The Politics of the Charter," *Supreme Court Law Review* 8 (1986): 474-76, 480, 483, 505; Hutchinson and Petter, "Private Rights/Public Wrongs," 278-80, 283-85, 294-97; Allan Hutchinson, "Mice under a Chair: Democracy, the Courts and the Administrative State," *University of Toronto Law Journal* 40 (1990): 375-76, 385-89; and David Beatty, "The Canadian Conception of Equality," *University of Toronto Law Journal* 46 (1996): 348-51, 371-72. The other main stream in the left-wing perspective is the Judicial Social Engineering position advanced by David Beatty.
44 Petter, "The Politics of the Charter," 473-505; Hutchinson, *Waiting for Coraf*, 37; Joel Bakan, *Just Words* (Toronto: University of Toronto Press, 1997), 9-10.
45 Mandel, *The Charter of Rights and the Legalization of Politics*, 38-40.
46 Hutchinson and Petter, "Private Rights/Public Wrongs," 297; Hutchinson, *Waiting for Coraf*, 3-7, 66-75.
47 Hutchinson, *Waiting for Coraf*, 403.
48 Andrew Petter, "Immaculate Deception: The Charter's Hidden Agenda," *Advocate* 45 (1987): 857.
49 Fudge, "The Canadian Charter of Rights," 351.
50 Mandel, *The Charter of Rights and the Legalization of Politics*, 71.
51 Ibid., 311.
52 *Retail, Wholesale and Department Store Union v. Dolphin Delivery*, cited in Peter H. Russell, Rainer Knopff, and Ted Morton, eds., *Federalism and the Charter: Leading Constitutional Decisions* (Ottawa: Carleton University Press, 1990), 461.
53 *Dunmore v. Ontario (Attorney General)*, [2001] 3 S.C.R. 1016, cited at http://www.lexum.umontreal.ca/csc-scc/cgi-bin.disp.pl/en/rec/html/dunmore.en.html?query.
54 *UFCW, Local 1518 v. Kmart Canada Ltd.*, [1999] 2 S.C.R. 1083 at 1084-85.
55 *RWDSU, Local 558 v. Pepsi-Cola Canada Beverages (West) Ltd.*, [2002] 1 S.C.R. 156, cited at http://www.lexum.umontreal.ca/csc-scc/cgi-bin.disp.pl/en/rec/html/pepsi.en.html?query=%.
56 Manfredi, *Judicial Power and the Charter*, 2nd ed., 25.
57 The point must be stressed that Morton and Knopff are critical of Charter *politics*, not the Charter as a document. This clearly distinguishes the position of conservative judicial critics from the Critical Legal Studies position, which is critical of the Charter as a liberal document and the liberal state in general. F.L. Morton is clear on this point in "Judicial Politics Canadian Style: The Supreme Court's Contribution to the Constitutional Crisis of 1992," where he is critical of Alan Cairns' collapsing the Charter into the Supreme Court of Canada's interpretation of the Charter: "Cairns confuses the Supreme Court's interpretation of the Charter with the Charter itself and identifies the latter as the cause of the new constitutional expectations of Charter groups. This is a mistake." In Curtis Cook, ed., *Constitutional Predicament* (Montreal and Kingston: McGill-Queen's University Press, 1994), 138.
58 F.L. Morton, "The Politics of Rights and What Canadians Should Know about the American Bill of Rights," *Windsor Review of Legal and Social Issues* 1 (1990): 70; Morton, "Judicial Politics Canadian Style," 133-34; and Christopher P. Manfredi, *Judicial Power and the Charter* (Toronto: McClelland and Stewart, 1993), 213, 217.
59 Rainer Knopff and F.L. Morton, "Permanence and Change in a Written Constitution: The 'Living Tree' Doctrine and the Charter of Rights," *Supreme Court Law Review* 1 (1990): 533-34, 538-39; and Rainer Knopff and F.L. Morton, *Charter Politics* (Scarborough, ON: Nelson Canada, 1992), 108-14.
60 Morton, "The Politics of Rights," 77.
61 F.L. Morton, "The Charter Revolution and the Court Party," *Osgoode Hall Law Journal* 30 (1992): 627-28, 649-50; Manfredi, *Judicial Power and the Charter*, 11.
62 Christopher P. Manfredi, "Adjudication, Policy Making and the Supreme Court of Canada: Lessons from the Experience of the United States," *Canadian Journal of Political Science* 22 (1989): 314-15.
63 F.L. Morton cited in Stephen Bindman, "Debate over New 'Juristocracy,'" *Montreal Gazette*, 10 January 1998.

64 Robin Elliot, "The Charter Revolution and the Court Party': Sound Critical Analysis or Blinkered Political Polemic?" *UBC Law Review* 35 (2002): 323.

65 James B. Kelly, "The Supreme Court of Canada's *Charter of Rights* Decisions, 1982-1999: A Statistical Analysis," in F.L. Morton, ed., *Law, Politics and the Judicial Process in Canada*, 3rd ed. (Calgary: University of Calgary Press, 2002), 503-4. I have updated the data in the Morton publication to include 2000 and 2002.

66 Roach, *Due Process and Victims' Rights*, 13-14. The crime control model places primary emphasis on the investigative techniques of the police and is directed to securing guilty pleas before a case goes to court. Factual guilt is given great weight in this model, and the role of the criminal justice system is to prevent crime. Due process, on the other hand, prioritizes the rights of the accused and administrative fairness. Guilt is established in the courtroom in an adversarial process that requires the state to prove its case. In other words, the crime control model is viewed as favouring the victims of crime, whereas due process is suggested to favour the accused.

67 *Egan*, 513-14.

68 *Egan*, 514.

69 *Adler v. Ontario*, [1996] 3 S.C.R. 609.

70 *Vriend v. Alberta*, [1998] 1 S.C.R. 493. Available at http://www.lexum.umontreal.ca/csc-scc/en/pub/1998/vol1/html/1998scr1_0493.html.

71 Roach, *The Supreme Court on Trial*, 97.

72 Patrick J. Monahan, "The Charter: Then and Now," in P. Bryden, S. Davis, and J. Russell, eds., *Protecting Rights and Freedoms* (Toronto: University of Toronto Press, 1994), 117-18; and Peter H. Russell, "Canadian Constraints on Judicialization from Without," *International Political Science Association* 15 (1994): 168-69, 170-71.

73 Peter H. Russell, "The Political Purposes of the Canadian Charter of Rights and Freedoms," *Canadian Bar Review* 61 (1983): 44-45.

74 Morton and Knopff, *The Charter Revolution and the Court Party*, 58.

75 Elliot, "The Charter Revolution and the Court Party,'" 272-74.

76 James B. Kelly, "The Supreme Court of Canada and the Complexity of Judicial Activism," in Patrick James, Donald E. Abelson, and Michael Lusztig, eds., *The Myth of the Sacred: The Charter, the Courts and the Constitution in Canada* (Montreal and Kingston: McGill-Queen's University Press, 2002), 113-14.

77 Gerald N. Rosenberg, *The Hollow Hope* (Chicago: University of Chicago Press, 1991), 28-30.

78 See Janet L. Hiebert, *Charter Conflicts* (Montreal and Kingston: McGill-Queen's University Press, 2002).

79 Ibid., 50-51.

80 Mary Dawson, "Governing in a Rights Culture," *Supreme Court Law Review*, 2nd ser., 14 (2001): 269.

81 Donald J. Savoie, *Governing from the Centre* (Toronto: University of Toronto Press, 1999), 72-108; Peter H. Russell, "A Democratic Approach to Civil Liberties," *University of Toronto Law Journal* 19 (1969): 128.

82 Elmer A. Driedger, "The Meaning and Effect of the Canadian Bill of Rights: A Draftman's Viewpoint," *Ottawa Law Review* 9 (1977): 306.

83 J.L.I.J. Edwards, "The Attorney General and the Charter of Rights," in Robert J. Sharpe, ed., *Charter Litigation* (Toronto: Butterworths, 1987), 47.

84 Grant Huscroft, "The Attorney General and *Charter* Challenges to Legislation: Advocate or Adjudicator?" *National Journal of Constitutional Law* 5 (1995): 135-36.

85 Author interviews with Senator Serge Joyal, Standing Senate Committee on Legal and Constitutional Affairs, 37th Parliament, 22 October 2002, Ottawa, ON; Senator Gérald Beaudoin, Standing Senate Committee on Legal and Constitutional Affairs, 37th Parliament, 22 October 2002, Ottawa, ON; Senator Arnell Andreychuk, Standing Senate Committee on Legal and Constitutional Affairs, 37th Parliament, 23 October 2002, Ottawa, ON.

86 Author interviews with Chuck Cadman, MP (Surrey North), Standing Committee on Justice and Human Rights, 37th Parliament, 23 October 2002, Ottawa, ON; Irwin Cotler, MP (Mont Royal), Standing Committee on Justice and Human Rights, 37th Parliament, 23 October 2002, Ottawa, ON.

87 Russell, "A Democratic Approach to Civil Liberties," 126. Janet Hiebert has renewed calls for the establishment of a Charter committee, as has James Kelly. See Janet L. Hiebert, "Wrestling with Rights: Judges, Parliament and the Making of Social Policy," in Paul Howe and Peter H. Russell, eds., *Judicial Power and Canadian Democracy* (Montreal and Kingston: McGill-Queen's University Press, 2001), 200-6; James B. Kelly, "Guarding the Constitution: Parliamentary and Judicial Roles under the Charter of Rights and Freedoms," in Harvey Lazar, Peter Meekison, and Hamish Telford, eds., *Canada: The State of the Federation, 2002* (Montreal and Kingston: McGill-Queen's University Press, 2004).

88 Author interviews with Joyal, Beaudoin, and Andreychuk.

89 Peter Aucoin, "Organizational Changes in the Machinery of Canadian Government: From Rational Management to Brokerage Politics," *Canadian Journal of Political Science* 19 (1986): 8-9; Ian D. Clark, "Recent Changes in the Cabinet Decision-Making System in Ottawa," *Canadian Public Administration* 28 (1985): 185-201.

90 Funston, "The Impact of the Charter of Rights and Freedoms," 609.

91 Dawson, "The Impact of the Charter on the Public Policy Process," 596-97.

92 Hon. Brian Dickson, "The Canadian Charter of Rights and Freedoms: Dawn of a New Era?" *Review of Constitutional Studies* 2 (1994): 11.

93 Savoie, *Governing from the Centre*, 3-8.

94 Kelly, "Bureaucratic Activism and the Charter of Rights and Freedoms," 486-90.

95 Brian Slattery, "A Theory of the Charter," *Osgoode Hall Law Journal* 25 (1987): 745.

Chapter 2: Constitutional Politics and the Charter

1 Anne F. Bayefsky, "Parliamentary Sovereignty and Human Rights in Canada: The Promise of the Canadian Charter of Rights and Freedoms," *Political Studies* 31 (1983): 239.

2 Berend Hovius and Robert Martin, "The Canadian Charter of Rights and Freedoms in the Supreme Court of Canada," *Canadian Bar Review* 61 (1983): 355-57.

3 *Canadian Bill of Rights*, 1960, c.44, preamble, cited in Walter Tarnopolsky, *The Canadian Bill of Rights*, 2nd ed. (Toronto: McClelland and Stewart, 1975), 353.

> The Parliament of Canada, affirming that the Canadian Nation is founded upon the principles that acknowledge the supremacy of God, the dignity and worth of human persons and the position of the family in a society of free men and free institutions;
> Affirming also that men and institutions remain free only when freedom is founded upon respect for moral and spiritual values and the rule of law;
> And being desirous of enshrining these principles and the human rights and fundamental freedoms derived from them, in a Bill of Rights which shall reflect the respect of Parliament for its constitutional authority and which shall ensure the protection of these rights and freedoms in Canada:
> THEREFORE Her Majesty, by and with the advice and consent of the Senate and House of Commons of Canada, enacts as follows.

4 F.L. Morton, Peter H. Russell, and Troy Q. Riddell, "The *Canadian Charter of Rights and Freedoms*: A Descriptive Analysis of the First Decade, 1982-1992," *National Journal of Constitutional Law* 5 (1994): 5.

5 The section states: "The Constitution of Canada is the supreme law of Canada, and any law that is inconsistent with the provisions of the Constitution is, to the extent of the inconsistency, of no force or effect." Cited in Patrick J. Monahan, *Constitutional Law*, 2nd ed. (Toronto: Irwin Law, 2002), 551-52.

6 Peter H. Russell, *Constitutional Odyssey*, 2nd ed. (Toronto: University of Toronto Press, 1993), 107, 111.

7 An important exception is Roy Romanow, John Whyte, and Howard Leeson, *Canada ... Notwithstanding: The Making of the Constitution 1976-1982* (Toronto: Carswell, 1984), 216-62. Janet Hiebert has presented a specific analysis of the reasonable limits clause. Please see Janet L. Hiebert, *Limiting Rights* (Montreal and Kingston: McGill-Queen's University Press, 1996), 10-31.

8 Hereafter referred to as simply the Special Joint Committee.
9 Edward McWhinney, "Dilemmas of Judicial Law-Making on the Canadian Charter of Rights," in Pierre Thibault, Benoit Pelletier, and Louis Perret, eds., *Essays in Honour of Gérald-A. Beaudoin: The Challenges of Constitutionalism* (Cowansville, QC: Éditions Yvon Blais, 2002), 315-17.
10 Lusztig refers to these differences as Mega Constitutional Orientations (MCOs). See Michael Lusztig, "Constitutional Paralysis: Why Canadian Constitutional Initiatives Are Doomed to Fail," *Canadian Journal of Political Science* 37 (1994): 747-71.
11 Lorraine Eisenstat Weinrib, "The Activist Constitution," in Paul Howe and Peter H. Russell, eds., *Judicial Power and Canadian Democracy* (Montreal and Kingston: McGill-Queen's University Press, 2001), 82-84.
12 Peter H. Russell, "Bold Statescraft, Questionable Jurisprudence," in Keith Banting and Richard Simeon, eds., *And No One Cheered* (Toronto: Methuen, 1983), 210.
13 Guy Laforest, *Trudeau and the End of a Canadian Dream* (Montreal and Kingston: McGill-Queen's University Press, 1995), 31-32.
14 Alan C. Cairns, *Disruptions: Constitutional Struggles, from the Charter to Meech Lake* (Toronto: McClelland and Stewart, 1991), 59-60.
15 Author interview with Roger Tassé, deputy minister of justice (1978-85), 2 October 1997, Ottawa, ON.
16 Donald Smiley, "A Dangerous Deed: The Constitution Act, 1982," in Keith Banting and Richard Simeon, eds., *And No One Cheered* (Toronto: Methuen, 1983), 76. Canada lacked a domestic amending formula until 1982, and all previous amendments to the *BNA Act* first required a resolution passed by the Parliament of Canada instructing the British parliament to make the requested changes. Based on constitutional practice, changes affecting federalism or the division of powers were only requested by the Parliament of Canada if unanimous provincial consent had first been secured. This constitutional convention was a significant part of the Supreme Court of Canada's decision in the *Patriation Reference* of 1981.
17 Patriation meant breaking the colonial relationship with the United Kingdom as it related to the constitution of Canada. In effect, the colonial constitution – the *British North America Act, 1867* – would be returned to Canada as the domestic constitution – the *Constitution Act, 1982*.
18 Author interview with Tassé.
19 *Attorney General Manitoba et al. v. Attorney General Canada et al.*, [1981] 1 S.C.R. 753 [*Patriation Reference*].
20 Continuing Committee of Ministers on the Constitution, Montreal, QC, 8-11 July 1980. *Statement by the Honourable Jean Chrétien.* Document 830-81/025 at 2.
21 *Background Notes, Charter of Rights and Freedoms.* Tabled by the delegation of the Government of Canada, 5 July 1980. Document 830-81/029 at 3.
22 Christopher P. Manfredi, *Judicial Power and the Charter*, 2nd ed. (Don Mills, ON: Oxford University Press, 2001), 34-35; F.L. Morton and Rainer Knopff, *The Charter Revolution and the Court Party* (Peterborough, ON: Broadview Press, 2000), 21-22.
23 Author interview with Tassé.
24 Ibid.
25 Continuing Committee of Ministers on the Constitution, Montreal, QC, 8-11 July 1980. *Rights and Freedoms within the Canadian Federation, Discussion Draft.* Tabled by the delegation of the Government of Canada, 4 July 1980. Document 830-81/027.
26 Ibid.
27 Ibid. The full text of the limitations clause for legal rights appeared as follows:

> 6(3) In times of serious public emergency threatening the life of the country, the existence of which is officially proclaimed by or pursuant to a law enacted to deal with such circumstances or by a law specifically referring to this subsection, the rights mentioned in this section other than the right to life and those mentioned in subparagraphs (1)(d)(i) and (ii) and (1)(e)(i)-(iii) and (v) and paragraphs (1)(f)(g)(h)(i) and (j) may be derogated from to the extent strictly required by the circumstances of the emergency.

28 Romanow, Whyte, and Leeson, *Canada ... Notwithstanding*, 242-43.
29 Continuing Committee of Ministers on the Constitution, Vancouver, BC, 22-24 July 1980. *Report by the Sub-Committee of Officials on a Charter of Rights, 24 July 1980*. Document 830-83/019. The phrase "due process" had been given a substantive interpretation by the United States Supreme Court, where the application and the effect of the act under review would be evaluated for its constitutionality. As a result, the phrase "principles of fundamental justice" was adopted to avoid a substantive interpretation and to ensure a narrow approach to legal rights under the Canadian Charter.
30 Continuing Committee of Ministers on the Constitution, Montreal, QC, 8-11 July 1980. *Rights and Freedoms within the Canadian Federation, Discussion Draft*. Tabled by the delegation of the Government of Canada, 4 July 1980. Document 830-81/027.
31 Ibid.
32 Ibid.
33 Ibid.
34 Ibid.
35 Ibid.
36 McWhinney, "Dilemmas of Judicial Law-Making," 311.
37 Continuing Committee of Ministers on the Constitution, Montreal, QC, 8-11 July 1980. *Rights and Freedoms within the Canadian Federation, Discussion Draft*. Tabled by the delegation of the Government of Canada, 4 July 1980. Document 830-81/027.
38 *Background Notes, Entrenching a Charter of Rights*. Tabled by the delegation of the Government of Canada. Document 830-81/026 at 2.
39 Ibid. at 3.
40 Troy Q. Riddell and F.L. Morton, "Reasonable Limitations, Distinct Society and the Canada Clause: Interpretive Clauses and the Competition for Constitutional Advantage," *Canadian Journal of Political Science* 31 (1998): 470-73; Rainer Knopff and F.L. Morton, "Nation Building and the Canadian Charter of Rights and Freedoms," in Alan C. Cairns and Cynthia Williams, eds., *Constitutionalism, Citizenship and Society in Canada* (Toronto: University of Toronto Press, 1985), 133-82.
41 Continuing Committee of Ministers on the Constitution, Vancouver, BC, 22-24 July 1980. *Report by the Sub-Committee of Officials on a Charter of Rights, 24 July 1980*. Document 830-83/019.
42 Ibid.
43 Ibid.
44 Continuing Committee of Ministers on the Constitution, Ottawa, ON, 26-29 August 1980. *The Canadian Charter of Rights and Freedoms, Federal Draft, 22 August 1980*. Document 830-84/004.
45 Bayefsky, "Parliamentary Sovereignty and Human Rights in Canada," 255; Hiebert, *Limiting Rights*, 21-26.
46 Alexander Alvaro, "Why Property Rights Were Excluded from the Canadian Charter of Rights and Freedoms," *Canadian Journal of Political Science* 24 (1991): 320-21. Alvaro argues that the NDP premiers were concerned that property rights would affect the ability of governments to promote public sector enterprises.
47 Continuing Committee of Ministers on the Constitution, Montreal, QC, 8-11 July 1980. *Rights and Freedoms within the Canadian Federation, Discussion Draft*. Tabled by the delegation of the Government of Canada, 4 July 1980. Document 830-81/027.
48 Continuing Committee of Ministers on the Constitution, Ottawa, ON, 26-29 August 1980. *The Canadian Charter of Rights and Freedoms, Federal Draft, 22 August 1980*. Document 830-84/004.
49 Ibid.
50 Continuing Committee of Ministers on the Constitution, Montreal, QC, 8-11 July 1980. *Rights and Freedoms within the Canadian Federation, Discussion Draft*. Tabled by the delegation of the Government of Canada, 4 July 1980. Document 830-81/027.
51 Christopher Dunn, *The Institutionalized Cabinet* (Montreal and Kingston: McGill-Queen's University Press, 1995).

52 Lorraine Eisenstat Weinrib, "The Supreme Court of Canada in the Age of Rights: Constitutional Democracy, the Rule of Law and Fundamental Rights under Canada's Constitution," *Canadian Bar Review* 80 (2001): 721.
53 *The Canadian Charter of Rights and Freedoms, Provincial Proposal (In the Event that There Is Going to Be Entrenchment), 28 August 1980.* Annex to Document 830-84/031.
54 Romanow, Whyte, and Leeson, *Canada ... Notwithstanding*, 244.
55 Continuing Committee of Ministers on the Constitution, Vancouver, BC, 22-24 July 1980. *Report by the Sub-Committee of Officials on a Charter of Rights, 24 July 1980.* Document 830-83/019.
56 Charter of Rights, *Report to Ministers by Sub-Committee of Officials, 29 August 1980.* Tabular Comparison of Charter of Rights Drafts. Document 830-84/031.
57 Ibid.
58 Ibid.
59 *The Canadian Charter of Rights and Freedoms, Provincial Proposal (In the Event that There Is Going to Be Entrenchment), 28 August 1980.* Annex to Document 830-84/031.
60 Federal-Provincial First Ministers' Conference, Ottawa, ON, 8-12 September 1980. *The Canadian Charter of Rights and Freedoms, Revised Discussion Draft, Federal, 3 September 1980.* Document 800-14/064.
61 Continuing Committee of Ministers on the Constitution, Vancouver, BC, 22-24 July 1980. *Report by the Sub-Committee of Officials on a Charter of Rights, 24 July 1980.* Document 830-83/019.
62 Ibid.
63 Honourable Sterling Lyon, *Federal-Provincial Conference of First Ministers on the Constitution,* Ottawa, ON, 8-12 September 1980. *Verbatim Transcript,* 478. Document 800-15/012.
64 Richard Sigurdson, "Left- and Right-Wing Charterphobia in Canada: A Critique of the Critics," *International Journal of Canadian Studies* 7 (1993): 101-2.
65 Honourable Allan Blakeney, *Federal-Provincial Conference of First Ministers on the Constitution,* Ottawa, ON, 8-12 September 1980. *Verbatim Transcript,* 487-88. Document 800-15/005.
66 Honourable Peter Lougheed, *Federal-Provincial Conference of First Ministers on the Constitution,* Ottawa, ON, 8-12 September 1980. *Verbatim Transcript,* 497. Document 800-15/009.
67 *Federal-Provincial Conference of First Ministers on the Constitution,* Ottawa, ON, 8-12 September 1980. *Verbatim Transcript,* 583-96. Only the premier of Manitoba completely rejected entrenching rights in the constitution.
68 Prime Minister's Remarks at Close of Discussion on the Charter of Rights, 10 September 1980. Document 800-14/078 at 5.
69 Pierre Elliott Trudeau, cited in Ron Graham, ed., *The Essential Trudeau* (Toronto: McClelland and Stewart, 1998), 153.
70 Ibid., 153-54.
71 Russell, *Constitutional Odyssey,* 111.
72 Continuing Committee of Ministers on the Constitution, Ottawa, ON, 26-29 August 1980. *Charter of Rights, Report to Ministers by Sub-Committee of Officials, 29 August 1980.* Document 830-84/031; *The Canadian Charter of Rights and Freedoms, Provincial Proposal (In the Event that There Is Going to Be Entrenchment), 28 August 1980.* Annex to Document 830-84/031.
73 *Proposed Resolution for Joint Address to Her Majesty the Queen, Respecting the Constitution of Canada.* Tabled in the House of Commons and the Senate, 6 October 1980. Catalogue no. YC3-321/5-57.
74 Ibid.
75 Ibid.
76 Federal-Provincial First Ministers' Conference, Ottawa, ON, 8-12 September 1980. *The Canadian Charter of Rights and Freedoms, Revised Discussion Draft, Federal, 3 September 1980.* Document 800-14/064.
77 *Proposed Resolution for Joint Address to Her Majesty the Queen, Respecting the Constitution of Canada.* Tabled in the House of Commons and the Senate, 6 October 1980. Catalogue no. YC3-321/5-57.

78 Federal-Provincial First Ministers' Conference, Ottawa, ON, 8-12 September 1980. *The Canadian Charter of Rights and Freedoms, Revised Discussion Draft, Federal, 3 September 1980.* Document 800-14/064.

79 Roger Tassé, "Intention of the Framers: A Political Analysis," paper presented at the Fourth Annual Conference on Human Rights and the Charter, 16-17 November 1992, 7.

80 Walter Tarnopolsky, "The Charter and the Supreme Court of Canada," in G. Beaudoin, ed., *The Charter: Ten Years Later* (Cowansville, QC: Les Éditions Yvon Blais, 1992), 63; Weinrib, "The Supreme Court of Canada in the Age of Rights," 721-22.

81 Janet L. Hiebert, "The Evolution of the Limitation Clause," *Osgoode Hall Law Journal* 28 (1990): 126-27.

82 Author interview with Tassé; Romanow, Whyte, and Leeson, *Canada ... Notwithstanding,* 112-13.

83 Author interview with Tassé.

84 Ibid.

85 Ibid.; Tassé, "Intention of the Framers," 8.

86 The Special Joint Committee of the Senate and the House of Commons on the Constitution of Canada, 1980-81. Report to Parliament and Proposed Resolution for a Joint Address to Her Majesty the Queen Respecting the Constitution of Canada, As Amended by the Committee, 13 February 1981. Cited in Anne F. Bayefsky, *Canada's Constitution Act 1982 and Amendments – A Documentary History* (Toronto: McGraw-Hill Ryerson, 1989), 786.

87 Ibid.

88 A special joint committee of the Senate and the House of Commons, referred to as the Molgat-MacGuigan Committee, was the first to incorporate public participation in the process of constitutional reform. It released its report in 1972 after the failure of the *Victoria Charter.*

89 The Special Joint Committee of the Senate and the House of Commons on the Constitution of Canada, 1980-81. Report to Parliament and Proposed Resolution for a Joint Address to Her Majesty the Queen Respecting the Constitution of Canada, As Amended by the Committee, 13 February 1981. Cited in Bayefsky, *Canada's Constitution Act 1982 and Amendments,* 785-86.

90 Russell, *Constitutional Odyssey,* 228.

91 Tassé, "Intention of the Framers," 8.

92 James McGrath, Special Joint Committee of the Senate and House of Commons on the Constitution of Canada Hearings, 12 November 1980, 3:15.

93 Svend Robinson, MP, SJC Hearings, 12 November 1980, 3:27.

94 Honourable Jean Chrétien, minister of justice, SJC Hearings, 12 November 1980, 3:27.

95 Ibid., 3:78.

96 Morton and Knopff, *The Charter Revolution and the Court Party,* 25.

97 Tassé, "Intention of the Framers," 10.

98 Honourable Justice Clyne, counsel, Canada West Foundation, SJC Hearings, 25 November 1980, 12:100.

99 Peter H. Russell, SJC Hearings, 8 January 1981, 34:148.

100 Ibid., 34:149.

101 Russell, *Constitutional Odyssey,* 114.

102 Riddell and Morton, "Reasonable Limitations, Distinct Society and the Canada Clause," 470-73; Hiebert, "The Evolution of the Limitation Clause," 122-24.

103 Gordon Fairweather, chief commissioner, Canadian Human Rights Commission, SJC Hearings, 14 November 1980, 5:8.

104 Ibid.

105 Lynn McDonald, NACSW, SJC Hearings, 20 November 1980, 9:58.

106 Walter Tarnopolsky, president, Canadian Civil Liberties Association, SJC Hearings, 18 November 1980, 7:9.

107 Ibid.

108 The Canadian Bar Association, 28 November 1980; Canadian Federation of Civil Liberties and Human Rights Associations, 8 December 1980; Coalition for the Protection of Human

Life, 9 December 1980; British Columbia Civil Liberties Association, 9 December 1980; Canadian Association for the Prevention of Crime, 11 December 1980.

109 Fairweather, SJC Hearings, 14 November 1980, 5A:3.

110 Tarnopolsky, SJC Hearings, 18 November 1980, 7:10.

111 Max Cohen, chairman, Select Committee on the Constitution of Canada of the Canadian Jewish Congress, SJC Hearings, 18 November 1980, 7:102.

112 Chief John Ackroyd, Canadian Association of Chiefs of Police, SJC Hearings, 27 November 1980, 14:8.

113 Ibid.

114 Fairweather, SJC Hearings, 14 November 1980, 5:9.

115 Alan Borovoy, general counsel, Canadian Civil Liberties Association, SJC Hearings, 18 November 1980, 7:12.

116 Ibid.; Fairweather, SJC Hearings, 14 November 1980, 5A:3-4; J.P. Nelligan, chairman, Special Committee on the Constitution of Canada, Canadian Bar Association, SJC Hearings, 28 November 1980, 15:8; Cohen, SJC Hearings, 18 November 1980, 7:89; David Sussman, Canadian Association for the Prevention of Crime, SJC Hearings, 11 December 1980, 24:43; Peter Maloney, member of the executive committee, Canadian Association of Lesbians and Gay Men, SJC Hearings, 11 December 1980, 24:23.

117 Borovoy, SJC Hearings, 18 November 1980, 7:13.

118 Peter H. Russell, "The Effect of a Charter of Rights on the Policy-Making Role of Canadian Courts," *Canadian Public Administration* 25 (Spring 1982): 22.

119 Fairweather, SJC Hearings, 14 November 1980, 5:10.

120 Ackroyd, SJC Hearings, 27 November 1980, 14:8.

121 *Hogan v. the Queen,* [1975] 2 S.C.R. 574.

122 Tarnopolsky, SJC Hearings, 18 November 1980, 7:11.

123 Ibid., 7:15.

124 Ibid., 7:27.

125 *R. v. Collins,* [1987] 1 S.C.R. 265.

126 *Bliss v. A.G. Canada,* [1979] 1 S.C.R. 183; *Lavell v. A.G. Canada,* [1974] S.C.R. 1349.

127 This recommendation was made by the Canadian Human Rights Commission, Canadian Jewish Congress, Canadian Bar Association, Saskatchewan Human Rights Commission, British Columbia Civil Liberties Association, Coalition for the Protection of Human Life, and the Canadian Association of Lesbians and Gay Men.

128 Fairweather, SJC Hearings, 14 November 1980, 5:16.

129 Doris Anderson, Canadian Advisory Council on the Status of Women, SJC Hearings, 20 November 1980, 9:124.

130 Ibid.

131 Mary Eberts, legal counsel, CACSW, SJC Hearings, 20 November 1980, 9:138.

132 Wayne Norman, chief commissioner, Saskatchewan Human Rights Commission, SJC Hearings, 5 December 1980, 20:17.

133 Romanow, Whyte, and Leeson, *Canada ... Notwithstanding,* 248.

134 Author interview with Senator Serge Joyal, 22 October 2002, Ottawa, ON.

135 Ron Irwin, MP, SJC Hearings, 8 January 1981, 34:152.

136 Russell, *Constitutional Odyssey,* 118.

137 The dates and names for the subsequent drafts of the Charter are as follows: (1) Consolidation of Proposed Resolution and Possible Amendments As Placed before the Special Joint Committee by the Minister of Justice (12 January 1981); (2) Proposed Resolution for a Joint Address to Her Majesty the Queen Respecting the Constitution of Canada, As Amended by the Committee (17 February 1981); (3) Consolidation of Proposed Constitutional Resolution Tabled by the Minister of Justice in the House of Commons on 13 February 1981, with the Amendments Approved by the House of Commons on 23 April 1981 and by the Senate on 24 April 1981 (24 April 1981); (4) Federal-Provincial First Ministers' Conference, Ottawa, ON, 2-5 November 1981. First Ministers' Agreement on the Constitution (5 November 1981); (5) Text of the Resolution Respecting the Constitution of Canada Adopted by the House of Commons on 2 December 1981 and by the Senate on 8 December 1981.

138 The Progressive Conservative Party proposed twenty-two amendments, with seven accepted, and the New Democratic Party proposed forty-three amendments, with two accepted. Special Joint Committee on the Constitution of Canada, Report to Parliament, 13 February 1981. Cited in Bayefsky, *Canada's Constitution Act 1982 and Amendments*, 785.

139 Minister of Justice and Attorney General of Canada. Statement by the Honourable Jean Chrétien, Minister of Justice, to the Special Joint Committee on the Constitution, 12 January 1981, 2.

140 Ibid., 3.

141 *Consolidation of Proposed Resolution and Possible Amendments As Placed before the Special Joint Committee by the Minister of Justice, 12 January 1981.* Together with Explanatory Notes at 3. Document on file with author.

142 Ibid.

143 Minister of Justice and Attorney General of Canada. Statement by the Honourable Jean Chrétien, Minister of Justice, to the Special Joint Committee on the Constitution, 12 January 1981, 3.

144 Ibid., 4.

145 Tassé, "Intention of the Framers," 10.

146 Minister of Justice and Attorney General of Canada. Statement by the Honourable Jean Chrétien, Minister of Justice, to the Special Joint Committee on the Constitution, 12 January 1981, 16.

147 Premiers' Conference, Ottawa, ON, 16 April 1981, Constitutional Accord: Canadian Patriation Plan, 16 April 1981, Document 850-19/002. Cited in Bayefsky, *Canada's Constitution Act 1982 and Amendments*, 805.

148 Tassé, "Intention of the Framers," 8-9.

149 Russell, *Constitutional Odyssey*, 118-19.

150 Russell, "Bold Statescraft, Questionable Jurisprudence," 210.

151 Federal-Provincial First Ministers' Conference, Ottawa, ON, 2-5 November 1981. First Ministers' Agreement on the Constitution, 5 November 1981. Document 800-15/021 at 1-2.

Chapter 3: Framers' Intent and the Parliamentary Arena

1 Pierre Elliott Trudeau, "The Values of a Just Society," in Thomas S. Axworthy and Pierre Elliott Trudeau, eds., *Towards a Just Society* (Toronto: Penguin Books, 1992), 412.

2 F.L. Morton and Rainer Knopff, *The Charter Revolution and the Court Party* (Peterborough, ON: Broadview Press, 2000), 13, 37-38; Christopher P. Manfredi, *Judicial Power and the Charter,* 2nd ed. (Don Mills, ON: Oxford University Press, 2001), 169.

3 Roger Tassé, "Intention of the Framers: A Political Analysis," paper presented at the Fourth Annual Conference on Human Rights and the Charter, 16-17 November 1992, 9.

4 Lorraine Eisenstat Weinrib, "Canada's *Charter of Rights:* Paradigm Lost," *Review of Constitutional Studies* 6 (2001): 123, 137.

5 Manfredi, *Judicial Power and the Charter,* 2nd ed., 108-13.

6 F.L. Morton, "Judicial Politics Canadian Style: The Supreme Court's Contribution to the Constitutional Crisis of 1992," in Curtis Cook, ed., *Constitutional Predicament* (Montreal and Kingston: McGill-Queen's University Press, 1994), 138.

7 Author interview with the Honourable Mr. Justice Barry Strayer, Federal Court of Canada, 22 August 2001, Ottawa, ON.

8 Patrick J. Monahan, *Constitutional Law,* 2nd ed. (Toronto: Irwin Law, 2002), 398.

9 James B. Kelly and Michael Murphy, "Confronting Judicial Supremacy: A Defence of Judicial Activism and the Supreme Court of Canada's Legal Rights Jurisprudence," *Canadian Journal of Law and Society* 16 (2001): 4-5.

10 Patrick J. Monahan, *Politics and the Constitution* (Toronto: Carswell, 1987), 77.

11 James B. Kelly, "The Supreme Court and the Complexity of Judicial Activism," in Patrick James, Donald E. Abelson, and Michael Lusztig, eds., *The Myth of the Sacred: The Charter, the Courts and the Constitution in Canada* (Montreal and Kingston: McGill-Queen's University Press, 2002), 121.

12 Kent Roach, *The Supreme Court on Trial* (Toronto: Irwin Law, 2001), 95.

13 Manfredi, *Judicial Power and the Charter,* 2nd ed., 25; Morton and Knopff, *The Charter Revolution and the Court Party,* 41.

14   This point is disputed in Berend Hovius and Robert Martin, "The Canadian Charter of Rights and Freedoms in the Supreme Court of Canada," *Canadian Bar Review* 61 (1983): 363.

15   Leslie A. Pal, *Interests of State* (Montreal and Kingston: McGill-Queen's University Press, 1993), 171-74.

16   Janet L. Hiebert, *Limiting Rights: The Dilemma at Judicial Review* (Montreal and Kingston: McGill-Queen's University Press, 1996), 12-13.

17   Alexander Hamilton, James Madison, and John Hay, Essay 78 in Clinton Rossiter, ed. *The Federalist Papers* (New York: New American Library, 1961), 469.

18   Author interview with the Right Honourable Pierre Elliott Trudeau, PC, QC, 5 September 1997, Montreal, QC.

19   Author interviews with former senior DOJ officials, 30 September and 2 October 1997, Ottawa, ON; Tassé, "Intentions of the Framers," 9-12. Tassé was deputy minister of justice and deputy attorney general of Canada from 1977 to 1985.

20   Lorraine Eisenstat Weinrib, "The Activist Constitution," *Policy Options* 20 (April 1999): 29-30.

21   Lorraine Eisenstat Weinrib, "Canada's Constitutional Revolution: From Legislative to Constitutional State," *Israel Law Review* 33 (1991): 45.

22   Weinrib, "Canada's *Charter of Rights*," 125.

23   *Canadian Bill of Rights,* 1960, c.44, s.1.

24   Manfredi provides an alternative analysis that accounts for judicial restraint under the Bill of Rights: "Although these structural features of the Bill of Rights (exclusive application to the federal government, recognition of 'existing' rights only, non-constitutional status) placed hurdles in the path of judicial review, they became insurmountable obstacles only because the Court as a whole viewed them as such." See Manfredi, *Judicial Power and the Charter,* 2nd ed., 16.

25   Charles R. Epp, *The Rights Revolution: Lawyers, Activists, and Supreme Courts in Comparative Perspectives* (Chicago: University of Chicago Press, 1998), 160.

26   James B. Kelly, "Bureaucratic Activism and the Charter of Rights and Freedoms: The Department of Justice and Its Entry into the Centre of Government," *Canadian Public Administration* 42 (1999): 490-91.

27   Pierre Elliott Trudeau, *Federalism and the French Canadians* (Toronto: Macmillan, 1968), 58.

28   F.L. Morton and Rainer Knopff, *The Charter Revelation and the Court Party* (Peterborough: Broadview Press, 2000); Manfredi, *Judicial Power and the Charter,* 2nd ed.

29   Morton and Knopff, *The Charter Revolution and the Court Party,* 34.

30   Ibid., 53.

31   Ibid., 23-24.

32   Ibid., 22. Manfredi also discusses the Charter revolution as the result of the Supreme Court of Canada succumbing to the "legal seduction of politics." See Manfredi, *Judicial Power and the Charter,* 2nd ed., 196.

33   Rainer Knopff and F.L. Morton, *Charter Politics* (Scarborough, ON: Nelson Canada, 1992), 111.

34   Morton and Knopff, *The Charter Revolution and the Court Party,* 40.

35   Ibid., 24.

36   Ibid., 59.

37   For a critique of the Court Party thesis, see Miriam Smith, *Lesbian and Gay Rights in Canada: Social Movements and Equality-Seeking, 1971-1995* (Toronto: University of Toronto Press, 1999), 16-21.

38   Manfredi, *Judicial Power and the Charter,* 2nd ed., 22.

39   *R. v. Big M Drug Mart Ltd.,* [1985] 1 S.C.R. 295.

40   Author interview with Trudeau.

41   Trudeau, *Federalism and the French Canadians,* 55-56.

42   Morton and Knopff, *The Charter Revolution and the Court Party,* 14.

43   Author interviews with former deputy minister of justice and associate deputy minister of justice, 30 September and 2 October 1997, Ottawa, ON.

44   Avigail I. Eisenberg, "Justice and Human Rights in the Provinces," in Christopher Dunn, ed., *Provinces: Canadian Provincial Politics* (Peterborough, ON: Broadview Press), 485-89; R.

Brian Howe and David Johnson, *Restraining Equality: Human Rights Commissions in Canada* (Toronto: University of Toronto Press, 2000), 9-22.

45 Lorraine Weinrib has provided a very strong critique of the right-wing position and its analysis of framers' intent: "The Charter provides new rights, and an exceptional, qualified, legislative override. The critics of judicial activism, in contrast, would prefer frozen or morality-based rights that are reflected in so-called enduring myths of human nature, general acceptable limits on those rights, and recourse to a legislative override released, not only from its built-in political sting, but also from the conventions that elected governments have built up against its use." See Weinrib, "The Activist Constitution," 30.

46 Weinrib, "Canada's *Charter of Rights,*" 123.

47 Roach, *The Supreme Court on Trial,* 226-29.

48 Roy Romanow, John Whyte, and Howard Leeson, *Canada ... Notwithstanding* (Toronto: Carswell, 1984), 216; Lorraine Eisenstat Weinrib, "Trudeau and the Canadian Charter of Rights and Freedoms: A Question of Constitutional Maturation," in Andrew Cohen and J.L. Granatstein, eds., *Trudeau's Shadow* (Toronto: Random House of Canada, 1998), 266-68.

49 Kelly, "The Supreme Court of Canada and the Complexity of Judicial Activism," 100-3.

50 Tassé, "Intentions of the Framers," 6.

51 Ibid.

52 Ibid.

53 Ibid., 6-7.

54 Honourable Sterling Lyon, "Opening Remarks," *Federal-Provincial Conference of First Ministers on the Constitution,* Ottawa, 8-12 September 1980, Document 800-15/012 at 476-78. The recorded opposition of the provincial premiers at the September conference is taken from *Federal-Provincial Conference of First Ministers on the Constitution, September 8-13, 1980. Verbatim Transcript.* The following premiers opposed the entrenchment of the Charter: Honourable Allan Blakeney (Saskatchewan), 484-91; Honourable Peter Lougheed (Alberta), 493-97; Honourable Angus MacLean (PEI), 566; Honourable John Buchanan (Nova Scotia), 569-73; Honourable Brian Peckford (Newfoundland), 573-83; Honourable René Lévesque (Quebec), 527; Honourable William Bennett (British Columbia), 554. Only the Honourable William Davis (Ontario), 498-502, and the Honourable Richard Hatfield (New Brunswick), 511, supported the entrenchment of rights and freedoms.

55 *Attorney General Manitoba et al. v. Attorney General Canada et al.,* [1981] 1 S.C.R. 753 [*Patriation Reference*].

56 Peter H. Russell, "Bold Statecraft, Questionable Jurisprudence," in Keith Banting and Richard Simeon, eds., *And No One Cheered* (Toronto: Methuen, 1983), 217-18.

57 Lorraine Eisenstat Weinrib, "The Supreme Court of Canada in the Age of Rights: Constitutional Democracy, the Rule of Law and Fundamental Rights under Canada's Constitution," *Canadian Bar Review* 80 (2001): 720-24.

58 Patrick Monahan elaborates on this "modified judicial realism" in his study *Politics and the Constitution:* "They had a relatively sophisticated and realistic view of the nature of the adjudicative process. For them, constitutional adjudication was far from mechanical or formalistic. They were aware of the significant degree of discretion available to courts in interpreting constitutional texts. Because some degree of judicial originality was inevitable, the drafters saw their task as making educated guesses as to how the courts might interpret particular constitutional language, and choosing the language which was most likely to secure for them the results they desired." Monahan, *Politics and the Constitution,* 78-79.

59 Author interview with Trudeau.

60 Trudeau, *Federalism and the French Canadians,* 58.

61 Tassé, "Intention of the Framers," 9.

62 I have elaborated on the issue of bureaucratic activism in Kelly, "Bureaucratic Activism and the Charter of Rights and Freedoms," 476-511.

63 Author interview with former senior DOJ official, 30 September 1997, Ottawa, ON.

64 *Background Notes, Entrenching a Charter of Rights.* Tabled by the delegation of the Government of Canada, 5 July 1980, Document 830-81/026 at 4.

65 Peter H. Russell, Rainer Knopff, and Ted Morton, *Federalism and the Charter: Leading Constitutional Decisions* (Ottawa: Carleton University Press, 1990), 19.

66 Honourable Jean Chrétien, minister of justice, Special Joint Committee of the Senate and House of Commons on the Constitution of Canada Hearings, 12 November 1980, 3:27.
67 Roger Tassé, deputy minister of justice, SJC Hearings, 12 November 1980, 3:28-29.
68 Chrétien, SJC Hearings, 15 January 1981, 38:42.
69 Ibid.
70 Tassé, SJC Hearings, 15 January 1981, 38:40.
71 Chrétien, SJC Hearings, 27 January 1981, 46:126-27.
72 Ibid., 46:127.
73 Manfredi, *Judicial Power and the Charter,* 2nd ed., 37-38.
74 Barry Strayer, associate deputy minister of justice, SJC Hearings, 27 January 1981, 46:36, 46:41-42.
75 Manfredi, *Judicial Power and the Charter,* 2nd ed., 34-38. *Reference Re s.94(2) of the British Columbia Motor Vehicles Act,* [1985] 2 S.C.R. 486.
76 Chrétien, SJC Hearings, 27 January 1981, 46:131.
77 *R. v. Prosper,* [1994] 3 S.C.R. 145 at 267.
78 Chrétien, SJC Hearings, 15 January 1981, 38:37.
79 Tassé, SJC Hearings, 29 January 1981, 48:84.
80 *Mahé v. Alberta,* [1990] 1 S.C.R. 342.
81 Manfredi, *Judicial Power and the Charter,* 2nd ed., 167.
82 Chrétien, SJC Hearings, 15 January 1981, 38:38.
83 Morton and Knopff, *The Charter Revolution and the Court Party,* 60.
84 Chrétien, SJC Hearings, 29 January 1981, 48:110.
85 Ibid., 11 December 1980, 3:18.
86 Ibid., 3:17.
87 Troy Riddell disagrees with this assessment of section 23(1). Please see Troy Q. Riddell, "Official Minority-Language Education Policy outside of Quebec: The Impact of Section 23 of the Charter and Judicial Decisions," *Canadian Public Administration* 46 (2003): 27-49.
88 Chrétien, SJC Hearings, 11 December 1980, 3:17.
89 Manfredi, *Judicial Power and the Charter,* 2nd ed., 168.
90 Ibid., 103-4.
91 *Egan v. Canada,* [1995] 2 S.C.R. 513. For a critical assessment of the effect of Charter review on the equality claims of gays and lesbians, please see the following: Smith, *Lesbian and Gay Rights in Canada,* 73-140; Brenda Cossman, "Lesbians, Gay Men, and the Canadian Charter of Rights and Freedoms," *Osgoode Hall Law Journal* 40 (2002): 223-49; Donald G. Casswell, "Moving toward Same-Sex Marriage," *Canadian Bar Review* 80 (2001): 810-56.
92 Tassé, "Intentions of the Framers," 10.
93 Manfredi, *Judicial Power and the Charter,* 2nd ed., 123.
94 *Statement by the Honourable Jean Chrétien.* Document 830-81/025 at 5.
95 Background Notes, Charter of Rights and Freedoms, tabled by the delegation of the Government of Canada, 5 July 1980, Document 830-81/029 at 2.
96 Minister of Justice and Attorney General of Canada, Statement by the Honourable Jean Chrétien, Minister of Justice, to the Special Joint Committee on the Constitution, 12 January 1981, 7.
97 Ibid., 9.
98 Tassé, SJC Hearings, 20 January 1981, 41:23-24.
99 Smith, *Lesbian and Gay Rights in Canada,* 67.
100 Morton and Knopff, *The Charter Revolution and the Court Party,* 43; F.L. Morton, "Vriend v. Alberta: Judicial Power at the Crossroads?" *Canada Watch* 7, 4-5 (1999), http://www.yorku.ca/robarts/projects/canada-watch/pdf.
101 Author interview with Strayer, 22 August 2001.
102 *Vriend v. Alberta,* [1998] 1 S.C.R. 493; *M. v. H.,* [1999] 2 S.C.R. 3.
103 Howe and Johnson, *Restraining Equality;* Donna Greschner, "The Right to Belong: The Promise of *Vriend,"* *National Journal of Constitutional Law* 9 (1999): 417-20.
104 Janet L. Hiebert, *Charter Conflicts* (Montreal and Kingston: McGill-Queen's University Press, 2002), 169.
105 Chrétien, SJC Hearings, 12 November 1980, 3:60.

106 Ibid., 29 January 1981, 48:31.
107 Svend Robinson, MP, SJC Hearings, 20 January 1981, 41:22.
108 Honourable Robert Kaplan, solicitor general, SJC Hearings, 20 January 1981, 41:23.
109 F.L. Morton, "Vriend: A Misinterpretation of the Charter," http://www.conservativeforum. org/EssaysForm.asp?ID=6080.
110 Ibid., 5.
111 Alberta Human Rights Commission, *Equal in Dignity and Rights: A Review of Human Rights in Alberta by the Alberta Human Rights Review Panel* (Edmonton, AB: Alberta Human Rights Commission, 1994), 71.
112 Ibid., 75.
113 Author interview with senior official, Alberta Human Rights and Citizenship Commission, 16 December 2002, Edmonton, AB.
114 Minister of Justice and Attorney General of Canada. Statement by the Honourable Jean Chrétien, Minister of Justice, to the SJC, 12 January 1981, 7.
115 Miriam Smith, "Recognizing Same-Sex Relationships: The Evolution of Recent Federal and Provincial Policies," *Canadian Public Administration* 45 (2002): 2.

Chapter 4: The Supreme Court and Police Conduct

1 Alan D. Gold and Michelle Fuerst, "The Stuff that Dreams Are Made of! Criminal Law and the Charter of Rights," *Ottawa Law Review* 24 (1992): 13-37; Christopher P. Manfredi, "Judicial Review and Criminal Disenfranchisement," *Review of Politics* 60 (1998): 284-92.
2 James B. Kelly, "The Supreme Court of Canada's *Charter of Rights* Decisions, 1982 to 1999: A Statistical Analysis," in F.L. Morton, ed., *Law, Politics and the Judicial Process in Canada,* 3rd ed. (Calgary: University of Calgary Press, 2002), 499. This trend continued from 2000 to 2003.
3 Christopher P. Manfredi, *Judicial Power and the Charter,* 2nd ed. (Don Mills, ON: Oxford University Press, 2001), 97.
4 James B. Kelly, "The Supreme Court of Canada and the Complexity of Judicial Activism," in Patrick James, Donald E. Abelson, and Michael Lusztig, eds., *The Myth of the Sacred: The Charter, the Courts and the Constitution in Canada* (Montreal and Kingston: McGill-Queen's University Press, 2002), 97-122.
5 Peter W. Hogg and Allison A. Bushell, "The *Charter* Dialogue between Courts and Legislatures," *Osgoode Hall Law Journal* 35 (1997): 75-124; Christopher P. Manfredi and James B. Kelly, "Six Degrees of Dialogue: A Response to Hogg and Bushell," *Osgoode Hall Law Journal* 37 (1999): 513-27.
6 Peter H. Russell, "The Effect of a Charter of Rights on the Policy-Making Role of Canadian Courts," *Canadian Public Administration* 25 (Spring 1982): 21.
7 Alan Young, "The Charter, the Supreme Court of Canada and the Constitutionalizing of the Investigative Process," in Jamie Cameron, ed., *The Charter's Impact on the Criminal Justice System* (Toronto: Carswell, 1996), 2.
8 Alan D. Gold, "Section 10(b) and the Right to Counsel: Post-Bartle," *Journal of Motor Vehicle Law* 7 (1996): 16; and Peter H. Russell, "Canadian Constraints on Judicialization from Without," *International Political Science Review* 15 (1994): 170-71.
9 Young, "The Charter, the Supreme Court of Canada and the Constitutionalizing of the Investigative Process," 2-3.
10 Patrick J. Monahan, *Constitutional Law,* 2nd ed. (Toronto: Irwin Law, 202), 398-99.
11 Kent Roach, *Due Process and Victims' Rights* (Toronto: University of Toronto Press, 1999), 42-48.
12 F.L. Morton and Rainer Knopff, *The Charter Revolution and the Court Party* (Peterborough, ON: Broadview Press, 2000), 37-40; Manfredi, *Judicial Power and the Charter,* 2nd ed., 75-102.
13 Kathy Brock, "Polishing the Halls of Justice: Sections 24(2) and 8 of the Charter of Rights," *National Journal of Constitutional Law* 2 (1992): 274-75.
14 Christopher P. Manfredi and Scott Lemieux, "Judicial Discretion and Fundamental Justice: Sexual Assault Jurisprudence in the Supreme Court of Canada," *American Journal of Comparative Law* 47 (1999): 491-94; Morton and Knopff, *The Charter Revolution and the Court Party,* 38-40.

15 Herbert Packer, *The Limits of Criminal Sanction* (Stanford: Stanford University Press, 1968), 177.
16 Ibid, 163-64.
17 Roach, *Due Process and Victims' Rights*, 52.
18 Don Stuart, "The Unfortunate Dilution of Section 8 Protection: Some Teeth Remain," *Queen's Law Journal* 25 (1999): 65-94.
19 F.L. Morton, "The Political Impact of the Canadian Charter of Rights and Freedoms," *Canadian Journal of Political Science* 20 (1987): 37; Manfredi, *Judicial Power and the Charter*, 2nd ed., 83-90; Robert Harvie and Hamar Foster, "Ties that Bind? The Supreme Court of Canada, American Jurisprudence, and the Revision of Canadian Criminal Law under the Charter," *Osgoode Hall Law Journal* 28 (1990): 763-64.
20 Lee Burgess, "Recent Developments in Drinking and Driving Law and the Right to Counsel," *Journal of Motor Vehicle Law* 5 (1995): 38.
21 Kent Roach, "The Evolving Fair Trial Test under Section 24(2) of the Charter," *Canadian Criminal Law Review* 1 (1996): 120-22.
22 Herbert Packer, "Two Models of the Criminal Process," *University of Pennsylvania Law Review* 113 (1964): 1.
23 Roach, *Due Process and Victims' Rights*, 2-50.
24 Manfredi, *Judicial Power and the Charter*, 2nd ed., 90-95, 180-81.
25 *Seaboyer v. The Queen*, [1991], 2 S.C.R. 577 at 620.
26 *R. v. Daviault*, [1994] 3 S.C.R. 63 at 103.
27 *R. v. O'Connor*, [1995] 4 S.C.R. 411; *R. v. Carosella*, [1997] 1 S.C.R. 80.
28 Dianne Martin, "Rising Expectations: Slippery Slope or New Horizon? The Constitutionalization of Criminal Trials in Canada," in Jamie Cameron, ed., *The Charter's Impact on the Criminal Justice System* (Toronto: Carswell, 1996), 87-121.
29 *R. v. Mills*, [1999] 3 S.C.R. 668; Janet L. Hiebert, *Charter Conflicts* (Montreal and Kingston: McGill-Queen's University Press, 2002), 115-16.
30 Manfredi, *Judicial Power and the Charter*, 2nd ed., 180.
31 *R. v. Collins*, [1987] 1 S.C.R. 265 [*Collins*].
32 James B. Kelly, "The *Charter of Rights and Freedoms* and the Rebalancing of Liberal Constitutionalism in Canada, 1982-1997," *Osgoode Hall Law Journal* 37 (1999): 625-95.
33 R.J. Delisle, "Collins: An Unjustified Distinction," *Criminal Reports* 56 (1987): 217-18; Richard Mahoney, "Problems with the Current Approach to s.24(2) of the Charter: An Inevitable Discovery," *Criminal Law Quarterly* 42 (1999): 443-77.
34 Roach, "The Evolving Fair Trial Test," 112-23.
35 Jack Watson, "Blood Samples: Are They Real or Not?" *Journal of Motor Vehicle Law* 2 (1990): 174.
36 *R. v. Stillman*, [1997] 1 S.C.R. 607 [*Stillman*] at 655.
37 For simplicity, I will refer to real/non-conscripted evidence as real evidence and will refer to non-conscripted only when discussing post-*Stillman* cases.
38 Hon. Marc Rosenberg, "The *Charter's* Impact on the Law of Evidence in Criminal Cases," in Jamie Cameron, ed., *The Charter's Impact on the Criminal Justice System* (Toronto: Carswell, 1996), 185-86.
39 *R. v. Therens*, [1985] 1 S.C.R. 613.
40 Ibid., 652.
41 Kent Roach, "Chief Justice Lamer and Some Myths about Judicial Activism," *Canadian Criminal Law Review* 5 (2000): 26-27.
42 *Collins*, 274.
43 Walter Tarnopolsky, president, Canadian Civil Liberties Association, SJC Hearings, 18 November 1980, 7:27.
44 *R. v. Brydges*, [1990] 1 S.C.R. 190 [*Brydges*].
45 *R. v. Manninen*, [1987] 1 S.C.R. 1233.
46 *Brydges*, 203.
47 Ibid., 216-17.
48 *R. v. Prosper*, [1994] 3 S.C.R. 236.
49 Ibid., 267.

50 *New Brunswick (Minister of Health and Community Services) v. G. (J.),* [1999] 3 S.C.R. 46 at para. 2.
51 *R. v. Clarkson,* [1986] 1 S.C.R. 383 at 395-96.
52 *R. v. Black,* [1989] 2 S.C.R. 138 at 158.
53 The knife was included because it is real evidence and, according to the principle of inevitable discoverability, real evidence is excluded only in cases of extreme rights violations, which the court did not conclude occurred in *Black.*
54 *R. v. Smith,* [1991] 1 S.C.R. 714.
55 Ibid., 728.
56 *R. v. Tremblay,* [1987] 2 S.C.R. 435.
57 Ibid., 439.
58 Ibid., 438.
59 Stanley A. Cohen, "Indirect Interrogation: Jailhouse Informers and the Right to Counsel," *Criminal Reports* 68 (1989): 58-66.
60 A critical analysis of the Supreme Court of Canada's decision to exclude cell statements is provided in John L. Gibson, "In Defense of Cell Statements," *Criminal Reports,* 3rd ser., 73 (1990): 381.
61 *R. v. Hebert,* [1990] 2 S.C.R. 151 [*Hebert*] at 152.
62 Ibid., 153
63 *R. v. Broyles,* [1991] 3 S.C.R. 595.
64 Ibid., 617.
65 *R. v. Liew,* [1999] 3 S.C.R. 227 [*Liew*] at para. 13.
66 The problems in using jailhouse informants are discussed in Christopher Sherrin, "Jailhouse Informants, Part 1: Problems with Their Use," *Criminal Law Quarterly* 40 (1997): 106-21.
67 *Hebert,* 184-85.
68 *Liew,* at para. 58.
69 *R. v. Fliss,* [2002] 1 S.C.R. 535 at para. 58-67.
70 R. Devonshire, "The Effects of Supreme Court Charter-Based Decisions on Policing: More Beneficial than Detrimental?" *Criminal Reports* 31 (1991): 97.
71 Ibid., 99.
72 *Hunter v. Southam Inc.,* [1984] 2 S.C.R. 145 at 160.
73 *Stillman.*
74 Ibid., 655.
75 David Paciocco, "Stillman, Disproportion and the Fair Trial Dichotomy under Section 24(2)," *Canadian Criminal Law Review* 2 (1997): 169-70.
76 *R. v. Feeney,* [1997] 2 S.C.R. 13 [*Feeney*].
77 Author interview with senior government official, 2 October 1997, Ottawa, ON; Sean Fine, "Top Court Extends Rights of Accused," *Globe and Mail,* 9 August 1997.
78 *Feeney,* 15-17.
79 Ibid., 68.
80 Author interview with senior government official, 1 October 1997, Ottawa, ON.
81 Hiebert, *Charter Conflicts,* 154-55.
82 Kent Roach, *The Supreme Court on Trial* (Toronto: Irwin Law, 2001), 178-79.
83 *R. v. Greffe,* [1990] 1 S.C.R. 755.
84 Ibid., 758-59 (emphasis in original).
85 *R. v. Simmons,* [1988] 2 S.C.R. 495 at 517.
86 Devonshire, "The Effects of Supreme Court Charter-Based Decisions on Policing," 99.
87 *R. v. Monney,* [1999] 1 S.C.R. 652 at 681-82.
88 *R. v. Pohoretsky,* [1987] 1 S.C.R. 945 at 949
89 Watson, "Blood Samples," 173-94.
90 *R. v. Dyment,* [1988] 2 S.C.R. 417 at 435.
91 *R. v. Dersch,* [1993] 3 S.C.R. 769.
92 Ibid., 779.
93 Renee M. Pomerance, "Searching in Vein: R. v. Dersch, Blood Samples, and Informational Privacy," *Journal of Motor Vehicle Law* 6 (1995): 75-103.

94   *R. v. Plant.,* [1993] 3 S.C.R. 281.
95   Ibid., 291-92.
96   Ibid., 291.
97   Ibid., 295.
98   *R. v. Wiley,* [1993] 3 S.C.R. 263; *R. v. Grant,* [1993] 3 S.C.R. 223; *R. v. Evans,* [1996] 1 S.C.R. 8.
99   *R. v. Silveria,* [1995] 2 S.C.R. 297.
100   Ibid., 345-46.
101   Ibid., 375.
102   Ibid.
103   *R. v. Edwards,* [1996] 1 S.C.R. 128.
104   Ibid., 140.
105   Ibid., 146-47.
106   *R. v. Duarte,* [1990] 1 S.C.R. 30.
107   Ibid., 59.
108   Ibid., 54.
109   *R. v. Wong,* [1990] 3 S.C.R. 36.
110   Ibid., 59.
111   Ibid., 63.
112   *R. v. Askov,* [1990] 2 S.C.R. 1199 at 1223.
113   *R. v. Morin,* [1992] 1 S.C.R. 771 [*Morin*] at 778-79.
114   Rainer Knopff and F.L. Morton, *Charter Politics* (Scarborough, ON: Nelson Canada, 1992), 219.
115   Carl Baar, "Criminal Court Delay and the Charter: The Use and Misuse of Social Facts in Judicial Policy Making," *Canadian Bar Review* 72 (1993): 305-36.
116   Russell, "Canadian Constraints on Judicialization from Without," 170-71.
117   *Morin,* 802-3.
118   Ibid., 809.
119   David M. Paciocco, "Morin: The Transitional Reasonableness of Excessive Systemic Delay," *Criminal Reports* 76 (1993): 58.
120   Of the twenty-two cases since *Askov* in which the court considered that a trial delay was unreasonable, only eleven cases specified what the actual time delay was. Therefore, the average of sixteen months is true for half the cases heard by the Supreme Court between 1990 and 2002.
121   *R. v. Frazer,* [1993] 2 S.C.R. 866 at 869-70. The same argument was advanced by Justice McLachlin in *R. v. Gallagher,* [1993] 2 S.C.R. 861 at 864: "The large number of appeals arising in the aftermath of *R. v. Askov* caused abnormal institutional delay. This was unfortunate, but largely unavoidable. It took several months to compile the necessary transcripts, a period which cannot in all circumstances be said to be much overlong."
122   *R. v. Potvin,* [1993] 2 S.C.R. 880 at 898.
123   Normally, the Crown must demonstrate why an individual should be denied reasonable bail. However, in a number of areas, such as narcotic trafficking, the Criminal Code places the onus on the accused to demonstrate why reasonable bail should not be denied. This is the essence of a reverse-onus provision in the Criminal Code as it relates to bail.
124   *R. v. Pearson,* [1992] 3 S.C.R. 665.
125   *R. v. Morales,* [1992] 3 S.C.R. 711 at 741.
126   *R. v. Hall,* [2002] 3 S.C.R. 309 at para. 4.
127   *R. v. Jones,* [1994] 2 S.C.R. 229.
128   Ibid., 292.
129   *Kindler v. Canada,* [1991] 2 S.C.R. 779 [*Kindler*]; *Reference Re Ng Extradition,* [1991] 2 S.C.R. 858.
130   *Kindler,* 839.
131   Ibid.
132   *United States v. Burns,* [2001] 1 S.C.R. 283.
133   *R. v. L.(D.O.),* [1993] 4 S.C.R. 419 at 472.
134   Jacqueline Castel, "The Use of Screens and Closed Circuit Television in the Prosecution of Child Sex Abuse Cases: Necessary Protection for Children or a Violation of the Rights of

the Accused?" *Canadian Journal of Family Law* 10 (1992): 285-87.

135 Christopher P. Manfredi and James B. Kelly, "Dialogue, Deference and Restraint: Judicial Independence and Trial Procedures," *Saskatchewan Law Review* 64 (2001): 343-45.

136 *R. v. Levogiannis*, [1993] 4 S.C.R. 475 at 491.

137 Ibid., 483.

138 Michelle Fuerst, "When Societal Interests Outweigh a Right to Confrontation: Charter Protection for Child Witnesses," in Jamie Cameron, ed., *The Charter's Impact on the Criminal Justice System* (Toronto: Carswell, 1996), 161-79.

139 Proposed Resolution for Joint Address to Her Majesty the Queen, Respecting the Constitution of Canada, tabled in the House of Commons and the Senate, 6 October 1980. Catalogue no. YC3-321/5-57.

Chapter 5: Guardians of the Constitution

1 *Vriend v. Alberta*, [1998] 1 S.C.R. 493 [*Vriend*] at 565.

2 Kent Roach, *The Supreme Court on Trial* (Toronto: Irwin Law, 2001), 175-204.

3 F.L. Morton and Rainer Knopff, *The Charter Revolution and the Court Party* (Peterborough, ON: Broadview Press, 2000), 37.

4 Brian Slattery, "A Theory of the Charter," *Osgoode Hall Law Journal* 25 (1987): 707.

5 *Hunter v. Southam Inc.*, [1984] 2 S.C.R. 145.

6 Janet L. Hiebert, *Charter Conflicts* (Montreal and Kingston: McGill-Queen's University Press, 2002), 43-51.

7 Hon. J. Laforest, "The Balancing of Interests under the Charter," *National Journal of Constitutional Law* 2 (1993): 134-59.

8 Hiebert, *Charter Conflicts*, 52-72.

9 *RJR-Macdonald Inc. v. Canada*, [1995] 3 S.C.R. 199 [*RJR-Macdonald*]; *Reference Re Provincial Court Judges*, [1997] 3 S.C.R. 3 [*Provincial Court Judges Reference*].

10 *R. v. Oakes*, [1986] 1 S.C.R. 103 [*Oakes*].

11 Peter W. Hogg, "Section 1 Revisited," *National Journal of Constitutional Law* 1 (1991-92): 1-24.

12 Donna Greschner, "The Right to Belong: The Promise of *Vriend*," *National Journal of Constitutional Law* 9 (1999): 419.

13 Hogg, "Section 1 Revisited," 17.

14 F.L. Morton, Peter H. Russell, and Troy Q. Riddell, "The *Canadian Charter of Rights and Freedoms*: A Descriptive Analysis of the First Decade, 1982-1992," *National Journal of Constitutional Law* 5 (1994): 30.

15 Patrick J. Monahan, "The Charter: Then and Now," in P. Bryden, S. Davis, and J. Russell, eds., *Protecting Rights and Freedoms* (Toronto: University of Toronto Press, 1994), 111-12.

16 *R. v. Edwards Books and Art Ltd.*, [1986] 2 S.C.R. 713 [*Edwards Books*]; *Irwin Toy v. A.G. Quebec*, [1989] 1 S.C.R. 927 [*Irwin Toy*].

17 *Edwards Books*, 781-82.

18 Ibid., 795.

19 Ibid.

20 Laforest, "The Balancing of Interests under the Charter," 146.

21 *Irwin Toy*, 993-94.

22 Ibid., 994.

23 Roach, *The Supreme Court on Trial*, 172.

24 Hiebert, *Charter Conflicts*, 90.

25 *RJR-Macdonald*, para. 168.

26 Ibid., 342.

27 *R. v. Sharpe*, [2001] 1 S.C.R. 45.

28 Ibid., para 97.

29 Hon. Beverly McLachlin, "Charter Myths," *UBC Law Review* 33 (1999): 29.

30 If the analysis is expanded to include constitutional protections outside the Charter, then the total number of invalidations increases to seventy-nine, as seven cases have involved Aboriginal rights protected in section 35(1) of the *Constitution Act*, and eight statutes have involved language and education rights.

31   Peter H. Russell, "Canadian Constraints on Judicialization from Without," *International Political Science Review* 15 (1994): 168.
32   Lorraine Eisenstat Weinrib, "The Canadian Charter's Transformative Aspirations," in Joseph Eliot Magnet, Gerald-A. Beaudoin, Gerald Gall and Christopher P. Manfredi, eds., *The Canadian Charter of Rights and Freedoms* (Toronto: Butterworths, 2003), 17-37.
33   *Trociuk v. British Columbia (Attorney General)*, [2003] 1 S.C.R. 835, cited at http://www.lexum.umontreal.ca/csc-scc/en/rec/html/2003scc034.wpd.html.
34   *Sauvé v. Canada (Chief Electoral Officer)*, [2002] 3 S.C.R. 519 [*Sauvé*].
35   Data on file with author. I have reviewed the date of enactment or last amendment of all statutes reviewed by the Supreme Court on Charter grounds, and the limited number enacted or last amended in the 1990s is a significant characteristic.
36   Charles Epp, *The Rights Revolution: Lawyers, Activists, and Supreme Courts in Comparative Perspectives* (Chicago: University of Chicago Press, 1998), 171-96.
37   Morton and Knopff, *The Charter Revolution and the Court Party*, 117-23.
38   Roach, *The Supreme Court on Trial*, 146.
39   James B. Kelly, "Governing with the *Charter of Rights and Freedoms*," *Supreme Court Law Review*, 2nd ser., 21 (2003): 299-337.
40   Christopher P. Manfredi, "Strategic Behaviour and the Canadian Charter of Rights and Freedoms," in Patrick James, Donald E. Abelson, and Michael Lusztig, eds., *The Myth of the Sacred: The Charter, the Courts and the Constitution in Canada* (Montreal and Kingston: McGill-Queen's University Press, 2002), 147-66.
41   Christopher P. Manfredi, "The Chrétien Court," *Policy Options* 21 (November 2000): 23.
42   There were three cases in this reference decision: *Reference Re Remuneration of Judges of the Provincial Court of Prince Edward Island*, [1997] 3 S.C.R. 3; *R. v. Campbell*, [1999] 2 S.C.R. 956; *Manitoba Provincial Judges Assn. v. Manitoba (Minister of Justice)*, [1997] 3 S.C.R. 3. The court considered the *Public Sector Pay Reduction Act* (PEI), the *Payment to Provincial Court Judges Amendment Regulation* (Alberta), and the *Public Sector Reduced Work Week and Compensation Management Act* (Manitoba) and in a majority decision (six to one), with Justice Laforest dissenting, concluded that the governments of Alberta, Manitoba, and Prince Edward Island had compromised judicial independence as established by the court in *R. v. Valente*. The salary reductions of provincial court judges were therefore unconstitutional as a violation of section 11(d).
43   *Provincial Court Judges Reference*, 104.
44   *R. v. Valente*, [1985] 2 S.C.R. 673.
45   *Provincial Court Judges Reference*, 104.
46   *Mackin v. New Brunswick (Minister of Finance)*, [2002] 1 S.C.R. 405.
47   Ibid., para 69.
48   Anthony A. Peacock, "Judicial Rationalism and the Therapeutic Constitution: The Supreme Court's Reconstruction of Equality and Democratic Process under the Charter of Rights and Freedoms," in Patrick James, Donald E. Abelson, and Michael Lusztig, eds., *The Myth of the Sacred: The Charter, the Courts and the Constitution in Canada* (Montreal and Kingston: McGill-Queen's University Press, 2002), 19-56.
49   Lorraine Eisenstat Weinrib, "The Supreme Court of Canada in the Age of Rights: Constitutional Democracy, the Rule of Law and Fundamental Rights under Canada's Constitution," *Canadian Bar Review* 80 (2001): 704.
50   James B. Kelly, "Bureaucratic Activism and the Charter of Rights and Freedoms: The Department of Justice and Its Entry into the Centre of Government," *Canadian Public Administration* 42 (1999): 476-511; Patrick J. Monahan and Marie Finkelstein, "The Charter of Rights and Public Policy in Canada," *Osgoode Hall Law Journal* 30 (1992): 510-16; Janet L. Hiebert, "Wrestling with Rights: Judges, Parliament and the Making of Social Policy," *Choices* 5 (1999): 3-10.
51   Morton, Russell, and Riddell, "The *Canadian Charter of Rights and Freedoms*," 29-32.
52   Robert Ivan Martin, *The Most Dangerous Branch* (Montreal and Kingston: McGill-Queen's University Press, 2003), 40-76.

53 *Singh v. Minister of Employment and Immigration*, [1985] 1 S.C.R. 177 [*Singh*]; *Libman v. Quebec*, [1997] 3 S.C.R. 569 [*Libman*]; *Little Sisters Book and Art Emporium v. Canada (Minister of Justice)*, [2000] 2 S.C.R. 1120 [*Little Sisters*]; *Eldridge v. British Columbia*, [1997] 3 S.C.R. 624 [*Eldridge*].
54 *Singh*, 198.
55 Ibid., 216.
56 Ibid., 217.
57 Ibid., 218.
58 *An Act to Amend the Immigration Act, 1976*, S.C. 1986, c.13, s.5.
59 Morton and Knopff, *The Charter Revolution and the Court Party*, 101.
60 *Libman*, para. 76-78.
61 Ibid., para. 86.
62 *Eldridge*, 682.
63 Christopher P. Manfredi and Antonia Maioni, "Courts and Health Policy: Judicial Policy Making and Publically Funded Health Care in Canada," *Journal of Health Politics, Policy and Law* 27 (2002): 229-31.
64 Kent Roach, "Remedial Consensus and Dialogue under the *Charter*: General Declarations and Delayed Declarations of Invalidity," *UBC Law Review* 35 (2002): 228-29.
65 Brenda Cossman, "Lesbians, Gay Men and the *Canadian Charter of Rights and Freedoms*," *Osgoode Hall Law Journal* 40 (2002): 239-42.
66 *Little Sisters*, para. 159.
67 *Osborne v. Canada (Treasury Board)*, [1991] 2 S.C.R. 69 at 88-89.
68 Ibid., 99.
69 Ibid., 105.
70 *R. v. Swain*, [1991] 1 S.C.R. 933 at 934.
71 Ibid., 1018-19.
72 Ibid.
73 *R. v. Heywood*, [1990] 3 S.C.R. 761 at 790.
74 Ibid., 804.
75 *Winko v. B.C. (Forensic Psychiatric Institute)* [1999] 2 S.C.R. 625.
76 Ibid., 686.
77 *R. v. Keegstra*, [1990] 3 S.C.R. 697 [*Keegstra*]; *R. v. Zundel*, [1992] 2 S.C.R. 731 [*Zundel*].
78 Kathleen Mahoney, "*R. v. Keegstra*: A Rationale for Regulating Pornography?" *McGill Law Journal* 37 (1992): 250-56 (emphasis in original).
79 *Keegstra*, 785-86.
80 Shannon Ishiyama Smithey, "Cooperation and Conflict: Group Activity in *R. v. Keegstra*," in Patrick James, Donald E. Abelson, and Michael Lusztig, eds., *The Myth of the Sacred: The Charter, the Courts and the Constitution in Canada* (Montreal and Kingston: McGill-Queen's University Press, 2002), 192-93.
81 *Zundel*, 765-66.
82 *UFCW, Local 1518 v. Kmart Canada Ltd.*, [1999] 2 S.C.R. 1083.
83 Ibid., para 50.
84 Ibid., para. 55.
85 Ibid., para. 77.
86 *Sauvé*, para. 55-56.
87 Roach, *The Supreme Court on Trial*, 201-4.
88 Martin, *The Most Dangerous Branch*, 7-8.
89 *Oakes*, 109.
90 *R. v. Martineau*, [1990] 2 S.C.R. 633 at 635.
91 *R. v. Vaillancourt*, [1987] 2 S.C.R. 636.
92 Ibid., 643.
93 Ibid., 646.
94 Ibid., 647.
95 *R. v. Logan*, [1990] 2 S.C.R. 731 at 738.
96 Ibid., 744.

97   *R. v. Morgentaler*, [1988] 1 S.C.R. 30 [*Morgentaler*].

98   Ibid., 48.

99   Thomas Flanagan, "The Staying Power of the Legislative Status Quo: Collective Choice in Canada's Parliament after *Morgentaler*," *Canadian Journal of Political Science* 30 (1997): 31-53.

100 Christopher P. Manfredi, *Judicial Power and the Charter* (Toronto: McClelland and Stewart, 1993), 119; Ian T. Urquhart, "Federalism, Ideology, and Charter Review: Alberta's Response to Morgentaler," *Canadian Journal of Law and Society* 4 (1989): 160-64.

101 *Morgentaler*, 72-73.

102 Ibid., 68.

103 Ibid., 95.

104 Ibid., 98.

105 Richard J. Schultz, *Federalism, Bureaucracy and Public Policy* (Montreal and Kingston: McGill-Queen's University Press, 1980), 147.

106 *Morgentaler*, 183.

107 Ibid., 128.

108 Flanagan, "The Staying Power of the Legislative Status Quo," 32.

109 *Attorney General (Quebec) v. Protestant School Boards*, [1984] 2 S.C.R. 66.

110 Ibid., 780.

111 Christopher P. Manfredi, "Constitutional Rights and Interest Advocacy: Litigating Educational Reform in Canada and the United States," in F. Leslie Seidle, ed., *Equity and Community* (Montreal: Institute for Research on Public Policy, 1993), 103.

112 Guy Laforest, *Trudeau and the End of a Canadian Dream* (Montreal and Kingston: McGill-Queen's University Press, 1995), 125-49.

113 Christopher P. Manfredi, *Judicial Power and the Charter*, 2nd ed. (Don Mills, ON: Oxford University Press, 2001), 40.

114 *Ford v. Quebec*, [1988] 2 S.C.R. 712.

115 Ibid., 780.

116 *Rocket v. Royal College of Dental Surgeons*, [1990] 2 S.C.R. 232 at 245. This case involved the constitutionality of provisions of the *Health Disciplines Act* restricting the ability of dentists to advertise. In *RJR-Macdonald v. Canada*, the Supreme Court did not accept that the total ban on tobacco product advertising was a reasonable limitation, nor did it accept, in *Committee for the Commonwealth of Canada v. Canada*, [1991] 1 S.C.R. 139, that the ban on soliciting at airports was a reasonable limitation on freedom of expression.

117 *Thompson Newspapers Company v. Canada (Attorney General)*, [1998] 1 S.C.R. 877 at para. 111.

118 Ibid., para. 122.

119 Ibid., para. 119.

120 Ibid., para. 130.

121 *Figueroa v. Canada (Attorney General)*, [2003] 1 S.C.R. 912 at para. 48-55, cited at http://www.lexum.umontreal.ca/csc-scc/en/rec/html/2003scc037.wpd.html.

122 *R. v. Nguyen*, [1990] 2 S.C.R. 906 at 913.

123 Ibid., 926.

124 *R. v. Daviault*, [1994] 2 S.C.R. 63 at 74.

125 Ibid., 74.

126 Cited in Richard Litkowski, "The Charter and Principles of Criminal Responsibility: A Long and Winding Road," in Jamie Cameron, ed., *The Charter's Impact on the Criminal Justice System* (Toronto: Carswell, 1996), 283.

127 *Dunmore v. Ontario (Attorney General)*, [2001] 3 S.C.R. 1016.

128 Ibid., para. 45

129 Ibid., para. 63.

130 Ibid., para. 64.

131 Timothy Macklem, "Vriend v. Alberta: Making the Private Public," *McGill Law Journal* 44 (1999): 225-26; Miriam Smith, *Lesbian and Gay Rights in Canada: Social Movements and Equality-Seeking, 1971-1995* (Toronto: University of Toronto Press, 1999), 99-100.

132 *Vriend*, para. 113.

133 *M. v. H.,* [1999] 2 S.C.R. 3 at para. 18.
134 Ibid., para. 73.
135 Ibid., para. 93.
136 Ibid., para. 116.
137 Ibid., para. 126.
138 Manfredi, *Judicial Power and the Charter,* 2nd ed., 135.
139 L. Martin Overby, "Free Voting in a Provincial Parliament: The Case of 'Same-Sex' Legislation in Ontario, 1994," *The Journal of Legislative Studies* 2 (1996): 176.
140 Ibid., 180.
141 Sujit Choudhry and Kent Roach, "Putting the Past behind Us? Prospective Judicial and Legislative Constitutional Remedies," *Supreme Court Law Review,* 2nd ser., 21 (2003): 233.
142 Morton and Knopff, *The Charter Revolution and the Court Party,* 163-66.

Chapter 6: The Charter and Canadian Federalism
  1 Peter W. Hogg, "Federalism Fights the Charter," in David Shugarman and Reg Whitaker, eds., *Federalism and Political Community* (Peterborough, ON: Broadview Press, 1989), 250.
  2 Guy Laforest, *Trudeau and the End of a Canadian Dream* (Montreal and Kingston: McGill-Queen's University Press, 1995), 134.
  3 James B. Kelly, "Reconciling Rights and Federalism during Review of the Charter of Rights and Freedoms: The Supreme Court of Canada and the Centralization Thesis, 1982 to 1999," *Canadian Journal of Political Science* 34 (2001): 321-26.
  4 Peter H. Russell, "The Political Purposes of the Charter: Have They Been Fulfilled?" in P. Bryden, S. Davis, and J. Russell, eds., *Protecting Rights and Freedoms* (Toronto: University of Toronto Press, 1994), 37.
  5 Janet L. Hiebert, *Limiting Rights* (Montreal and Kingston: McGill-Queen's University Press, 1996), 137-38; Katherine E. Swinton, *The Supreme Court and Canadian Federalism* (Toronto: Carswell, 1990), 345-46.
  6 Donna Greschner, "The Supreme Court, Federalism and Metaphors of Moderation," *Canadian Bar Review* 79 (2000): 55.
  7 Rainer Knopff and F.L. Morton, "Nation Building and the Canadian Charter of Rights and Freedoms," in Alan C. Cairns and Cynthia Williams, eds., *Constitutionalism, Citizenship and Society in Canada* (Toronto: University of Toronto Press, 1985), 147.
  8 Alain Gagnon and Guy Laforest, "The Future of Federalism: Lessons from Canada and Quebec," *International Journal* 28 (1993): 477-78.
  9 F.L. Morton, "The Effects of the Charter of Rights on Canadian Federalism," *Publius* 25 (1995): 179-80.
 10 Yves de Montigny, "The Impact (Real or Apprehended) of the Canadian Charter of Rights and Freedoms on the Legislative Authority of Quebec," in David Schneiderman and Kate Sutherland, eds., *Charting the Consequences* (Toronto: University of Toronto Press, 1997), 9-10.
 11 Laforest, *Trudeau and the End of a Canadian Dream,* 134.
 12 Morton, "The Effects of the Charter of Rights on Canadian Federalism," 181.
 13 F.L. Morton, "Judicial Politics Canadian Style: The Supreme Court's Contribution to the Constitutional Crisis of 1992," in Curtis Cook, ed., *Constitutional Predicament* (Montreal and Kingston: McGill-Queen's University Press, 1994), 139.
 14 *Attorney General (Quebec) v. Protestant School Boards,* [1984] 2 S.C.R. 66.
 15 *Ford v. Quebec,* [1988] 2 S.C.R. 712.
 16 *Devine v. Quebec (A.G.),* [1988] 2 S.C.R. 790.
 17 Peter H. Russell, "Standing Up for Notwithstanding," *Alberta Law Review* 29 (1991): 304.
 18 Tsvi Kahana, "The Notwithstanding Mechanism and Public Discussion: Lessons from the Ignored Practice of Section 33 of the Charter," *Canadian Public Administration* 44 (2001): 256-57. Kahana disputes that the notwithstanding clause has only been used twice and contends that it has been used sixteen times at the provincial level.
 19 Laforest, *Trudeau and the End of a Canadian Dream,* 134-35, 147-48.
 20 Russell, "The Political Purposes of the Charter," 37.

21 Peter W. Hogg and Allison A. Bushell, "The *Charter* Dialogue between Courts and Legislatures," *Osgoode Hall Law Journal* 35 (1997): 82.
22 Christopher P. Manfredi and James B. Kelly, "Six Degrees of Dialogue: A Response to Hogg and Bushell," *Osgoode Hall Law Journal* 37 (1999): 520-21.
23 *Libman v. Quebec*, [1997] 3 S.C.R. 569.
24 Shannon Ishiyama Smithey, "The Effects of the Canadian Supreme Court's Charter Interpretation on Regional and Intergovernmental Tensions in Canada," *Publius* 26 (1996): 90-91; Josée Legault, "How to Deny Quebec's Right to Self-Determination," *Globe and Mail* (Montreal), 21 August 1998.
25 B.L. Strayer, "Life under the Canadian Charter: Adjusting the Balance between Courts and Legislatures," *Public Law* (1988): 359.
26 *Thibault v. Corp. Professionel Médicins du Québec*, [1988] 1 S.C.R. 1033; *Edmonton Journal v. Alberta*, [1989] 2 S.C.R. 1326; *Andrews v. Law Society (B.C.)*, [1989] 1 S.C.R. 143; *Black v. Law Society (Alberta)*, [1989] 1 S.C.R. 591.
27 *Rocket v. Royal College of Dental Surgeons*, [1990] 2 S.C.R. 232.
28 Hogg and Bushell, "The *Charter* Dialogue between Courts and Legislatures," 117.
29 Peter H. Russell, "Canadian Constraints on Judicialization from Without," *International Political Science Review* 15 (1994): 173.
30 James B. Kelly, "The *Charter of Rights and Freedoms* and the Rebalancing of Liberal Constitutionalism in Canada, 1982-1997," *Osgoode Hall Law Journal* 37 (1999): 646-47.
31 *Dunmore v. Ontario (Attorney General)*, [2001] 3 S.C.R. 1016 [*Dunmore*]; *UFCW, Local 1518 v. Kmart Canada Ltd.*, [1999] 2 S.C.R. 1083.
32 *Nova Scotia (Workers' Compensation Board) v. Martin*, [2003] 2 S.C.R. 504 [*Nova Scotia v. Martin*].
33 *Vriend v. Alberta*, [1998] 1 S.C.R. 493; *M. v. H.*, [1999] 2 S.C.R. 3.
34 *Eldridge v. British Columbia*, [1997] 3 S.C.R. 624.
35 *Reference Re Public Schools Act (Manitoba), ss.79(3), (4), and (7)*, [1993] 1 S.C.R. 839; *Arsenault-Cameron v. Prince Edward Island*, [2000] 1 S.C.R. 3.
36 There were three cases in this reference decision: *Reference Re Remuneration of Judges of the Provincial Court of Prince Edward Island*, [1997] 3 S.C.R. 3; *R. v. Campbell*, [1999] 2 S.C.R. 956; and *Manitoba Provincial Judges Assn. v. Manitoba (Minister of Justice)*, [1997] 3 S.C.R. 3. See note 42 in Chapter 5.
37 *Mackin v. New Brunswick (Minister of Finance)*, [2002] 1 S.C.R. 405.
38 *R. v. Sharpe*, [2001] 1 S.C.R. 45 at para. 129.
39 *Little Sisters Book and Art Emporium v. Canada (Minister of Justice)*, [2000] 2 S.C.R. 1120 at para. 159.
40 Kent Roach, "Remedial Consensus and Dialogue under the *Charter*: General Declarations and Delayed Declarations of Invalidity," *UBC Law Review* 35 (2002): 220-21.
41 Timothy Macklem, "Vriend v. Alberta: Making the Private Public," *McGill Law Journal* 44 (1999): 225-27.
42 Steve Chase, "Notwithstanding Clause: Klein Ponders Overruling Courts on Gay Rights," *Calgary Herald*, 7 April 1998, A1.
43 Brian Laghi, "Alberta to Let Court Ruling on Gay Rights to Stand," *Globe and Mail* (Toronto), 10 April 1998, A5.
44 Brian Laghi, "Debate on Gay Rights Polarizes Albertans," *Globe and Mail* (Toronto), 2 April 1998, A12.
45 F.L. Morton and Rainer Knopff, *The Charter Revolution and the Court Party* (Peterborough, ON: Broadview Press, 2000), 165-66.
46 *Edmonton Journal*, 30 March 1999, A1.
47 Miriam Smith, "Recognizing Same-Sex Relationships: The Evolution of Recent Federal and Provincial Policies," *Canadian Public Administration* 45 (2002): 9, 18.
48 *Trociuk v. British Columbia (Attorney General)*, [2003] 1 S.C.R. 835.
49 Janet L. Hiebert, *Charter Conflicts* (Montreal and Kingston: McGill-Queen's University Press, 2002), 184-96.
50 Smith, "Recognizing Same-Sex Relationships," 2-3, 18.
51 Author interviews with departmental officials in provincial ministries: Department of Justice, Government of Newfoundland and Labrador, 11-12 February 2002, St. John's NF;

Ministry of the Attorney General, Government of Ontario, 21 May 2002, Toronto, ON; Ministry of Justice and Attorney General, Government of Alberta, 18 December 2002, Edmonton, AB; Department of Justice, Government of Saskatchewan, 13-14 February 2003, Regina, SK; Department of Justice, Government of Manitoba, 17-19 February 2003, Winnipeg, MB; Office of the Attorney General, Government of Prince Edward Island, 28-29 April 2003, Charlottetown, PEI; Department of Justice, Government of New Brunswick, 25-26 September 2003, Fredericton, NB.

52 Christopher P. Manfredi and Antonia Maioni, "Courts and Health Policy: Judicial Policy Making and Publicly Funded Health Care in Canada," *Journal of Health Politics, Policy and Law* 27 (2002): 213-40.

53 Roach, "Remedial Consensus and Dialogue under the Charter," 229.

54 Greschner, "The Supreme Court, Federalism and Metaphors of Moderation," 59-60.

55 Peter H. Russell, "The Effect of a Charter of Rights on the Policy-Making Role of Canadian Courts," *Canadian Public Administration* 25 (1982): 18.

56 Hiebert, *Limiting Rights*, 137-38; Patrick J. Monahan, *Constitutional Law*, 2nd ed. (Toronto: Irwin Law, 2002), 406-7, 414-22.

57 Swinton, *The Supreme Court and Canadian Federalism*, 342-43.

58 *Adler v. Ontario*, [1996] 3 S.C.R. 609 [*Adler*]; *Eaton v. Brant County Board of Education*, [1997] 1 S.C.R. 241; *R. v. Jones*, [1986] 2 S.C.R. 285 [*Jones*].

59 *Reference Re Public Service Employee Relations Act*, [1987] 1 S.C.R. 313; *RWDSU v. Saskatchewan*, [1987] 1 S.C.R. 460. The Alberta statutes challenged were the *Public Service Employee Relations Act*, R.S.A. 1980; the *Labour Relations Act*, R.S.A. 1980; and the *Police Officers Collective Bargaining Act*, S.A. 1983. The Saskatchewan statute challenged was *The Dairy Workers Act*, S.S. 1983-1984.

60 *Reference Re Workers' Compensation Act, 1983*, [1989] 2 S.C.R. 335; *Irwin Toy v. A.G. Quebec*, [1989] 1 S.C.R. 927.

61 *Gosselin v. Quebec*, [2002] 4 S.C.R. 429.

62 *B.(R.) v. Children's Aid Society of Metropolitan Toronto*, [1995] 1 S.C.R. 315; *Winnipeg Child and Family Services v. K.L.W.*, [2000] 2 S.C.R. 519.

63 *Reference Re Provincial Electoral Boundaries (Saskatchewan)*, [1991] 2 S.C.R. 158; *Mackay v. Manitoba*, [1989] 2 S.C.R. 357.

64 *R. v. Hufsky*, [1988] 1 S.C.R. 621; *R. v. Ladouceur*, [1990] 1 S.C.R. 1257.

65 *Reference Re Bill 30, An Act to Amend the Education Act (Ontario)*, [1987] 1 S.C.R. 1149 [*Reference Re Bill 30*].

66 Section 29 of the Charter says: "Nothing in this Charter abrogates or derogates from any rights or privileges guaranteed by or under the Constitution of Canada in respect of denominational, separate or dissentient schools."

67 *Reference Re Bill 30*, 1197.

68 Ibid., 1207.

69 *Ontario Home Builders' Association v. York Region Board of Education*, [1996] 2 S.C.R. 929 at 941.

70 *Adler*, 642.

71 *Ell v. Alberta*, [2003] 1 S.C.R. 857 at para. 18.

72 *Jones*, 304.

73 *R. v. Edwards Books and Art Ltd.*, [1986] 2 S.C.R. 713.

74 Ibid., 802.

75 *R. v. S.(S.)*, [1990] 2 S.C.R. 254; *R. v. Turpin*, [1989] 1 S.C.R. 1296; *R. v. Lyons*, [1989] 2 S.C.R. 309.

76 For similar analysis of these cases, see Hiebert, *Limiting Rights*, 133-34.

77 *R. v. S.(S.)*, 255-56.

78 Ibid., 288.

79 Ibid., 289.

80 *McKinney v. University of Guelph*, [1990] 3 S.C.R. 229 [*McKinney*]; *Stoffman v. Vancouver General Hospital*, [1990] 3 S.C.R. 483.

81 In *McKinney*, only Justice Wilson found that mandatory retirement policies did not constitute a reasonable limitation on section 15(1).

82 *McKinney*, 314.
83 *Haig v. Canada*, [1993] 2 S.C.R. 995.
84 Ibid., 1023.
85 Ibid., 1024.
86 Ibid., 1046.
87 *Dunmore*, para. 64.
88 *R. v. Advance Cutting & Coring Ltd.*, [2001] 3 S.C.R. 209.
89 Ibid., 239.
90 Ibid., para. 275.
91 Ibid.
92 *Nova Scotia v. Martin*, para. 110. Legislative objectives the court rejected as pressing and substantial based on submissions in the case were (1) the need to ensure the financial viability of the Workers' Compensation Fund; (2) the need to establish a consistent administrative response for evaluating chronic pain claims; and (3) the need to implement early medical treatments to facilitate optimal returns to work. Only the need to prevent fraudulent claims was accepted as pressing and substantial.
93 Ibid., para. 113.
94 Ibid.
95 Ibid.
96 *R. v. Morgentaler*, [1988] 1 S.C.R. 30.
97 Christopher P. Manfredi, *Judicial Power and the Charter* (Toronto: McClelland and Stewart, 1993), 119, 163; Ian T. Urquhart, "Federalism, Ideology, and Charter Review: Alberta's Response to Morgentaler," *Canadian Journal of Law and Society* 4 (1989): 160-61.
98 The exception to this statement would be *R. v. Feeney*, [1997] 2 S.C.R. 13, in which provincial warrant requirements were affected by the court's ruling. In *New Brunswick (Minister of Health and Community Services) v. G.(J.)*, [1999] 3 S.C.R. 46 [*New Brunswick v. G.(J.)*], the court placed an obligation, in limited circumstances, to provide state-funded counsel.
99 *R. v. Brydges*, [1990] 1 S.C.R. 190 at 216-17.
100 Ibid., 212.
101 *R. v. Bartle*, [1994] 3 S.C.R. 173; *R. v. Wozniak*, [1994] 3 S.C.R. 310 [*Wozniak*]; and *R. v. Cobham*, [1994] 3 S.C.R. 360.
102 *Wozniak*, 319.
103 Ibid.
104 *R. v. Prosper*, [1994] 3 S.C.R. 236.
105 Ibid., 267.
106 Ibid., 265.
107 *New Brunswick v. G.(J.)*, para. 2.
108 *R. v. Matheson*, [1994] 3 S.C.R. 328; *R. v. Latimer*, [1997] 1 S.C.R. 217 [*Latimer*].
109 *Latimer*, 236-37.
110 Hogg and Bushell, "The *Charter* Dialogue between Courts and Legislatures," 79-81.
111 Mary Dawson, "Governing in a Rights Culture," *Supreme Court Law Review*, 2nd ser., 21 (2001): 251-80; Janet L. Hiebert, "Legislative Scrutiny: An Alternative Approach for Protecting Rights," in Joseph F. Fletcher, ed., *Ideas in Action: Essays on Politics and Law in Honour of Peter Russell* (Toronto: University of Toronto Press, 1999), 298-307.
112 James B. Kelly, "Governing with the Charter of Rights and Freedoms," *Supreme Court Law Review*, 2nd ser., 21 (2003): 299-337.
113 Kent Roach, *The Supreme Court on Trial* (Toronto: Irwin Law, 2001), 146.
114 Torbjörn Vallinder, "The Judicialization of Politics – A World-Wide Phenomenon: Introduction," *International Political Science Review* 15 (1994): 91.
115 Sujit Choudhry and Claire E. Hunter, "Measuring Judicial Activism on the Supreme Court of Canada: A Comment on Newfoundland (Treasury Board) v. NAPE," *McGill Law Journal* 48 (2003): 547.
116 The organizational name varies considerably at the provincial level, with Department of Justice, Department of the Attorney General, Office of the Attorney General, and Department of Justice and Attorney General employed in several provinces. For simplicity, I will refer to provincial departments of Justice and use the precise name when discussing specific provinces.

117 I conducted a total of 100 interviews at both the federal and provincial levels. The provincial interviews were conducted between 11 February 2002 and 20 November 2003, and seventy-three public servants participated. The provincial participants were mainly drawn from departments of Justice, executive counsel offices, and legislative counsel offices, if they were separate offices, as in the case of Nova Scotia. Only one department of Justice declined to participate, and that was Nova Scotia's. However, I did conduct interviews with members of the Office of Legislative Counsel and the Executive Counsel Office. The federal interviews involved public servants (twenty) and members of parliament (seven) and occurred between 30 September 1997 and 19 September 2003. The interviews in September 2003 with Justice officials verified the findings of the 1997 research and identified any changes in Charter review functions during the design of legislation since 1997.

118 Author interviews with departmental officials: Department of Justice, Newfoundland and Labrador, 11 February 2002; Department of Justice, Saskatchewan, 11 February 2003; Department of Justice, Manitoba, 17 February 2003.

119 Author interview with departmental officials in the Ministry of Justice, Government of Quebec, 20 November 2003, Ste.-Foy, QC. This point was made often in interviews with departmental officials in each province: Department of Justice, Newfoundland and Labrador, 11-12 February 2002; Ministry of the Attorney General, Ontario, 21 May, 8 and 26-28 November 2002; Ministry of Attorney General, Government of British Columbia, 9-11 December 2002, Victoria, BC; Ministry of Justice and Attorney General, Alberta, 16-18 December 2002; Department of Justice, Saskatchewan, 10-14 February 2003; Department of Justice, Manitoba, 17-19 February 2003; Office of the Attorney General, Prince Edward Island, 28-30 April 2003; Department of Justice, New Brunswick, 25-26 September, 10 October 2003. This point was also made in interviews with the Executive Council Office and the Office of Legislative Counsel, Government of Nova Scotia, 27 November 2003, Halifax, NS.

120 Patrick J. Monahan and Marie Finkelstein, "The Charter of Rights and Public Policy in Canada," *Osgoode Hall Law Journal* 30 (1992): 501-44; Julie Jai, "Policy, Politics and Law: Changing Relationships in Light of the Charter," *National Journal of Constitutional Law* 9 (1996): 11-12; Grant Huscroft, "The Attorney General and *Charter* Challenges to Legislation: Advocate or Adjudicator?" *National Journal of Constitutional Law* 5 (1995): 135-38; Ian Scott, "Law, Policy, and the Role of the Attorney General: Constancy and Change in the 1980s," *University of Toronto Law Review* 39 (1989): 109-26.

121 The following Alberta ministries have seconded solicitors from Justice and Attorney General: Energy, Environment, Health and Wellness, Municipal Affairs.

122 Author interviews with departmental officials: Ministry of the Attorney General, Ontario, 21 May 2002; Ministry of Justice, Quebec, 20 November 2003.

123 Author interview with departmental officials in the Ministry of the Attorney General, Ontario, 30 May, 8 and 26 November 2002.

124 Author interview with departmental officials in the Ministry of Justice, Quebec.

125 Author interview with departmental officials in the Ministry of the Attorney General, Ontario, 26 November 2002.

126 Ibid., 30 May, 26 November 2002.

127 Ibid., 30 May, 8 November 2002.

128 Ibid., 30 May, 8 and 26 November 2002.

129 Author interviews with departmental officials: Ministry of Justice, Quebec, 20 November 2003; Quebec Human Rights Commission, Government of Quebec, 3 November 2003, Montreal, QC.

130 Author interview with departmental officials in the Ministry of Justice, Quebec, 20 November 2003.

131 Author interviews with departmental officials: Ministry of Justice, Quebec; Ministry of the Executive Council, Government of Quebec, 20 November 2003, Québec, QC.

132 Ibid.

133 Ibid.

134 Ibid.

135 Author interview with departmental officials in the Quebec Human Rights Commission, Montreal, QC, 3 November 2003.

136 R. Brian Howe and David Johnson, *Restraining Equality: Human Rights Commissions in Canada* (Toronto: University of Toronto Press, 2000), 48-49.

137 When provincial human rights codes provide a review function for human rights commissions, it is generally a monitoring mechanism that evaluates the functioning of acts. Thus, the Quebec Human Rights Commission comments on the development and functioning of acts, whereas the remaining provincial human rights commissions have a much more limited function after an act is proclaimed into law.

138 Author interviews with departmental officials in the Quebec Human Rights Commission, Montreal, QC, 2 November 2003.

139 Smithey, "The Effects of the Canadian Supreme Court's Charter Interpretation on Regional and Intergovernmental Tensions in Canada," 92.

140 Sheila A. Gallagher, "The Public Policy Process and Charter Litigation," in Patrick J. Monahan and Marie Finkelstein, eds., *The Impact of the Charter on the Public Policy Process* (Concord, ON: Beckers Associates, 1993), 85.

141 British Columbia, Ministry of Attorney General, Office of Legislative Counsel, *Guide to Preparing Drafting Instructions for Legislation* (August 2000), 4. This document is on file with the author.

142 Author interview with departmental officials in the Ministry of Attorney General, British Columbia, 9 December 2002.

143 Request for Legislation, Government of British Columbia, 2. Document on file with author.

144 Donald J. Savoie, *Governing from the Centre* (Toronto: University of Toronto Press, 1999), 3-4; Christopher Dunn, *The Institutionalized Cabinet* (Montreal and Kingston: McGill Queen's University Press, 1995), 243-44.

145 For an account of Charter vetting in Saskatchewan, see Graeme Mitchell, "The Impact of the Charter on the Public Policy Process: The Attorney General," in Patrick J. Monahan and Marie Finkelstein, eds., *The Impact of the Charter on the Public Policy Process* (Concord, ON: Beckers Associates, 1993), 78-80.

146 Author interviews with departmental officials: Department of Justice, Newfoundland and Labrador, 11-12 February 2002; Ministry of Justice and Attorney General, Alberta, 16-18 December 2002; Department of Justice, Saskatchewan, 11 and 13 February 2003; Department of Justice, Manitoba, 17-19 February 2003; Office of the Attorney General, Prince Edward Island, 28-29 April 2003; Department of Justice, New Brunswick, 25-26 September, 10 October 2003; Executive Council Office, Nova Scotia, 31 October 2003; Office of Legislative Counsel, Nova Scotia, 27 November 2003.

147 See, for example, Saskatchewan, Department of Justice, Office of Legislative Drafting, *Drafting Style Guide*, 10:2. Document on file with author.

148 Author interviews with departmental officials: Department of Justice, Newfoundland and Labrador, 13 February 2003; Department of Justice, Saskatchewan, 11 and 13 February 2003; Department of Justice, Manitoba, 17-18 February 2003; Office of the Attorney General, Prince Edward Island, 28-29 April 2003.

149 Author interviews with departmental officials: Department of Justice, Saskatchewan, 13 February 2003; Department of Justice, Manitoba, 17 February 2003; Office of the Attorney General, Prince Edward Island, 28 April 2003.

150 Author interview with the Right Honourable Pierre Elliott Trudeau, PC, QC, 5 September 1997, Montreal, QC.

151 Alain C. Cairns, "The Judicial Committee and Its Critics," *Canadian Journal of Political Science* 3 (1971): 319.

Chapter 7: Governing with the Charter of Rights

1 Janet L. Hiebert, "Why Must a Bill of Rights Be a Contest of Political and Judicial Wills? The Canadian Alternative," *Public Law Review* 10 (1999): 23-24.

2 Peter W. Hogg and Allison A. Bushell, "The *Charter* Dialogue between Courts and Legislatures (Or Perhaps the *Charter* Isn't Such a Bad Thing After All)," *Osgoode Hall Law Journal* 35 (1997).

3 Donald J. Savoie, *Governing from the Centre* (Toronto: University of Toronto Press, 1999).

4 Peter Aucoin, "Organizational Changes in the Machinery of Canadian Government: From Rational Management to Brokerage Politics," *Canadian Journal of Political Science* 19 (1986): 3-27.

5 James B. Kelly, "Guarding the Constitution: Parliamentary and Judicial Roles under the Charter of Rights and Freedoms," in Harvey Lazar, Peter Meekison, and Hamish Telford, eds., *Canada: The State of the Federation, 2002* (Montreal and Kingston: McGill-Queen's University Press, 2004), 77-110.

6 James B. Kelly, "Bureaucratic Activism and the Charter of Rights and Freedoms: The Department of Justice and Its Entry into the Centre of Government," *Canadian Public Administration* 42 (1999): 476-511.

7 For a recent account of this issue see Peter Aucoin and Lori Turnbull, "The Democratic Deficit: Paul Martin and Parliamentary Reform," *Canadian Public Administration* 46 (2003): 427-49.

8 Author interviews with departmental officials: Department of Justice, Government of Canada, 19 September 2003, Ottawa, ON; Ministry of the Attorney General, Government of Ontario, 8 and 26 November 2002, Toronto, ON.

9 Author interviews with departmental officials: Department of Justice, 19 September and 31 October 2003, 29 September and 1 October 1997; Legal Service Unit, Department of Justice, Government of Canada, 1 and 7 October 1997, Ottawa, ON; Privy Council Office, Government of Canada, 8 October 1997, Ottawa, ON. Author interview with former DOJ official, 8 October 1997, Ottawa, ON. See also John Tait, "Policy Development and the Charter," *Perspectives on Public Policy* 7 (1995): 9-10; Honourable Brian Dickson, "The Canadian Charter of Rights and Freedoms: Dawn of a New Era?" *Review of Constitutional Studies* 2 (1994): 11-12.

10 A central agency is also referred to as an executive-support agency because it supports the prime minister and, to a lesser degree, the cabinet.

11 Donald Savoie, *The Politics of Public Spending in Canada* (Toronto: University of Toronto Press, 1990), 77.

12 Savoie, *Governing from the Centre,* 7, 72, 260.

13 Aucoin, "Organizational Changes in the Machinery of Canadian Government," 10-11; Ian D. Clark, "Recent Changes in the Cabinet Decision-Making System in Ottawa," *Canadian Public Administration* 28 (1985): 194; Paul Thomas, "Central Agencies: Making a Mesh of Things," in James P. Bickerton and Alain G. Gagnon, eds., *Canadian Politics* (Peterborough, ON: Broadview Press, 1994), 289-90; and Donald J. Savoie, "Central Agencies: A Government of Canada Perspective," in Jacques Bourgault, Maurice Demers, and Cynthia Williams, eds., *Public Administration and Public Management Experiences in Canada* (Ste.-Foy, QC: Publications du Québec, 1997), 60.

14 G. Bruce Doern, "From Sectoral to Macro Green Governance: The Canadian Department of the Environment as an Aspiring Central Agency," *Governance* 6 (1993): 180-83.

15 Aucoin, "Organizational Changes in the Machinery of Canadian Government," 3-27.

16 Savoie, *Governing from the Centre,* 72-74.

17 Ibid., 338.

18 Peter H. Russell, "The Effect of a Charter of Rights on the Policy-Making Role of Canadian Courts," *Canadian Public Administration* 25 (1982): 14.

19 Howard Leeson, "Section 33, the Notwithstanding Clause: A Paper Tiger?" *Choices* 6 (2000): 14-16; Tsvi Kahana, "The Notwithstanding Mechanism and Public Discussion: Lessons from the Ignored Practice of Section 33 of the Charter," *Canadian Public Administration* 44 (2001): 259-72.

20 Kelly, "Guarding the Constitution," 98-103.

21 Patrick J. Monahan and Marie Finkelstein, "The Charter of Rights and Public Policy in Canada," *Osgoode Hall Law Journal* 30 (1992): 510-11.

22 Author interview with departmental official in the Privy Council Office, 8 October 1997. Author interview with former DOJ official, 8 October 1997.

23 Ibid.

24 Kelly, "Bureaucratic Activism and the Charter of Rights and Freedoms," 491.

25 Author interviews with departmental officials: Department of Justice, 19 September 2003; Legal Service Unit, DOJ, 2 October 1997. Author interview with former DOJ official, 2 October 1997, Ottawa, ON.
26 B.L. Strayer, "Life under the Canadian Charter: Adjusting the Balance between Legislatures and Courts," *Public Law* (1988): 359.
27 Thomas, "Central Agencies," 289.
28 Author interviews with departmental officials: Department of Justice, 31 October 2003 and 1 October 1997; Privy Council Office, 8 October 1997. Author interviews with former DOJ officials, 22 August 2001, 7-8 October 1997, and 30 September 1997, Ottawa, ON.
29 Jeremy Croft, *Whitehall and the Human Rights Act, 1998: The First Year* (London: Constitution Unit, 2000), 10-16.
30 Author interview with former DOJ official, 22 August 2001 and 30 September 1997.
31 Mary Dawson, "The Impact of the Charter on the Public Policy Process and the Department of Justice," *Osgoode Hall Law Journal* 30 (1992): 597.
32 Author interview with departmental official in the Department of Justice, 19 September 2003. Author interviews with former DOJ officials, 22 August 2001, 2 October 1997, and 30 September 1997.
33 This was the *Statute Law (Canadian Charter of Rights and Freedoms) Amendment Act,* R.S.C. 1985, c.31 (1st Supp.).
34 See Minister of Justice and Attorney General of Canada, *Equality Issues in Federal Law: A Discussion Paper* (Ottawa: Department of Justice, 1985).
35 Author interviews with departmental officials: Legal Service Unit, DOJ, 29 September 1997; Privy Council Office, 29 September 1997.
36 Author interviews with departmental officials: Department of Justice, 19 September 2003; Privy Council Office, 8 October 1997; Legal Service Unit, DOJ, 7 October 1997. Author interviews with former DOJ officials, 22 August 2001, 8 October 1997, 30 September 1997.
37 Author interviews with departmental officials: Legal Service Unit, DOJ, 7 October 1997; Privy Council Office, 8 October 1997. Author interview with former DOJ official, 8 October 1997.
38 Author interview with departmental official in the Privy Council Office, 8 October 1997. Author interviews with former DOJ official, 2 and 8 October 1997.
39 Author interviews with former DOJ official, 22 August 2001 and 30 September 1997.
40 Mary Dawson, "Governing in a Rights Culture," *Supreme Court Law Review,* 2nd ser., 14 (2001): 269-75.
41 Author interviews with former DOJ official, 22 August 2001 and 30 September 1997.
42 Ibid.
43 Savoie, *Governing from the Centre,* 338-39.
44 *Schacter v. Canada,* [1992] 2 S.C.R. 679.
45 Ian Brodie, "The Charter and the Policy Process," paper presented at the annual meeting of the Canadian Political Science Association, June 1995, 27-28.
46 Author interviews with departmental officials in the Department of Justice, 30 September and 1 October 1997. This point was reiterated in recent interviews with DOJ officials, 19 September 2003. Author interview with former DOJ officials, 30 September and 2 October 1997. John Tait was deputy minister of justice and deputy attorney general of Canada between 1988 and October 1994.
47 Dawson, "The Impact of the Charter on the Public Policy Process," 595-96.
48 Author interviews with departmental officials in the Department of Justice, 19 September 2003 and 29 September 1997; Legal Service Unit, DOJ, 7 October 1997; Privy Council Office, 8 October 1997. Author interview with former DOJ official, 8 October 1997. The Charter checklist is not a public document but an internal document available only to Justice officials and members of LSUs.
49 Author interviews with former DOJ official, 22 August 2001 and 30 September 1997.
50 Author interviews with departmental officials: Department of Justice, 19 September 2003 and 29 September 1997; Legal Service Unit, DOJ, 7 October 1997.

51 Author interviews with departmental officials: Department of Justice, 29 September 1997; Legal Service Unit, DOJ, 7 October 1997; Privy Council Office, 8 October 1997. Author interview with former DOJ official, 8 October 1997.

52 Author interviews with departmental officials: Department of Justice, 19 September 2003 and 30 September 1997; Legal Service Unit, DOJ, 7 October 1997.

53 Department of Justice, *A Guide to the Making of Federal Acts and Regulations* (1995), http://www.canada.justice.gc.ca/en/jus/far/index.htm. Author interviews with departmental officials: Department of Justice, 19 September 2003 and 1 October 1997; Privy Council Office, 8 October 1997. Author interview with former DOJ official, 8 October 1997.

54 Author interview with departmental official in the Privy Council Office, 8 October 1997. Author interview with former DOJ official, 8 October 1997. See Privy Council Office, *Memoranda to Cabinet: A Drafter's Guide* (2005), B19.

55 Dawson, "The Impact of the Charter on the Public Policy Process," 597.

56 Author interview with departmental official in the Department of Justice, 29 September 1997.

57 Department of Justice, "Preparation and Enactment of Bills," Chapter 3 of *A Guide to the Making of Federal Acts and Regulations,* http://www.canada.justice.gc.ca/en/jus/far/Guidd05.htm.

58 Author interview with departmental official in the Department of Justice, 30 September 1997.

59 Author interviews with departmental officials: Department of Justice, 19 September 2003 and 30 September 1997; Department of the Solicitor General, Government of Canada, 1 October 1997, Ottawa, ON; Legal Service Unit, DOJ, 7 October 1997; Privy Council Office, 8 October 1997.

60 Author interviews with departmental officials: Department of Justice, 19 September and 31 October 2003; Department of the Solicitor General, 1 October 1997.

61 Richard Schultz, "Prime Ministerial Government, Central Agencies and Operating Departments: Towards a More Realistic Analysis," in Thomas Hockin, ed., *Apex of Power* (Toronto: Prentice-Hall, 1971), 229-76.

62 Author interviews with departmental officials in the Department of Justice, 19 September 2003 and 30 September 1997.

63 Author interviews with departmental officials: Department of Justice, 19 September 2003; Legal Service Unit, DOJ, 7 October 1997.

64 Ibid.

65 Author interviews with departmental officials: Department of Justice, 31 October and 19 September 2003, 1 October and 29 September 1997; Legal Service Unit, DOJ, 7 October 1997.

66 Author interview with departmental official in the Department of Justice, 19 September 2003.

67 Author interview with departmental official in the Department of Justice, 19 September 2003. Author interview with former DOJ official, 2 October 1997.

68 Ibid.

69 Author interview with departmental official in the Privy Council Office, 8 October 1997. Author interview with former DOJ official, 8 October 1997.

70 Thomas, "Central Agencies," 289.

71 Lorraine Eisenstat Weinrib, "Canada's Constitutional Revolution: From Legislative to Constitutional State," *Israel Law Review* 33 (1999): 22-25.

72 Ran Hirschl, *Towards Juristocracy: The Origins and Consequences of the New Constitutionalism* (Cambridge, MA: Harvard University Press, 2004), 50-99.

73 *R. v. Hall,* [2002] 3 S.C.R. 309.

74 *Sauvé v. Canada,* [2002] 3 S.C.R. 519 at para. 19.

75 Ibid., para. 37.

76 Ibid., para. 163-74.

77 *R. v. Sharpe,* [2001] 1 S.C.R. 45 at para. 98-100.

78 Ibid., para. 115.

79 *Figueroa v. Canada (Attorney General)*, [2003] 1 S.C.R. 912 at para. 80-89.

80 Croft, *Whitehall and the Human Rights Act*, 3-4; David Kinley, "Parliamentary Scrutiny of Human Rights: A Duty Neglected?" in Philip Alston, ed., *Promoting Human Rights through Bills of Rights* (Oxford: Oxford University Press, 1999), 158-84.

81 Department of Justice, *A Guide to the Making of Federal Acts and Regulations*, 3-4, http://www.canada.justice.gc.ca/en/jus/far/Index.htm.

82 Grant Huscroft, "The Attorney General and *Charter* Challenges to Legislation: Advocate or Adjudicator?" *National Journal of Constitutional Law* 5 (1995): 135-36.

83 Author interview with Senator Serge Joyal, Standing Senate Committee on Legal and Constitutional Affairs, 37th Parliament, 22 October 2002, Ottawa, ON.

84 Author interview with Honourable Margaret Wilson, attorney general of New Zealand, 12 May 2004, Wellington, New Zealand. The advice provided by the Ministry of Justice and Crown Law Office to the attorney general of New Zealand is available at http://www.justice.govt.nz.

85 Paul Rishworth, Grant Huscroft, Scott Optican, and Richard Mahoney, *The New Zealand Bill of Rights* (Melbourne: Oxford University Press, 2003), 195-201.

86 Author interview with Justice and Electoral Select Committee, New Zealand Parliament, 5-6 May 2004, Wellington, New Zealand.

87 Department of Justice, "Principles and Policies," Chapter 2 of *A Guide to the Making of Federal Acts and Regulations*, http://www.canada.justice.gc.ca/en/jus/far/Guidd04.htm.

88 C.E.S. Franks, "Parliament, Intergovernmental Relations, and National Unity" (Working Paper Series, Institute of Intergovernmental Relations, Queen's University, Kingston, ON, 1999), 10, http://www.iigr.ca/iigr.php/.

89 Department of Justice, "Notes for the Minister of Justice's Appearance before the Special Senate Committee on the Subject Matter of Bill C-36 Evidence" (speaking notes for the Honourable Anne McLellan, Minister of Justice and Attorney General of Canada), 29 October 2001, http://canada.justice.gc.ca/en/news/sp/2001/doc_27854.html.

90 For an account of this, see Kent Roach, *September 11: Consequences for Canada* (Montreal and Kingston: McGill-Queen's University Press, 2003), 56-84.

91 Justice Canada, "Concluding Comments from the Department of Justice," in Ronald J. Daniels, Patrick Macklem, and Kent Roach, eds., *The Security of Freedom: Essays on Canada's Anti-Terrorism Bill* (Toronto: University of Toronto Press, 2001), 435-45.

92 Special Senate Committee on the Subject Matter of Bill C-36, "First Report of the Committee," 1 November 2001, http://www.parl.gc.ca/37/1/parlbus/commbus/senate/com-e/sm36-e/rep-e/rep01oct01-e.htm.

93 Department of Justice, "Amendments to Bill C-36" (news release), 20 November 2001, http://canada.justice.gc.ca/en/news/nr/2001/doc_27902.html.

94 For a related analysis of the benefits of a parliament-centred approach, see Janet L. Hiebert, "Parliament and Rights," in Tom Campbell, Jeffrey Goldsworthy, and Adrienne Stone, eds., *Protecting Human Rights* (Oxford: Oxford University Press, 2003), 234-41.

95 C.E.S. Franks, "Representation and Policy-Making in Canada," in C.E.S. Franks, J.E. Hodgetts, O.P. Dwivedi, D. Williams, and W. Seymour Wilson, eds., *Canada's Century: Governing in a Maturing Society – Essays in Honour of John Meisel* (Montreal and Kingston: McGill-Queen's University Press, 1995), 72-73.

96 Hogg and Bushell, "The *Charter* Dialogue between Courts and Legislatures," 75-124; Janet C. Hiebert, "A Relational Approach to Constitutional Interpretation: Shared Legislative and Judicial Responsibilities," *Journal of Canadian Studies* 35 (2001): 161-81.

97 *R. v. Mills*, [1999] 3 S.C.R. 668 at para. 59.

98 *R. v. O'Connor*, [1995] 4 S.C.R. 411.

99 Christopher P. Manfredi and Scott Lemieux, "Judicial Discretion and Fundamental Justice: Sexual Assault Jurisprudence in the Supreme Court of Canada," *American Journal of Comparative Law* 47 (1999): 506-7.

100 Donald J. Savoie, "The Rise of Court Government in Canada," *Canadian Journal of Political Science* 32 (1999): 635-36.

101 Jonathon Malloy, "Reconciling Expectations and Reality in House of Commons Committees: The Case of the 1989 GST Inquiry," *Canadian Public Administration* 39 (1999): 318-19, 330-31.

102   *United States v. Burns,* [2001] 1 S.C.R. 283.

103   Ibid., para. 132.

104   Ibid., para. 129.

105   Ibid., para. 134.

106   George Williams, *A Bill of Rights for Australia* (Sydney: University of New South Wales Press, 2000), 45.

107   Standing Senate Committee on Legal and Constitutional Affairs, "Proceedings," Issue 60 (10 March 1999), 11, http://www.parl.gc.ca/36/1/parlbus/commbus/senate/com-e/lega-e/60ev-e.htm?Language=E&Parl=36&Ses=1&comm_id=11.

108   Ibid., Issue 63 (18 March 1999), 2-3, http://www.parl.gc.ca/36/1/parlbus/commbus/senate/com-e/lega-e/63cv-e.htm?Language=E&Parl=36&Ses=1&comm_id=11.

109   Ibid., Issue 62 (17 March 1999), 19-20, http://www.parl.gc.ca/36/1/parlbus/commbus/senate/com-e/lega-e/62ev-e.htm?Language=E&Parl=36&Ses=1&comm_id=11.

110   Ibid., Issue 63 (18 March 1999), 9.

111   Ibid., 15.

112   Standing Senate Committee on Legal and Constitutional Affairs, "Twenty-Third Report of the Committee," Issue 64 (25 March 1999), 1, http://www.parl.gc.ca/36/1/parlbus/commbus/senate/com-e/lega-e/64rp-e.htm?Language=E&Parl=36&Ses=1&comm_id=11.

113   For an analysis of rights vetting at the provincial level, see Huscroft, "The Attorney General and *Charter* Challenges to Legislation," 135-41.

114   Aisling Reidy and Meg Russell, "Second Chambers As Constitutional Guardians and Protectors of Human Rights," *The Constitution Unit* (June 1999) at 2-3, 10-13.

115   Geoffrey Palmer and Matthew Palmer, *Bridled Power,* 4th ed. (Wellington, NZ: Oxford University Press, 2004), 13-18.

116   Charles R. Epp, *The Rights Revolution: Lawyers, Activists, and Supreme Courts in Comparative Perspectives* (Chicago: University of Chicago Press, 1998), 156-57.

117   For a comparative assessment of the problems of executive dominance in Westminster democracies, see Geoffrey Palmer, *Unbridled Power: An Interpretation of New Zealand's Constitution and Government* (Don Mills, ON: Oxford University Press, 1999). Interestingly, after surveying the impact of electoral change in New Zealand and the introduction of the statutory *New Zealand Bill of Rights,* Sir Geoffrey changed the title in the fourth edition. See Palmer and Palmer, *Bridled Power.*

118   Author interview with Joyal.

Conclusion

1   Peter H. Russell, Special Joint Committee of the Senate and House of Commons on the Constitution of Canada Hearings, 8 January 1981, 34:148.

2   New Zealand, Justice and Law Reform Select Committee, *Inquiry into the White Paper – A Bill of Rights for New Zealand* (interim report of the committee), 1987.

3   Brian Slattery, "A Theory of the Charter," *Osgoode Hall Law Journal* 25 (1987): 701-47.

4   Christopher P. Manfredi and James B. Kelly, "Misrepresenting the Supreme Court's Record? A Comment on Sujit Choudhry and Claire E. Hunter, 'Measuring Judicial Activism on the Supreme Court'," *McGill Law Journal* 49 (2004): 12-14.

5   James B. Kelly, "Reconciling Rights and Federalism during Review of the Charter of Rights and Freedoms: The Supreme Court of Canada and the Centralization Thesis, 1982 to 1999," *Canadian Journal of Political Science* 34 (2001): 321-55.

6   Privy Council Office, *Ethics, Responsibility, Accountability: An Action Plan for Democratic Reform* (2004), http://www.pco-bcp.gc.ca/default.asp?Language=E&Page=Publications&doc=dr-rd/dr-rd_e.htm.

7   Stephen Gardbaum, "The New Commonwealth Model of Constitutionalism," *American Journal of Comparative Law* 49 (2001): 709.

8   Julie Debeljak, "Rights Protection without Judicial Supremacy: A Review of the Canadian and British Models of Bills of Rights," *Melbourne University Law Review* 26 (2002): 285-324.

9   Mark Tushnet, "Non-Judicial Review," *Harvard Journal on Legislation* 40 (2003): 492.

10   Paul Rishworth, Grant Huscroft, Scott Optican, and Richard Mahoney, *The New Zealand Bill of Rights* (Melbourne: Oxford University Press, 2003), 116-67.

Bibliography

Government Documents

Alberta Human Rights Commission. *Equal in Dignity and Rights: A Review of Human Rights in Alberta by the Alberta Human Rights Review Panel*. Edmonton, AB: Alberta Human Rights Commission, 1994.

Background Notes, Charter of Rights and Freedoms. Tabled by the Delegation of the Government of Canada, 5 July 1980. (Document 830-81/029).

Background Notes, Entrenching a Charter of Rights. Tabled by the Delegation of the Government of Canada, 5 July 1980. (Document 830-81/026).

Charter of Rights, *Report to Ministers by Sub-Committee of Officials*. 29 August 1980. Tabular Comparison of Charter of Rights Drafts. (Document 830-84/031).

Consolidation of Proposed Constitutional Resolution Tabled by the Minister of Justice in the House of Commons on 13 February 1981, with the Amendments Approved by the House of Commons on 23 April 1981 and by the Senate on 24 April 1981.

Consolidation of Proposed Resolution and Possible Amendments As Placed before the Special Joint Committee by the Minister of Justice, 12 January 1981. Together with Explanatory Notes. (Document on file with author.)

Continuing Committee of Ministers on the Constitution, Montreal, QC, 8-11 July 1980. *Rights and Freedoms within the Canadian Federation, Discussion Draft*. Tabled by the Delegation of the Government of Canada, 4 July 1980. (Document 830-81/027).

Continuing Committee of Ministers of the Constitution, Montreal, QC, 8-11 July 1980. *Statement by the Honourable Jean Chrétien*. (Document 830-81/025).

Continuing Committee of Ministers on the Constitution, Vancouver, BC, 22-24 July 1980. *Report by the Sub-Committee of Officials on a Charter of Rights, 24 July 1980*. (Document 830-83/019).

Continuing Committee of Ministers on the Constitution, Ottawa, ON, 26-29 August 1980. *The Canadian Charter of Rights and Freedoms, Federal Draft, 22 August 1980*. (Document 830-84/004).

Department of Justice. "Notes for the Minister of Justice's Appearance before the Special Senate Committee on the Subject Matter of Bill C-36 Evidence." Speaking notes for the Honourable Anne McLellan, Minister of Justice and Attorney General of Canada, 29 October 2001, http://canada.justice.gc.ca/en/news/sp/2001/doc_27854.html.

Federal-Provincial First Ministers' Conference, Ottawa, ON, 8-12 September 1980. *The Canadian Charter of Rights and Freedoms, Revised Discussion Draft, Federal, 3 September 1980*. (Document 800-14/064).

Federal-Provincial First Ministers' Conference, Ottawa, ON, 2-5 November 1981. *First Ministers' Agreement on the Constitution, 5 November 1981*. (Document 800-15/021).

Federal-Provincial Conference of First Ministers on the Constitution, Ottawa, ON, 8-12 September 1980. Verbatim Transcript.

Government of Saskatchewan, Department of Justice, Office of Legislative Drafting. *Drafting Style Guide*. October 2001.

Honourable Allan Blakeney, *Federal-Provincial Conference of First Ministers on the Constitution, Ottawa, 8-12 September 1980*. (Document 800-15/005).

Honourable Peter Lougheed. *Federal-Provincial Conference of First Ministers on the Constitution, Ottawa, 8-12 September 1980*. (Document 800-15/009).

Honourable Sterling Lyon. *Federal-Provincial Conference of First Ministers on the Constitution, Ottawa, 8-12 September 1980*. (Document 800-15/012).

Minister of Justice and Attorney General of Canada. *Statement by the Honourable John Chrétien, Minister of Justice, to the Special Joint Committee on the Constitution*. 12 January 1981.

New Zealand, Justice and Law Reform Select Committee. *Inquiry into the White Paper – A Bill of Rights for New Zealand*. Interim report of the Committee. New Zealand House of Representatives, 1987.

Premiers' Conference, Ottawa, ON. *Constitutional Accord: Canadian Patriation Plan, 16 April 1981*. (Document 850-19/002).

Prime Minister's Remarks at Close of Discussion on the Charter of Rights, 10 September 1980. (Document 800-14/078).

Privy Council Office, Government of Canada. Ottawa, ON (29 September and 8 October 1997).

–. *Memoranda to Cabinet: A Drafter's Guide*. 2005.

–. *Ethics, Responsibility, Accountability: An Action Plan for Democratic Reform* (2004), http://www.pco-bcp.gc.ca/default.asp?Language=E&Page=Publications&doc=dr-rd/dr-rd_e.htm.

Proposed Resolution for Joint Address to Her Majesty the Queen Respecting the Constitution of Canada. Tabled in the House of Commons and the Senate, 6 October 1980. (Catalogue no. YC3-321/5-57).

Proposed Resolution for a Joint Address to Her Majesty the Queen Respecting the Constitution of Canada, As Amended by the Committee. 13 February 1981.

Report to Parliament and Proposed Resolution for a Joint Address to Her Majesty the Queen Respecting the Constitution of Canada, As Amended by the Committee. The Special Joint Committee of the Senate and the House of Commons on the Constitution of Canada, 1980-81. 13 February 1981.

Special Joint Committee on the Constitution of Canada, Senate and House of Commons, 1980-81, 1st session, 32nd Parliament.

Special Senate Committee on the Subject Matter of Bill C-36. "First Report of the Committee." 1 November 2001, http://www.parl.gc.ca/37/1/parlbus/commbus/senate/com-e/sm36-e/rep-e/rep01oct01-e.htm.

Text of the Resolution Respecting the Constitution of Canada. Adopted by the House of Commons on 2 December 1981 and by the Senate on 8 December 1981. (Catalogue no. CP45-22/1981).

The Canadian Charter of Rights and Freedoms, Provincial Proposal (In the Event that There Is Going to Be Entrenchment). 28 August 1980. (Annex to Document 830-84/031).

Interviews

Alberta Human Rights and Citizenship Commission, Government of Alberta. Edmonton, AB (16 December 2002).

Andreychuk, Senator Raynell. Standing Senate Committee on Legal and Constitutional Affairs, 37th Parliament. Ottawa, ON (23 October 2002).

Barnett, Tim, MP (Christchurch Central). Chair of Justice and Electoral Select Committee, Parliament of New Zealand. Wellington, NZ (6 May 2004).

Beaudoin, Senator Gérald. Standing Senate Committee on Legal and Constitutional Affairs, 37th Parliament. Ottawa, ON (22 October 2002).

Cadman, Chuck, MP (Surrey North). Member of Standing Committee on Justice and Human Rights, 37th Parliament. Ottawa, ON (23 October 2002).

Collins, Judith, MP (Clevedon). Member of Justice and Electoral Select Committee, Parliament of New Zealand. Wellington, NZ (6 May 2004).

Cotler, Irwin, MP (Mont Royal). Member of Standing Committee on Justice and Human Rights, 37th Parliament. Ottawa, ON (23 October 2002).

Crown Law Office, Government of New Zealand. Wellington, NZ (6 May 2004).

Department of Justice, Government of Canada. Ottawa, ON (31 October 2003; 19 September 2003; 22 August 2001; 1-2, 7-8 October 1997; 19, 29-30 September 1997).

Department of Justice, Government of Manitoba. Winnipeg, MB (17-19 February 2003).

Department of Justice, Government of New Brunswick. Fredericton, NB (10 October 2003; 25-26 September 2003).

Department of Justice, Government of Newfoundland and Labrador. St. John's, NF (11-14 February 2002).

Department of Justice, Government of Saskatchewan. Regina, SK (10-14 February 2003).

Department of the Solicitor General, Government of Canada. Ottawa, ON (1 October 1997).

Executive Council Office, Government of Manitoba. Winnipeg, MB (18 February 2003).

Executive Council Office, Government of Nova Scotia. Halifax, NS (27 November 2003).

Executive Council Office, Government of Prince Edward Island. Charlottetown, PEI (27 November 2003).

Fairbrother, Russell, MP (Napier). Member of Justice and Electoral Select Committee, Parliament of New Zealand. Wellington, NZ (6 May 2004).

Joyal, Senator Serge. Standing Senate Committee on Legal and Constitutional Affairs, 37th Parliament. Ottawa, ON (22 October 2002).

Legal Service Units, Department of Justice, Government of Canada. Ottawa, ON (29 September to 7 October 1997).

Maloney, John, MP (Erie Lincoln). Member of Standing Committee on Justice and Human Rights, 37th Parliament. Ottawa, ON (23 October 2002).

McKay, John, MP (Scarborough East). Member of Standing Committee on Justice and Human Rights, 37th Parliament. Ottawa, ON (22 October 2002).

Ministry of Attorney General, Government of British Columbia. Victoria, BC (9-11 December 2002).

Ministry of the Attorney General, Government of Ontario. Toronto, ON (8 and 26 November 2002; 21 and 30 May 2002).

Ministry of Justice and Attorney General, Government of Alberta. Edmonton, AB (16-18 December 2002).

Ministry of Justice, Government of New Zealand. Wellington, NZ (4-5 and 11-12 May 2004).

Ministry of Justice, Government of Quebec. Ste. Foy, QC (20 November 2003).

Ministry of the Executive Council, Government of Quebec. Québec, QC (20 November 2003).

New Zealand Human Rights Commission. Wellington, NZ (4 May 2004).

Office of Legislative Counsel, Government of Nova Scotia. Halifax, NS (27 November 2003).

Office of the Attorney General, Government of Prince Edward Island. Charlottetown, PEI (28-29 April 2003).

Palmer, Sir Geoffrey, former Prime Minister of New Zealand. Wellington, NZ (6 May 2004).

Palmer, Matthew, Dean. Faculty of Law, Victoria University of Wellington. Wellington, NZ (12 May 2004).

Parliamentary Counsel Office, Government of New Zealand. Wellington, NZ (12 May 2004).

Quebec Human Rights Commission, Government of Quebec. Montreal, QC (3 November 2003).

Strayer, Honourable Mr. Justice Barry. Federal Court of Canada. Ottawa, ON (22 August 2001).

Tassé, Roger, former deputy minister of justice, PC, QC. Ottawa, ON (2 October 1997).

Trudeau, Right Honourable Pierre Elliott, PC, QC. Montreal, QC (5 September 1997).

Wilson, Honourable Margaret, attorney general of New Zealand. Wellington, NZ (12 May 2004).

Secondary Sources

Ajzenstat, Janet. "Reconciling Parliament and Rights: A.V. Dicey Reads the Canadian Charter of Rights and Freedoms." *Canadian Journal of Political Science* 30 (1997): 645-62.

Alvaro, Alexander. "Why Property Rights Were Excluded from the Canadian Charter of Rights and Freedoms." *Canadian Journal of Political Science* 24 (1991): 309-29.

Aucoin, Peter. "Organizational Changes in the Machinery of Canadian Government: From Rational Management to Brokerage Politics." *Canadian Journal of Political Science* 19 (1986): 3-27.

Aucoin, Peter, and Lori Turnbull. "The Democratic Deficit: Paul Martin and Parliamentary Reform." *Canadian Public Administration* 46 (2003): 427-49.

Baar, Carl. "Criminal Court Delay and the Charter: The Use and Misuse of Social Facts in Judicial Policy Making." *Canadian Bar Review* 72 (1993): 305-36.

Bakan, Joel. *Just Words.* Toronto: University of Toronto Press, 1997.

Bayefsky, Anne F. "Parliamentary Sovereignty and Human Rights in Canada: The Promise of the Canadian Charter of Rights and Freedoms." *Political Studies* 31 (1983): 239-63.

–. *Canada's Constitution Act 1982 and Amendments – A Documentary History.* Toronto: McGraw-Hill Ryerson, 1989.

Beatty, David. "The Canadian Conception of Equality." *University of Toronto Law Journal* 46 (1996): 349-74.

Bindman, Stephen. "Debate over New 'Juristocracy.'" *Gazette* (Montreal), 10 January 1998.

Bork, Robert H. *Coercing Virtue.* Toronto: Random House Canada, 2002.

Brazier, Rodney. "New Labour, New Constitution?" *Northern Ireland Legal Quarterly* 49 (1998): 1-22.

Brock, Kathy. "Polishing the Halls of Justice: Sections 24(2) and 8 of the Charter of Rights." *National Journal of Constitutional Law* 2 (1992): 265-303.

Brodie, Ian. "The Charter and the Policy Process." Paper presented at the annual meeting of the Canadian Political Science Association, June 1995.

–. "Interest Group Litigation and the Embedded State: Canada's Court Challenges Program." *Canadian Journal of Political Science* 34 (2001): 357-76.

–. *Friends of the Court: The Privileging of Interest Group Litigants in Canada.* Albany, NY: SUNY Press, 2002.

Burgess, Lee. "Recent Developments in Drinking and Driving Law and the Right to Counsel." *Journal of Motor Vehicle Law* 5 (1995): 25-38.

Cairns, Alan C. "The Judicial Committee and Its Critics." *Canadian Journal of Political Science* 3 (1971): 301-45.

–. *Disruptions: Constitutional Struggles, from the Charter to Meech Lake.* Toronto: McClelland and Stewart, 1991.

Casswell, Donald G. "Moving toward Same-Sex Marriage." *Canadian Bar Review* 80 (2001): 810-56.

Castel, Jacqueline. "The Use of Screens and Closed Circuit Television in the Prosecution of Child Sex Abuse Cases: Necessary Protection for Children or a Violation of the Rights of the Accused?" *Canadian Journal of Family Law* 10 (1992): 283-301.

Chase, Steve. "Notwithstanding Clause: Klein Ponders Overruling Courts on Gay Rights." *Calgary Herald,* 7 April 1998, A1.

Choudhry, Sujit, and Claire E. Hunter. "Measuring Judicial Activism on the Supreme Court of Canada: A Comment on Newfoundland (Treasury Board) v. NAPE." *McGill Law Journal* 48 (2003): 525-62.

Choudhry, Sujit, and Kent Roach. "Putting the Past behind Us? Prospective Judicial and Legislative Constitutional Remedies." *Supreme Court Law Review,* 2nd ser., 21 (2003): 205-66.

Clark, Ian D. "Recent Changes in the Cabinet Decision-Making System in Ottawa." *Canadian Public Administration* 28 (1985): 185-201.

Cohen, Stanley A. "Indirect Interrogation: Jailhouse Informers and the Right to Counsel." *Criminal Reports,* 3rd ser., 68 (1989): 58-66.

Cossman, Brenda. "Lesbians, Gay Men, and the *Canadian Charter of Rights and Freedoms*." *Osgoode Hall Law Journal* 40 (2002): 223-49.

Croft, Jeremy. *Whitehall and the Human Rights Act, 1998*. London: The Constitution Unit, 2000.

Davidov, Guy. "The Paradox of Judicial Deference." *National Journal of Constitutional Law* 12 (2001): 133-64.

Dawson, Mary. "The Impact of the Charter on the Public Policy Process and the Department of Justice." *Osgoode Hall Law Journal* 30 (1992): 595-603.

–. "Governing in a Rights Culture." *Supreme Court Law Review*, 2nd ser., 14 (2001): 251-80.

De Montigny, Yves. "The Impact (Real or Apprehended) of the Canadian Charter of Rights and Freedoms on the Legislative Authority of Quebec." In David Schneiderman and Kate Sutherland, eds., *Charting the Consequences*, 3-33. Toronto: University of Toronto Press, 1997.

Debeljak, Julie. "Rights Protection without Judicial Supremacy: A Review of the Canadian and British Models of Bills of Rights." *Melbourne University Law Review* 26 (2002): 285-324.

Delisle, R.J. "Collins: An Unjustified Distinction." *Criminal Reports* 56 (1987): 216-19.

Devonshire, R. "The Effects of Supreme Court Charter-Based Decisions on Policing: More Beneficial than Detrimental?" *Criminal Reports* 31 (1991): 82-104.

Dicey, A.V. *An Introduction to the Study of the Law of the Constitution*. Indianapolis: Liberty Fund Classics, 1982.

Dickson, Honourable Brian. "The Canadian Charter of Rights and Freedoms: Dawn of a New Era?" *Review of Constitutional Studies* 2 (1994): 3-20.

Doern, G. Bruce. "From Sectoral to Macro Green Governance: The Canadian Department of the Environment as an Aspiring Central Agency." *Governance* 6 (1993): 172-93.

Driedger, Elmer A. "The Meaning and Effect of the Canadian Bill of Rights: A Draftsman's Viewpoint." *Ottawa Law Review* 9 (1977): 303-20.

Dunn, Christopher. *The Institutionalized Cabinet*. Montreal and Kingston: McGill-Queen's University Press, 1995.

Edwards, J.L.I.J. "The Attorney General and the Charter of Rights." In Robert J. Sharpe, ed., *Charter Litigation*, 45-68. Toronto: Butterworths, 1987.

Eisenberg, Avigail I. "Justice and Human Rights in the Provinces." In Christopher Dunn, ed., *Provinces: Canadian Provincial Politics*, 478-502. Peterborough, ON: Broadview Press, 1996.

Elliot, Robin. "'The Charter Revolution and the Court Party': Sound Critical Analysis or Blinkered Political Polemic?" *UBC Law Review* 35 (2002): 271-327.

Epp, Charles R. *The Rights Revolution: Lawyers, Activists, and Supreme Courts in Comparative Perspectives*. Chicago: University of Chicago Press, 1998.

Ewing, K.D. "The Unbalanced Constitution." In Tom Campbell, K.D. Ewing, and Adam Tomkins, eds., *Sceptical Essays on Human Rights*, 103-17. Oxford: Oxford University Press, 2001.

Fine, Sean. "Top Court Extends Rights of Accused." *Globe and Mail*, 9 August 1997.

Flanagan, Thomas. "The Staying Power of the Legislative Status Quo: Collective Choice in Canada's Parliament after Morgentaler." *Canadian Journal of Political Science* 30 (1997): 31-53.

Fletcher, Joseph F., and Paul Howe. "Canadian Attitudes towards the Charter and the Courts in Comparative Perspective." *Choices* 6 (2000): 1-29.

Franks, C.E.S. "Representation and Policy-Making in Canada." In C.E.S. Franks, J.E. Hodgetts, O.P. Dwivedi, D. Williams, and V. Seymour Wilson, eds., *Canada's Century: Governing in a Maturing Society: Essays in Honour of John Meisel*, 68-83. Montreal and Kingston: McGill-Queen's University Press, 1995.

–. "Parliament, Intergovernmental Relations, and National Unity." Working Paper Series, Institute of Intergovernmental Relations, Queen's University, Kingston, ON, 1999. http://www.iigr.ca/iigr.php/.

Fudge, Judy. "The Canadian Charter of Rights: Recognition, Redistribution, and the Imperialism of the Courts." In Tom Campbell, K.D. Ewing, and Adam Tomkins, eds., *Sceptical Essays on Human Rights*, 335-58. Oxford: Oxford University Press, 2001.

Fuerst, Michelle. "When Societal Interests Outweigh a Right to Confrontation: Charter Protection for Child Witnesses." In Jamie Cameron, ed., *The Charter's Impact on the Criminal Justice System*, 161-79. Toronto: Carswell, 1996.

Funston, Bernard W. "The Impact of the Charter of Rights and Freedoms on Policy Development in the Northwest Territories." *Osgoode Hall Law Journal* 30 (1992): 605-11.

Gagnon, Alain, and Guy Laforest. "The Future of Federalism: Lessons from Canada and Quebec." *International Journal* 28 (1993): 470-91.

Gallagher, Sheila A. "The Public Policy Process and Charter Litigation." In Patrick J. Monahan and Marie Finkelstein, eds., *The Impact of the Charter on the Public Policy Process*, 85-95. Concord, ON: Beckers Associates, 1993.

Gardbaum, Stephen. "The New Commonwealth Model of Constitutionalism." *American Journal of Comparative Law* 49 (2001): 707-60.

Gibson, John L. "In Defense of Cell Statements." *Criminal Reports*, 3rd ser., 73 (1990): 379-82.

Gold, Alan D. "Section 10(b) and the Right to Counsel: Post-Bartle." *Journal of Motor Vehicle Law* 7 (1996): 15-32.

Gold, Alan D., and Michelle Fuerst. "The Stuff that Dreams Are Made Of! Criminal Law and the Charter of Rights." *Ottawa Law Review* 24 (1992): 13-37.

Graham, Ron, ed. *The Essential Trudeau*. Toronto: McClelland and Stewart, 1998.

Greschner, Donna. "The Right to Belong: The Promise of *Vriend*." *National Journal of Constitutional Law* 9 (1999): 417-40.

–. "The Supreme Court, Federalism and Metaphors of Moderation." *Canadian Bar Review* 79 (2000): 47-56.

Hamilton, Alexander, James Madison, and John Hay. *The Federalist Papers*. Edited by Clinton Rossiter. New York: New American Library, 1961.

Harvie, Robert, and Hamar Foster. "Ties that Bind? The Supreme Court of Canada, American Jurisprudence, and the Revision of Canadian Criminal Law under the Charter." *Osgoode Hall Law Journal* 28 (1990): 730-88.

Hein, Gregory. "Interest Group Litigation in Canada, 1988-1998." *Choices* 6 (March 2000): 1-32.

Hiebert, Janet L. "The Evolution of the Limitation Clause." *Osgoode Hall Law Journal* 28 (1990): 103-34.

–. *Limiting Rights: The Dilemma of Judicial Review*. Montreal and Kingston: McGill-Queen's University Press, 1996.

–. "Legislative Scrutiny: An Alternative Approach for Protecting Rights." In Joseph F. Fletcher, ed., *Ideas in Action: Essays on Politics and Law in Honour of Peter Russell*, 294-312. Toronto: University of Toronto Press, 1999.

–. "Why Must a Bill of Rights Be a Contest of Political and Judicial Wills? The Canadian Alternative." *Public Law Review* 10 (1999): 22-36.

–. "Wrestling with Rights: Judges, Parliament and the Making of Social Policy." *Choices* 5 (1999): 1-36.

–. "A Relational Approach to Constitutional Interpretation: Shared Legislative and Judicial Responsibilities." *Journal of Canadian Studies* 35 (2001): 161-81.

–. *Charter Conflicts*. Montreal and Kingston: McGill-Queen's University Press, 2002.

–. "Parliament and Rights." In Tom Campbell, Jeffrey Goldsworthy, and Adrienne Stone, eds., *Protecting Human Rights*, 231-46. Oxford: Oxford University Press, 2003.

Hirschl, Ran. *Towards Juristocracy: The Origins and Consequences of the New Constitutionalism*. Cambridge, MA: Harvard University Press, 2004.

Hogg, Peter W. *Constitutional Law of Canada*. 2nd ed. Toronto: Carswell, 1985.

–. "The Charter of Rights and American Theories of Interpretation." *Osgoode Hall Law Journal* 25 (1987): 87-113.

–. "Federalism Fights the Charter." In David Shugarman and Reg Whitaker, eds., *Federalism and Political Community*, 249-66. Peterborough, ON: Broadview Press, 1989.

–. "Section 1 Revisited." *National Journal of Constitutional Law* 1 (1991-92): 1-24.

Hogg, Peter W., and Allison A. Bushell. "The *Charter* Dialogue between Courts and Legislatures (Or Perhaps the Charter Isn't Such a Bad Thing After All)." *Osgoode Hall Law Journal* 35 (1997): 75-124.

Hovius, Berend, and Robert Martin. "The Canadian Charter of Rights and Freedoms in the Supreme Court of Canada." *Canadian Bar Review* 61 (1983): 354-76.

Howe, R. Brian, and David Johnson. *Restraining Equality: Human Rights Commissions in Canada*. Toronto: University of Toronto Press, 2000.

Huscroft, Grant. "The Attorney General and Charter Challenges to Legislation: Advocate or Adjudicator?" *National Journal of Constitutional Law* 5 (1995): 125-62.

–. "The Attorney General, the Bill of Rights, and the Public Interest." In Grant Huscroft and Paul Rishworth, eds., *Rights and Freedoms: The New Zealand Bill of Rights Act 1990 and the Human Rights Act 1993*, 133-70. Wellington, NZ: Brooker's, 1995.

Hutchinson, Allan. "Mice under a Chair: Democracy, the Courts and the Administrative State." *University of Toronto Law Journal* 40 (1990): 374-411.

–. *Waiting for Coraf*. Toronto: University of Toronto Press, 1996.

Hutchinson, Allan, and Andrew Petter. "Private Rights/Public Wrongs: The Liberal Lie of the Charter." *University of Toronto Law Journal* 23 (1988): 278-97.

Jackman, Martha. "Protecting Rights and Promoting Democracy: Judicial Review under Section 1 of the *Charter*." *Osgoode Hall Law Journal* 34 (1996): 661-80.

Jai, Julie. "Policy, Politics and Law: Changing Relationships in Light of the Charter." *National Journal of Constitutional Law* 9 (1996): 1-25.

Justice Canada. "Concluding Comments from the Department of Justice." In Ronald J. Daniels, Patrick Macklem, and Kent Roach, eds., *The Security of Freedom: Essays on Canada's Anti-Terrorism Bill*, 435-45. Toronto: University of Toronto Press, 2001.

Kahana, Tsvi. "The Notwithstanding Mechanism and Public Discussion: Lessons from the Ignored Practice of Section 33 of the Charter." *Canadian Public Administration* 44 (2001): 255-91.

Kelly, James B. "Bureaucratic Activism and the Charter of Rights and Freedoms: The Department of Justice and Its Entry into the Centre of Government." *Canadian Public Administration* 42 (1999): 476-511.

–. "The *Charter of Rights and Freedoms* and the Rebalancing of Liberal Constitutionalism in Canada, 1982-1997." *Osgoode Hall Law Journal* 37 (1999): 625-95.

–. "Reconciling Rights and Federalism during Review of the Charter of Rights and Freedoms: The Supreme Court of Canada and the Centralization Thesis, 1982 to 1999." *Canadian Journal of Political Science* 34 (2001): 321-55.

–. "The Supreme Court of Canada and the Complexity of Judicial Activism." In Patrick James, Donald E. Abelson, and Michael Lusztig, eds., *The Myth of the Sacred: The Charter, the Courts and the Constitution in Canada*, 97-122. Montreal and Kingston: McGill-Queen's University Press, 2002.

–. "The Supreme Court of Canada's *Charter of Rights* Decisions, 1982-1999: A Statistical Analysis." In F.L. Morton, ed., *Law, Politics and the Judicial Process in Canada*, 496-512. 3rd ed. Calgary: University of Calgary Press, 2002.

–. "Governing with the Charter of Rights and Freedoms." *Supreme Court Law Review*, 2nd ser., 21 (2003): 299-337.

–. "Guarding the Constitution: Parliamentary and Judicial Roles under the Charter of Rights and Freedoms." In Harvey Lazar, Peter Meekison, and Hamish Telford, eds., *Canada: The State of the Federation, 2002*, 77-110. Montreal and Kingston: McGill-Queen's University Press, 2004.

Kelly, James B., and Michael Murphy. "Confronting Judicial Supremacy: A Defence of Judicial Activism and the Supreme Court of Canada's Legal Rights Jurisprudence." *Canadian Journal of Law and Society* 16 (2001): 3-27.

Kinley, David. "Parliamentary Scrutiny of Human Rights: A Duty Neglected?" In Philip Alston, ed., *Promoting Human Rights through Bills of Rights*, 158-84. Oxford: Oxford University Press, 1999.

Knopff, Rainer, and F.L. Morton. "Nation Building and the Canadian Charter of Rights and Freedoms." In Alan C. Cairns and Cynthia Williams, eds., *Constitutionalism, Citizenship and Society in Canada*, 133-82. Toronto: University of Toronto Press, 1985.

–. "Permanence and Change in a Written Constitution: The 'Living Tree' Doctrine and the Charter of Rights." *Supreme Court Law Review* 1 (1990): 533-46.

–. *Charter Politics.* Scarborough, ON: Nelson Canada, 1992.

–. "Ghosts and Straw Men: A Comment on Miriam Smith's 'Ghosts of the Judicial Committee of the Privy Council.'" *Canadian Journal of Political Science* 35 (2002): 31-42.

Laforest, Guy. *Trudeau and the End of a Canadian Dream.* Montreal and Kingston: McGill-Queen's University Press, 1995.

Laforest, Honourable Justice. "The Balancing of Interests under the Charter." *National Journal of Constitutional Law* 2 (1993): 133-62.

Laghi, Brian. "Debate on Gay Rights Polarizes Albertans." *Globe and Mail* (Toronto), 2 April 1998, A12.

–. "Alberta to Let Court Ruling on Gay Rights to Stand." *Globe and Mail* (Toronto), 10 April 1998, A5.

Leeson, Howard. "Section 33, the Notwithstanding Clause: A Paper Tiger?" *Choices* 6 (2000): 1-24.

Legault, Josée. "How to Deny Quebec's Right to Self-Determination." *Globe and Mail* (Montreal), 21 August 1998.

Litkowski, Richard. "The Charter and Principles of Criminal Responsibility: A Long and Winding Road." In Jamie Cameron, ed., *The Charter's Impact on the Criminal Justice System*, 271-92. Toronto: Carswell, 1996.

Lusztig, Michael. "Constitutional Paralysis: Why Canadian Constitutional Initiatives Are Doomed to Fail." *Canadian Journal of Political Science* 37 (1994): 747-71.

Macklem, Timothy. "Vriend v. Alberta: Making the Private Public." *McGill Law Journal* 44 (1999): 197-230.

McLachlin, Honourable Beverly. "Charter Myths." *UBC Law Review* 33 (1999): 23-36.

MacLennan, Christopher. *Toward the Charter.* Montreal and Kingston: McGill-Queen's University Press, 2003.

McWhinney, Edward. "Dilemmas of Judicial Law-Making on the Canadian Charter of Rights." In Pierre Thibault, Benoît Pelletier, and Louis Perret, eds., *Essays in Honour of Gérald-A. Beaudoin: The Challenges of Constitutionalism*, 307-31. Cowansville, QC: Éditions Yvon Blais, 2002.

Mahoney, Kathleen. "*R. v. Keegstra:* A Rationale for Regulating Pornography?" *McGill Law Journal* 37 (1992): 247-69.

Mahoney, Richard. "Problems with the Current Approach to s.24(2) of the Charter: An Inevitable Discovery." *Criminal Law Quarterly* 42 (1999): 443-77.

Malloy, Jonathan. "Reconciling Expectations and Reality in House of Commons Committees: The Case of the 1989 GST Inquiry." *Canadian Public Administration* 39 (1999): 314-55.

Mandel, Michael. *The Charter of Rights and the Legalization of Politics in Canada.* Toronto: Thompson Educational Publishing, 1994.

Manfredi, Christopher P. "Adjudication, Policy Making and the Supreme Court of Canada: Lessons from the Experience of the United States." *Canadian Journal of Political Science* 22 (1989): 313-35.

–. "Constitutional Rights and Interest Advocacy: Litigating Educational Reform in Canada and the United States." In F. Leslie Seidle, ed., *Equity and Community*, 91-113. Montreal: Institute for Research on Public Policy, 1993.

–. *Judicial Power and the Charter.* Toronto: McClelland and Stewart, 1993.

–. "Judicial Review and Criminal Disenfranchisement." *Review of Politics* 60 (1998): 277-305.

–. "The Chrétien Court." *Policy Options* 21 (2000): 23-24.

–. *Judicial Power and the Charter.* 2nd ed. Don Mills, ON: Oxford University Press, 2001.

–. "Strategic Behaviour and the Canadian Charter of Rights and Freedoms." In Patrick James, Donald E. Abelson, and Michael Lusztig, eds., *The Myth of the Sacred: The Charter, the Courts and the Constitution in Canada*, 147-67. Montreal and Kingston: McGill-Queen's University Press, 2002.

–. *Feminist Activism in the Supreme Court.* Vancouver: UBC Press, 2004.

Manfredi, Christopher P., and James B. Kelly. "Six Degrees of Dialogue: A Response to Hogg and Bushell." *Osgoode Hall Law Journal* 37 (1999): 513-27.

–. "Dialogue, Deference and Restraint: Judicial Independence and Trial Procedures." *Saskatchewan Law Review* 64 (2001): 323-46.

–. "Misrepresenting the Supreme Court's Record? A Comment on Sujit Choudhry and Claire E. Hunter, 'Measuring Judicial Activism on the Supreme Court.'" *McGill Law Journal* 49 (2004): 741-64.

Manfredi, Christopher P., and Scott Lemieux. "Judicial Discretion and Fundamental Justice: Sexual Assault Jurisprudence in the Supreme Court of Canada." *American Journal of Comparative Law* 47 (1999): 487-514.

Manfredi, Christopher P., and Antonia Maioni. "Courts and Health Policy: Judicial Policy Making and Publically Funded Health Care in Canada." *Journal of Health Politics, Policy and Law* 27 (2002): 213-40.

Martin, Dianne. "Rising Expectations: Slippery Slope or New Horizon? The Constitutionalization of Criminal Trials in Canada." In Jamie Cameron, ed., *The Charter's Impact on the Criminal Justice System,* 87-121. Toronto: Carswell, 1996.

Martin, Robert Ivan. *The Most Dangerous Branch.* Montreal and Kingston: McGill-Queen's University Press, 2003.

Mitchell, Graeme. "The Impact of the Charter on the Public Policy Process: The Attorney General." In Patrick J. Monahan and Marie Finkelstein, eds., *The Impact of the Charter on the Public Policy Process,* 77-83. Concord, ON: Beckers Associates, 1993.

Monahan, Patrick J. *Politics and the Constitution.* Toronto: Carswell, 1987.

–. "The Charter: Then and Now." In P. Bryden, S. Davis, and J. Russell, eds., *Protecting Rights and Freedoms,* 105-28. Toronto: University of Toronto Press, 1994.

–. *Constitutional Law.* 2nd ed. Toronto: Irwin Law, 2002.

Monahan, Patrick J., and Marie Finkelstein. "The Charter of Rights and Public Policy in Canada." *Osgoode Hall Law Journal* 30 (1992): 501-44.

Morton, F.L. "The Political Impact of the Canadian Charter of Rights and Freedoms." *Canadian Journal of Political Science* 20 (1987): 31-53.

–. "The Politics of Rights and What Canadians Should Know about the American Bill of Rights." *Windsor Review of Legal and Social Issues* 1 (1990): 61-96.

–. "The Charter Revolution and the Court Party." *Osgoode Hall Law Journal* 30 (1992): 627-52.

–. "The Effect of the Charter of Rights on Canadian Federalism." *Publius* 25 (1995): 173-88.

–. "Judicial Politics Canadian Style: The Supreme Court's Contribution to the Constitutional Crisis of 1992." In Curtis Cook, ed., *Constitutional Predicament,* 132-48. Montreal and Kingston: McGill-Queen's University Press, 1994.

–. "Vriend v. Alberta: Judicial Power at the Crossroads?" *Canada Watch* 7, 4-5 (1999), http://www.yorku.ca/robarts/projects/canada-watch/.

Morton, F.L., and Avril Allen. "Feminists and the Courts: Measuring Success in Interest Group Litigation in Canada." *Canadian Journal of Political Science* 34 (2001): 55-84.

Morton, F.L., and Rainer Knopff. *The Charter Revolution and the Court Party.* Peterborough, ON: Broadview Press, 2000.

Morton, F.L., Peter H. Russell, and Troy Q. Riddell. "The *Canadian Charter of Rights and Freedoms*: A Descriptive Analysis of the First Decade, 1982-1992." *National Journal of Constitutional Law* 5 (1994): 1-60.

Overby, L. Martin. "Free Voting in a Provincial Parliament: The Case of 'Same-Sex' Legislation in Ontario, 1994." *Journal of Legislative Studies* 2 (1996): 172-83.

Paciocco, David. "Morin: The Transitional Reasonableness of Excessive Systemic Delay." *Criminal Reports,* 3rd ser., 76 (1993): 56-63.

–. "Stillman, Disproportion and the Fair Trial Dichotomy under Section 24(2)." *Canadian Criminal Law Review* 2 (1997): 163-82.

Packer, Herbert. "Two Models of the Criminal Process." *University of Pennsylvania Law Review* 113 (1964): 1-68.

–. *The Limits of Criminal Sanction.* Stanford: Stanford University Press, 1968.

Pal, Leslie A. *Interests of State.* Montreal and Kingston: McGill-Queen's University Press, 1993.

Palmer, Geoffrey. *Unbridled Power: An Interpretation of New Zealand's Constitution and Government*. Don Mills, ON: Oxford University Press, 1999.

Palmer, Geoffrey, and Matthew Palmer. *Bridled Power*. 4th ed. Wellington, NZ: Oxford University Press, 2004.

Peacock, Anthony A. "Judicial Rationalism and the Therapeutic Constitution: The Supreme Court's Reconstruction of Equality and Democratic Process under the Charter of Rights and Freedoms." In Patrick James, Donald E. Abelson, and Michael Lusztig, eds., *The Myth of the Sacred: The Charter, the Courts and the Constitution in Canada*, 17-66. Montreal and Kingston: McGill-Queen's University Press, 2002.

Petter, Andrew. "The Politics of the Charter." *Supreme Court Law Review* 8 (1986): 474-505.

–. "Immaculate Deception: The Charter's Hidden Agenda." *Advocate* 45 (1987): 857-65.

Pomerance, Renee M. "Searching in Vein: *R. v. Dersch*, Blood Samples, and Informational Privacy." *Journal of Motor Vehicle Law* 6 (1995): 75-103.

Reidy, Aisling, and Meg Russell. "Second Chambers as Constitutional Guardians and Protectors of Human Rights." *The Constitution Unit*, June 1999: 1-14.

Riddell, Troy Q. "Official Minority-Language Education Policy Outside of Quebec: The impact of Section 23 of the Charter and Judicial Decisions." *Canadian Public Administration* 46 (2003): 27-49.

Riddell, Troy Q., and F.L. Morton. "Reasonable Limitations, Distinct Society and the Canada Clause: Interpretive Clauses and the Competition for Constitutional Advantage." *Canadian Journal of Political Science* 31 (1998): 467-93.

Rishworth, Paul, Grant Huscroft, Scott Optican, and Richard Mahoney. *The New Zealand Bill of Rights*. Melbourne: Oxford University Press, 2003.

Roach, Kent. "The Evolving Fair Trial Test under Section 24(2) of the Charter." *Canadian Criminal Law Review* 1 (1996): 117-34.

–. *Due Process and Victims' Rights*. Toronto: University of Toronto Press, 1999.

–. "The Attorney General and the Charter Revisited." *University of Toronto Law Journal* 50 (2000): 1-40.

–. "Chief Justice Lamer and Some Myths about Judicial Activism." *Canadian Criminal Law Review* 5 (2000): 21-40.

–. *The Supreme Court on Trial*. Toronto: Irwin Law, 2001.

–. "The Uses and Audiences of Preambles in Legislation." *McGill Law Journal* 47 (2001): 129-59.

–. "Remedial Consensus and Dialogue under the *Charter*: General Declarations and Delayed Declarations of Invalidity." *UBC Law Review* 35 (2002): 211-69.

–. *September 11: Consequences for Canada*. Montreal and Kingston: McGill-Queen's University Press, 2003.

Romanow, Roy, John Whyte, and Howard Leeson. *Canada ... Notwithstanding: The Making of the Constitution 1976-1982*. Toronto: Carswell, 1984.

Rosenberg, Gerald N. *The Hollow Hope*. Chicago: University of Chicago Press, 1991.

Rosenberg, Honourable Marc. "The *Charter's* Impact on the Law of Evidence in Criminal Cases." In Jamie Cameron, ed., *The Charter's Impact on the Criminal Justice System*, 181-99. Toronto: Carswell, 1996.

Russell, Peter H. "A Democratic Approach to Civil Liberties." *University of Toronto Law Journal* 19 (1969): 105-31.

–. "The Effect of a Charter of Rights on the Policy-Making Role of Canadian Courts." *Canadian Public Administration* 25 (Spring 1982): 1-33.

–. "Bold Statecraft, Questionable Jurisprudence." In Keith Banting and Richard Simeon, eds., *And No One Cheered*, 210-38. Toronto: Methuen, 1983.

–. "The Political Purposes of the Canadian Charter of Rights and Freedoms." *Canadian Bar Review* 61 (1983): 31-54.

–. "Standing Up for Nothwithstanding." *Alberta Law Review* 24 (1991): 293-309.

–. *Constitutional Odyssey*. 2nd ed. Toronto: University of Toronto Press, 1993.

–. "Canadian Constraints on Judicialization from Without." *International Political Science Review* 15 (1994): 165-75.

–. "The Political Purposes of the Charter: Have They Been Fulfilled?" In P. Bryden, S. Davis, and J. Russell, eds., *Protecting Rights and Freedoms*, 33-43. Toronto: University of Toronto Press, 1994.

Russell, Peter H., Rainer Knopff, and Ted Morton, eds. *Federalism and the Charter: Leading Constitutional Decisions*. Ottawa: Carleton University Press, 1990.

Savoie, Donald J. *The Politics of Public Spending in Canada*. Toronto: University of Toronto Press, 1990.

–. "Central Agencies: A Government of Canada Perspective." In Jacques Bourgault, Maurice Demers, and Cynthia Williams, eds., *Public Administration and Public Management Experiences in Canada*. Ste.-Foy, QC: Publications du Québec, 1997.

–. *Governing from the Centre*. Toronto: University of Toronto Press, 1999.

–. "The Rise of Court Government in Canada." *Canadian Journal of Political Science* 32 (1999): 635-64.

Schultz, Richard J. "Prime Ministerial Government, Central Agencies and Operating Departments: Towards a More Realistic Analysis." In Thomas Hockin, ed., *Apex of Power*, 229-36. Toronto: Prentice-Hall, 1971.

–. *Federalism, Bureaucracy and Public Policy*. Montreal and Kingston: McGill-Queen's University Press, 1980.

Scott, Ian. "Law, Policy, and the Role of the Attorney General: Constancy and Change in the 1980s." *University of Toronto Law Review* 39 (1989): 109-26.

Sherrin, Christopher. "Jailhouse Informants, Part I: Problems with Their Use." *Criminal Law Quarterly* 40 (1997): 106-21.

Sigurdson, Richard. "Left- and Right-Wing Charterphobia in Canada: A Critique of the Critics." *International Journal of Canadian Studies* 7 (1993): 95-115.

Slattery, Brian. "A Theory of the Charter." *Osgoode Hall Law Journal* 25 (1987): 701-47.

Smiley, Donald. "A Dangerous Deed: The Constitution Act, 1982." In Keith Banting and Richard Simeon, eds., *And No One Cheered*, 74-95. Toronto: Methuen, 1983.

Smith, Miriam. *Lesbian and Gay Rights in Canada: Social Movements and Equality-Seeking, 1971-1995*. Toronto: University of Toronto Press, 1999.

–. "Ghosts of the Judicial Committee of the Privy Council: Group Politics and Charter Litigation in Canadian Political Science." *Canadian Journal of Political Science* 35 (2002): 3-29.

–. "Partisanship as Political Science: A Reply to Rainer Knopff and F.L. Morton." *Canadian Journal of Political Science* 35 (2002): 43-48.

–. "Recognizing Same-Sex Relationships: The Evolution of Recent Federal and Provincial Policies." *Canadian Public Administration* 45 (2002): 1-23.

Smithey, Shannon Ishiyama. "The Effects of the Canadian Supreme Court's Charter Interpretation on Regional and Intergovernmental Tensions in Canada." *Publius* 26 (1996): 83-100.

–. "Cooperation and Conflict: Group Activity in *R. v. Keegstra*." In Patrick James, Donald E. Abelson, and Michael Lusztig, eds., *The Myth of the Sacred: The Charter, the Courts and the Constitution in Canada*, 189-204. Montreal and Kingston: McGill-Queen's University Press, 2002.

Strayer, B.L. "Life under the Canadian Charter: Adjusting the Balance between Legislatures and Courts." *Public Law* (1988): 345-69.

Stuart, Don. "The Unfortunate Dilution of Section 8 Protection: Some Teeth Remain." *Queen's Law Journal* 25 (1999): 65-94.

Swinton, Katherine E. *The Supreme Court and Canadian Federalism*. Toronto: Carswell, 1990.

Tait, John C. "Policy Development and the Charter." *Perspectives on Public Policy* 7 (1995): 1-23.

Tarnopolsky, Walter. *The Canadian Bill of Rights*. 2nd ed. Toronto: McClelland and Stewart, 1975.

–. "The Charter and the Supreme Court of Canada." In G. Beaudoin, ed., *The Charter: Ten Years Later*, 63-70. Cowansville, QC: Les Éditions Yvon Blais, 1992.

Tassé, Roger. "Intention of the Framers: A Political Analysis." Paper presented at the Fourth Annual Conference on Human Rights and the Charter, 16-17 November 1992.

Thomas, Paul. "Central Agencies: Making a Mesh of Things." In James P. Bickerton and Alain G. Gagnon, eds., *Canadian Politics*, 129-47. Peterborough, ON: Broadview Press, 1994.

Trudeau, Pierre E. *A Canadian Charter of Human Rights*. Ottawa: Queen's Printer, 1968.

–. *Federalism and the French Canadians*. Toronto: Macmillan, 1968.

–. "The Values of a Just Society." In Thomas S. Axworthy and Pierre Elliott Trudeau, eds., *Towards a Just Society*, 401-29. Toronto: Penguin Books, 1992.

Tushnet, Mark. "Non-Judicial Review." *Harvard Journal on Legislation* 40 (2003): 453-92.

Urquhart, Ian T. "Federalism, Ideology, and Charter Review: Alberta's Response to Morgentaler." *Canadian Journal of Law and Society* 4 (1989): 157-63.

Vallinder, Torbjörn. "The Judicialization of Politics – A World-Wide Phenomenon: Introduction." *International Political Science Review* 15 (1994): 91-99.

Vaughan, Frederick. "Judicial Politics in Canada: Patterns and Trends." *Choices* 5 (1999): 1-20.

Watson, Jack. "Blood Samples: Are They Real or Not?" *Journal of Motor Vehicle Law* 2 (1990): 173-94.

Weinrib, Lorraine Eisenstat. "The Supreme Court of Canada and Section One of the Charter." *Supreme Court Law Review* 10 (1988): 469-513.

–. "Learning to Live with the Override." *McGill Law Journal* 35 (1990): 541-71.

–. "The Activist Constitution." *Policy Options* 20 (1999): 29-30.

–. "Canada's Constitutional Revolution: From Legislative to Constitutional State." *Israel Law Review* 33 (1999): 13-50.

–. "Trudeau and the Canadian Charter of Rights and Freedoms: A Question of Constitutional Maturation." In Andrew Cohen and J.L. Granatstein, eds., *Trudeau's Shadow*, 257-82. Toronto: Random House of Canada, 1999.

–. "Canada's *Charter of Rights*: Paradigm Lost?" *Review of Constitutional Studies* 6 (2001): 119-78.

–. "The Supreme Court of Canada in the Age of Rights: Constitutional Democracy, the Rule of Law and Fundamental Rights under Canada's Constitution." *Canadian Bar Review* 80 (2001): 699-748.

–. "The Canadian Charter's Transformative Aspirations." In Joseph Eliot Magnet, Gerald-A. Beaudoin, Gerald Gall, and Christopher P. Manfredi, eds., *The Canadian Charter of Rights and Freedoms*, 17-37. Toronto: Butterworths, 2003.

Williams, George. *A Bill of Rights for Australia*. Sydney: University of New South Wales Press, 2000.

Young, Alan. "The Charter, the Supreme Court of Canada and the Constitutionalizing of the Investigative Process." In Jamie Cameron, ed., *The Charter's Impact on the Criminal Justice System*, 1-33. Toronto: Carswell, 1996.

Cases Cited

Adler v. Ontario, [1996] 3 S.C.R. 609.

Andrews v. Law Society (B.C.), [1989] 1 S.C.R. 143.

Arsenault-Cameron v. Prince Edward Island, [2000] 1 S.C.R. 3.

Attorney General Manitoba et al. v. Attorney General Canada et al., [1981] 1 S.C.R. 753 [*Patriation Reference*].

Attorney General (Quebec) v. Protestant School Boards, [1984] 2 S.C.R. 66.

Benner v. Canada, [1997] 1 S.C.R. 358.

Black v. Law Society (Alberta), [1989] 1 S.C.R. 591.

Bliss v. A.G. Canada, [1979] 1 S.C.R. 183.

B.(R.) v. Children's Aid Society of Metropolitan Toronto, [1995] 1 S.C.R. 315.

Committee for the Commonwealth of Canada v. Canada, [1991] 1 S.C.R. 139.

Devine v. Quebec (A.G.), [1988] 2 S.C.R. 790.

Dunmore v. Ontario (Attorney General), [2001] 3 S.C.R. 1016.

Eaton v. Brant County Board of Education, [1997] 1 S.C.R. 241.

Edmonton Journal v. Alberta, [1989] 2 S.C.R. 1326.

Egan v. Canada, [1995] 2 S.C.R. 513.

Eldridge v. British Columbia, [1997] 3 S.C.R. 624.
Ell v. Alberta, [2003] 1 S.C.R. 857.
Figueroa v. Canada (Attorney General), [2003] 1 S.C.R. 912.
Ford v. Quebec, [1988] 2 S.C.R. 712.
Gosselin v. Quebec, [2002] 4 S.C.R. 429.
Haig v. Canada, [1993] 2 S.C.R. 995.
Hogan v. The Queen, [1971] 2 S.C.R. 574.
Hunter v. Southam Inc., [1984] 2 S.C.R. 145.
Irwin Toy v. A.G. Quebec, [1989] 1 S.C.R. 927.
Kindler v. Canada, [1991] 2 S.C.R. 779.
Lavell v. A.G. Canada, [1974] S.C.R. 1349.
Libman v. Quebec, [1997] 3 S.C.R. 569.
Little Sisters Book and Art Emporium v. Canada (Minister of Justice), [2000] 2 S.C.R. 1120.
Mackay v. Manitoba, [1989] 2 S.C.R. 357.
Mackin v. New Brunswick (Minister of Finance), [2002] 1 S.C.R. 405.
Mahé v. Alberta, [1990] 1 S.C.R. 342.
Manitoba Provincial Judges Assn. v. Manitoba (Minister of Justice), [1997] 3 S.C.R. 3.
McKinney v. University of Guelph, [1990] 3 S.C.R. 229.
M. v. H., [1999] 2 S.C.R. 3.
New Brunswick (Minister of Health and Community Services) v. G.(J.), [1999] 3 S.C.R. 46.
Nova Scotia (Workers' Compensation Board) v. Martin, [2003] 2 S.C.R. 504.
Ontario Home Builders' Association v. York Region Board of Education, [1996] 2 S.C.R. 929.
Osborne v. Canada (Treasury Board), [1991] 2 S.C.R. 69.
Reference Re Bill 30, An Act to Amend the Education Act (Ontario), [1987] 1 S.C.R. 1149.
Reference Re s.94(2) of the British Columbia Motor Vehicle Act, [1985] 2 S.C.R. 486.
Reference Re Ng Extradition, [1991] 2 S.C.R. 858.
Reference Re Provincial Court Judges, [1997] 3 S.C.R. 3.
Reference Re Provincial Electoral Boundaries (Saskatchewan), [1991] 2 S.C.R. 158.
Reference Re Public Schools Act (Manitoba), ss.79(3), (4) and (7), [1993] 1 S.C.R. 839.
Reference Re Public Service Employee Relations Act, [1987] 1 S.C.R. 313.
Reference Re Remuneration of Judges of the Provincial Court of Prince Edward Island, [1997] 3 S.C.R. 3.
Reference Re Workers' Compensation Act, 1983, [1989] 2 S.C.R. 335.
Retail, Wholesale and Department Store Union v. Dolphin Delivery, [1986] 2 S.C.R. 573.
Retail, Wholesale and Department Store Union v. Pepsi-Cola Canada Beverages Ltd., [2002] 1 S.C.R. 156.
RJR-Macdonald Inc. v. Canada, [1995] 3 S.C.R. 199.
Rocket v. Royal College of Dental Surgeons of Ontario, [1990] 2 S.C.R. 232.
R. v. Advance Cutting & Coring Ltd., [2001] 3 S.C.R. 209.
R. v. Askov, [1990] 2 S.C.R. 1199.
R. v. Bartle, [1994] 3 S.C.R. 173.
R. v. Big M. Drug Mart Ltd., [1985] 1 S.C.R. 295.
R. v. Black, [1989] 2 S.C.R. 138.
R. v. Broyles, [1991] 3 S.C.R. 595.
R. v. Brydges, [1990] 1 S.C.R. 190.
R. v. Campbell, [1999] 2 S.C.R. 956.
R. v. Carosella, [1997] 1 S.C.R. 80.
R. v. Clarkson, [1986] 1 S.C.R. 383.
R. v. Cobham, [1994] 3 S.C.R. 360.
R. v. Collins, [1987] 1 S.C.R. 265.
R. v. Daviault, [1994] 3 S.C.R. 63.
R. v. Dersch, [1993] 3 S.C.R. 769.
R. v. Duarte, [1990] 1 S.C.R. 30.
R. v. Dyment, [1988] 2 S.C.R. 417.
R. v. Edwards, [1996] 1 S.C.R. 128.
R. v. Edwards Books and Art Ltd., [1986] 2 S.C.R. 713.

R. v. Evans, [1996] 1 S.C.R. 8.
R. v. Feeney, [1997] 2 S.C.R. 13.
R. v. Fliss, [2002] 1 S.C.R. 535.
R. v. Frazer, [1993] 2 S.C.R. 866.
R. v. Gallagher, [1993] 2 S.C.R. 861.
R. v. Généreux, [1992] 1 S.C.R. 259.
R. v. Grant, [1993] 3 S.C.R. 223.
R. v. Greffe, [1990] 1 S.C.R. 755.
R. v. Hall, [2002] 3 S.C.R. 309.
R. v. Hebert, [1990] 2 S.C.R. 151.
R. v. Heywood, [1990] 3 S.C.R. 761.
R. v. Hufsky, [1988] 1 S.C.R. 621.
R. v. Jones, [1994] 2 S.C.R. 229.
R. v. Jones, [1986] 2 S.C.R. 285.
R. v. Keegstra, [1990] 3 S.C.R. 697.
R. v. Ladouceur, [1990] 1 S.C.R. 1257.
R. v. Latimer, [1997] 1 S.C.R. 217.
R. v. L.(D.O.), [1993] 4 S.C.R. 419.
R. v. Levogiannis, [1993] 4 S.C.R. 475.
R. v. Liew, [1999] 3 S.C.R. 227.
R. v. Logan, [1990] 2 S.C.R. 731.
R. v. Lyons, [1987] 2 S.C.R. 309.
R. v. Manninen, [1987] 1 S.C.R. 1233.
R. v. Martineau, [1990] 2 S.C.R. 633.
R. v. Matheson, [1994] 3 S.C.R. 328.
R. v. Mills, [1999] 3 S.C.R. 668.
R. v. Monney, [1999] 1 S.C.R. 652.
R. v. Morales, [1992] 3 S.C.R. 711.
R. v. Morgentaler, [1988] 1 S.C.R. 30.
R. v. Morin, [1992] 1 S.C.R. 771.
R. v. Nguyen, [1990] 2 S.C.R. 906.
R. v. Oakes, [1986] 1 S.C.R. 103.
R. v. O'Connor, [1995] 4 S.C.R. 411.
R. v. Pearson, [1992] 3 S.C.R. 665.
R. v. Plant, [1993] 3 S.C.R. 281.
R. v. Pohoretsky, [1987] 1 S.C.R. 945.
R. v. Potvin, [1993] 2 S.C.R. 880.
R. v. Prosper, [1994] 3 S.C.R. 236.
R. v. S.(S.), [1990] 2 S.C.R. 254.
R. v. Sharpe, [2001] 1 S.C.R. 45.
R. v. Silveria, [1995] 2 S.C.R. 297.
R. v. Simmons, [1988] 2 S.C.R. 495.
R. v. Smith, [1991] 1 S.C.R. 714.
R. v. Stillman, [1997] 1 S.C.R. 607.
R. v. Swain, [1991] 1 S.C.R. 933.
R. v. Therens, [1985] 1 S.C.R. 613.
R. v. Tremblay, [1987] 2 S.C.R. 435.
R. v. Turpin, [1989] 1 S.C.R. 1296.
R. v. Vaillancourt, [1987] 2 S.C.R. 636.
R. v. Valente, [1985] 2 S.C.R. 673.
R. v. Wiley, [1993] 3 S.C.R. 263.
R. v. Wong, [1990] 3 S.C.R. 36.
R. v. Wozniak, [1994] 3 S.C.R. 310.
R. v. Zundel, [1992] 2 S.C.R. 731.
RWDSU v. Saskatchewan, [1987] 1 S.C.R. 460.
RWDSU, Local 558 v. Pepsi-Cola Canada Beverages (West) Ltd., [2002] 1 S.C.R. 156.

Sauvé v. Canada, [1992] 2 S.C.R. 438; [2002] 3 S.C.R. 519.
Schacter v. Canada, [1992] 2 S.C.R. 679.
Seaboyer v. The Queen, [1991] 2 S.C.R. 577.
Singh v. Minister of Employment and Immigration, [1985] 1 S.C.R. 177.
Stoffman v. Vancouver General Hospital, [1990] 3 S.C.R. 483.
Thibault v. Corp. Professionel Médicins du Québec, [1988] 1 S.C.R. 1033.
Thompson Newspapers Company v. Canada (Attorney General), [1998] 1 S.C.R. 877.
Trociuk v. British Columbia (Attorney General), [2003] 1 S.C.R. 835.
UFCW, Local 1518 v. Kmart Canada Ltd., [1999] 2 S.C.R. 1083.
United States v. Burns, [2001] 1 S.C.R. 283.
Vancouver Society of Immigrant and Visible Minority Women v. M.N.R., [1999] 1 S.C.R. 10.
Vriend v. Alberta, [1998] 1 S.C.R. 493.
Winko v. B.C. (Forensic Psychiatric Institute), [1999] 2 S.C.R. 625.
Winnipeg Child and Family Services v. K.L.W., [2000] 2 S.C.R. 519.

Index

Printed and bound in Canada by Friesens

Set in Stone by Artegraphica Design Co. Ltd.

Copy editor: Audrey McClellan

Proofreader: Dallas Harrison

Indexer: Christine Jacobs